Praise for Peter Manseau's

ONE NATION, UNDER GODS

One of *Publishers Weekly*'s Best Books of the Year

"Lively, refreshing....The image of a city upon a hill evokes a founding idea of America: an exceptional nation of pilgrims contending with the wilderness, united in their faith. *One Nation, Under Gods* dispels that tidy image....With tales of secret faiths, false tolerance, and quiet yet formidable dissent, each chapter is a window onto lives that were lived on the margin of Christian narratives." — Damaris Colhoun, *New York Times Book Review*

"Riveting....With a novelist's verve and a historian's precision, Manseau deftly guides us through a cacophonous religious landscape, studded with encounters so unexpected and bizarre that they could be the stuff of speculative fiction....*One Nation, Under Gods* is crammed with enthralling tales of dissenters and outliers reinventing religious traditions to make sense of their often desperate circumstances....Much more than a simple catalog of diversity, *One Nation, Under Gods* is a stunning history of religious cross-pollination." — Tanya Erzen, *Bookforum*

"Here at last is the rest of the American story, in one great kaleidoscope of a book. Peter Manseau has revealed the many too often obscured by 'one nation.' The truth is so much more vast and strange and funny and fascinating than that, and Manseau, a brilliant writer of great wit, curiosity, and learning, is the perfect guide." — Jeff Sharlet, author of *The Family*

"Truth telling and riveting storytelling don't always go hand in hand, but they do in this necessary history of America's stunningly diverse religious heritage." — Cathleen Medwick, *More*

"An unusual work of history....Fascinating....Most key points in our national narrative involve a non-Christian element if you look closely, Manseau maintains....Each chapter tells the story of a person considered a heretic, blasphemer, atheist, or heathen, who nevertheless helped in some way to shape the course of American history."
— Laura Miller, *Salon*

"The United States is arguably the most religiously diverse nation in the world. Peter Manseau shows how this has always been the case. *One Nation, Under Gods* is a refreshing, compelling, and surprising reexamination of our nation's history that puts lie to the oft-quoted idea that America was founded as 'a Christian nation.'"
— Reza Aslan, author of *No god but God* and
Zealot: The Life and Times of Jesus of Nazareth

"Accessible and insightful....A richer, more complex, and compelling viewpoint that is reminiscent of Howard Zinn's *A People's History of the United States*....This significant and timely work is important for those who wish to understand the complete and diverse landscape of religious history in America—but even more valuable for those who don't."
— Erin Entrada Kelly, *Library Journal*

"Manseau artfully packs each profile with context, adding the occasional soupçon of drama to ensure maximal, enthralling readability."
— *Booklist*

"*One Nation, Under Gods* is one of those too-rare works of innovative history that also manage to be works of literary art. Its series of interlocking stories, rich in color and depth, combine to offer a new picture of America, both past and present."
— Adam Goodheart, author of *1861*

"What the author endeavors to do here—and does so with deep-running stories told with verve and dash—is to square that narrative with a religious syncretism that provides a more colorful, distinct, eccentric, not to mention truthful, historical record....An eye-opener. After reading Manseau, readers will see the influences he writes about not only dot, but shape, the landscape."
— *Kirkus Reviews*

"Manseau's writing is lively....He finds a place for the religiously disaffected, for atheists like William Livingston, and for the seriously addled hucksters who sponsored cosmic awareness and 'Be-Ins' in the sixties. One is not surprised to find the attitude of the deist Thomas Jefferson recommended in the book's epigraph: 'It does me no injury for my neighbor to say there are twenty gods, or no god.' An entire chapter is devoted to Jefferson's gift of his library to the nation in 1814 and the congressional battles it generated—a foretaste of present-day culture wars."

—Luke Timothy Johnson, *Commonweal*

"Subversive and much-needed....A tour de force. A thorough reimagining of our nation's religions....Engagingly written, with a historian's eye for detail and a novelist's sense of character and timing, this history from another perspective reexamines familiar tales and introduces fascinating counternarratives."

—*Publishers Weekly*

"Brilliant."

—Ed Simon, *Tikkun*

"A beautifully written account of our interfaith country."

—Eboo Patel, *Sojourners*

"*One Nation, Under Gods* is a tour de force, definitely in the must-read category....Dissecting five hundred years of history, Manseau presents scholarly research as compelling storytelling that presents a controversial view: the notion that the United States was founded as a Christian nation is a myth."

—Najwa Margaret Saad, *Arab Weekly*

ALSO BY PETER MANSEAU

Rag and Bone

Songs for the Butcher's Daughter

Vows

Killing the Buddha (with Jeff Sharlet)

ONE NATION, UNDER GODS

A NEW AMERICAN HISTORY

PETER MANSEAU

BACK BAY BOOKS
Little, Brown and Company
New York • Boston • London

Back Bay Books / Little, Brown and Company
Hachette Book Group
1290 Avenue of the Americas, New York, NY 10104
littlebrown.com

Originally published in hardcover by Little, Brown and Company, January 2015
First Back Bay paperback edition, February 2016

Back Bay Books is an imprint of Little, Brown and Company, a division of Hachette Book Group, Inc. The Back Bay Books name and logo are trademarks of Hachette Book Group, Inc.

The publisher is not responsible for websites (or their content) that are not owned by the publisher.

Library of Congress Cataloging-in-Publication Data

Manseau, Peter.
    One nation, under gods : a new American history / Peter Manseau.—First Edition.
        pages cm
    Includes bibliographical references.
    ISBN 978-0-316-10003-8 (hardcover) / 978-0-316-10001-4 (paperback)
    1. United States—Religion—History.   I. Title.
    BL2525.M357 2015
    200.973—dc23   2014020469

10 9 8 7 6 5 4 3 2 1

RRD-C

Printed in the United States of America

For my daughters.

But it does me no injury for my neighbor to say there are
  twenty gods, or no god.
It neither picks my pocket nor breaks my leg.
  —Thomas Jefferson

. . . the forest is unconverted.
  —Derek Walcott

Contents

ONE NATION, UNDER GODS

Unearthing History

In the dry red soil of Chimayo, New Mexico, there is a hole in the ground that some call holy. They intend no pun, no play on words. The hole is a serious matter; the locals who tend to it would no more joke about their humble opening in the earth than they would a hole in the head, or the heart.

An arm's length in diameter and just deep enough that the temperature seems to drop when you lean in for a closer look, the hole has been here for centuries. The dirt in this valley has been regarded as sacred since before the birth of the Republic of which it is now a part; it has been revered as the physical nature of the spirit world since before the Spanish missionaries arrived with their own notions of embodied divinity; it was holy even before the first Europeans looked on the people of an unmapped continent and declared that they must know nothing of God.

Though it has a long and eclectic spiritual history, the hole sits today in the back corner of a Roman Catholic Church, El Santuario de Chimayo, which is among the most frequently visited religious pilgrimage sites in America. Hundreds of thousands of true believers and curious souls visit every year to line up in a small side chapel strewn with pictures of loved ones lost. They crowd into a closet-sized space around the hole, bend at the knees, dip their hands into the cool of the gap below, and pull up big handfuls of dirt. Some of it ends up in Ziploc bags, some in Tupperware tubs to be taken home on airplanes to every corner of this improbable nation. Much of it ends up in the mouths of the faithful. Visitors to Chimayo believe that eating the dirt brings miracles; as evidence they point to the crutches hanging from the walls.

Some would call this practice folk religion—not the real or legitimate orthopraxy of a Christian church but an indigenous corruption of the sanctioned sacrament of Communion. Others might suggest it is in fact something more complicated: a distinctly American form of religious syncretism, a blending of faith traditions so complete that it is difficult to separate one from the other. Implicit in each of these explanations is a more obvious physical truth. The church at Chimayo was built over a hole in the ground that has history both connected to and independent of the structure around it.

To extend the metaphor: In thinking about religion in American history, we have too often focused only on the church standing above the hole and not on the hole itself, nor on the people lining up to make the soil within a part of their blood, their bones. The United States is a land shaped and informed by internal religious diversity—some of it obvious, some of it hidden—and yet the history we have all been taught has mostly failed to convey this. We have learned history from the middle rather than the margins, though it is the latter from which so much of our culture has been formed.

We need only look to the point often seen as the beginning to know this is true. It is the story we memorized in school: *In fourteen hundred and ninety-two, Columbus sailed the ocean blue*...and he did so, we all have been taught, on orders and at the expense of Ferdinand and Isabella, the Catholic monarchs of Spain. The largest of his ships was named for the mother of the Christian savior (its full name was *Santa María de la Inmaculada Concepción*, Holy Mary of the Immaculate Conception). In his journal, which begins in the form of a prayer, "In the Name of Our Lord Jesus Christ," Columbus writes of standards bearing the cross brought onto the lands he was soon to conquer.

Less well known are the men who sailed with Columbus who did not call this symbol their own. No less than America would be, Europe at the time was a place endlessly conflicted over its multireligious past. Having shaped so much of Iberian culture, practitioners of Judaism and Islam provided Spain's Catholics with a daily reminder that their world was not made by the church alone. Whether this reminder was mere embarrassment or existential threat, it was reason enough to force them out. Columbus devotes the first words of his diary to praising Spain for evicting its religious minorities in the same year he began his voyage, and yet his own adventure could not have been accomplished without men drawn from the very peoples he was so pleased to see driven from their homes. It was precisely their connections to exiled faiths that led several of his crewmen to join a mission that was less likely to end in riches than a watery grave.

Even less well known are the spiritual practices of the Taino Indians who paddled their boats out to greet the newly arrived ships. Columbus declared that the people he encountered could easily be converted to the faith of Christendom because they obviously had none of their own. In fact, they merely had no faith he recognized, and so he was as blind to it as history books have often been.

The dominance of the Christian narrative of Columbus over the more complicated quilt of beliefs present at the earliest encounter between the places called the Old World and the New illustrates a neglected aspect of the American story. At every major turning point in the nation's narrative of encounter and expansion, an alternate spiritual history can be told. From a distance it is easy to see only the Christian elements of much of American history. The church stands above — as unavoidable as any twice-told tale — obscuring the more beguiling story within.

For another example, look no further than the well-known drama of the separatist Christians who left England to practice what they considered a purified version of the Protestant faith. Their establishment of a theocracy in New England intended as a "city upon a hill" usually serves as the Exodus story within the scripture of American history: England as Egypt; the ocean as desert; Massachusetts as the promised land. Mostly forgotten is that within a single generation, heterodoxy rather than uniformity of spiritual purpose became the rule. Banishments from the heavenly cities established in Plymouth and Massachusetts Bay began almost as soon as the passengers of the *Mayflower* and the *Arabella* came ashore. As for those not forced into exile to brave the supposedly godless wilderness, colonists in both New England and Virginia made desperate attempts to maintain religious order by imposing harsh punishments on anyone who posed a threat to divinely ordained authority. Death sentences were threatened for the first offense of church robbing, as well as for the third offense of blasphemy. Though history is quick to identify this entire era as

"Puritan," the more persuasive ideologies of the time may have been antipathy or indifference to the religious baggage that had come with muskets across the sea. The American experiment was frequently shaped by a rejection of old ways and openness to the new. In religious terms, this rejection created over time a nation unique in its ability to absorb and be built by those of different beliefs; people who believed there were many gods, or none at all.

To be sure, the American talent for the absorption of faiths and cultures has rarely resulted in the kind of peaceful pluralism most hope for today. The story of how a global array of beliefs came to occupy the same ocean-locked piece of land is more often one of violence than of toleration. There can be no clearer illustration of this than what occurred during the three centuries of slavery, which gave the nation its most enduring spiritual wounds. Twenty percent of the U.S. population was enslaved at the Republic's inception, and few were Christians when they arrived. Most were born of religious histories as rich and complex as Christendom— followers of Islam, Yoruba, and a dozen other lesser-known faiths. During this era, there was a forced transplantation of African beliefs and practices into the growing body of American religion. Yet the loss of such ancient traditions is often overlooked in the discussion of what was wrought by that painful period in our history. So too is the question of whether these traditions were truly lost at all: Much as the "secret Jews" Christianized by the Spanish Inquisition came to influence Catholicism in the Old World, the newly converted men and women held in bondage dramatically changed the faith into which they were forced. Beliefs driven underground have a way of maintaining their power; they rise again in myriad guises, known to the faithful even when the faith is called by different names.

The story of so many minority religious traditions living in the shadow of a single dominant creed may seem an epic only of repression and subjugation. However, it is in that tension—between the marginal and the mainstream—that the nation so many faiths have come to call home has forged its commitment, clear on paper if not always in practice, to become a place where, paradoxically, belief matters both very much and not at all, because we have the right to believe as we please.

As Walt Whitman famously wrote, "The United States themselves are essentially the greatest poem." Though no corner of

America is so tidy as a line of verse, no single life or community is so well-ordered as any metered rhythm, no alliances are so secure that they can be thought an enduring rhyme, his meaning nonetheless rings true when surveying the vast landscape of faiths that together comprise the nation. In the century and a half since Whitman offered that reflection, the American poem has only grown in character and complexity. We might now think of the United States less as a poem than as a massive multigenerational novel. The plot of this novel, and so the plot of this book, is how the repeated collision of conflicting systems of belief, followed frequently by ugly and violent conflict, has somehow arrived, again and again, not merely at peaceful coexistence but at striking moments of inter-influence.

These moments come along unexpectedly, often imperceptibly, to those involved. Some can be recognized only at a distance of centuries. Considering them now, we might view them as reminders that the process by which many peoples become one, *E pluribus unum*, is not merely the gathering of populations or regions within one border. It is the many living among and learning from each other. It is every strident orthodoxy making room for strange ways and exotic creeds. It is the recognition that, to paraphrase Thomas Jefferson, those who believe in one God, those who believe in twenty gods, and those who believe in no God, are bound together by something more significant than their own individual beliefs.

The Burning of Hatuey by the Spaniards at Yara, Cuba, on February 2, 1512. Engraving by Théodore de Bry, 1664.

CHAPTER 1

A Meeting of the Gods

1492–1512

They carved their scriptures from the world around them. With conch shells, mangrove trees, coral rock, true believers in a faith now forgotten made images of the gods who lived in the sky. There were among the people men called *behiques* whose role it was to determine if a branch of wood, a block of stone, or a mound of clay had sufficient power to serve this vital purpose. If satisfied, the behique would then coax a human form or sacred shape from the abode of spirits to the physical realm, inviting ever more deities to serve and protect the 400,000 men, women, and children who knew themselves as the Taino, original inhabitants of the islands that would become stepping-stones to the place now called America.

It pleased the gods to be among them. In gratitude for their creation, these small statues — called *zemies* — were believed to speak to their makers, teaching them to find order in the chaos of life just as they had found form in the formless materials of the earth. The zemies told the Taino their history: that people, too, had once been gods. In stories passed from one generation to the next, their Eden was a cave at the center of the island later called Hispaniola, where in bygone days they had lived together with the spirits they now revered.

Like the men in ships they would soon encounter, their myth of origins was one of exile. It was said that long ago the gods had ventured from their cave only under cover of darkness to eat from the limbs of the jobo tree. One night a few of their number found the fruit too sweet to turn from as dawn approached. They kept eating until morning and when the sun shone on their skin they became human, made mortal by their desire.

According to legends recorded later, the zemies informed the Taino not only of the beginning but also of the coming end. A tale was told of two chiefs, called *caciques*, who fasted for fifteen days in order to win sufficient favor with the gods that they might learn something of the future. Under the guidance of a behique shaman, the caciques inhaled sacred powder ground from the seeds of the jobo tree. Growing as tall as sixty feet, with pale yellow flowers and thorny bark, the jobo, also called cohoba, is a powerful entheogen — from the Greek, meaning something that "creates God within" — and it was at the center of Taino religious practice.

Following a ritual in which one chief blew the powder into the nose of the other, the caciques soon had visions in which the zemies told them that the world as they knew it would not last much longer. The prophecy the chiefs reported when their trance had ended was that the time of the Taino living in peace, with only the drama of the jobo ceremony to disrupt their days, soon would pass. A description of the Taino prophecy can be found in the 1511 chronicle of Peter Martyr d'Anghiera, an Italian-born historian of the Spanish explorations of the New World. "Within a few years," the chiefs told their people, "a race of men wearing clothes would land on the island and would overthrow their religious rites and ceremonies, massacre their children, and make them slaves."

For a time, the Taino believed this revelation referred to the torments they suffered at the hands of the Caribs, a rival tribe that made occasional raids from neighboring islands. So feared were these warriors that they had found a place in the bogeyman stories Taino parents told their children. Unlike the Taino, who had spears of crudely sharpened cane used only for hunting, the Caribs carried long-handled, hatchet-like clubs they used, as one account put it, "to trample the head of their enemies," and wielded bows with arrows made lethal by the toxic sap of the manchineel tree, also known as "the death apple." They were the worst demons the Taino could imagine, the only fitting denizens of their visions of apocalypse — at least, until the ships arrived.

The year 1492 was one of endings as well as beginnings. While the Taino mystics took their communion of cohoba powder and beseeched the zemies for a vision of what would come next through the door of the future, another set of doors was closing on the other side of the world.

The gates of the great palace of Alhambra, the "red fortress" of the Moors, were last shut to their makers as the banner of the cross was raised overhead. After centuries of hostility, the Roman Catholic rulers of Spain had successfully forced the final emir of the Islamic Nasrid dynasty from his seat of power in Granada, on the southern coast of the Iberian Peninsula. With the seizure of Alhambra, the five-hundred-year campaign known as the Reconquista, the reversion of Spain from Islamic dominance to Christian control, was complete. That this would have anything to do with a people four thousand miles away, who had yet to hear the names of either Jesus or Muhammad, seems as unlikely as the proverbial flap of a butterfly's wings changing the weather. Yet such is the religious history of the world: As the author of the Gospel of John said, spirits blow where they will; when beliefs are suppressed, the ripples can often be felt to the ends of the earth.

In January of 1492, an ambitious forty-one-year-old weaver's son known to the Spanish as Cristóbal Colón was present as King Ferdinand and Queen Isabella watched Sultan Abu 'abd-Allah Muhammad XII abandon his palace, the crowning achievement of Moorish culture, for exile in Africa. As he departed, the sultan paused to breathe an anguished cry of regret, the infamous "Moor's last sigh," for the loss of Europe's only Muslim kingdom.

Colón, whom we know as Christopher Columbus, was certainly in a better mood. Islam's loss would be Christendom's gain, and it might be his as well. The Catholic Monarchs, as King Ferdinand and Queen Isabella are often called, were aware of Columbus's ambitions to sail west to reach the East. At a time that can be seen as the beginning of the phenomenon we now call globalization, when control over global trade routes was key to a kingdom's fortunes, Columbus proposed replacing the dangerous overland route to Asia with a supposedly placid trip across the sea. Six years earlier, the Spanish Crown had turned down his request for financing—as had the Portuguese, the English, the Venetians, and the Genoese. The reasons they had given were that the trip would be prohibitively expensive and that it would be almost guaranteed to fail. Court-appointed experts insisted that Columbus had miscalculated the distance between Europe and the Orient, and thus any trip he might take would far exceed his proposed budget.

At the time, no one among the educated classes doubted that circumnavigation of the earth was possible. It was only later myth-making (not least of all by the American folk writer Washington Irving) that created the impression of Columbus as a geographic visionary, rare in his possession of the knowledge that the world was round. Yet still the royals ruled Columbus's adventure unworthy of the cost at a time when the kingdom was stretched thin by its ongoing conflict with the Moors.

It was logical, then, that Columbus would look upon the Catholic acquisition of the riches of Alhambra as a first step toward turning the monarchs' no to a yes. That same month—January 1492—he revisited the idea with the king and queen, providing them with information concerning, as he later wrote, "the countries of India and of a Prince, called Great Khan, which in our language signifies King of Kings, how, at many times he and his predecessors had sent to Rome soliciting instructors who might teach him our holy faith, and the holy Father had never granted his request, whereby great numbers of people were lost, believing in idolatry and doctrines of perdition."

Columbus's report to the Spanish court was full of errors both of history and geography. To begin with, Christian missionaries had been visiting the countries he called "India"—which today, we know, refers mostly to China—since early in the fourteenth century. Yet while Columbus may have had a hazy understanding of the past, his intention here is clear: With the mention of "doctrines of perdition" on the rise in "India," he hoped to suggest to the Catholic Monarchs that the vast, mysterious East was in danger of falling irredeemably under Muslim influence, a turn of events that would significantly dim the glow of the recent Catholic conquest of Alhambra. Moreover, Columbus's suggestion that the pope himself had long neglected to take this crucial step in the ongoing struggle between Christianity and Islam may have appealed to pious Isabella's spiritual vanity. If the "Great Khan" could be converted through her intervention, then she even more than the Holy Father might be seen as the world's preeminent defender of the faith.

With veiled threat and open flattery, Columbus convinced them. It certainly helped that Ferdinand and Isabella, like the would-be explorer himself, knew next to nothing about the people, governance, or culture of Asia. Very likely when Columbus referred to the "Great Khan" he meant Kublai Khan, the Mongol conqueror who loomed large over the most famous text of early European encounter with the East, *The Book of Marvels* by the late medieval Venetian merchant Marco Polo. A Latin edition of Polo's travelogue was among the prized possessions of Columbus's youth. His copy, in the collection of the Columbine Library of Seville, contains comments in the explorer's own hand that show just how inspiring this book of tall tales and exaggeration was to the man whose own exploits would become part of the mythology of America itself.

That Kublai Khan was long dead and his dynasty finished for more than one hundred years would have been news to Columbus and his patrons, but no matter. The specter of the Great Khan converting to "doctrines of perdition" and thus becoming predisposed to strike out against Christian kingdoms was enough to alter perception of what might be gained if Columbus was successful in his mission. According to Columbus's journal, permission was granted to him that very month, though it remained unclear how the funding for an ongoing exploration of uncharted lands and waters might be maintained.

A further step toward Columbus's voyage occurred later that same year, in the same palace. Following the advice of Tomás de Torquemada, the Dominican priest who was the Grand Inquisitor of the Spanish Inquisition, the Catholic Monarchs signed the Alhambra Decree, the order of expulsion of all Jews from the kingdom. For years, Torquemada had been the scourge of religious minorities in Spain, making particular targets of converts from Judaism and Islam. The Inquisitor's motivating fear was that though many Jews and Muslims had become Christian in name, they had done so for the entirely practical reason of avoiding persecution, rather than as the result of a genuine conversion to the faith. So-called crypto-Muslims (Moriscos) and crypto-Jews (Marranos) were thought to be everywhere, and Torquemada oversaw a campaign of torture and execution to root them out. While the Inquisition had no official authority over the nonbaptized, the original communities from which Moriscos and Marranos came were seen to be the source of the problem. Hebrew and Arabic religious texts were burned in town squares, and the readers of those texts frequently found themselves following their books into the flames.

With the decree issued in March of 1492, all the Jews in Spain were given six months to leave. Two hundred thousand would ultimately abandon their homes and livelihoods in the only land their families had known for generations. Like the riches of Alhambra, much of the wealth of Jews fleeing Torquemada's fires fell into royal hands, which in turn financed Columbus's expedition of commerce and evangelism.

Of those few converted Jews allowed to remain, some of whom were friends and advisors to the Crown, many felt obliged to contribute personally to the voyage. Foremost among these was Luís de Santángel, finance minister to the royal court, who supported Columbus's case for the necessity of converting the Mongol Empire, and put up a sizable portion of his own fortune — 17,000 ducats — as a sign of loyalty to the kingdom and the faith.

It would be too easy to conclude that the voyage of Columbus was the result of simple cause and effect, but chronology does tell a tale. When Columbus first sought Spanish resources for his expedition, none were to be found. After the capture of Muslim and Jewish wealth, the way was suddenly clear. With funds gained from the confiscation of Moorish treasures and the expulsion of Spain's Jews, Columbus was free to take his journey. Without the two-pronged assault on the religious diversity of the kingdom, it seems unlikely Columbus's ships would have ever left port.

Yet, like the larger history of the world about to be born, this is not merely an account of the attempted destruction of the weak by the strong. It is, also, a story of resilience.

The Grand Inquisitor Torquemada was not wrong when he assumed that Jews and Muslims were flouting the authority of the church through pro forma baptisms that did little to change their religious practices or beliefs. Throughout Spain, and later in nearly all the lands to which the Spanish would travel, entire communities of nominal Christians were found to avoid pork, pray in non-Latin tongues, read forbidden books, and generally maintain their spiritual heritage despite the threat of such marvels of medieval technology as the Judas Cradle or the Heretic's Fork. Over time, as one generation of keepers of a hidden faith gave way to the next, Marranos and Moriscos often lost awareness of who their forebears had been, and yet remnants of the old ways of worship survived. In fact, the Grand Inquisitor may have had personal experience of this. Torquemada's grandmother was a baptized Jew, as were others in his extended family. His zeal for hunting Marranos, then, likely arose, at least in part, from a strategy of self-preservation.

*   *   *

The possibility that Columbus himself had Jewish roots has been the subject of heated debate among historians. Those who think it likely roll out the fact that the family name, Colón, had a distinctly Jewish ring to it at the time; likewise, the family business, wool weaving, was one of the few occupations open to Jews in their native Genoa. Others point to the support Columbus received from well-placed baptized Jews in the court of Ferdinand and Isabella, and to the presence of markings that appear to be Hebrew letters on several extant documents written in his hand.

Circumstantial evidence aside, the Jewish Columbus will likely never be more than speculation. Far more certain is the fact that even if Columbus himself was inarguably as Christian as the Catholic Monarchs who finally approved his journey across the sea, the men who helped him get there were less so. The ability of marginal traditions to persevere in the face of persecution was so strong that expeditions conceived and undertaken for the purpose of extending the reach of the church unwittingly facilitated the spread not only of religious orthodoxy but spiritual dissent as well. It was not just a Muslim palace and Jewish ducats that helped Columbus on his way, but a few of the souls the Catholic Monarchs had attempted to rid themselves of earlier that same eventful year.

When they set sail from Spain—on the very day that served as the deadline for Jews to leave—Columbus's small fleet served as unlikely life rafts for a handful of men of Jewish birth who would have preferred to continue their lives as not only Jews but Spaniards. Those who signed on to sail with Columbus included not only criminals given amnesty for the purpose but Marranos and perhaps Moriscos as well. While most were professional sailors with miles of sea behind them, many were marginal men who surely had reasons to take the risk. Boarding the *Niña*, the *Pinta*, and the *Santa Maria* offered a kind of deliverance for these men. They were fleeing a place of religious persecution and sailing for an unknown land that offered freedom in its mystery.

Columbus, too, saw something of an Exodus narrative in his journey. As he writes in his journal, after two months at sea, the crew began to "murmur" just as the Hebrews did against Moses as he led them endlessly through the desert. They had begun to see tantalizing signs of land, but it seemed the winds had died and they might progress no farther. In the sky above, they noted turtle doves and pelicans, birds that rarely wandered far from shore; in the waters below, they saw weeds poking up from the depths, busy with crabs clinging to patches of green oasis in the desert of the empty ocean. But signs of land are a far cry from land itself. If neither gale nor current moved them, the three ships would float aimlessly, with little hope of reaching new ground or turning back the way they came. Later that day, Columbus writes, when the sea rose and began to move without wind, the crew was astonished—and relieved. The Admiral thought it was a very good sign, because, he remembered, such things often happened to the prophets of scripture. In his estimation, he was not merely a mariner, but a spiritual titan leading the way toward the Promised Land.

That Christopher Columbus believed he was on a mission from God is evident in nearly every document he has left us. It was not just a line he sold to Ferdinand and Isabella. Whatever his material ambitions—which were so considerable he believed himself personally entitled to 10 percent of anything he found—his real motivation seems to have been a fervent, and at times fanatical, devotion to his faith. Eventually he came to believe the accidental propaganda of his name. He was the namesake of the third-century Christian saint who, according to legend, had once carried a small but unbelievably heavy boy across a dangerous river. The boy, as this pious folktale explained, was Jesus himself, making an appearance centuries after his death, holding the weight of the world within him. For this reason, the saint was called Christopher, literally, "the bearer of Christ." Columbus believed the burden of carrying the savior across the waters had now fallen to him.

Neither the Admiral nor the sailors under his command could have known this, but they would not be the first to bring alien religious traditions to the New World.

Though the suggestion was once ridiculed, it is today well known that Norsemen visited North America five hundred years before Columbus set sail. As Geraldine Barnes notes in her history *Viking America*, the fact that Leif Erikson's longship had arrived long before the *Niña*, the *Pinta*, or the *Santa Maria* was seen throughout the nineteenth century as a challenge to "the image of America as a land unseen, unnamed and otherwise without mortal creator before 1492...imping[ing] on questions of national history and identity." That great mythmaker Washington Irving, whose best-selling book about Columbus gave him an obvious interest in maintaining the singularity of the Admiral as the discoverer of the Americas, scoffed at Viking tales of encounter with the native tribes of Canada as mere legends. At best, he insisted, Erikson had enjoyed "transient glimpses of the new world...in a little time lost again to mankind." Another doubter of the day dismissed supposed evidence to the contrary as "the sublime of humbuggery."

The confidence of the naysayers could not prevent the facts from becoming more widely known. Around the year 1000, Leif Erikson came ashore and established a Viking foothold with an encampment he called Vinland, which today is thought to have been in Newfoundland. *The Saga of the Greenlanders* describes the exploits of the Erikson clan—Leif, Thorvald, and Thorstein, the sons of Erik the Red—as they explored and inhabited Vinland, and eventually ran afoul of its occupants. It is thanks to the volley of arrows that cut Thorvald down, or more precisely to the funeral that followed, that we know something of the religious practices he and his brothers imported. The Eriksons arrived in North America at the precise moment their people were becoming Christianized, converted from their traditional belief in the gods of Scandinavian mythology through contact with the European mainland. And so as Thorvald lay dying, he asked to be brought to a spot where he had imagined building a home. "There shall ye bury me," he said, "and set up crosses at my head and feet." The Vikings, then, were the first Christians in America. And this new faith may not have been the only religion they carried across the sea. The buried man's very name, which means "the power of Thor," suggests they also brought gods they had known far longer than Christ.

The possibility that still another Old World faith arrived before Columbus is suggested by tales of North African Muslims who allegedly stumbled upon the Americas not long after the Eriksons. The eleventh-century geographer Abu Abdallah Muhammad Ibn Muhammad Ibn Abdallah Ibn Idrisi, commonly referred to as Idrisi, alludes to lands on the far side of the Atlantic in a geography and travelogue with a title just barely longer than his name: *The going out of a Curious Man to explore the Regions of the Globe, its Provinces, Islands, Cities and their Dimensions and Situation*, abbreviated variously as *"The Amusement of him who Desires to Traverse the Earth," "The Peregrinations of one who longs to Penetrate New Horizons,"* and also simply as "Roger's Book," in honor of his patron, Roger II of

Sicily. At Roger's direction and on his dime, Idrisi selected "certain intelligent men, who were despatched on travels and were accompanied by draftsmen." When these travelers and mapmakers returned, Idrisi inserted their descriptions into his narrative and reworked his vision of the world accordingly. Though sponsored by a Christian king, Idrisi made clear from the opening words whom he hoped to glorify through his work. "All grace goes back to Allah," he writes, "the essentially great and powerful being." Viewing exploration as a fundamentally Islamic enterprise, he dated his manuscript in relation to the prophetic career of Muhammad, explaining that it was completed in the year "548 of Hijra." A man of a faith perhaps even more fervently missionary than that of his patron, Idrisi thus found it fitting to send Muslim explorers into the unknown ocean he referred to as the "Gloomy Sea," otherwise known as the Atlantic. "No one knows what lies beyond it," he wrote, because of "the great expanse of its waters, the plethora of its horrors, the reach of its beasts, and the frenzy of its winds." However, when his commissioned explorers returned, he was able to note that they had been held captive for a time on an island on the other side of the darkness and fog, where the navigators saw "people with red skin" with "not much hair on their bodies." The women of the island, he further noted, "were extraordinarily beautiful."

Similarly, the Arabic-inscribed maps of the Ottoman cartographer Ahmed Muhiddin Piri showed the northeast coast of South America in relationship to the West coast of Africa as early as 1513. Considered in the context of the work of Idrisi, who elsewhere described China in obsessive detail and argued with confidence that the world was round but not perfectly spherical ("the Earth is," he wrote, "plunged in space like the yoke in a middle of an egg"), such maps provide evidence of an era of Islamic geographic awareness predating Columbus that has nearly been lost to history. Moreover, the collaboration of the Christian King Roger and the Muslim scholar Idrisi, as well as the speed with which later maps crossed between cultures, suggest the porousness of religious boundaries despite the ongoing hostilities between Christendom and the Islamic world.

Perhaps the most developed of the legends of the ancient exploration of the Americas involves Chinese seamen, who unlike Western adventurers would have sailed east toward the New World.

Chinese maps created one thousand years before Columbus embarked describe a land known as Fusang, across the Pacific from the Middle Kingdom. After initial discovery, it was said that Buddhist priests made a journey to Fusang to establish their faith, and "carried with them their books and sacred images and the ritual... and so changed the manners of the inhabitants." In the eighteenth century, European historians and mapmakers argued over the theory of French sinologist Joseph de Guignes, author of the comprehensive *History of the Huns, Mongols, and Turks,* that Fusang referred to the west coast of the Americas. Advocates of the Fusang-as-America hypothesis pointed to ancient descriptions of long-horned cattle very much like American buffalo, and to the place these same texts referred to as the "Country of Women," which European intellectuals of the day assumed to be the Amazon. De Guignes, it should be noted, also believed that China itself began as a colony of the ancient Egyptians; such eighteenth-century theories are, in the opinion of Chinese historian Joseph Needham, "youthful indiscretions at which modern sinology is accustomed to blush."

True or not, the legend of Fusang—like the once-dismissed tale of Norse discovery and the still-speculative accounts of North African adventurers—is a reminder that the land first brought to the attention of southern Europe a little more than five hundred years ago has been a part of the world's religions much longer than that. Perhaps one thousand years before Columbus, the possibility of America already had religious meanings that had nothing to do with the faith he brought with him. Not only did the land's original inhabitants have their own notions concerning the spiritual significance of the places they called home; every culture for which the land beyond the waters served as the great unknown had made it a part of its own mythology and aspirations. In response to these, there may have been a constellation of discoveries: the Vikings in the Northeast; navigators from the Pacific in the Southwest; the southern Europeans in the Southeast, all of whom "found" a land that had not been lost, a fruitfully inhabited place more vast and diverse—geographically and spiritually—than any of the great discoverers could have imagined.

These possibilities, however, do nothing to lessen the drama of the only fully known moment of first contact, when the people of Europe met the people of the world they would mistakenly call new, and the gods of each learned they were not alone in the heavens.

Late in the night of October 12, 1492, in the crow's nest high on the main mast of the *Pinta*, the fastest of Columbus's ships, it was one of the crew's Marranos, Rodrigo de Triana, who spotted a reflected light on the horizon, the moon's glow on beach sand. "Tierra! Tierra!" he called out. *Land!*

The first man to make such a sighting had been promised a substantial bonus, but Columbus, in keeping with his self-identification with Moses—the first to lay eyes on the Land of Canaan—claimed to have seen the light earlier that evening. When the full crews of all three ships began to search the horizon, others began to see the light as well. The first glimpse they had of what would soon be called the "Fourth Part of the World"—a mysterious new land added to the current understanding of the earth as consisting of Europe, Asia, and Africa—resembled only the light of "a wax candle rising and falling." According to the Admiral's journal, many doubted this tiny glimmer could be the land they had all but given up hope of reaching. Both Columbus and Triana believed, however, even if only one would be rewarded.

Triana's response to the slight of being denied his bonus, which Columbus claimed for himself, went undocumented. However, stories told about him for centuries have attempted to fill in the gaps. After the journey home, disappointed to return to a country still hostile to his religious ancestry, Triana is said to have drifted to North Africa, where reports began to circulate that the first European to see the New World had begun to follow Islam. As a nineteenth-century account put it, "It is hardly to be wondered at, that one treated so unjustly should abandon his native land and new religion, to seek shelter with the Moors, whom he counted less inclined to take from a poor man his just deserts." Born a Jew, living as a Christian, destined to die as a Muslim, he was a man with a hidden spiritual arc to his life that is mostly missing from tales of Europe's discovery of the continent.

The differences between the three faiths of Rodrigo de Triana would have been incomprehensible to the Taino, a people who had many gods because the world had many needs. They may have found the warring theologies of Spain impoverished in their singularity, despite the obvious wealth of those who brought them.

When the Taino spotted three great wooden vessels drifting toward their lands, groups of young men swam out to investigate, calling back to those on shore. The words they used were unintelligible to those whose memory would win the day—but of those on board the ships, at least one believed the Taino were singing about them as if they were zemies made flesh. Columbus alone thought he could understand the cries of the Taino. He recorded the initial interactions of the Old World and the New in his meticulous journal of the voyage: "Come and see the men who have come from the heavens!" he later claimed to have heard them shout.

Despite his questionable interpretation of the words that greeted him, Columbus would soon also say that as far as he could tell, the Taino were a people without religion—an assessment, we now know, that would be no more true of Rome.

In an era when one's creed was much less a matter of choice than we might assume it is today, being without religion was nearly unheard of; the very possibility was an indication that the world may not be as it seemed. The universe of Columbus's time was divided neatly among Christians, Jews, Muslims, and Mongols. Theologically, the assumption that the Taino had no religion raised for Columbus the question of whether or not such people had souls, which in turn suggested that they may not be human at all.

One can see in Columbus's own writings how this unmoored him. In the years that followed his first encounter with the Taino, his understanding of where he had been, and whom he had met, would change wildly. For a time he believed he had found Paradise itself; he imagined the world at the time not as an almost perfect sphere but rather as a shape closer to a pear, with the vestiges of Eden poking up from the top of the globe like, in his words, a nipple on a breast. Alternately, he wondered if he had found a spot inhabited by the lost tribes of Israel. He would devote his later years to the production of a text, written in collaboration with a cloistered monk, proving through biblical citation that his discoveries had ensured that Jerusalem would be retaken for Christendom, bringing about the second coming of Christ. In his largely forgotten *Book of Prophecies,* Columbus identifies himself as a figure whose arrival is hinted at throughout scripture. "I have already said that for my voyage to the Indies neither intelligence nor mathematics nor world maps were of any use to me," he wrote. "It was the fulfillment of the prophecy of the Prophet Isaiah."

All these thoughts had their beginnings as he looked upon the Taino and heard their awestruck shouts as hosannas of welcome, believing they were overjoyed to see a man so grand he must be their savior.

Very likely they believed quite the opposite. If the Taino had feared their neighbors the Caribs as lethal goblins from the under-world, bringers of the end of days, what would they have thought of this new "race of men wearing clothes"? What would the zemies say such men might do to their children and their gods?

On this score, there is no need to speculate. At least some among the Taino looked upon the three ships of Columbus as Christians might have looked upon the Four Horsemen of the Apocalypse, forms given to the fears of a culture nearing its end.

Peter Martyr d'Anghiera, the Italian-born chronicler of the final days of the Taino, wrote in 1511, "When the Spaniards landed the islanders then referred the prophecy to them, as being the peo-ple whose coming was announced. And in this they were not wrong...for under the domination of the Christians, those who resisted have been killed."

Soon after landing—though not immediately—Columbus realized he was nowhere near the place he called "India" or the prince he called "the Great Khan." One wonders if the frustration and befud-dlement he felt at this revelation could have rivaled the emotions that inspired the fabled "Moor's last sigh." That earlier lament had been offered for a kingdom and a fortune lost; Columbus's grief now was for a kingdom and fortune of his own that never would be. If he had not reached the lands known as the East, there would be no large-scale conversion of the Mongol Empire. The lucrative new trade route with the Orient he had promised his royal patrons was now proved a fiction. Judged by its initial intentions, Colum-bus's mission was a failure both spiritually and commercially. The only way to salvage his reputation would be to find some way to wring profit from an otherwise disastrous expedition. After a mostly fruitless search for gold, he chose the only commodities readily available: land and bodies. To claim the former, he planted the same Catholic standards he had seen raised over Alhambra, and established beneath them a fort he named for the birth of Christ, Navidad. To claim the latter, he took five hundred Taino by force and shipped them back to Spain. More than half died on the way—a horrific rate of survival that nonetheless offered better chances than those faced by all who remained, for whom murder, disease, and forced labor were the immediate implications of life under the banner of Christendom.

As it was chronicled by the sixteenth-century Dominican historian Bartolomé de las Casas in his *A Brief Account of the Destruction of the Indies*, the decades that followed Columbus's arrival rivaled any torment dreamed up by the Inquisition. "The *Spaniards* first assaulted the innocent Sheep...like most cruel Tygers, Wolves and Lions hunger-starv'd," las Casas wrote, "studying nothing, for the space of Forty Years, after their first landing, but the Massacre of these Wretches, whom they have so inhumanely and barbarously butchered and harassed with several kinds of Torments never before known or heard...that of Three Millions of Persons, which lived in *Hispaniola* itself, there is at present but the inconsiderable remnant of scarce Three Hundred." Elsewhere in the Caribbean, las Casas continues, three hundred would have seemed a multitude:

> The Isle of *Cuba*, which extends as far as *Valledolid* in *Spain* is distant from *Rome*, lies now uncultivated, like a Desert, and intomb'd in its own Ruins. You may also find the Isles of St. *John*, and *Jamaica*, both large and fruitful places, unpeopled and desolate. The *Lucayan* Islands on the North Side, adjacent to *Hispaniola* and *Cuba*, which are Sixty in number...is now laid waste and uninhabited; and whereas, when the *Spaniards* first arriv'd here, about Five Hundred Thousand Men dwelt in it, they are now cut off, some by slaughter, and others ravished away by Force and Violence, to work in the Mines of *Hispaniola*, which was destitute of Native Inhabitants...There are other Islands, Thirty in number, and upward bordering upon the Isle of St. *John*, totally unpeopled; all which are above Two Thousand miles in Length, and yet remain without Inhabitants.

Las Casas was all but alone among the Spanish in his attempt to look to his faith for sources of sympathy for a vanishing people. He compared them to the hermits of the early church for the holy simplicity of their lives, and noted the zeal and fervor of their spiritual sentiments. Far more common than his approach to the native population, however, was the use of religion as the justification for, and even the methodology of, their subjugation. On the island of Hispaniola, in the shadow of the fort Columbus had named for the birth of Christ, specially designed gallows were constructed to hang the Taino thirteen at a time, "in Honour and Reverence" to the "Redeemer and his Twelve Apostles." The executioners made sure these gibbets were "large, but low made," so that the feet of the dead almost reached the ground, where "they made a Fire to burn them to Ashes," oblivious to the fact that this tableau of thirteen souls arranged in a line transformed the classic depiction of the Last Supper into an icon of death.

That religion was the cudgel with which they were being beaten was not lost on the Taino. While at first many among them may have, as las Casas notes, "reverenced [the Spanish] as Persons descended from Heaven," within a generation it was clear that the newcomers and their God had only ill intentions.

In 1511, on the island of Cuba, a cacique named Hatuey who had escaped the torments on Hispaniola gathered his people together to discuss rumors that the Spanish would soon be upon them. While there was general agreement that they were "cruelly and wickedly inclined," no one could guess why this was so. Pressing the issue, Hatuey asked, "Do you not know the cause and reason of their coming?" They did not, the people replied. "They adore a certain Covetous Deity," Hatuey explained, "whose cravings are not to be satisfied by a few moderate offerings, but they may answer his Adoration and Worship, demand many unreasonable things of us, and use their utmost endeavors to subjugate and afterwards murder us." Hatuey then took up a chest full of gold and gems and showed them its glittering contents. "This is the Spaniards' God," he said. "If we Worship this Deity...we shall be destroyed. Therefore I judge it convenient, upon mature deliberation, that we cast it into the River." And with agreement from all, this is just what they did.

Yet though the symbol of the alien god had been easily fed to the waters and swept away, its emissaries would not be so easily dispatched. Hatuey led an armed resistance against the Spanish across the island but soon was captured and condemned. Bound to a post with kindling strewn about his feet, he was again confronted with the newcomers' God, this time in the person of a Franciscan priest. The friar spoke to him of "eternal glory" and everlasting life open to those who believe. As Las Casas records the conversation that followed: "After Hatuey had been silently pensive sometime, he asked the Monk whether the Spaniards also were admitted into Heaven."

"The Gates of Heaven are open to all that are Good and Godly," the monk answered.

Hearing this, Hatuey "replied without further consideration." He would rather go to hell, he said, than risk sharing heaven with "so Sanguinary and Bloody a Nation."

Far from an aberration, Hatuey's story of spiritual resistance is the norm in las Casas's history, which serves as a catalogue not only of the torments inflicted by the Spanish but of the lengths to which the people of the Americas would go in order to maintain their traditional practices and beliefs even in the face of certain slaughter. Rather than die at the hands of Christians preaching their love of a God of mercy as they unsheathed their swords, Taino by the "multitude," in las Casas's estimation, took their own lives to "put an end to those Calamities." Because of the ferocity of just one particular "Spanish tyrant," las Casas adds, "above Two Hundred *Indians* hang'd themselves of their own accord." Peter Martyr d'Anghiera adds that it was not merely for the living that the Taino took such extreme actions but for those yet to be born. The treatment by the Spanish, he wrote, "is killing them in great numbers and reducing the others to such a state of despair that many kill themselves, or refuse to procreate their kind. It is alleged that the pregnant women take drugs to produce abortion, knowing that the children they bear will become the slaves of the Christians."

This battle of religious will was fought not only over lives but over objects of devotion. Ramón Pané describes attempting to convert a Taino village by presenting it with a collection of sacred images and asking the villagers to keep them safe. No sooner had the missionary left, however, than several men among the Taino threw the images on the ground, covered them with dirt, and urinated on them, mocking the missionary's attempts to plant his faith in this soil by saying, "Now will you yield good and abundant fruit?" *A Brief Account of the Destruction of the Indies* further recounts tales of zemies and other religious items that were defended as zealously as a mother defended her daughter when "a profligate Christian attempted to devirginate the Maid." In every case, such altercations ended well for no one: mother, daughter, or the believers protecting the objects of their devotion. For the mother's offense of preventing rape, las Casas notes, "the Spaniard[,] enraged, cut off her Hand with a short Sword, and stab'd the Virgin in several places, till she Expir'd, because she obstinately opposed and disappointed his inordinate Appetite." The same might be said of the native beliefs that resisted Christian advances. Though their holiest objects were merely small statues fashioned from the world around them, they seemed to the faithful to suffer and die as surely as if they were flesh and bone.

Near the end of his treatise las Casas writes with exhausted finality, "This Deep, Bloody *American* Tragedy is now concluded." But of course it had only just begun.

The events that today suggest Columbus, wittingly or not, initiated a genocide are well known. Yet there remains something useful, even hopeful, in an untold meeting that occurred before the worst of this history began.

Within a week of his arrival in the islands of North America, Columbus sent an interpreter to try to communicate with the native people. Because he imagined himself taking part in a religious adventure that would complete narratives begun in the Bible, the interpreter Columbus had chosen to bring on this journey, Luis de Torres, was himself a secret Jew — and among the languages with which he was familiar were Hebrew and Arabic. It was through this translator that the first prolonged encounter between Europe and the Americas took place.

To see the world as Columbus saw it — with himself divinely ordained to find a place he at times believed to be Eden — requires a significant leap of the imagination. It takes far less to imagine what transpired when Columbus's Marrano translator made his way cautiously into the Taino village. The first greeting would have been offered in one of the non-Christian languages that de Torres had been brought to speak. It has become a popular trope of Jewish American humor to propose that he may have said "shalom." Yet given his linguistic repertoire, and the symbolic connections the Spanish would soon begin making between Indians and the Arab world (to be discussed in the next chapter), de Torres just as likely hailed them as a Muslim might, with the words "*a salaam aleikum.*"

Whatever his language, this greeting and the unrecorded response of the Taino were likely spoken under the banner of the cross—as all words on these islands soon would be. On balance, it cannot be denied that the beliefs brought ashore by Columbus had a greater impact on the future of the land and the people who would come to live here than did those of the man in the crow's nest who traded one faith for another, or the men, women, and children whose faith would soon seemingly disappear. Yet like the beliefs and practices of Jews and Muslims in Catholic Spain, many of the ways of the Taino did not simply vanish; they went underground. Even as the newcomers to the island fulfilled the prophecy heard by the caciques by capturing and slaughtering those who had been there for generations, certain elements of indigenous spiritual practices remained. Soon not just forts but churches were built by the European conquerors, and in their shadow small statues of stone or wood continued to be carved and imbued with religious significance.

Over time, the people who made the statues ceased calling them zemies, giving them instead a name more in keeping with the culture that had come to rule the land. The statues the true believers prayed to and beseeched for visions of the future were now called santos, images of Christian saints carved from conch shells, mangrove trees, coral rock; three-dimensional scriptures made from the formless materials of the earth. They can be seen in churches and bodegas from Havana, to Los Angeles, to the place the descendants of the Spanish and the Taino would later call *Nueva York*. They are relics of a faith forced into exile, still hiding in plain sight.

Cortes, with the Moorish soldier Estevanico, entering Mexico, c. 1550. Mexican School/Bibliothèque Nationale, Paris/ The Bridgeman Art Library.

CHAPTER 2

An American Jihad

1513-1540

When Mustafa Zemmouri was a boy, he saw the towering masts of invading gunships become as much a part of the Azemmour skyline as its minarets. Three days on foot from Casablanca (then known in the Berber language as Anfa), the walled Moroccan port city was named for the groves of wild olive trees, *azemur*, that grew in the surrounding countryside. It would later become infamous as a slave market, where thousands would be sold into captivity and sent on the often fatal journey to the Americas. But in 1513, the occupation of Azemmour by the Portuguese was only just beginning, the trans-Atlantic slave trade not yet born, and the lone individual enslavement of enduring significance soon to take place in the city was that of a Muslim boy not much older than thirteen.

Disappeared into the dark hold of a European ship as thousands of others like him would be, young Mustafa surely should have been forgotten by history, just another casualty of the ancient grudge between the forces of Caliphates and Christendom. Instead, precisely because of his ability to move between faiths, he survived the confines of slavery to become the first man of the Old World to make his way across the vast expanse of the New.

For nearly a millennium, the city that gave this boy the name Zemmouri had been a place known for its blending of beliefs. From the earliest arrival of Islam in Morocco in the seventh century, Azemmour became home to a variant of the Muslim faith that commingled the teachings of the Prophet Muhammad with doctrines borrowed from Judaism and Christianity, while also making free use of the ancient astrology that guided the nomadic tribes of the region as well as popular rituals of magic and witchcraft.

Moroccan religious life was remarkable mainly because of a syncretic system of local devotion known as maraboutism, named for *murabits*, mystic teachers largely of the Sufi school of Islam who gathered followers within fortified strongholds called *ribats*. Within these ribats, which were built in coastal cities like Azemmour as bulwarks against European invasion, each mubarit instructed his disciples with his own idiosyncratic interpretations of the many religious experiences available at the time. They were linked by a common element: the training of disciples as defenders against crusaders from the north. Guided by maraboutism, Azemmour for centuries had been open to the blending of practices and belief within, but watchful for the imposition of faith from without.

Closer to Mustafa Zemmouri's time, Azemmour served as a refuge for Jews and Muslims driven from Catholic Spain. A city of thousands in the year of his birth, it remained home to sizable Jewish and Christian minorities, who lived more or less in peace among the Muslim majority, a miniature *convivencia* — coexistence — that had proved tragically ephemeral across the Strait of Gibraltar.

Yet the peace of Azemmour was challenged throughout the years of Zemmouri's childhood. After a failed attempt to take the city in 1508, and a refusal by local leaders to pay tribute to a Christian monarch, the Portuguese returned in force in 1513. As the sixteenth-century diplomat and historian Leo Africanus described the onset of the invasion, "the king sent another navy of two hundred sail well furnished, at the very sight whereof the citizens were so discomfited, that they all betook themselves to flight." Addressing his reader, he notes, "Neither could you...have refrained from teares, had you seene the weak women, the silly old men, and the tender children run away bare-footed and forlorn." If Mustafa Zemmouri and his family were among those trying to escape, they would have been disappointed. "The throng was so great at their entrance of the gates, that more than fourscore citizens were slain therein," Leo Africanus writes, "and so the Christians obtained the city."

In the aftermath of the naval invasion (which counted among its 15,000-strong landing force Ferdinand Magellan, just six years before he set off to circumnavigate the globe), economic conditions became dire enough that children of working age sold themselves into slavery, trading their poverty and freedom for the possibility of food and shelter.

This, it seems, was the decision made by young Mustafa Zemmouri, or perhaps by his parents, or else by those who had either economic or legal control over the boy and his family. The circumstances that led to his departure were part of a systematic assault on the culture of the region, a set of repressive measures that soon would lead the locals to wage an armed insurgency against the Christian invaders. As in other places at other times where devout Muslims had attached religious significance to their guerrilla campaigns, those fighting against the Portuguese identified themselves by the same term that had been used for the disciples of the *murabits* within the ramparts of religious and military instruction: mujahideen. And they knew their mission by the Arabic word for struggle: jihad.

Zemmouri would not be there to join this struggle, or to revel in its success when the Portuguese evacuated in 1541. He would see neither his city nor his family again. He was transported out of Africa, first to Portugal and then Spain—and, in the process, became someone new. Like virtually all of the Muslims brought in bondage to a land that had chased Islam from its shores just a generation before, he was converted to Catholicism, either by the slaver who sold him or by the man who bought him. If by the former, his conversion was likely accomplished for marketing purposes: A Christian slave had fewer restrictions placed on where he could live and work, and so was a more portable asset. If, on the other hand, he was converted by his new owner, it was likely for the belief that a slave of one's own faith was easier to control. Conversions at the time were most often practical and pro forma; they said little conclusively about the convert's loyalties or his beliefs, as Spain's obsessive fear of secret Jews and crypto-Muslims well proved.

Regardless of the sincerity of his conversion, Zemmouri became known in his captivity as Esteban, the name of the first Christian martyr, and sometimes by the diminutive Estebanico, "Little Stephen." Yet even after he had been renamed, he still was frequently referred to simply as "the Arab," "the black," or "the Moor." The place he had come from, the color of his skin, and the faith he had professed when he boarded the slave ship in

Azemmour, these were the things that defined him—certainly to others, and likely to himself.

It was fitting, then, that he would soon find himself undertaking a righteous struggle of his own—not for faith but for his freedom. While his countrymen had fought for their own land, the jihad of Mustafa Zemmouri would take him across an ocean, and into the heart of America.

To understand what became of the boy from Azemmour in the mostly unknown place to which he was soon sent, we need to return for a moment to the earliest encounter between Europe and the New World. Within twenty years of Columbus's collision with the Taino people, the Spanish began to realize they had stumbled onto more than a scattering of islands. And while Columbus himself had fixated, until his death in 1506, on his own imagined individual role as a divinely inspired explorer-king predicted by biblical prophecy, the religiously obsessed civilization that had birthed this "Christ-bearer" had its own preoccupations.

The vast interior of North America was thought by some to be home to the Seven Cities of Cibola, which according to legend were not only kingdoms made entirely of gold but were, like Mustafa Zemmouri's exile from Azemmour, born of the clash of Christendom and the Islamic world. As pious stories passed down for generations told the tale, some eight hundred years before, seven bishops had fled the Iberian Peninsula ahead of invading Moorish armies. Each had escaped along with a crowd of the faithful on vessels left by their attackers at Gibraltar. As the legend continued, these bishops and their followers, upon reaching an island in the "sea of darkness," had burned their ships to ashes to avoid the temptation of return. They then built seven cities, each home to a single bishop and the souls in his care, each rich with treasures saved by Christians from the infidel hordes.

This saga was undoubtedly a fairy tale, albeit one of epic proportions. The supposed site of the seven bishops' landing and subsequent construction of their cities had island-hopped across the Atlantic in the European imagination with each successive discovery of terra incognita. Placed variously on the Canary Islands and the Azores, the mythical cities also cast a shadow in the form of the most enduring lost civilization story, Atlantis. As recorded in perhaps the first-ever global depiction of the earth's geography, the

German cartographer Martin Behaim placed the cities on the island of Antilia:

> In the year 734 of Christ when the whole of Spain had been won by the heathen of Africa, the above island Antilia called Septa Citade [Seven Cities] was inhabited by an archbishop from Porto in Portugal, with six other bishops and other Christians, men and women, who had fled thither from Spain by ship, together with their cattle, belongings and goods. 1414 a ship from Spain got near it without being endangered.

Far from confirming that these legends were nothing but the daydreams of devout imaginations, the inability to substantiate the rumors of their existence became proof that they must lie somewhere in the expanse of the newly discovered territories. The hope of finally locating the Cities of Cibola was one of the earliest and most provocative enticements to undertake the arduous exploration of the North American continent.

The journey into a region subsequent explorers came to refer to as the Northern Mystery was not only about laying claim to riches or mapping the unknown. It was, for the Iberian adventurers who began the European plunder of America, about the recovery of a supposedly lost religious heritage. If found, the cities would of course make their rediscoverers rich. More importantly, their reclamation would ease the centuries-old national embarrassment of having lost "the whole of Spain" to "the heathen of Africa" and their alien faith, Islam. The enduring rivalry between these two empires of belief made the position of anyone with a foot in each world particularly precarious yet also particularly open to the possibility of transformation — as the boy from Azemmour would soon discover.

While the facts of his youth can only be conjectured, it is certain that upon leaving North Africa the young Moroccan eventually arrived in Spain, where he was sold into the service of a man roughly his own age, the nobleman Andrés Dorantes. Though only in his twenties, Dorantes had already seen his share of fighting, and had the scars to prove it. He wore the mark of a saber slash across his face from his experience suppressing an uprising of

Castilians against the youthful King Charles V during a clash known as the Revolt of the Comuneros of 1520. As it is likely Zemmouri had come into the service of Dorantes before or during the battle that left the latter disfigured, it is possible that the two men were already comrades-in-arms by the time they set sail for America seven years later.

Peers they were not, however. The choice to join such an expedition belonged to Dorantes alone. When the apparently adventure-hungry Spaniard was invited by a fellow veteran of the Comunero revolt to join some six hundred soldiers, sailors, and slaves on a voyage to New Spain, Zemmouri had no choice but to go along. Had he been asked, he would have had ample reasons to decline. To begin with, a person owned was far less likely to return from such a voyage than the one who owned him. Moreover, the family history of the man responsible for their participation — Álvar Núñez Cabeza de Vaca — might have seemed a bad omen for what lay ahead.

Cabeza de Vaca, ten years senior to Zemmouri and Andrés Dorantes, was to be treasurer of the expedition and would later become its accidental scribe as the author of a chronicle of one of the most calamitous journeys in history. In the 1542 *relación* he wrote about the ordeal, he is also cast as the expedition's hero.

To the men who struggled with him, this was likely not a surprise. Taking credit for the exploits of others was written into his very name. According to possibly apocryphal tradition, his odd moniker, which literally means "Head of the Cow," had been earned through one of the violent intersections of faith that punctuate Spanish history. Passed down for centuries on his mother's side, the honorific "Cabeza de Vaca" had been bestowed originally on a medieval Iberian shepherd named Martin Halaja, who once infamously used a bovine skull to mark a hidden pass to an encampment of Moors, allowing the Catholic armies of the Reconquista to march under cover of darkness, surprise their enemy at daybreak, and kill them in their tents. Thus awarded a dubious title, Halaja passed it down to his heirs, and they to theirs, ten generations of Cows' Heads until the Moor-killing legend of Cabeza de Vaca was carried across the sea. It is a great joke of the fates that we know of Zemmouri's life mostly because of Cabeza de Vaca's account of their journey together. They were a Morisco and a man named for a slaughter of Muslims, joined by disaster.

Together with Dorantes, Cabeza de Vaca, and some six hundred others, Zemmouri set out in late 1527 as part of a mission to explore, colonize, and gain the riches of the New World, though doubtless he knew none of this wealth would be his. Most of it would go to the expedition's official leader, Pánfilo Narváez, who had served in the Spanish territories before, as lieutenant governor of Cuba, and was returning now for a piece of what he considered his due.

Eight years earlier, Narváez had been sent on an ill-fated mission to arrest the conquistador Hernán Cortés for the crime of keeping too much plundered Aztec gold as personal property. His hope at the time might have been to garner some of those riches for his own use, but he ended up losing more than he had gained. Cortés had bribed much of Narváez's forces into defection, then routed those who remained in a vicious inter-Spanish battle. With many of his men lying dead around him, Narváez was fortunate to lose only an eye.

Now he set his sights — limited by injury, blinkered by greed — on the vast interior of North America, surmising that treasures similar to those Cortés had won could be found in the region rumored to be home to the Seven Cities of Cibola. In 1527, Narváez was named governor of all that lay north of modern-day Texas and Florida. While in theory rule over this domain made him one of the most powerful men on earth, in practice it would cost him everything, including his life.

The folly now known as the Narváez Expedition was doomed from the start. Beginning with five ships and six hundred voyagers, Narváez saw more than a hundred men flee his command immediately upon their arrival on the island of Santo Domingo. Rumors of the cruelty of Indian attacks in the land they hoped to conquer passed among his sailors like a virus, causing a quarter of the fighting force to either brave the return journey across the ocean or to seek out less dangerous missions. Others simply remained in the Caribbean and disappeared into the original American melting pot, a place where Indians, Africans, and Europeans were already blending to create the culture for which the region now is known.

Following the loss of personnel in Santo Domingo, the expedition sailed on to Cuba, a short voyage that saw two of the five ships sink in a hurricane. Along with the ships, sixty soldiers and twenty horses disappeared into the deep. The Narváez Expedition had not even seen the shore of the Northern Mystery, but already the resources upon which they would rely were cut nearly in half. And it only got worse when they finally reached the mainland.

The early European expeditions into the Americas are generally thought of today as excuses for gold lust, but their unmistakably religious nature has been largely forgotten. One reminder can be found in the requirement of all Spanish explorers to read an official declaration of faith upon each encounter with native peoples. The Requerimiento, as this declaration was called, was put forth in 1513, the same year Azemmour was conquered by the Portuguese, and also the year in which the conquistador Juan Ponce de León arrived in Florida, twenty-one years after Columbus came ashore on the islands to the south. By royal decree, all those conquering the terra incognita on behalf of the Catholic monarchs were called upon to make use of a prepared text that at once announced their intentions and offered a bargain before the inevitable killing began:

> We the servants [of King Ferdinand of Aragon and his daughter Queen Joanna of Castile] notify and make known to you, as best we can, that the Lord our God, Living and Eternal, created the Heaven and the Earth, and one man and one woman, of whom you and we, and all the men of the world, were and are descendants, and all those who come after us.

It started, ecumenically enough, with an acknowledgment that both those who delivered this notification and those who heard it were, at least, all part of the same human family. This genealogy would become a matter of some debate through the century that followed, when certain Spanish philosophers argued that indigenous Americans were not truly human at all and thus did not have souls worthy of concern. The notion that Christians and the inhabitants of a supposedly godless land shared a common ancestor was nearly progressive for its day, but that is the extent of positive things that might be said of the Requerimiento. Its nod toward common ground soon proved to be little more than the throat clearing of a people who intended to turn the Americans' world upside down. The text continued:

> Of all these nations God our Lord gave charge to one man…that he should be Lord and Superior of all the men in the world, that all should obey him, and that he should be the head of the whole human race, wherever men should live, and under whatever law, sect, or belief they should be and he gave him the world for his kingdom and jurisdiction. And he commanded him to place his seat in Rome, as the spot most fitting to rule the world from; but also he permitted him to have his seat in any other part of the world, and to judge and govern all Christians, Moors, Jews, Gentiles, and all other sects. This man was called Pope.

As historian Ralph T. Twitchell noted with some understatement, it is a "remarkable document," recounting as it does the history of the universe, a justification for the papacy, and the governance of the earth with nary a pause for breath. Its supposed purpose was to give the natives of this new land an opportunity to accept the Christian religion, and in so doing to receive the protection of both the pope and the Spanish Crown. "As best we can, we ask and require you that you consider what we have said to you," the Requerimiento continues, "and that you take the time that shall be necessary to understand and deliberate upon it, and that you acknowledge the Church as the Ruler and Superior of the whole world."

Because this offer of protection was made in the tongue of the invaders, often in the dead of night before entry into an Indian village, at times while natives watched from a wary distance, there was never much possibility that its tenets would be accepted. Nonetheless, the Spaniards' sense of protocol, to say nothing of their desire to feel justified in the righteousness of their actions, made this proclamation necessary. As god-fearing Christians of the time would have seen it, not only the natives' souls but their own hung in the balance. And so the offer of deliverance was made whenever there was an encounter between those who carried the banner of Christ and those who fell under its shadow.

"If you do accept this, you will do well," the Requerimiento goes on to say. "We shall receive you in all love and charity, and shall leave you, your wives, and your children, and your lands, free without servitude, that you may do with them and with yourselves freely that which you like and think best." However, as the commanding officer of any exploratory mission into the American mainland would hasten to add:

> If you do not do this, and maliciously make delay in it, I certify to you that, with the help of God, we shall powerfully enter into your country, and shall make war against you in all ways and manners that we can, and shall subject you to the yoke and obedience of the Church and of their Highnesses.
>
> We shall take you and your wives and your children, and shall make slaves of them, and as such shall sell and dispose of them as their Highnesses may command; and we shall take away your goods, and shall do you all the mischief and damage that we can, as to vassals who do not obey, and refuse to receive their lord, and resist and contradict him; and we protest that the deaths and losses which shall accrue from this are your fault, and not that of their Highnesses, or ours, nor of these cavaliers who come with us.

The Requerimiento ends with a bureaucratic flourish, declaring that the time and place of the statement's recitation should be notarized. Both those who had comprehended the words and those who had not were understood as having served as witnesses that the conquerors had attended to all proper legalities; the dismantling of a culture could commence only after the proper forms had been filed.

Scholars regard the Requerimiento as a legal formality, a necessary statement of the terms that would thereafter govern Spanish treatment of the native peoples they encountered. Most modern observers might retrospectively note, however, that the promise of "love and charity" proffered in the message was not a legal fiction but an outright lie. As the Spanish conquest continued through the sixteenth and into the seventeenth century, Native Americans who agreed to convert to Christianity were surely not safe from the "mischief and damage" that would be done by the men who had come from across the sea, despite promises to the contrary. Nor were Christians of the day unanimous in their agreement with this approach to spreading the faith. As the first historian of the Americas, Bartolomé de las Casas said of the Requerimiento, one is not sure whether to laugh or weep at its audacious departure from the fundamentals of the Christian faith. It was as if, he observed, Jesus had supplemented his order to preach the Gospel to all lands with a directive that his apostles should offer far-off people a choice between baptism or the sword.

Even so, to those who delivered the Requerimiento—as the members of the Narváez Expedition did on Good Friday of 1528, in what is now St. Petersburg, Florida—it was not necessarily the example of bald hypocrisy that it may seem today. To Zemmouri it must have instead sounded like an honest statement of the logic upon which Christendom rested, and thus the underlying system of thought upon which the entire colonial enterprise would depend. Through the conversion process that had provided him with the Christian name Esteban, he no doubt had been given much the same offer, made with the understanding that those who did not believe in Christ were lost, and those who did believe bore responsibility for souls they failed to save.

Europeans brought with them across the ocean a set of taken-for-granted facts about the world and its order that they could not unlearn simply because they had traveled to a new place and now addressed a people to whom such facts would have been utterly nonsensical in any language. Without granting any measure of absolution, it should be remembered that a civilization ignorant of the rules of order the Requerimiento described would not have seemed to the Spanish to be a civilization at all. The Europeans who arrived in America as the fifteenth century turned to the sixteenth lacked adequate categories for understanding who and what they had encountered. Most of them barely knew where they were on the globe, so it should come as no surprise that the moral compass of these explorers was similarly misaligned. The Requerimiento may have assumed ignorance on the part of those for whom it was intended, but it survives as evidence of the failings—both ethical and imaginative—of those who delivered it.

In the spring of 1528, the Spanish governor of all North America decided to separate his land forces from their vessels, their lifelines back to the Spanish stronghold of Cuba. The result was disastrous:

Within weeks, their cohort had been decimated. Scores of explorers were killed by disease or native attacks.

With provisions quickly exhausted, the explorers slaughtered support animals for meat ("after we had eaten the dogs," Cabeza de Vaca later wrote, "it seemed to us that we had enough strength to go further on"), and soon the hunger of some members of the expedition turned even to the human dead. On a particularly harrowing note, Cabeza de Vaca mentions five soldiers cut off from the rest, who in their desperation killed and ate each other one by one. Of the others, he notes, "One-third of our people were dangerously ill, getting worse hourly, and we felt sure of meeting the same fate, with death as our only prospect, which in such a country was much worse yet."

In a last-ditch effort to find their way home, the two hundred or so yet living decided they would be better off getting as far as possible from the land that seemed intent on their demise. They built a makeshift forge—with flues made of hollowed-out logs and bellows sewn from deerskin—and melted military equipment including "stirrups, spurs, cross-bows and other iron implements" into the nails, saws, and hatchets with which they began to cut down as many pines, junipers, and palmettos as they could gather. They then butchered their remaining horses, wove the hair of manes and tails into ropes, and used these to bind together the tree trunks into several barges, each large enough to carry fifty men.

Though hewn of superhuman effort and ingenuity, and labored over for nearly two months, two of these barges quickly sank in the Gulf of Mexico. ("None of us knew how to build ships," Cabeza de Vaca admitted.) The supposed leader of this expedition, the bungling one-eyed Narváez, was among those lost beneath the storm-tossed waves. The remaining barges ran aground on an island off the Texas coast, most likely present-day Galveston, which the survivors came to call Isla de Malhado, the Island of Misfortune.

By November of 1528, a force that once numbered in the hundreds had been reduced to little more than a dozen. As Cabeza de Vaca later described the situation of these survivors, they had seen most of their number die brutal deaths on land or disappear into the sea, and "the rest of us, as naked as we had been born, had lost everything." With winter approaching, bitter wind and ravenous hunger seemed likely to accomplish what five thousand miles and months of suffering had not. "We were in such a state that every bone could easily be counted," Cabeza de Vaca wrote, "and we looked like death itself."

But at this point something unexpected happened. The original inhabitants of the Island of Misfortune, a tribe known as the Karankawa, approached the beachside encampment where the explorers had all expected to die. They could not have looked more menacing to the vulnerable castaways. "They seemed to be giants," Cabeza de Vaca wrote. They also were apparently impervious to pain: "The men have one of their nipples perforated from side to side and sometimes both. Through this hole is thrust a reed as long as two and a half hands and as thick as two fingers; they also have the under lip perforated and a piece of cane in it as thin as the half of a finger."

Yet despite their warlike appearance, they did not attack. "Upon seeing the disaster we had suffered in our misery and distress, the Indians sat down with us and all began to weep out of compassion for our misfortune," Cabeza de Vaca wrote. "For more than half an hour they wept so loud and so sincerely that it could be heard far away. Truly, to see beings so devoid of reason, untutored, so savage, yet so deeply moved by pity for us, it increased my feelings and those of others in my company."

Occurring long before the first Thanksgiving, that myth of shared maize and cross-cultural kindness, it was a moment of awareness on the part of the Europeans that the people they encountered in the New World might be able to teach them something about surviving within it. "When the lament was over, I spoke to the others and asked them if they would like me to beg the Indians to take us to their homes," Cabeza de Vaca wrote. The Karankawa took them to their village, installed them in a new hut, and then "they began to dance and to make a great celebration that lasted the whole night." The starved explorers, however, could not believe these unlikely people might be their salvation. Despite the apparent goodwill of the Indians, "there was neither pleasure, feast, nor sleep in it for us," Cabeza de Vaca wrote, "since we expected to be sacrificed in the morning."

They were not sacrificed, but most of them never did make it out of the Karankawa village. Weakened by malnutrition and disease, the last members of the Narváez Expedition began dying by the day, until only four remained. Those men were the three who were veterans of the Comunero rebellion—Andrés Dorantes,

Cabeza de Vaca, and Mustafa Zemmouri—and a fourth, a doctor's son called Castillo, who like the two other Spaniards had crossed the ocean hoping to make his fortune and his name.

Of these men, only Zemmouri had already experienced the degradations of bondage they all soon would know. Only he had lived for years in the space between faiths, which is exactly where they all would soon find themselves when they realized they were no longer the guests of the natives but their prisoners. Only Zemmouri had moved through cultures, languages, and systems of belief in order to survive.

While the challenge of communicating with a people who did not fit into preexisting categories cannot be overstated, the Spanish were obviously not unaware of the religious differences between themselves and the people they encountered in America. In some ways, in fact, the religious assumptions at work in their interactions were more complex than they might initially seem. They are still not very sympathetic from a twenty-first-century perspective, but nonetheless it is useful to consider that when Spanish explorers looked upon the people to whom the Requerimiento was read, they did not always see them as people lacking religion. Rather, the more often they saw them, the more they came to see—or thought they were seeing—signs of a familiar difference.

The Spanish invaders looked upon Native Americans and sometimes thought they saw the difference by which their own culture had been most profoundly shaped: the divide between one set of religious assumptions and another. As unlikely as it seems, they frequently reacted as if the people encountered on the other side of the Atlantic were Muslims. This is not to say they truly believed the Indians had any connection to Islam. Rather, because the Spanish saw humanity defined and separated by known religious differences, they lacked a category for the native peoples of the Americas, and so used one of their existing categories to make sense of a form of difference they were encountering for the first time. In the documents detailing the exploration, whenever a native site of obvious religious or ceremonial significance is described, the Spanish word for church is never used. The word mosque—*mezquita*—on the other hand, appears again and again. In some ways this is not at all unusual. The Spanish language had developed over the course of centuries of alternating Muslim and

Christian dominance over the Iberian Peninsula, resulting in thousands of words of Arabic origin in common usage (even the prototypical Spanish exclamation *olé* is thought by some to derive from the *wa-Allah*, "by God"). Naturally, some Arabic elements of the language might have been used by the conquistadors without intention or even awareness of their implications.

Yet as Ana Marcos Maíllo of the Universidad de Salamanca has noted, in written accounts of the New World, "Arabic terms have been found to be used more often when the conquerors wanted to name what they found especially exotic or different." For example, when explorers described the costumes and accoutrements of shamans and others performing a ritual role, the ornate vestments of Spanish Catholic priests are never invoked, even though they might have provided readers of these accounts with the most familiar analogy. Instead, the terms used most often relate to Islamic customs of decoration and appearance. As Bernal Díaz del Castillo, chronicler of the conquests of Hernán Cortés, wrote, the clothes of those they met in the region then known as New Spain were *"a la manera de albornoces moriscos"* ("in the style of Moorish robes"); and the women who danced at ceremonial gatherings were *"muy bien vestidas a su manera y que parecían moriscas"* ("very well dressed in their own way and seemed like Moorish women").

Another example can be found in the writings of the Spanish historian Francisco López de Gómara, who interviewed Cortés and other conquistadors to compile his *History of the Conquest of Mexico*. Describing dances similar to those observed by Bernal, López de Gómara notes that it was not merely the dancers but their very movements that were like *"la zambra de los moros"* ("the zambra of the Moors"). In the centuries since these words were recorded, "zambra" has come to refer to a specific kind of dance associated with Iberian music and culture generally. At the time, however, the name of the dance itself had unmistakable religious significance: The zambra was the mark of identity among Muslims who had converted to Christianity to avoid expulsion from Spain yet had maintained most of their beliefs and traditions. Not merely a dance of leisure or celebration, the zambra was a ceremony performed in hiding to keep the spark of communal history alive despite legal strictures on its existence. Performing the zambra, in fact, appears on a long list of heretical activities that marked Muslim converts to Christianity as stubbornly clandestine adherents of Islam. Documents of the Spanish Inquisition known as Edicts of Faith warned specifically against those who have "married or betrothed through the rite and custom of the Moors, and have sung songs of the Moors, or have danced the prohibited zambras." The comparison of Native American dances to a Moorish ritual was not just about similarities in rhythm or movement; it concerned a form of religiosity regarded as an existential threat to Catholic Spain. This threat was made most explicit in the use of Arabic-derived terms to describe the ways in which the Spanish were resisted. Though the natives encountered had no advanced metalwork, their weapons were often called *alfanjes,* the same term that would be used for an ornate curved scimitar inscribed with Quranic verses. As early as 1517, friars on Hispaniola made the connection plain when they spoke of the island's native inhabitants as *estos moros,* "these Moors."

Given the number of times the dress, customs, and even the facial features of the natives are described in specifically Islamic terms, one would think that it was not Christian bishops who were believed to have fled Spain to build the mythical Seven Cities of Cibola but Muslim imams. The historian Patricia Seed goes so far as to suggest that the Requerimiento itself, as a "military and political ritual" expressed in religious terms asking not just for surrender but "submission," had more in common with the means through which Islam had spread across Iberia than with any other European approach to conquest. "The first formal step of jihad," she writes, "is that a messenger must be sent announcing one's intentions to the enemy.... Hence, Islamic rules on the Iberian Peninsula insisted strictly upon the sending of an announcement.... Like the Requirement it was a public ritual, addressing itself in a highly stylized way to the unbelievers." The Requerimiento might then be considered a reenactment of that earlier ritual between "believers" and "unbelievers," though now with Indians standing in for Muslims, and the roles symbolically reversed.

The Spanish conquest of the Americas is often considered the opening of a new act in the drama of world history. Seen with a fuller view of the history of which it was a part, however, it was also a restaging of the tragedies that had long defined Europe. This was never truer than in the case of the role the centuries-old fight against Islam played in the psyche of Spanish Christians. The generation of sailors, priests, and military men that came to explore and colonize the Americas had been raised in the shadow of the glorious Reconquista of previous generations. Having no more Muslims at home to fight, they needed to venture into the world to find a Reconquista of their own, a Crusade against the Islamic ghosts that still haunted their imaginations. The European adventure in America began as a kind of proxy war—or perhaps, more damningly, it was closer to a trip to a shooting range with the images of an uncatchable villain affixed to the targets. The conquistador Cortés made a particular effort to frame his actions in terms that made his personally enriching conquests seem a victory over Islam. Tasked by the governor of Cuba, Diego Velázquez de Cuéllar, with reporting back on any houses of worship (*"mezquitas"*) or masters of religious knowledge (*"alfaquíes"*) he found, Cortés claimed to have seen over four hundred mosques in a land known as Anahuac.

Today we know Anahuac as Texas and Mexico. While the region would not be home to actual mosques for almost five hundred years, the man who first explored its northern reaches for the Spanish was indeed an *alfaquí* of a sort, a Morisco called Mustafa Zemmouri.

As later recounted by Cabeza de Vaca, the few survivors of the Narváez Expedition would eventually travel for years through North America, passing months at a time as prisoners and slaves of one tribe, then traded to another. Having already made their way from their Florida landing site to the Texas coast, they now were moved about through what would become the borderlands between the United States and Mexico. In the process, they became among the earliest observers of American civilization.

Through the years of their wandering, the lost explorers mostly made note of differences between the world they had come from and the one in which they were now stranded. Had they paused to consider it, however, they might have found signs that this civilization was not entirely dissimilar from their own. Complete with regional differences of language, governance, tradition, and belief, the land through which these four survivors trod was at the time very much like Catholic Spain in at least one other significant way: It was a home to cultures that had risen and fallen, and now faced uncertain futures.

Unknowingly, they had crossed through lands that once had been home to bustling urban centers on both sides of the Mississippi. The mound-building cultures that dominated the southeastern woodlands from the ninth century to the fifteenth had produced cities with populations in the tens of thousands. They would have been rivals to all but the largest of European cities at the time, and would not be matched in North America until Philadelphia surpassed 20,000 inhabitants around 1760. Indeed, the total population of the territory of which Narváez had absurdly been declared governor would not be equaled by the descendants of European settlers for nearly three hundred years.

With a few notable exceptions, the cities that large numbers of this vast population once called home have become invisible to all but archaeologists. Many were already in ruins by the time Zemmouri landed in Florida. Yet far more of what remained of these civilizations could have been seen then than now. The major structures at sites today found scattered throughout the American south—in Georgia, Alabama, and Mississippi—were ceremonial mounds, some as tall as one hundred feet, the height of a ten-story building. Surrounding these mounds were villages built of thatch and mud, filled with people who created and sustained sophisticated agricultural systems. The mounds themselves were built in formations that defined a large central plaza, which served as the locus of religion and governance. They were, in a sense, the cathedrals of the Americas, sites of both political and spiritual power, which also, like any medieval cathedral, served the further purpose of attracting commerce of all kinds.

For a time the mound-building cultures were so successful their problems seem disconcertingly modern: runaway populations, overuse of resources, rising political rivalries, war, famine, and disease. Despite the persistence of the narrative that native cultures knew no such trouble before the arrival of Europeans, it is worth remembering that none of the mound-builders' cities was utopia. Ceremonial mounds the size of the U.S. Capitol do not form themselves, and it is doubtful they were built because the thousands involved in their construction wanted to spend their days hauling the heavy clay of the Mississippi watershed. They were formed instead by a society segmented and enforced through religious hierarchy. Long before the arrival of the Spanish and their Requerimiento, America was a place already grappling with the demands of men who claimed to speak for the gods.

Zemmouri, Cabeza de Vaca, and the other survivors of the Narváez Expedition endured five years of captivity and forced labor at the hands of a number of native peoples. They were passed and traded from one tribe to another, each man becoming at times a curiosity and a possession of distinction, but most often treated as mere chattel. They were put to work carrying heavy loads and doing other chores the tribes felt beneath them, and often were beaten for sport. True to the Spanish explorers' tendency to turn to religious conflicts of the past to make sense of the present, Cabeza de Vaca noted that they "were there made slaves and forced to serve with more cruelty than the Moor would have used."

But soon they began to perform other tasks as well. While the Spanish lay dying on the sands of the Island of Misfortune, the Karankawa had watched from a distance as the one remaining priest of the Narváez Expedition went from man to man blessing each with the sign of the cross. Apparently impressed with this ritual, and believing it must have some curative power, the elders of the tribe insisted the survivors should make use of this same magic in exchange for the hospitality they had received.

"On the island I have spoken of," Cabeza de Vaca wrote, "they wanted to make medicine men of us without any examination or asking for our diplomas." They believed the priests they had seen could "cure diseases by breathing on the sick, and with that breath and their hands they drive the ailment away. So they summoned us to do the same in order to be at least of some use." Trained as military men, the Spanish balked at the suggestion that they had spiritual powers. "We laughed, taking it for a jest, and said that we did not understand how to cure."

Yet the Karankawa persisted. As four survivors of hundreds, Zemmouri and the others were seen as having been clearly set apart for some special purpose. This purpose fit naturally with the Karankawa understanding of the world, in which medicine men were so ontologically distinct from other people that they were even treated differently in death. "Their usual custom is to bury the dead," Cabeza de Vaca wrote, "except those who are medicine men among them. These they burn, and while the fire is burning, all dance and make a big festival, while some work grinding the bones to powder. At the end of the year, when they celebrate the anniversary, they scarify themselves and give to the relatives the pulverized bones to drink in water."

The Karankawa and other tribes soon came to believe the bodies of the four survivors were similarly powerful. What choice did they have but to try? The form their attempts at faith healing ultimately took became yet another example of American religious syncretism: "The way we treated the sick was to make over them the sign of the cross while breathing on them, recite a Pater Noster and Ave Maria, and pray to God, Our Lord, as best we could to give them good health," Cabeza de Vaca's *Relación* recounts. "All those for whom we prayed, as soon as we crossed them, told the others that they were cured and felt well again. For this they gave us good cheer."

As Cabeza de Vaca wrote, among the various tribes with whom the four survivors interacted, Zemmouri soon came to take on a unique role. Born into a city at the crossroads of the world's cultures and customs, he was a natural intermediary. He spoke for the group, becoming the lone necessary member of the expedition, even as the narrator and self-imagined hero of the adventure rarely deigned to call him by name. "It was the negro who talked to them all the time," Cabeza de Vaca wrote. "He inquired about the road we should follow, the villages — in short, about everything we wished to know."

The Spaniards would later maintain that they had Zemmouri speak for them because they believed their authority could be maintained only by remaining aloof. But considering how low they had been brought by their experiences, it is difficult to imagine they believed themselves to have any authority left. Zemmouri, on the other hand, was increasingly finding himself in a role that might have been familiar to anyone from Azemmour. The Narváez Expedition may not have truly discovered mosques and *alfaquíes* in the land of Anahuac, but they did encounter a people who regarded the comingling of diverse prayers and rituals with an attitude of openness to spiritual innovation similar to that of those practicing the maraboutism of Morocco. And like the mujahideen back home who drew on the eclectic teachings of Sufi masters to defend their land against crusaders from the north, Zemmouri found a way to use the blending of beliefs in service of his own struggle, the jihad that would, for a time, set him free.

*   *   *

In September 1534, more than six years after their disastrous land-ing in Florida, the four survivors of the Narváez Expedition finally escaped their captors. Slipping off into the wilderness, they fol-lowed the sun in a direction they hoped would lead south and west to New Spain. Apparently by this point their reputation as medi-cine men had preceded them throughout the region: Wherever they traveled during the months that followed, they were welcomed as healers. Zemmouri even began carrying the symbolic marker of a shaman, a sacred gourd rattle that Cabeza de Vaca later described as a ceremonial object of great importance, used only "at dances, or as medicine, to cure," which "nobody dares touch" except the rightful owner. Made from a calabash strung with dried cascabel chiles, these rattles were said to have the power to call down spirits from the heavens; Zemmouri carried one because the Indians he met increasingly came to believe he had come from the heavens himself. He continued to make the sign of the cross over those who hoped to be healed, but now the gesture was less a marker of the Christian identity forced upon him than a signifier of his growing separation from it.

He and the rest of his troupe of accidental faith healers began to be followed by a crowd of Indians wherever they went. If Cabeza de Vaca's accounting is to be trusted, these processions sometimes numbered thousands. Even assuming the likelihood of exaggera-tion, the following these shipwrecked survivors amassed must have been a sight to behold.

It was during one such procession, eighteen months after their escape, that the leaders of this strange parade happened upon the first Christians they had seen in years: a Spanish slave-hunting expedition on the coast of the Gulf of California. With their crowd of acolytes bereft at their departure, the four survivors followed the slavers to Mexico City, where three of the four men received a hero's welcome.

Not so for Zemmouri. For the better part of a decade he had been made first an equal by circumstance, and then a leader by necessity. To return now to the "land of Christians," as Cabeza de Vaca called it, was to lose all that he had gained. He was perhaps relieved, then, when he was directed to join another scouting mission back into the Northern Mystery.

The journey that followed completed one of the most remarkable transformations in history. Though it is often said that there are no second acts in American lives, here was Zemmouri, beginning not only his second or his third but his fourth. Born in Africa, a slave in Europe, an explorer in the first of his American expeditions, what else was there for him to become?

The final act in the life of Mustafa Zemmouri began almost as soon as the four survivors found themselves in the relative safety of New Spain, near what is now Mexico City. While they had arrived empty-handed, the three Spaniards were full of stories of dangerous peoples, sufferings endured, and places that seemed unimaginably exotic even to their fellow adventurers. Of particular interest to their astonished audiences were the notes in their saga that suggested that the objects of that ancient Iberian desire — the Seven Cities of Cibola — were finally within reach.

Some of the descriptions the three Spaniards offered referred to things they had actually seen — particularly intriguing was "a hawkbell of copper, thick and large, figured with a human face," which Andrés Dorantes had been given in exchange for a healing — while other details were pure hearsay, full of rumors filtered through miscommunication and overstatement. Dorantes's bell, they had been told, was made of a material in great abundance in regions to the north, where plates of precious metal could be found everywhere buried in the ground. Cabeza de Vaca likewise claimed to have heard that there were "pearls and great riches on the coast…and all the best and most opulent countries are near there."

These tales were not merely the stuff of idle talk reliving past glories. They were also repeated in official testimony given to the first viceroy of New Spain, Antonio de Mendoza. According to a *relación* left by Pedro de Castañeda, Dorantes and Cabeza de Vaca regaled the ranking Spanish official in the hemisphere with accounts of "large and powerful villages, four and five stories high of which they had heard a great deal in the countries they had crossed." Free to editorialize when writing his account twenty years after the fact, Castañeda added that the survivors of the Narváez Expedition had likewise reported "other things very different from what turned out to be the truth."

While the three Spanish survivors obviously told these tall tales for their own self-aggrandizement, it is possible that Zemmouri had the most to gain from the exaggeration. Had it not been for the lies of his fellow travelers, he would likely have returned merely to servitude and obscurity. He probably would not have gone on to blaze a trail into the heart of the continent.

After hearing the accounts that seemed to suggest the Seven Cities of Cibola might be within reach, Viceroy Mendoza arranged for a reconnaissance trip north. Planning to personally preserve any glory that might be gained through this mission, he called for it to be led by men who, he hoped, would not dream of claiming wealth or status for themselves: two Franciscan friars and a slave.

One of the friars assigned to this mission was Father Marcos. According to Castañeda's account: "The negro Estéban had been ordered by the viceroy to obey Friar Marcos in everything, under pain of serious punishment." Like Cabeza de Vaca before him, the priest left a *relación* that consigns Zemmouri to a supporting role. Father Marcos instructed him to travel ahead, and the two devised a code by which they could communicate what he found across a great distance.

"I sent Estéban de Dorantes, the black, whom I instructed to follow to the north for fifty or sixty leagues, to see if by that route he would be able to learn of any great thing such as we sought," Father Marcos wrote, "and I agreed with him that if he received any information of a rich, peopled land, that was something great, he should not go farther, but that he return in person or send me Indians with this signal, which we arranged: that if the thing was of moderate importance, he send me a white cross the size of a hand; if it was something great he send me one of two hands; and if it was something bigger and better than New Spain, he send me a large cross."

As it would turn out, the man from Azemmour would show himself unwilling to play the part of obedient servant to other men in search of glory.

Zemmouri departed on Passion Sunday, two weeks before Easter. Four days later, messengers arrived in Friar Marcos's camp with "a very large cross, of the height of a man." The messengers told the priest Zemmouri had advised that he follow immediately, "because he had reached people who gave him information of the greatest thing in the world." The report Marcos heard was "that there are seven very large cities... with large houses of stone and lime; the smallest one-story high, with a flat roof above, and others two and three stories high, and the house of the lord four stories high.... And on the portals of the principal houses there are many designs of turquoise stones, of which he says they have a great abundance. And the people in these cities are very well clothed." According to the report the Franciscan heard that day, the slave from Azemmour had found "the first city of that country, which city he said was called Cibola."

The excitement likely caused by this news cannot be overstated. The object of decades of Spanish exploration now seemed tantalizingly close. Zemmouri then sent another cross, bigger than the last. At every village Father Marcos encountered they told him of the great cities to be found only a few days ahead. For weeks the friars traveled this way, with both Zemmouri and the prize of the Seven Cities always just out of reach.

This story of separation and dislocation seems in the Franciscan's telling to be the inevitable outcome of attempts to communicate across the expanse of an unknown land. Yet the other side of the story emerges in the account of Castañeda: "It seems that, after the friars I have mentioned and the negro had started, the negro did not get on well with the friars, because he took the women that were given him and collected turquoises, and got together a stock of everything." Even before the friar suggested he travel ahead, it seems Zemmouri had made preparations. "Besides, the Indians in those places through which they went got along with the negro better, because they had seen him before," Castañeda continues. "This was the reason he was sent on ahead to open up the way and pacify the Indians, so that when the others came along they had nothing to do except to keep an account of the things for which they were looking."

As the Spanish came to understand the story, after Zemmouri took his leave of the friars, "he thought he could get all the reputation and honor himself, and that if he should discover those settlements with such famous high houses, alone, he would be considered bold and courageous. So he proceeded with the people who had followed him and attempted to cross the wilderness."

While the Spanish were searching for Cibola, however, it is possible Zemmouri was searching for something else — perhaps a place not unlike a *ribat*, the desert fortress well known in the

Morocco of his youth, at once a hostel for travelers, a refuge for mystics, and a garrison from which mujahideen could repel Christian invaders. Carved of sand-colored stone with small square windows set high in walls tall enough to provide a view of any who approached, the North African *ribat*'s physical resemblance to the cliff dwellings built by some of the native tribes of the American Southwest is of course entirely coincidental, but even to a man without memories of similar outposts, such "high houses" would have seemed an obvious place to find protection.

In short order, "he was so far ahead of the friars" that he had traveled "80 leagues beyond" where Father Marcos had instructed him to remain. For Mustafa Zemmouri, it seems, this was not a scouting mission undertaken for the Viceroy of New Spain but an elaborate escape plan all his own, a journey to a place where he would not be seen as the slave he was when he arrived in America but recognized for what he had become.

If Zemmouri remembered anything by this point of the religious traditions of the country in which he was born, he would have recalled the way the marabout found within each *ribat* was rewarded for his ability to blend the beliefs and practices around him. Moreover, the power of the marabout was thought to intensify as he ventured far from home, and so it is a role that has found particular resonance through immigration. Centuries later, the place of the marabout within some Muslim cultures is largely unchanged. As Donald Martin Carter wrote in his recent study of North African Muslims in Europe, they are known primarily by what their followers believe about them. "Marabout are assumed to have mystical powers.... Marabout are assumed to be able to perform miracles and alter the course of worldly events. The Marabout may intercede for the follower in a whole range of activities." As a Moroccan-raised man with devoted followers who, it was later said, "believ[ed] that under his protection they could traverse the whole world without danger," it seems that something like a marabout is precisely what he considered himself to be.

What happened next is hazy. The two Spanish accounts — the *relación* of Friar Marcos and that of Castañeda written many years later — both indicate that Zemmouri attempted to find refuge among the Zuni people in what is now New Mexico. "They lodged him in a little hut they had outside their village, and the older men and the governors heard his story and took steps to find out the reason he had come to that country," Castañeda writes.

> For three days they made inquiries about him and held council. The account which the negro gave them of two white men who were following him, sent by a great lord, who knew about the things in the sky, and how these were coming to instruct them in divine matters, made them think that he must be a spy or a guide from some nations who wished to come and conquer them, because it seemed to them unreasonable to say that the people were white in the country from which he came and that he was sent by them, being black.

In both accounts, the Zuni kill Zemmouri, throwing his sacred gourd rattle to the ground as if in rejection of his newly attained spiritual status. Yet stories gathered from the people whom he hoped to join appear to have different implications. One describes not his execution but the continuation of his career as a healer. During subsequent Spanish forays into North America, men still searching for the elusive Seven Cities of Cibola found instead tales of "a black man with a beard, wearing things that sounded, rattles, bells, and plumes, on his feet and arms—the regular outfit of a southwestern medicine man"—and also, it so happens, that of a North African marabout. Another story recounts an event that was ambiguously remembered as either his expulsion or his forced return to the spirit world. It was said that the wise men of the village in which he sought refuge took him to the edge of their pueblo at night and then "gave him a powerful kick, which sped him through the air to the south whence he came." Still another story suggests that among the Zuni he found neither death nor exile but apotheosis. His image has been linked to one of the many divine spirits of the kachina religion of the Pueblo people, of which the Zuni were a part. In legends from native mythology enacted in elaborate dance ceremonies, the figure possibly inspired by Zemmouri, a kachina called Chakwaina, is depicted with black skin and carrying a sacred rattle—an indication, perhaps, that his career as a god lasted longer than the time he had spent as a slave. According to at least one tale from the oral tradition of the Pueblo, he "lived on among the Zunis for many years, finally dying an old deity." The life of a god can be difficult, however. Legends of Chak-waina also suggest that his followers so feared that he would leave them that they cut off his feet to keep him in their village. When he could no longer move among those needing healing, they "placed him flat on his back and worshipped him as a god." In all these stories, no matter his ultimate fate, it seems likely Zemmouri's days ended as he had lived, with him attempting yet another transfor-mation in an ongoing struggle for survival.

Whether he is remembered as a victim, a god, or some combi-nation of both, the significance of Mustafa Zemmouri's adventure does not end with him. His use of the spiritual resources accumu-lated during his travels to subvert the plans of the priests and sol-diers who hoped to control him prefigured the efforts of the most significant resistance fighter the Spanish would encounter as they colonized the Southwest. Beginning in 1680 not far from where Zemmouri met his mysterious end, the Pueblo religious leader Popé led a guerrilla campaign against Christian attempts to eradi-cate native beliefs. While it cannot be known if Popé was directly inspired by tales of the dark-skinned stranger who had tricked the friars pursuing him, his campaign included the crafting of dark masks, like those depicting Chakwaina, for a revival of suppressed kachina dances. He also encouraged the Pueblo who had been converted to wash off their baptisms by scrubbing themselves with yucca root in the Rio Grande. The means as well as the ends of his insurrection have led some historians to call Popé's rebel-lion a "holy war." Like Zemmouri, he transformed the symbols of an alien religion in his fight against those who had forced it upon him.

Even in his own time, though he was singular in many ways, Mustafa Zemmouri was not unique. For evidence of this we need only look at the expedition that sought to follow the trail he had blazed to the mythical Cities of Cibola. A multitude of perhaps a thousand men like him—born in Africa, converted in Spain, carry-ing the versatility of those caught between cultures with them into unknown lands—followed in his footsteps.

In February 1540, a great army gathered at Compostela, west of Mexico City, on the Pacific coast of New Spain. As George Parker Winship, the translator of Castañeda's chronicle of the expedition, explains, "The general in command, Francisco Vazquez Coronado rode at the head of some two hundred and fifty horsemen, and

seventy Spanish foot soldiers armed with crossbows and harque-
buses. Besides these there were three hundred or more native allies,
and upward of a thousand negro and Indian servants..."

In the end this army did not find the Seven Cities—because, of
course, they did not exist. But it did set the course, for better or
worse, of all that would follow. The same account of Coronado's
journey goes on to take an unexpectedly philosophical turn:

> I always notice, and it is a fact, that for the most part when
> we have something valuable in our hands, and deal with it
> without hindrance, we do not value or prize it as highly as
> if we understood how much we would miss it after we had
> lost it... but after we have lost it and miss the advantages of
> it, we have a great pain in the heart, and we are all the time
> imagining and trying to find ways and means by which to
> get it back again. It seems to me that this has happened to
> all or most of those who went on the expedition in search
> of the Seven Cities.... Granted they did not find the riches
> of which they had been told, but they found a place in
> which to search for them and the beginning of a good
> country to settle in, so as to go farther from there.

This was true not only of the conquistadors but of the army
they had brought with them. We may never know if any of that
thousand-strong force did as Mustafa Zemmouri had done—devised
a way to escape to the relative freedom of this vast land over the
confinement and slavery of the world from which they had come.
But nonetheless we know that they stood there for a time, making
their lives forever a part of the story of the nation that would be
built atop their footprints. Unlike Cabeza de Vaca, Pedro de Castañeda, or Father Marcos, none of those men who had so much in
common with the slave of Azemmour left a *relación*. They recorded
no words of their own that might tell us, nearly five hundred years
later, what they experienced in the New World or hoped the future
might hold. And so the best we can do is to imagine them there on
the route trod by Coronado: in Texas, in New Mexico, perhaps as far
north as Kansas and Nebraska, an army of men born as Muslims,
marching through the middle of America as if toward Mecca, nearly
a century before other religious travelers dreamed of making a New
Jerusalem of their city on a hill.

Anne Hutchinson Preaching in Her House in Boston, 1637. Lithograph by Howard Pyle, published in *Harper's Magazine,* 1901.

CHAPTER 3

Strange Opinions in the City on a Hill

1630–1660

Roughly one hundred years after the doomed ships of the Narváez Expedition crashed into the figurative rocks of the New World and sank beneath its depths, long after the four survivors had died and the tales of their adventure had been surpassed by others in the mounting saga of conquest and colonization, another man sent to govern a land he had never seen stood in the salty air and warned his people that they risked a similar fate. The shipwreck they faced, however, was not to be nautical but divine. Even after they reached their destination, the danger of being capsized and swallowed by the waves of competing religious ideas would be all around them.

"Now the only way to avoid this shipwreck, and to provide for our posterity," Governor John Winthrop told the prospective settlers of the Massachusetts Bay Colony in 1630, "is to follow the counsel of Micah: to do justly, to love mercy, to walk humbly with our God." Invoking the biblical prophet best known for swords beaten into ploughshares, the recently chosen leader of North America's newest colony seemed to offer an alternative to the bloody exploits of the Spanish territories to the south. Unafflicted by the fever for finding lost cities, they would build one of their own, a godly community in the supposedly godless wilderness.

The threat of a spiritual shipwreck was a lesser-known note in Winthrop's famous "city upon a hill" sermon, "A Model of Christian Charity," delivered aboard the *Arabella* as it approached Massachusetts. The potential disaster described by the governor was not as dramatic as the one suffered by those stranded on the Island of Misfortune a century before. Yet in Winthrop's estimation, its consequences would be no less bleak. As he addressed the future New Englanders, he could imagine no fate worse than that which would befall them if they broke the covenant they had made with each other and with God. To speak even metaphorically of a vessel's destruction during a three-week ocean passage undoubtedly would have seemed a disquietingly odd choice for a man supposedly invested in keeping morale high, but the true "shipwreck," Winthrop said, would come only if they used their journey across the Atlantic in pursuit of "carnal intentions" and "seeking great things." To do so would mean ruin in the only sense that mattered to these pious folk. "The Lord will surely break out in wrath against us," he said, "and be revenged of such a people, and make us know the price of the breach of such a covenant."

The idea of the covenant was a central theme in the religious and social organization of the group of reform-minded Christians we have come to know as the Puritans, who in the wake of the English Reformation—that turbulent time in which the Anglican Church broke, reaffiliated, and then split irrevocably with Rome—sought to purify English religious life of lingering Catholic influence. Used in the broadest sense, the label Puritan in the American context applies to both the separatists of William Bradford's Plymouth Colony, who had arrived on the *Mayflower* ten years before, and the colonists of Massachusetts Bay, who believed no less that the existing English church was corrupt, but hoped it could be transformed without formal schism. The Puritans were a people who viewed the particulars of affiliation as matters of life and death. According to their covenantal theology, the relationship between God and humanity was based upon a series of promises and obligations, contracts made in scripture that continued to outline the responsibility of Christians to uphold divine law. This responsibility was not limited to religious practice but had bearing on all aspects of life, including economics and governance.

The covenant that led Winthrop's band of Puritans out of England in 1630 was no less spiritually preoccupied than the protocols that had directed Spanish exploration during the previous century had been, but the terms of each put them in stark contrast. While the Spanish, guided by their Requerimiento, focused on the New World as a place full of heathen souls to be converted, conquered, or both, the English were more inward-looking. They were aware, of course, that the Massachusett and Wampanoag tribes, their new neighbors, might provide opportunities for spreading the Gospel, but they were more invested in the question of what this "errand in the wilderness," as the Puritan experiment is often called, would mean for their own community of faith. Moreover, while the Spanish had sought to discover hidden glories, the English would attempt to build utopia from scratch. The covenant through which this would be accomplished was twofold, involving human duties to God as well as the duty of members of society often at odds with one another, the rich and the poor particularly, to work toward the common good.

"For this end, we must be knit together, in this work, as one man," Winthrop preached. "We must entertain each other in brotherly affection. We must be willing to abridge ourselves of our superfluities, for the supply of others' necessities. We must uphold a familiar commerce together in all meekness, gentleness, patience and liberality. We must delight in each other; make others' conditions our own; rejoice together, mourn together, labor and suffer together, always having before our eyes our commission and community in the work, as members of the same body."

A layman and a lawyer, Winthrop had no formal training in ministry, yet his sermon has come to be regarded by many as the starting point of a distinctly American religious literature, providing a singular metaphor for considering the divine favor allegedly enjoyed by the nation that arose from the English colonies. The primary reason for this is a brief use of a scriptural image to describe the kind of society the colonists would attempt to establish after safely crossing the sea. One sentence in particular is far more often recalled than Winthrop's warnings against spiritual shipwreck, though the latter may be closer to the point of the sermon as a whole. "For we must consider that we shall be as a city upon a hill, the eyes of all people are upon us," he preached, "so that if we shall deal falsely with our God in this work we have undertaken and so cause him to withdraw his present help from us, we shall be made a story and a byword through the world."

Nearly four hundred years since these words were spoken, Winthrop's notion of a city upon a hill occupies a hallowed place in our national self-understanding. The seemingly self-evident prophecy of its message has not only become the current creed of our civil religion but continues to influence commonly held assumptions about even the earliest moments in our prehistory. If we assume "the eyes of all people" are on the United States now, then Winthrop's suggestion that his community should consider themselves the pinnacle of civilization do indeed seem prescient. Having found their way into the religiously-infused rhetoric of both political parties, his words are often offered as evidence equally for American exceptionalism and the supposed Christian roots of the Republic.

This is not, however, the way Winthrop himself used his most famous phrase; nor is it the way it was considered throughout most of American history. Though it has become part of the creation myth of a nation, the idea of the city upon a hill has, like any myth, been interpreted in different ways by different people depending upon the needs of the time.

As anyone in his primary audience would have known, Winthrop used the phrase in reference to a New Testament parable. It is taken from one of the most famous passages of scripture, the Sermon on the Mount, in the fifth chapter of the Gospel according to Matthew. In the biblical text, Jesus exhorts his followers to be exemplars from whom others might learn how to live. "You are the light of the world. A city on a hill cannot be hidden," he tells them. "Neither do people light a lamp and put it under a bowl. Instead they put it on its stand, and it gives light to everyone in the house. In the same way, let your light shine before men, that they may see your good deeds and praise your Father in heaven."

There are multiple meanings at play here. The first, and certainly the one that has been most often applied to Winthrop's allusion, is that it is the responsibility of those who would consider themselves sources of light or moral instruction to set themselves apart from the crowd so that others may see them clearly enough to learn from them. The second meaning, which is also present in Winthrop's sermon but less often noted, is that a city on a hill, because it is a place set apart, is necessarily conspicuous. While this means that its residents' good works will be known far and wide, it also ensures that their mistakes will be instantly evident even to those beyond the city walls. To acknowledge that one hopes to build a city upon a hill is to be aware that though one may aspire to greatness, there is an equal if not greater chance that one will achieve infamy instead. As Jesus applies the phrase to his disciples, "city upon a hill" implies at once a compliment (they are "the light of the world"), a challenge (he calls on them to "let your light shine"), and a warning (they should never forget that, for good or for ill, they "cannot be hidden").

The ambiguity within Winthrop's reference is further complicated by the question of what it would have meant to his immediate audience, those joining him in the adventure of establishing a religiously oriented city so far from the lands that had both birthed and challenged their faith. For a fuller sense of what they hoped to accomplish, and why, it is worth looking briefly at an earlier set of writings usually ascribed to Winthrop's pen. "Arguments for the Plantation of New England," published the year before the *Arabella*'s departure, describes in greater detail than "A Model for Christian Charity" what the Puritans bound for Massachusetts intended. In lawyerly prose that suggests his prior career as a member of his father's London legal practice, Winthrop proposes nine theses in favor of further English settlement in North America, despite the recent failure of similar expeditions. He then moves through a series of objections and answers, making his case for a community that would provide at once a defensive safe haven for those within in it and a counteroffensive against the forces that would do them harm.

The most important points of Winthrop's nine "Arguments" were these: first, that a Puritan colony would establish "a bulwark against the kingdom of Anti-Christ" and the efforts of "Jesuits" — in other words, the Roman Catholic Church, which controlled the southern regions of the new land through the Spanish and, through the French, seemed poised to do the same in the north. Second, the rest of Europe was in such a bad state that "God hath provided this place to be a refuge for many whom he means to save out of the general calamity." Though it is often forgotten in favor of the narrative of the Puritan search for religious liberty, a fervent apocalypticism can be found just beneath the surface of the decision to brave the ocean and the wilderness on the other side. Finally, Winthrop said, "this land grows weary of her inhabitants." Life in England had become so corrupt and difficult, in the Puritan

estimation, that one could no longer live there honestly and survive. The theme joining all Winthrop's Arguments was the threat
from a complex of outside forces, both religious and economic.
Winthrop and his people risked the spiritual "shipwreck" of crossing the ocean because not to do so seemed even more hazardous to
their souls.

To the Puritans, the dangers and benefits of establishing themselves as a covenantal community in the biblical mold would
have been taken for granted. This is perhaps one reason why
Winthrop's sermon, regarded as immortal now, seemed to its
immediate audience less than memorable. It is telling that, though
today the phrase "City on a Hill" is synonymous with the
Massachusetts Bay Colony and all that came after it, the sermon
that marked its birth did not receive much notice at the time. "A
Model of Christian Charity" was not published until more than
two centuries after it was written. As recent biographers have noted,
only a single mention of the sermon can be found among contemporary documents related to the colony's origins. While Winthrop
hoped his settlement might be seen by all as a moral exemplar, it
would take centuries for this to come to fruition — perhaps because
it took that long to forget the realities the Puritans faced. If a city
upon a hill is a place one might look to as a prototype of a peaceful, upright, and successful community, it does not seem that
Winthrop's colony was viewed as such by anyone living there at
the time.

The sermon so commonly invoked as a statement of the singular purpose of those who came across the ocean to settle a new
land was actually concerned foremost with the problem of variation. Not only did Winthrop begin with a three-part explanation
of why God would make a world in which humanity would find
itself divided along economic and religious lines (in part because
God is "delighted to show forth the glory of his wisdom in the
variety and difference of the creatures"), he describes a covenantal
system of governance built on difference, so long as it is tightly
controlled. While mankind would always be split into rich and
poor, and between those who are "high and eminent in power and
dignity" and "others mean and in submission," he notes, nonetheless they were called to create something together. "The work we
have in hand...is by a mutual consent, through a special overvalu-
ing providence and a more than an ordinary approbation of the

churches of Christ, to seek out a place of cohabitation and consort-ship under a due form of government both civil and ecclesiastical. In such cases as this, the care of the public must oversway all private respects, by which, not only conscience, but mere civil pol-icy, doth bind us. For it is a true rule that particular estates cannot subsist in the ruin of the public."

Winthrop likewise ended with a note concerning difference, this time a warning about the hazards of straying too far from the communal religious norms. In a surprising turn given the wide-spread assumptions about Puritan religious uniformity, he quickly segued from reminding the founding inhabitants of the colony of Massachusetts that "the eyes of all people" were on them to warn-ing against worshipping "other gods":

> But if our hearts shall turn away, so that we will not obey, but shall be seduced, and worship other Gods, our pleasure and profits, and serve them; it is propounded unto us this day, we shall surely perish out of the good land whither we pass over this vast sea to possess it.

The gods Winthrop had foremost in mind at the time were "pleasure and profits," by which he meant not merely the pursuit of such things but individual longing at the expense of the communal need. To have other gods in the context of the Puritan covenant was to ignore that crucial commandment that "care of the public must oversway all private respects." However, given that neither pleasure nor profit had been found in either public or private abun-dance in English America by that point, it is likely that Winthrop was concerned with other actual divinities as well.

He should have been. Not only were he and his people intend-ing to establish a univocal faith in a land already filled with a cacophony of religious voices, in short order the Puritans them-selves would discover that even they, though they are remembered foremost for their strict adherence to doctrine, were in fact seeth-ing with spiritual discord. Winthrop's own fixation on difference as a divine creation suggests that this was perhaps inevitable. After all, he and those he led to Massachusetts were spiritual descen-dants of the disruption that had come to define the civilization from which they came, and would continue to influence the one they hoped to build.

*   *   *

New England's Puritans were the grandchildren of the Reformation. Just as the conquests of the southern coast of North America can be seen as born of the ancient religious disputes of the Iberian Peninsula, the settlement of the English colonies should be considered in the context of the equally tumultuous atmosphere of northern Europe in the sixteenth and seventeenth centuries. In the very years Mustafa Zemmouri was wandering through Texas transforming himself from a slave to a healer to a god, another shape-shifting religious figure was transforming the Christian faith—his own and eventually the world's—thousands of miles away.

By the 1530s, the French theologian John Calvin had begun his work of pushing the revolution started a generation before by Martin Luther toward its logical conclusion. The Protestant Reformation, which had begun as a challenge to papal authority when Luther nailed his famous 95 Theses to the door of a Wittenberg church in 1517, had left unanswered the question of what should fill the void if Rome no longer served as universal arbiter of divine intentions. Luther's creed of *sola scriptura*—by scripture alone—was fine as far as it went in shaping individual relationships with God, but it was less effective when it came to keeping the trains running on time. Calvin solved this problem, or attempted to, by offering an understanding of the relationship between religious and civil authority that eventually took concrete form in a theocratic government established in his adopted city of Geneva.

If one wants to find the true founding city upon a hill in American history, Calvin's Geneva might fit the bill better than Winthrop's Boston. Long before the *Arabella* or even the *Mayflower* set sail, it was Geneva that gave refuge to a group of Protestants from England, fleeing the reign of the Catholic queen Mary Tudor in 1553. These so-called Marian exiles drank deep the waters of Calvin's theocracy, and when they returned to England a few years later they sought to replicate his unrelenting approach to reform. The Anglican Church remained, in their estimation, too much like the Catholic Church in its beliefs and outward devotions, and so they hoped to purify it of any trapping that seemed unaffected by the transformation of the faith Luther and Calvin had achieved. Finding this impossible, and making few friends through the effort, followers of Calvinist ministers including John Cotton, as well as laymen like John Winthrop, took the extreme step of sailing into the unknown with scripture as their map and Geneva as their blueprint.

They would have done well to note the darker moments in the history of Calvin's city on a hill, however. A scourge of the papacy (the Roman pontiff, he wrote, "is the leader and standard-bearer of an impious and abominable kingdom"), Calvin nonetheless came quickly to be derided and feared as the "Pope of Geneva." In that mold, he allowed his theocracy to mimic the worst excesses of Rome, including the execution of the Spanish physician, theologian, and literal Renaissance man Michael Servetus as a heretic for his questioning of the Trinity. As a follower of Calvin lamented, Servetus's ideas posed a risk because they "infected both heaven and earth." After Servetus was burned at the stake, Calvin faced criticism from some fellow reformers, and responded as Torquemada might have in the previous century, with the threat of a widened net: "Whoever shall now contend that it is unjust to put heretics and blasphemers to death will knowingly and willingly incur their very guilt." Like many reformers before and since, Calvin was apparently chagrined not to be the final advocate of change.

So too in New England. No sooner had Winthrop's Puritans established their new godly community than they discovered that the Reformation that had made them began to repeat itself in miniature. Only now, the reformers were the ones desperately trying to maintain the status quo. An indication of this can be seen in the words of a minister who had arrived in Massachusetts shortly after Winthrop. In his preface to a 1644 pamphlet on the spiritual errors at large in the colony, Thomas Weld succinctly told the history of the tumultuous fifteen years since the colonists' departure from England:

> After we had escaped the cruel hands of persecuting prelates, and the dangers at sea, and had prettily well outgrown our wilderness troubles in our first plantings in New England; and when our commonwealth began to be founded, and our churches sweetly settled in peace (God abounding to us in more happy enjoyments than we could have expected), lest we should now grow secure, our wise God (who seldom suffers His own in this their wearisome pilgrimage to be long without trouble) sent a new storm after us, which proved the sorest trial that ever befell us since we left our native soil.

The new trial was this: Within the first year of the colony's existence, there began to appear among the orthodox believers people who were judged "full fraught with many unsound and loose opinions." Some of these troublemakers had brought their dangerous ideas with them like stowaways across the sea; others seem to have reacted to the unimaginable freedom of being separated from England by developing new notions in response to their environment. No matter where their notions came from, Weld writes, soon they "began to open their packs and freely vend their wares to any that would be their customers."

These were not a few isolated cranks out to cause a stir but, in Weld's telling, the beginnings of a movement: "Multitudes of men and women, church members and others, having tasted of their commodities were eager after them and were straight infected before they were aware, and some being tainted conveyed the infection to others."

Just as the Spanish feared the spiritual contamination of Muslims and Jews in the New World as early as the fifteenth century, and the Calvinists of Geneva had feared Servetus had "infected both heaven and earth" in the sixteenth, now the English Calvinists feared, and likewise identified as "infection," difference of opinion over such foundational Christian issues as the nature of salvation and grace. "Thus that plague first began amongst us," Weld wrote. "Had not the wisdom and faithfulness of him that watcheth over our vineyard night and day, and by the beams of his light cleaned and purged the aire, certainly we haf not have been able to have breathed there much longer."

Though remembered too simply today as a community unified by the strict enforcement of belief, the Massachusetts Bay Colony thought of itself from the very beginning as beset by a plague that today we might simply call religious difference. John Winthrop's journal, *The History of New England from 1630 to 1649*, is anything but the account of religious uniformity the label "Puritan" calls to mind. Its pages are full of accounts of spiritual disagreement and increasing hostility toward established ecclesial authority. On December 13, 1638, for example, Winthrop writes of the elders of the community calling for a general fast. "The chief occasion was," he writes "the much sickness of pox and fevers spread through the country" and "the apparent decay of the power of religion."

This decay could be readily observed in two ways: The very persistence of sicknesses such as smallpox was taken as evidence that colonists' prayers had become less efficacious, no doubt because of their own sinful nature; and the power of religion also seemed to suffer decay in its ability to inspire and regulate uniform belief among the members of the community. Judging from Winthrop's journal, uniformity was not nearly taken for granted by Puritans themselves, regardless of how they have come to be viewed in history.

"The devil would never cease to disturb our peace, and to raise up instruments one after another," Winthrop wrote. These instruments, more often than not, were threats to religious authority and the homogeneous practices and beliefs upon which authority rested. Winthrop describes one woman from Salem—five decades before the troubles for which that town would become best known—"who had suffered somewhat in England for refusing to bow at the name of Jesus." The woman, named only as the wife of a man named Oliver, repeatedly makes a nuisance of herself by disregarding accepted doctrine while demanding that she still be given the same right to attend meetings as other community members. She might have been more of an "instrument to have done hurt," Winthrop notes, "but that she was poor and had little acquaintance."

This unnamed dissenting woman seems to have been absorbed back into well-ordered Puritan society without further incident, but others followed the path of spiritual nonconformity into social mayhem. To cite an infamous example: Though she was known for her "good esteem for godliness," Dorothy Talbye began claiming to have visions distinct from church teachings. Cast out of her Salem congregation because of these visions, she was driven mad by "melancholy or spiritual delusions" and ultimately murdered her own child so that "she might free it from future misery." We would surely take it as a warning sign today that Talbye had named the three-year-old girl "Difficult." This word also captured the short life of the mother, who was hanged in 1638. While her crime was murder, the pastor of the community from which she had been exiled used her in a subsequent sermon to warn his congregants of the dangers of excommunication and the temptation of heeding revelations received outside the church.

If the seeds of spiritual disruption were not present at the landing of the *Arabella* in 1630, they were not long in arriving. In February of 1631, at a time when "the poorer sort of people," as Winthrop wrote, "were much afflicted with the scurvy, and many died," another ship dropped anchor in Boston's harbor. This ship, called the *Lyon*, carried a cargo of lemon juice to help those afflicted, who "lay long in tents" through the winter. Also on board was a twenty-eight-year-old preacher by the name of Roger Williams, who would soon put a sour taste in the mouths of the Puritan elite, even while providing a jolt of the kind of spiritual vitamins necessary for the English community to expand beyond its parochial limitations.

Williams was pronounced an appropriately pious man by Winthrop not long after he stepped off the *Lyon*, but the governor of the neighboring colony of Plymouth was perhaps more accurate when he said that this new arrival was "a man godly and zealous, having many precious parts, but very unsettled in judgment." His judgment was, in fact, a constant work in progress. A separatist from the Church of England, Williams refused to be associated with Winthrop's own Church of Boston, preferring the more austere community that had been established in Salem. Even there, though, Williams ran into trouble by questioning the role of religion in civil government, a crime that had more than once been punished by torture in Calvin's Geneva.

When Williams was called before the general court to answer for his "divers opinions," it was ruled that "the said opinions were adjudged by all, magistrates and ministers…to be erroneous, and very dangerous." Showing "a great contempt of authority," Williams was charged with proposing that "a church might run into heresy, apostasy, or tyranny, and yet the civil magistrate could not intermeddle." This to the Puritans sounded like nothing so much as anarchy. For these infractions against Calvinist orthodoxy, Williams was driven from the colony. He avoided deportation to England only by slipping off into the wilderness of southern New England, a region still peopled by the Wampanoag and Narragansett Indians, where further lessons in religious difference awaited him.

Leaving Winthrop's colony, Roger Williams set off on his own errand in the wilderness, specifically in the woodlands between Boston and the future site of the city of Providence, where he lived for a time among the Narragansett. From the outset, Williams attempted to make sense of their place in his theologically informed understanding of history, while taking their own beliefs into account. "From Adam and Noah that they spring, it is granted on all hands," he wrote of his native hosts. "But...they say themselves, that they have sprung and growne up in that very place, like the very trees of the wildernesse. They say that their Great God Cowtantowwit created those parts."

Williams at first attempted to understand the Indians in terms of another preexisting difference. While some Spanish explorers had once seen the shadow of Islam wherever they looked in the New World, it seems a certain variety of English clergyman was predisposed to look upon Indians and believe he was seeing Jews.

"Others (and myselfe) have conceived some of their words to hold affinitie with the Hebrew," Williams wrote. "Secondly, they constantly anoint their heads as the Jewes did. Thirdly, they give Dowries for their wives as the Jewes did. Fourthly, (and which I have not so observed amongst other nations as amongst the Jewes, and these) they constantly separate their women (during the time of their monthly sicknesse) in a little house alone by themselves foure or five dayes, and hold it an Irreligious thing for either Father or Husband or any Male to come near them."

In other ways, however, Williams found the Narragansett to be nearly Christian, particularly in their reverence for one prophet above all others. "They have many strange Relations of one Wetucks, a man that wrought great Miracles amongst them," he wrote. Making particular note that this Wetucks was known for "walking upon the waters," Williams proposed that this was an indigenous spiritual figure "with some kind of broken resemblance to the Sonne of God."

In fact, this resemblance was more than broken. The story itself may well have been a native response to Christian efforts to lead the Indians to the Bible, which after all had been ongoing for generations by then. In one version of Wetucks's infancy narrative, for example, it was said that his birth must have great significance because he was born to a woman well past childbearing years, making him a parallel for biblical figures including John the Baptist, born of Elizabeth, who was "well stricken in years," and Isaac, whose mother, Sarah, was ninety. Moments in Wetucks's later life meanwhile seem taken straight from the Gospels: He disappears for a time, not to the desert but to the sea, and during his absence his true power is revealed. While still a boy he calls the elders around and teaches them. He instructs them in healing and ritual and is generally the father of all their sacred traditions.

Despite his eagerness to find echoes of the Christian faith within Narragansett mythology, Williams at other times was content to let native beliefs speak for themselves. He did not insist that the Narragansett were Jews who had wandered far afield of the Holy Land or followers of a form of proto-Christianity. Instead, he recognized that they had a religion all their own, and were open to many manifestations of divinity. Williams claims to have counted thirty-seven deities but names only a dozen: "They branch their Godhead into many Gods," he wrote. Foremost among these was "Kautantowwit, The great South West God." The southwest, Williams records, was the direction in which all souls go, and from which all came. Other gods included: "Wompanand, The Easterne God. Chekesuwand, The Western God. Wunnanameanit, The Northern God. Sowwanand, The Southern God. Wetuomanit, The house God. Keesuckquand, The Sun God. Nanepaushat, The Moon God. Paumpagussit, The Sea God. Yotaanit, The fire God..."

His Puritan counterparts would try endlessly to fit the natives of New England into their own black-and-white theology, but Williams was willing to acknowledge the complexity of this alien faith. "Even as the Papists have their He and Shee Saint Protectors as St. George, St. Patrick, St. Dennis, Virgin Mary," Williams noted, the Indians had their own gendered and familial notions of divinity: There was "Squauanit, The Womans God," for example, and "Muckquachuckquand, the Children's God." Of this last, Williams makes a poignant observation: "I was once with a Native dying of a wound, given him by some of the murderous English, who robbed him and run him through with a Rapier....This Native dying called much upon Muckquachuckquand, which of other Natives I understood, (as they believed) had appeared to the dying young man, many years before, and bid him whenever he was in distress call upon him."

For all this variety of belief, Williams could find no moral fault in them. "I could never discern that excess of scandalous sins amongst them which Europe aboundeth with. Drunkenness, and gluttony generally they knew not what sinnes they be; and although they have not so much to restrain them both in respect of a knowledge of God and the laws of men, as the English have, yet a man shall never hear of such amongst them as robberies, murthers, adulteries, etc., as amongst the English."

Among the Puritans, Williams had been a mere critic; his interactions with these Indians led him to the earliest statement of religious toleration on the American continent. To force conversion on such people, he wrote, would be like using coercion or violence to make "an unwilling spouse to enter into forced relations."

Ultimately, as a Christian clergyman, Williams would have preferred to see Indians converted of their own free will, but he understood that they, too, could make a religious choice while respecting the religious choices of others. "They will generally confess that God made all," he writes. "Although they deny not that Englishmen's God made English men, and the heavens and earth, yet their Gods made them, and the heaven and the earth where they dwell."

The natives of America, Williams discovered, had also built communities they considered divinely ordained and ordered. No less than John Winthrop, they lived in their own cities on a hill.

Of all the spiritual dissenters in the early years of the Massachusetts Bay Colony, none shook Governor Winthrop as significantly as Anne Hutchinson. She was "a woman of a ready wit and bold spirit," as Winthrop himself said, and to his chagrin she used that wit to argue in favor of her right to interpret religion as she saw fit. She suggested that overconcern with the law amounted to a denial of the necessity of divine grace for salvation, which was most vexing to those charged with encouraging upright behavior and morality in the fledgling community. The notion that God's favor could be earned by humanity was, in Hutchinson's estimation, a belief in the power of "works." This was no minor allegation, but implied sympathy for a Catholic system of moral accounting that had its most shameless expression in the sale of indulgences—the very issue that had sparked the Reformation.

Like Dorothy Talbye, Hutchinson had begun her life in New England as a respected and godly woman. She had brought her family across the ocean to be nearer to the preacher John Cotton, under whose thrall she had fallen in Lincolnshire before his emigration. Aligned with Cotton, she was at the center of Boston society. Hutchinson's apparent defection from the straight and narrow to more heterodox views was thus a major blow to New England's spiritual status quo.

Hutchinson was the focal point of the antinomian controversy, which amounted to a dispute over how and why individuals might consider themselves saved, and, more importantly, who should be allowed to voice their opinions concerning this process. Winthrop held that it was beyond the role of women to speak of such things. Hutchinson begged to differ, and many others took her side. Her followers, mostly women, also included men such as Henry Vane, who himself served as governor for a time. Though she had based her own view of salvation on the inefficacy of "works," it is likely that it was precisely her own works that made her such an influential figure in the colony. She served as a midwife, and so had access to women of the colony when they were perhaps most in need of the kind of spiritual comfort no male clergyman could provide.

As Thomas Weld assessed her place within a genealogy of the spiritual "infections" suffered by the colony:

> The last and worst of all, which most suddenly diffused the venom of these opinions into the very veins and vitals of the people in the country, was Mistress Hutchinson's double weekly lecture, which she kept under a pretense of repeating sermons, to which resorted sundry of Boston and other towns about, to the number of fifty, sixty, or eighty at once. Where, after she had repeated the sermon, she would make her comment upon it, vent her mischievous opinions as she pleased, and wreathed the scriptures to her own purpose; where the custom was for her scholars to propound questions and she (gravely sitting in the chair) did make answers thereunto.
>
> The great respect she had at first in the hearts of all, and her profitable and sober carriage of matters, for a time made this her practice less suspected by the godly magistrates and elders of the church there, so that it was winked at for a time (though afterward reproved by the Assembly and called into Court), but it held so long, until she had spread her leaven so far that had not providence prevented, it had proved the canker of our peace and ruin of our comforts.

Because the source of her authority could be found in the intensity of the relationships she had fostered as a midwife, the first attacks against her were made concerning this very work, implying that her spiritual "infection" could be seen in the infants whose mothers she assisted at birth. Weld continued, "God Himself was pleased to step in...by testifying His displeasure against their opinions and practices, as clearly as if He had pointed with His finger." This divine displeasure could be seen, it was claimed, in God's causing pregnant women in Hutchinson's care "to produce out of their wombs, as before they had out of their brains, such monstrous births as no chronicle (I think) hardly ever recorded the like."

One of these afflicted mothers, Mary Dyer, was in Winthrop's estimation "a very proper and fair woman," yet she was also "notoriously infected with Mrs. Hutchinson's errors, and very censorious and troublesome." Adding a classic assessment of a man believing a woman should know her place, he added that, "being of a very proud spirit," Dyer was "much addicted to revelations."

While under Hutchinson's care, Dyer had delivered a stillborn baby girl, two months premature, apparently suffering from a number of birth defects. Among those already suspicious of the midwife's influence, rumors quickly spread that the infant was "a monster" composed of "a fish, a beast, and a fowl, all woven together in one, and without an head." As the body had been buried before anyone but Hutchinson, another midwife called Mrs. Hawkins, and a third unnamed woman had seen it, the leaders of the colony interrogated Mrs. Hawkins until she produced a sufficiently monstrous description:

It was of ordinary bigness; it had a face, but no head, and the ears stood upon the shoulders and were like an ape's; it had no forehead, but over the eyes four horns, hard and sharp; two of them were above one inch long, the other two shorter; the eyes standing out, and the mouth also; the nose hooked upward; all over the breast and back full of sharp pricks and scales, like a thornback; the navel and all the belly, with the distinction of the sex, were where the back should be, and the back and hips before, where the belly should have been; behind, between the shoulders, it had two mouths, and in each of them a piece of red flesh sticking out; it had arms and legs as other children; but, instead of toes, it had on each foot three claws, like a young fowl, with sharp talons.

The credulous leaders of the colony had Dyer's child exhumed six months after the day of her birth and death. In Winthrop's view, there were signs of some deformity but nowhere near, it seems, the level described by the midwife. They could not ask her to clarify, however, as she had disappeared after her interrogation, perhaps to avoid further investigations, for she was known to give the women in her care potions that might have had less than positive effects on the unborn. Nonetheless, Winthrop and others aligned against Anne Hutchinson preferred another explanation for the unfortunate events. No man had been present for Mary Dyer's labor, yet Winthrop wrote confidently of a scene he imagined as a moment of demonic possession:

> When it died in the mother's body, which was about two hours before the birth, the bed whereon the mother lay did shake, and withal there was such a noisome savor, as most of the women were taken with extreme vomiting and purging, so as they were forced to depart; and others of them their children were taken with convulsions, which they never had before nor after.

In his account years later, Thomas Weld added the detail that Anne Hutchinson herself had given birth to monsters—not just one, as Mary Dyer did, but "thirty monstrous births or thereabouts at once, some of them bigger, some lesser, some of one shape, some of another, few of any perfect shape, none at all of them (as far as I could ever learn) of human shape." Needless to say, neither Weld nor any man was ever present at Hutchinson's laboring bedside.

For her supposed crimes, Anne Hutchinson was brought to trial at the General Court at Newton, the highest in authority in Massachusetts Bay Colony, in 1637. Performing the interrogation of this one woman were Governor Winthrop as Chair of the Court, the Deputy Governor Thomas Dudley, five assistants, and five other deputies. Also in attendance were several of Boston's religious notables, including the preacher Hutchinson had followed from England, Reverend Cotton. Though he remained her minister and had inspired her troublemaking behavior, he had never faced anything remotely like Hutchinson's trial. Eventually he turned on his acolyte, preserving enough respectability that over time he and his family became symbols of New England piety.

Five decades before his grandson and namesake Cotton Mather would inspire another scare over troublesome women in nearby Salem, John Cotton watched as Hutchinson sat alone and debated the full force of the Puritan establishment. Her interrogation by Governor Winthrop and his associates reads today like a drama scripted to illustrate the intersection of sanctioned religious authority and willful individual rights, all framed within the barely spoken assumptions of the appropriate roles of women and men.

After a lengthy preamble in which Winthrop accused Hutchinson of having "troubled the peace of the commonwealth and the churches here" and of speaking "divers things, as we have been informed, very prejudicial to the honour of the churches and ministers" and finally of having held instructive gatherings in her home, an act "not tolerable nor comely in the sight of God nor fitting for your sex," Hutchinson responded as if the governor had not spoken at all.

"I am called here to answer before you," she said, "but I hear no things laid to my charge."

Winthrop, apparently fuming, replied, "I have told you some already and more I can tell you."

"Name one, Sir," Hutchinson said.

"Have I not named some already?" Winthrop replied.

"What have I said or done?" Hutchinson demanded.

"Why, for your doings," Winthrop sputtered. "This you did harbor and countenance those that are parties in this faction that you have heard of."

"That's matter of conscience, Sir."

It was her conscience, she told them, that brought her to lead Bible studies in her home. In this small rebellion were the seeds of a form of quiet dissent that threatened the very basis of Puritan society. Despite what the Reformation had established, Winthrop believed it was not up to each individual to determine what was just and right in the eyes of God. That duty belonged to the community, he maintained, as led by men chosen for that task by the knowledgeable consent of other men. If every woman who thought she knew something about holiness began instructing the impressionable, he feared, it would lead to spiritual lawlessness. This was the underlying reason for Winthrop's seeming incomprehension in the face of Hutchinson's obstinance. As the covenantally sanctioned leader of the colony, he believed he knew what was best for her, and it was certainly not the promulgation of heterodox views.

After observing the verbal sparring between Winthrop and the accused, Deputy Governor Thomas Dudley entered the fray. He put it plainly: Hutchinson had been a danger to Massachusetts Bay from the moment she arrived, and possibly before.

"About three years ago we were all in peace," Dudley said. "Mrs. Hutchinson, from that time she came hath made a disturbance, and some that came over with her in the ship did inform me what she was as soon as she was landed....Within half a year after, she had vented divers of her strange opinions and had made parties in the country."

Her strange opinions — that was the real issue here, because, as it happened, her opinions were not merely strange but tremendously attractive.

"Mrs. Hutchinson hath so forestalled the minds of many by their resort to her meeting," Dudley continued, "that now she hath a potent party in the country."

She was guilty, in other words, of establishing an alternate spiritual authority. People — women especially — had come to seek her out at the expense of their allegiances to more conventional religious voices. In this, Hutchinson was the foundation of a rising tower of spiritual dissent, rivaling the city upon a hill in its height. The only solution was to cast her out. "We must take away the foundation," Dudley said, "and the building will fall."

The expulsion of Anne Hutchinson was far from the end of the problem of religious diversity. Mary Dyer, "the woman which had the monster," in Winthrop's words, at first followed her teacher and friend from Massachusetts but later reappeared as if to haunt the men who had so abused the memory of her unfortunate child. When she returned, she was no longer merely a participant in a nameless protest against Puritan authority. She had become a member of the Quakers, at the time the most hated religious group in England and America because of their belief in an "inner light" that made teachers of all Christians and led to ceaseless questioning of the professional religious class. Along with three others, she was hanged from a tree in 1660, making Winthrop's Boston more like Calvin's Geneva than was perhaps intended.

Even after such harsh response, heterodoxies, heresies, and blasphemies bloomed and spread like spores across New England and then beyond in the years following. Even with rabble-rousers like Roger Williams and Anne Hutchinson gone more than ten years, fears of theological error were so widespread in 1651 that the Massachusetts General Court called for a day of repentance. The official reason was a succinct statement of the two most pressing dangers Puritan society believed it faced: witchcraft and strange opinions, both of which were simply synonyms for the kinds of religious differences that eventually showed themselves to be not aberrations but the norm.

John Winthrop's city upon a hill turned out to be built on a veritable volcano. Like the colonies and the nation it would come to represent, it was from the very start filled with heterodox religious practices, idiosyncratic beliefs, and doubts about the reigning doctrinal assumptions the Puritans had brought across the sea. With the force of heat and energy hidden just beneath the surface, this volcano blew more than once in the decades following the birth of the colony, exploding to rubble any hope of uniformity, and in the process redistributing the English population on the continent. Roger Williams responded to his exile by establishing a new colony in Rhode Island. Anne Hutchinson and her family traveled to Dutch New York. Killed in an Indian attack, she was said by her Puritan opponents to have gotten what was coming to her, but her death did not come before she had brought her message of individual religious insight beyond the jurisdiction of those who would suppress it. Of course, Mary Dyer never left Massachusetts again after her decision to return brought her to the gallows, but her willful incitement of the colony's wrath created the atmosphere in which the Quaker William Penn would establish a colony built on religious freedom — Pennsylvania — a generation after her death. The ideas brought to each of these colonies all fell away from the Puritan theocracy like debris from a crumbling city on a hill, spreading as if by gravity the true gospel of the American experiment: not religious agreement but dissent.

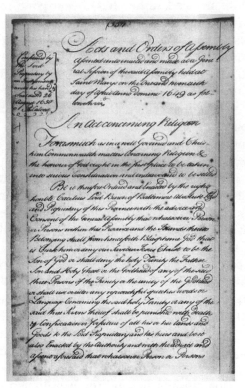

An Act Concerning Religion, 1649. Maryland's law has been remembered as an "Act of Toleration," but it made blasphemy a crime punishable by death.

CHAPTER 4

Blasphemy

1658

When Jacob Lumbrozo sailed for North America in the winter of 1656, the Province of Maryland must have seemed a good choice for a man such as himself. A Portuguese Jew whose family had once fled the anti-Semitism of the Iberian Peninsula, he perhaps would have been drawn to the colony's rhetoric of religious toleration. While its actual policies on that front were far from perfect, as he soon would discover, it nonetheless may have appeared slightly more enlightened than most other options at the time. If Christians elsewhere in America terrorized each other over minor differences in doctrine, what might they do to those who had not much use for Jesus at all?

A man of dark complexion, described as "black" in at least one court record and so possibly of North African ancestry, Lumbrozo similarly might have found it reassuring that in this colony, unlike its neighbors, the color of a man's skin did not yet seem destined to become a determinant of his legal rights. He also may have chosen his new home on entirely practical, economic grounds. Though he would eventually become a trader, a lawyer, a landowner, and a cultivator of corn and tobacco, he was trained as a physician. Maryland was still a small colony of fewer than a thousand souls, with only a handful of doctors. It was certain to grow, and as it did, it would surely be in need of his services. If rumors of compensation had ways of spreading through a profession then as they do now, he likely would have heard that men with similar skills had been given hundreds of acres and bushels of corn simply for transporting themselves into the province to practice their art.

Given all these logical reasons for his choice of a colony in which to settle, it is unlikely Jacob Lumbrozo was prepared for the possibility that in Maryland he would face precisely the kind of Inquisition his forebears had attempted to leave behind: an accusation and arrest on charges of blasphemy that threatened to end his life.

During the court proceedings against him, the first documented Jew in a colony founded by Catholics would show himself to be a reason-driven man, suspicious of overly symbolic meanings when literal explanations would suffice. And yet in his ordeal Jacob Lumbrozo himself became something of a symbol, raising a question that would determine the future of the land he had made his own: Would the New World offer merely another iteration of the most ancient of Old World hatreds, or could it find another way?

Though of Portuguese descent and born in Lisbon, Lumbrozo seems to have come to Maryland from London, then home to a small Jewish community newly reestablished following the end of a three-century ban prohibiting Jews from living in England. The Jews that returned upon formal readmission, as well as those who had been there secretly all along, were the descendants of those who had fled the ecclesiastical harassment found in the Catholic kingdoms of Spain and Portugal. The Iberian states throughout this time were in seemingly endless political upheaval, joining together under a common Crown and splitting apart again within less than a century. No matter the sovereign, however, the persecution of Jews continued, with special animosity reserved for *conversos*, also known as New Christians, who were often accused of being Christians in name alone, holding abiding allegiance to the faith they had renounced. Not infrequently, this was actually the case.

Pushed by these forces, pockets of Sephardic Jews—Jews originally from the regions known by the Hebrew term for the Iberian Peninsula, Sepharad—established themselves in the traditional centers within Ashkenaz, the medieval Jewish name for Germany, which when used more broadly as a signifier of a particular strain of Jewish identity has come to include the rest of northern and eastern Europe. Though distinctly Sephardic, the Lumbrozo name could by this time be found in England, Germany, and Holland, where Jacob's sister Rebecca was then living, and which had become a safe haven for the Jewish communities fleeing the Inquisitors' dangerous attentions. Amsterdam, especially, had emerged late in the previous century as a place where Spanish and Portuguese Jews, arriving as refugees from church-sponsored violence, eventually built a stronghold of relative freedom and prosperity. Emboldened by their improved security and social standing, many of the Jewish families who had practiced the rituals of Judaism covertly for generations now came to openly reembrace the faith.

Elsewhere in the Jewish world, others who had fled the Inquisition were not so lucky. In the Portuguese colony of Brazil, many *conversos* had arrived early in the sixteenth century, hoping that putting an ocean between themselves and the church tribunals would provide some protection. When the Inquisition arrived in Brazil in 1579, however, they were driven even further underground.

It was from these two communities of devotion — Amsterdam and Brazil, one whose Jewishness had been reclaimed, another in which it remained largely hidden — that the earliest and largest Jewish population in North America was drawn. Like almost all of colonial history in the New World, the path that first brought Jews to New Amsterdam, as New York City was then called, was an unexpected consequence of longstanding European rivalries playing out in a new arena.

For much of the seventeenth century, the Netherlands had been vying with Portugal over the sugar-producing regions of Brazil. After taking control of the northeast portion of the Amazon River basin, the Dutch West India Company encouraged immigration to establish Dutch culture and economic life in an area that was otherwise solidly under the control of the kingdoms of southern Europe. As a result, more than a thousand Jews had traveled there by 1645. As they had done in Amsterdam, they quickly created a vibrant cultural center, which included the first synagogue in the Americas, Kahal Zur Israel in the city of Recife. Only then did the New Christians who had been there for generations return to open expression of their faith. When the Portuguese regained control ten years later, however, the Jewish population once again was forced into exile, fearing the worst from the Catholic powers their ancestors had escaped.

Twenty-seven of these transplanted Amsterdam Jews pleaded with a Dutch ship captain to bring them out of Brazil to the oldest Dutch colony in the Americas: New Netherlands. When they landed in the settlement of New Amsterdam, however, the colony's governor, Peter Stuyvesant, was not happy to see them. There were already a small number of Jews living under his authority, but these refugees had the makings of a congregation. Not only did they present the possibility of religious difference organized into a potentially troublesome faction, they brought more immediate controversy as well. Upon arrival in port, the ship's captain claimed his passengers had not paid sufficient fare for their passage from Brazil and sued to recover his costs. Stuyvesant had the Jews' belongings seized and sold at auction to pay the damages, and wanted nothing more than for these new arrivals to leave the colony as quickly as possible.

Saddled with penniless newcomers from a population he feared would bring only spiritual contamination, Stuyvesant wrote to his sponsors in the Dutch West India Company. Seeking their support in the removal of the Jews for fear they might begin their "customary usury and deceitful trading with the Christians," Stuyvesant said that he "deemed it useful to require them in a friendly way to depart."

Of course, considering how few other options the Jews from Recife had, it is difficult to see anything "friendly" about it. Nor did Stuyvesant maintain this fiction when explaining to his backers why he felt they had to go. His reasons ranged from the practical — because of the Jews' "present indigence," he said, "they might become a charge in the coming winter" — to the theological: "Such hateful enemies and blasphemers of the name of Christ," he opined, should "be not allowed to further infect and trouble this new colony."

Like the Spanish to the south, like the English to the north, this Dutchman's primary concern was that allowing certain religious differences into the colony would amount to a spiritual infection that must be treated with extreme measures. His sponsors, however, saw things differently.

Unbeknownst to the governor, the refugees had outflanked him. They, too, had written back to Amsterdam, asking members of their community there to remind the colony's backers not only that Jews were allowed to live in Holland unmolested but that, more to the point, Jews were among the founders and investors in the very institution from which Stuyvesant had sought relief. The heads of the company wrote back to Stuyvesant on April 26, 1655:

> We would have liked to effectuate and fulfill your wishes and request that the new territories should no more be allowed to be infected by people of the Jewish nation, for we foresee there from the same difficulties which you fear, but after having further weighed and considered the matter, we observe that this would be somewhat unreasonable and unfair, especially because of the considerable loss sustained by this nation, with others, in the taking of Brazil, as also because of the large amount of capital which they still have invested in the shares of this company.

The leadership of the company concluded that, contrary to Stuyvesant's wishes, the "Portuguese Jews" should be allowed to "travel and trade to and in New Netherlands and live and remain there." The only solace they offered to the aggrieved governor was that this policy would be implemented on the condition that "the poor among them shall not become a burden to the company or to the community, but be supported by their own nation." In further correspondence, they agreed with Stuyvesant that under no circumstances should these religious outliers practice their religion.

Jews were permitted to live among the Christians of New Netherlands, in other words, but could not flaunt their spiritual differences. Clearly unsatisfied, Stuyvesant continued to complain about their presence for months, noting a year later that "[t]hey have many times requested of us the free and public exercise of their abominable religion, but this cannot yet be accorded to them."

Despite his obvious antipathy toward a people he referred to as "that deceitful race," however, it was soon determined that the problem of religion in New Netherlands was henceforth to be a matter of "don't ask, don't tell." As a law passed at this time declared:

> No man shall raise or bring forward any question or argument on the subject of religion, on pain of being placed on bread and water three days in the ship's galley. And if any difficulties should arise out of the said disputes, the author thereof shall be arbitrarily punished.

While the Jews of New Amsterdam eventually did win the right not only to remain in the colony but to openly practice some elements of their faith, the earliest form this practice took was the establishment of a Jewish cemetery in 1656. Still unhappy about being forced to allow Jews to live in his colony, Peter Stuyvesant was apparently less bothered with letting them die there.

Jacob Lumbrozo was no doubt aware of the treatment received by the New Netherlands' Brazilian refugees when he set sail from England in 1656. He also likely knew that the colony established twelve years earlier on the Chesapeake Bay envisioned itself as a place in stark contrast to the colonies whose residents were then basing hopes for the future on the idea of religious homogeneity.

The Province of Maryland had been founded by George Calvert and his son Cecil, the first and second Barons of Baltimore, as something of a safety valve for the ongoing persecution of Catholics in England. The very name of the province speaks of the fraught inter-religious history that brought it into being. Upon granting the elder Calvert a charter for a colony near Virginia, King Charles I proposed naming it for his Catholic wife, Henrietta Maria of France. The king had received no shortage of criticism for marrying a Catholic, an act that fostered fears that he would tip the scales in their favor in the ongoing struggle for religious control of the Crown. While his decision to name the new colony after her was a confirmation of her influence, his first suggestion of a name, Mariana, was deemed ill-advised by his court. Though more euphonious than other possibilities (which included "Crescentia" and "Terra Henriettae"), it also called to mind an infamous Jesuit of the day, Juan Mariana, whose writings encouraged regicide. Considering the fate Charles I eventually met (he lost his head in 1649), the name would have been morbidly prescient, but he settled instead on Terra Mariae, "Mary's Land."

George Calvert died two months before the charter could be finalized, and so the task of bringing the establishment of the colony to fruition fell to his son, who was referred to throughout the colonies thereafter as Lord Baltimore.

The first ships full of those taking advantage of the protection he offered, the *Ark* and the *Dove*, traveled to Maryland by way of the West Indies in 1634. Lord Baltimore's instructions to these earliest arrivals listed the peaceful coexistence between religious factions as a requirement for the colony:

> His Lordship requires his said Governor & Commissioners that in their voyage to Mary Land they be very careful to preserve unity & peace amongst all the passengers on Shipboard, and that they suffer no scandal nor offence to be given to any of the Protestants… and that for that end, they cause all Acts of Roman Catholic Religion to be done as privately as may be, and that they instruct all the Roman Catholics to be silent upon all occasions of discourse concerning matters of Religion; and that the said Governor & Commissioners treat the Protestants with as much mildness and favor as Justice will permit. And this to be observed at Land as well as at Sea.

Writing three years after Winthrop penned "A Model of Christian Charity" aboard the *Arabella*, Lord Baltimore gave advice concerning how religion ought to be lived in the New World precisely opposite to Winthrop's approach. Under no circumstances, in Calvert's opinion, should Catholics act as if they were establishing a city upon a hill, with the light of their convictions on display for all to see. On the contrary, though they shared a creed with the colony's founder and protector, their faith should be kept out of sight for the sake of preserving the peace.

This is not exactly what happened. Upon landing, the Catholics aboard the *Ark* and the *Dove* hewed a large cross from Maryland timber and held an open-air mass in its shadow, likely the first time the Catholic sacraments were administered in the English settlements of North America. Though this would seem precisely the kind of conspicuous "Acts of Roman Catholic Religion" Lord Baltimore had required "be done as privately as may be," there were no significant disputes over the matter. Indeed, the only distress suffered by the priest who had performed the mass that day was that a small boat carrying maids sent to shore to wash his church linens—altar cloth, chasuble, stole, and other ritual elements apparently soiled during the ocean passage—had capsized. The maids were recovered, but, to the priest's chagrin, the linens were lost.

With the feud between those divided by the Reformation seeming to be solved, at least for now, by Catholics mostly practicing discreetly and Protestants looking the other way when they did not, some among the settlers turned their attention to the new varieties of religious difference all around them. None other than the Jesuit priest who had performed the first mass, Father Andrew White, became the earliest chronicler of the region, and reported on the customs and beliefs of the local Yaocomico tribe in great detail.

"Upon the whole, they cultivate generous minds," he wrote of his colony's hosts, from whom the English had purchased land soon after landing. "Whatever kindness you may confer, they repay. They determine nothing rashly, or when actuated by a sudden impulse of mind, but with reflection; so that when any thing of moment is, at any time, proposed, they are for a time silent in a thoughtful manner; then they answer briefly, Yes or No, and are very firm of their purpose."

Yet for all their straightforwardness, White admitted, there was a gap in his Jesuit understanding. "They are possessed with a wonderful desire of civilization," he noted, but "ignorance of their language renders it still doubtful for me to state what views they entertain concerning religion."

Despite the seeming détente between the Old World adversaries, White did not trust "Protestant interpreters" in this important matter, and so what he knew of Native American beliefs was limited to what he could glean from observation and interpretation. "These few things we have learned at different times: They recognise one God of heaven, whom they call 'Our God,' nevertheless, they pay him no external worship, but by every means in their power, endeavor to appease a certain evil spirit which they call Okee, that he may not hurt them. They worship corn and fire, as I am informed, as Gods wonderfully beneficent to the human race."

Others among the early settlers were sufficiently comfortable with the religious differences the Yaocomico represented that they took part in a native ceremony at a site the English referred to as a "temple" near the Patuxent River. It was there, on an apparent day of celebration, that a large number of men, women, and children gathered around a great fire. The children first formed a ring around the flames, with their elders behind. A piece of deer fat was then thrown into the fire, causing the gathering place to fill with smoke, and the flames to jump with the greasy fuel. As all hands and voices rose in response, a procession around the fire began behind a medicine man carrying a sacred pouch of tobacco. The children followed his movements, singing in what White found to be "an agreeable voice." When the procession ended, pipes were lit with the holy leaves, and smoke was blown on all in attendance, apparently consecrating Indians and Englishmen alike.

The Jesuit White records all this with great sympathy and a remarkably anthropological eye. Unlike Puritan missionaries to the north, or even other Catholics in the Spanish or French territories, his first priority seems not to have been conversion. As a consequence of coming from a persecuted minority, the English Catholics were far more concerned with their own spiritual survival.

It was this concern that led to the creation, a dozen years after White made note of local beliefs and rituals, of the 1649 Act Concerning Religion, Maryland's statute protecting those of a variety of sects—a variety of *Christian* sects, that is—from the negative attention of the colonial government. Though often referred to as the Toleration Act, in fact it tolerated only those "professing to believe in Jesus Christ." These believers, and only these believers, would henceforth be protected from being "troubled, Molested or discountenanced for or in respect of his or her religion nor in the free exercise thereof within this Province…nor any way compelled to the belief or exercise of any other Religion against his or her consent…"

Conspicuously intended to protect Catholics at a time when their liberty and even their safety was far from guaranteed, the Toleration Act also reflected a broader reality that no one religious group could count on maintaining a majority within the quickly shifting demographics of colonial populations. This reality was underscored just five years later, when Catholics lost control of Maryland's governance for a time, and a law opposite in its intentions was passed. The Act Concerning Religion of 1654 again preserved toleration for all varieties of Christians, with the exception of "the Popish Religion commonly known by the name of the Roman Catholick Religion," adherents of which would not "be protected in this Province by the Lawes of England." This act, in turn, was repealed when Lord Baltimore reclaimed control just four years later. Within a decade of Jacob Lumbrozo's arrival, religious freedoms were granted, rescinded, and granted again.

Fickle laws of toleration aside, the members of the colony established, almost from the beginning, a reputation for being not only relatively broadminded but frequently scornful of the Old World's orthodoxies. Back in Massachusetts Bay, for example, visiting Marylanders had more than once ruffled the feathers of the devout. Try as he might to keep his colony free of religious difference, Governor Winthrop found it washing against the shores of Massachusetts as frequently as the tides, occasionally on board vessels from the Calverts' colony. Writing in his journal, Winthrop lamented that the shipmates of a vessel from Maryland jeered at Bostonians in the port, mocking their religiosity.

"It was informed the governour," he wrote, referring to himself as he often did in the third person, "that some of our people, being aboard the bark of Maryland, the sailors did revile them, calling them holy brethren, the members, etc., and withal did course and swear most horribly, and use threatening speeches against us." Unable to determine who the offending sailors were, the governor asked the ship's captain to "bring no more disordered persons among us."

Ten years later, Winthrop noted that no less a representative of Maryland than Lord Baltimore himself made a more veiled comment on religious life in Massachusetts when he "made tender of land in Maryland to any of ours that would transport themselves thither, with free liberty of religion, and all other privileges which the place afforded." Winthrop fumed at the implication that his colonists had any reason to desire such a thing. Dismissing the idea as a heresy bordering on absurdity, Winthrop wrote, "Our captain had no mind to further his desire therein, nor had any of our people temptation that way."

Others did not take Baltimore's offer so lightly, however. This same year, a group of Puritans from Anglican-controlled Virginia fled to Maryland, where they established the city of Providence, later called Annapolis. Virginia Quakers likewise fled persecution at the invitation of Lord Baltimore and settled on the eastern shore of the Chesapeake Bay. Such rapidly accumulating diversity seemed for a time to guarantee that Maryland truly would be, as in the early twentieth-century historian Hester Dorsey Richardson's too sunny assessment of the province's early days, "the only spot on the earth where the principle of Live and Let Live was the law of the land."

* * *

The growing population of religious dissenters of a number of persuasions might have made Maryland an excellent choice for Jacob Lumbrozo, except for one small detail: Under Maryland's so-called Act of Toleration, the penalty for blasphemy, defined simply as any denial of the central tenets of the Christian faith, was death:

> Bee it therefore ordayned and enacted...that whatsoever person or persons within this province and the islands thereunto belonging, shall from henceforth blaspheme God, that is, to curse him, or shall deny our Savior Jesus Christ to be the Son of God, or shall deny the Holy Trinity, the Father, Son, and Holy Ghost, or the Godhead or any of the sayd Three Persons of the Trinity, or the Unity of the Godhead, or shall use or utter any reproachful speeches, words or languages concerning the Holy Trinity, or any of the sayd three persons thereof, shall be punished with death, and confiscation or forfeiture of all his or her land and goods to the lord proprietary and his heires.

In other words, whatever Maryland's various laws concerning religion might have done to avoid the kinds of faith-based attacks colonists regularly made against each other in places like Massachusetts Bay, they offered no protection to a Jewish doctor who made the possibly fatal mistake of saying that Jesus Christ was nothing but a glorified magician, his miracles a sham, his resurrection a legend built upon lies.

Lumbrozo's troubles began when he had been in Maryland less than a year. On a summer evening in 1657, he was in the company of fellow colonists John Hoffsett, Josias Cole, and Richard Preston Jr. and their conversation took a theological turn. The setting was apparently Preston's home (it is referred to in court documents as "ye house of Mr. Preston"), or perhaps the home of his father, also named Richard Preston. The latter's house served throughout the period as a semi-official seat of provincial government, owing to the elder Preston's standing in the community. Preston-on-the-Patuxent, as this home was known, was the place to which residents of the province would travel in order to argue a tariff or petition for a regulation, such as the law adopted that year which made it legal to kill wolves by "meanes in any kind whatsoever," or the law that made it illegal to "beguile or deceive" authorities about the size of one's tobacco crop, punishable by a fine of 1,000 pounds of tobacco for every cask or hogshead concealed. Whether for these or similar reasons, a new resident like Lumbrozo had ample reason to visit.

Whatever brought him to Preston's home and into the company of Cole and Hoffsett, Lumbrozo seems to have fallen into a conversation about something other than wolves or tobacco. Perhaps goading Lumbrozo, or perhaps sincerely curious to hear the opinion of the only Jew he had likely ever met, Hoffsett asked the doctor his thoughts on various religious matters. Hoffsett was at the time a man in his mid-forties, so one might suppose he was old enough to put away childish things, but there nonetheless seems a measure of mischief in his attempt to push Lumbrozo's buttons. What, he wanted to know, did the good doctor think of "our Blessed Savior, Christ"? Hoffsett himself professed that anyone should agree that Jesus "was more than a man." For evidence, he simply pointed toward the fact of his death and resurrection. How else could his disciples have found an empty tomb on Easter morning?

Apparently not one to hold his tongue, Lumbrozo replied to Hoffsett that the disappearance of Jesus's body, and hence the moment that sparked the legend of the resurrection, could be very easily explained on natural rather than supernatural grounds. And then the only Jew in Maryland began methodically to dig his own grave.

"His disciples stole him away," Lumbrozo said.

The astonished Hoffsett, perhaps hearing more irreverence than he had hoped to incite, answered with piqued astonishment: "Yet no man ever did such miracles as he!"

With the air of a man recently arrived in the backward American provinces from the civilized cities of Europe, Lumbrozo attempted to enlighten his conversation partner. "Such works might be done," he said, "by necromancy or sorcery."

To this, Hoffsett could only answer that it was surely Lumbrozo himself who must be the necromancer to say such a thing. Lumbrozo simply laughed at the accusation, as if he put more faith in the colony's supposed spirit of religious toleration than in its willingness to ruthlessly carry out the letter of its laws.

That might have been the end of it, but Hoffsett was not the only man in Maryland who claimed to have had such a conversation with Lumbrozo. Significantly, Richard Preston Jr. later did not recall this conversation occurring at the Preston house at all, as Hoffsett had suggested. As the eldest son of one of the more prominent colonists, he perhaps had reason to distance such goings-on from their family home. In Preston's recollection, he was traveling with Lumbrozo and Josias Cole when Cole pointedly asked the "Jew doctor" whether or not Jews waited for the coming of the messiah.

Lumbrozo replied with an unambiguous affirmation that they did, which suggests that he was fully open with his faith, even proud to declare it. He may have even explained that every day, three times a day, observant Jews pray the Amidah, which alludes specifically to the coming of the messiah. However, to Jews the word messiah, *mashiach*, simply means the anointed one, not the son of God Christians believe in. This response already might have labeled the doctor a blasphemer, but his self-incrimination had only begun. As if springing a trap, Cole then peppered Lumbrozo with questions, eager to lead him to ever greater perdition.

"And what was he that was crucified at Jerusalem?"

"He was a man."

"But then how did he do all his miracles?"

"He did them by the art of magic," Lumbrozo said.

"How did his disciples do the same miracles after Jesus was crucified?"

The answer was apparently clear enough to Lumbrozo. Just as other, more experienced physicians had taught him the medical arts, surely one of history's great practitioners of magic would teach his techniques to pupils eager to learn.

"He taught them his art," Lumbrozo replied matter-of-factly.

In popular memory of these events, it should be noted, the men are often depicted as well into their cups by this point. Though the historical record nowhere reflects this, this might explain Lumbrozo's steady ratcheting up of the level of irreverence throughout his interrogation. It seems at times as if he was truly trying to get their goat, making a game of finding precisely the answer that would most upset his antagonists, paying no heed to the consequences.

But the consequences were dire: Harmless as these exchanges now seem, at a time when the meaning of religious toleration was shifting beneath the feet of this Jewish doctor and his Christian interlocutors, the conversation was enough to see Lumbrozo arrested and charged with blasphemy.

Curiously, the arrest seems to have occurred six months after he made his supposedly damning remarks. Why the delay? Lumbrozo had come to Maryland in the wake of New Amsterdam's Jewish refugees feeling the effects of far-off hostilities between the Dutch and the Portuguese. He was caught in the current of political changes that seemed to have little to do with him. When he committed his alleged blasphemy, the original Act Concerning Religion had been repealed by the Protestant regime. He was brought to trial only after Lord Baltimore's reclaimed control of the province allowed the Toleration Act to be restored. At the time Lumbrozo made his comments, in other words, blasphemy was not punishable by death, but then suddenly it was once more. In this, the Jewish doctor was an unintended victim of the ongoing dispute between Catholics and Protestants in England. Had he been executed for his crime, he would have been collateral damage of a fight over religious tolerance unfolding an ocean away.

Lumbrozo, however, had enough affinity for the law to mount a spirited defense. Hearing the testimony against him, he admitted that he had indeed spoken of Jesus's death and other religious questions with his accusers. Despite the differences in their accounts, Preston and Hoffsett were united against him, so a simple denial would have gotten Lumbrozo nowhere. Yet, with the benefit of some distance on that possibly drunken night, he insisted that he had not sought to force his views on them. They had asked his opinion, and he had given it honestly "to some particular demands when urged."

As the court documents explain, when pressed further on the matter of magic and miracles, Lumbrozo shrewdly suggested that his supposedly impious and offensive answers were actually scriptural references. Far from calling Jesus a necromancer, he had only "declared what remains written concerning Moses and ye Magicians of Egypt" — a reference to the Exodus story of the duel, of sorts, between the Liberator of Israel, his brother Aaron, and the sorcerers Pharaoh summoned to discredit the signs Moses used as demonstrations of God's power:

> The LORD said to Moses and Aaron, "When Pharaoh says to you, 'Perform a miracle,' then say to Aaron, 'Take your staff and throw it down before Pharaoh,' and it will become a snake."

So Moses and Aaron went to Pharaoh and did just as the LORD commanded. Aaron threw his staff down in front of Pharaoh and his officials, and it became a snake. Pharaoh then summoned wise men and sorcerers, and the Egyptian magicians also did the same things by their secret arts: Each one threw down his staff and it became a snake. But Aaron's staff swallowed up their staffs.

Using a scriptural reference anyone hearing him would have known, Lumbrozo suggested that he had only compared Jesus to Moses, which, if a blasphemy, was one Saint Paul was guilty of as well. Moreover, Lumbrozo insisted, he "said not anything scoffingly, or in derogation of Him Christians acknowledge for the Messiah." According to his testimony, he could not have spoken any other way, for he answered "by his profession"—not as a blasphemer but as a Jew.

Lumbrozo's defense, in other words, rested on two planks: First, that by reason of his faith, he could not have answered otherwise when asked such questions. Second, the texts upon which he based his beliefs and his answers to the specific questions he had been asked were also a cornerstone of the faith of those who had demanded he answer. Citing a biblical precedent even for his supposed blasphemy, he played the barbaric law of toleration against itself—conjuring a snake of his own, perhaps, to eat those of his accusers.

Neither Preston's nor Hoffsett's responses to this argument were recorded, but we do know something of their own religious commitments that makes the very fact of their accusation rather surprising. One of the most striking things about this episode is that those leading the charge against Lumbrozo—at least one of the men who testified against him, and two of those who are mentioned in the proceedings—were neither Catholics nor Puritans, but Quakers. They were themselves a religious minority threatened elsewhere in the colonies; members of a group who had been chased out of Massachusetts and Virginia and had only recently arrived in Maryland. Having come at the invitation of Lord Baltimore just as the Act Concerning Religion was repealed, rewritten, and then restored, they would have rightly wondered what the extent of toleration in the colony might be. There might have been less dramatic means of testing these waters than accusing a Jew of blasphemy, but nevertheless the Lumbrozo affair eventually provided an answer.

With little fanfare, Lumbrozo was ultimately pardoned. It is unlikely his freedom came as the result of his efforts to offer biblical justification for describing Jesus as a magician. More likely he was freed during a general amnesty offered as part of yet another power struggle for control of the kingdom of England. Just eight days after he heard Lumbrozo's case, the governor of Maryland heeded the new law of the land as decreed an ocean away, declaring, "I doe hereby pardon & acquit All & Every person or persons wch this Court in any Criminal Cause stood indicted Convicted or condemned to dye Resyding att this time within this province." Arrested as part of the ongoing struggle for control of Maryland, he was freed because of a dispute under way even farther from home, namely the Restoration, the ongoing turmoil over the Crown and its religious affiliation that consumed the middle decades of the century.

Lumbrozo went on to live another eight years in Maryland. During that time, as if in confirmation that a lasting peace had been reached between himself and his neighbors, he was permitted to conduct himself openly as a Jew in a province caught in a tug of war between two kinds of Christians. Moreover, he was granted letters of denization that allowed him to own land and hold public office. He acquired a plantation of his own and named it, intriguingly, Lumbrozo's Discovery.

It is tempting to think that what Jacob Lumbrozo had discovered is that a little tolerance can be a dangerous thing. Or perhaps he had discovered what so many spiritual outliers in American history have realized since: that survival often depends on following Lord Baltimore's advice to practice religion "as privately as may be." Before his death in 1666, the outspoken Lumbrozo frequently found himself involved in disputes with fellow colonists, but there was never again a disagreement so theologically charged. In this way, it might be said that the man known as Jacob Lumbrozo was indeed put to death following his dispute as a supposed blasphemer: Following his pardon, he changed his name to John.

Whether or not this adoption of an alias should be taken as an indication that Lumbrozo was the first Jewish immigrant to attempt assimilation in America, his experience does point beyond the fate of just one individual. The 1649 Act Concerning Religion, which nearly cost a blameless man his life, is generally regarded as a precursor to the U.S. Constitution's First Amendment guarantee of religious liberty. Yet it bears remembering that, just as the Toleration Act did nothing to protect non-Christians, the First Amendment itself did not immediately offer religious freedom to all, as the status of Jews in Maryland long after Lumbrozo's trial clearly shows. In 1723, the colony passed an act proposing that those denying the divinity of Christ should be punished with tongue-boring; for the second offense, the blasphemer was to be branded on the forehead with the letter *B*. Even the Maryland state constitution, adopted just months after American independence was declared in 1776, offers a striking echo of earlier ambivalent intentions. "No other test or qualification ought to be required" of those wishing to serve the new government, it declares, than an "oath of support and fidelity to this state" and "a declaration of belief in the Christian religion." Gone, of course, was the penalty of death, but no less than in 1649, non-Christians were automatically disqualified from full protection under the law.

Further rights for the spiritual descendants of Maryland's first Jews were not secured until fifty years after the Revolution, when another piece of dubiously named legislation, the Jew Bill of 1826, sought "to extend to the sect of people professing the Jewish religion the same rights and privileges that are enjoyed by Christians." When the act passed, barely, it served as a reminder that if not for the willingness, and perhaps the occasional chutzpah, of those on the margins of the dominant faith to maintain their beliefs, the freedoms the majority takes for granted might be strangled, as Jacob Lumbrozo nearly was, in a noose of selective toleration.

Tituba Teaching the First Act of Witch-craft. Sketch from *Witchcraft Illustrated,* by Henrietta D. Kimball. Boston: Geo. A. Kimball, 1892. Artist unknown. (Library of Congress)

CHAPTER 5

Witches and Indians

1692

A half century after John Winthrop stood on the deck of the *Arabella* and warned a ship full of pious settlers about the risks involved in making and breaking covenants with God, it seemed that divine retribution had come to his colony at last.

Beginning at midnight on August 8, 1679, a fire sparked to life in an outer room of one of Boston's dockside taverns, a small establishment owned by the publican Clement Gross, which he called the Three Mariners. It was the second time in four months that some unknown vandal had attempted to damage this particular house of ale and ill repute. In the first instance, the tavern keeper had stamped down the blaze without much trouble, smothering it before larger questions of its significance could kindle in his mind. He might have dismissed it as happenstance, the inevitable outcome of drunken men discarding clay pipe stems broken while tobacco still smoldered inside. But then, before the summer was out, it happened again. This second fire seemed more malign in its intent, and its consequences were incalulably more severe. In minutes, it spread to the inner tavern walls and then took the roof. Due to the hunger of the flames, the dry summer night on which it was set, or simply the willful refusal of Providence to intervene, the conflagration grew in size and intensity until Gross's entire building was engulfed, flashing on the harbor's edge like a beacon calling further misfortune to shore.

Boston at the time was a city built of sticks. The timber of Massachusetts forests made a ready resource, but it had made the quickly growing village as tinder-stocked as a smelting furnace. Thanks to the colonists' residual tendency to pack their dwellings and businesses as close together as if they were still in London, Bostonians had known a number of fiery catastrophes before, calling more than one of them "the Great Fire," as if in hope that each new holocaust would be the last. The first few of these great fires had been in the 1650s, when many of the colony's original arrivals watched in horror as the parts of a city it had taken a generation to build were consumed within hours; another had occurred just three years before the current calamity. Called "the greatest fire that ever happened in Boston," the great fire of 1676 destroyed a "meeting house of considerable bigness" and forty-six homes, including that of Increase Mather, the most prominent clergyman of the time. So susceptible was the city to this form of disaster, in fact, that a popular rhyming play on its name captured the general fear of its fate. "Lost-town," they called it, and it had never seemed so lost as in 1679, when a series of apparent arsons characterized by one early chronicler as a "grand triumph of incarnate desire and ambition" had resulted in the "most terrible devastation of property."

In this burning season, the "grand climax" was reached when the fire ignited at the Three Mariners spread to surrounding buildings. The blaze soon ravaged every warehouse in an active harbor — as many as seventy, by some counts — along with adjoining businesses and eighty homes. Many of these homes held households of ten or more (the average Puritan birthrate was eight children for every marriage, and single men were encouraged to board with families lest they be left to their own carnal inclinations), and the fire ultimately destroyed a not insignificant portion of the total shelter for a city of fewer than five thousand souls. When the flames reached the ships at dock, it seemed even the natural bulwark against such devastation — a whole ocean of water — was no match for whatever malevolent force had served as incendiary.

By daybreak on August 9, the first city of Massachusetts Bay looked as if fire and brimstone had rained down on it from above in recompense for some grievous sin. Any Puritans inclined to doubt might have wondered if they had built less an American facsimile of Calvin's Geneva than New England's very own Sodom and Gomorrah. Increase Mather, perhaps still smarting from the loss of his own home three years before, took this most recent fire as a cue to ask what had "provoked the Lord to bring His Judgments on New-England," while his son, the soon to be equally esteemed Cotton Mather, would later say of his city's remains, "Ah, Boston! Thou hast seen the vanity of all worldly possessions. One fatal morning, which laid *fourscore* of thy dwelling-houses and seventy of thy warehouses in a ruinous heap, gave thee to read it in fiery characters....Never was a town under the cope of heaven more liable to be laid to ashes, whether by the carelessness or wickedness of them who sleep in it. That such a *Combustible heap* of Contiguous Houses yet stands, it may be called A *Standing Miracle*."

Miracle or no, for a city upon a hill convinced of its place in the favor of the divine, the port blaze was only the latest in a series of setbacks that called into question the entire enterprise of occupying North America. In the classic jeremiad in which he pondered the source of the divine displeasure they were experiencing, Increase Mather went on to enumerate the "judgements" they had received. "That God hath a Controversy with his New-England People is undeniable," he said, "the Lord having written his displeasure in dismal Characters against us." Those "dismal Characters" included not only the most recent fire and those before it but a long line of agonies that made sense to the Puritan mind only if they were considered as punishments: King Philip's War, for example, which had been fought against the Wampanoag and other local tribes in 1675–76, had decimated the English population. In the years immediately following, a smallpox epidemic nearly replicated this awful casualty rate. A people given to see the hand of the divine in all things inevitably began to look about their Lost-town for reasons why they might deserve God's wrath.

To the elder Mather, the answers were obvious. To begin with, the August fire had started at a tavern. It stood to reason that all the activities one might find in such a place should be considered as shameful causes of such a terrible effect. "There is much Intemperance," he wrote. "The heathenish and Idolatrous practice of Health-drinking is too frequent. That shamefull iniquity of sinfull Drinking is become too general a Provocation."

Of course, it was not just the act of drinking "huzzahs" that warranted rebuke but the company one kept while doing so. "There are other heinous breaches of the seventh Commandment," he said. "Temptations thereunto are become too common, viz. such as immodest Apparel, Laying out of hair, Borders, naked Necks and Arms, or, which is more abominable, naked Breasts, and mixed Dancings, light behaviour and expressions, sinful Company-keeping with light and vain persons, unlawfull Gaming, an abundance of Idleness, which brought ruinating judgement upon Sodom."

Likewise, the aftereffects of a night at a place like the Three Mariners were without question to blame: "There is great profaneness, in respect of irreverent behaviour in the solemn Worship of God. It is a frequent thing for men...to sit in prayer time, and some with their heads almost covered, and to give way to their own sloth and sleepiness, when they should be serving God with attention and intention." Such activities and others, including "Inordinate Passions" and "Inordinate Affection for the World," Mather warned, were the sort that "brings wrath, Fires and other judgements upon a professing People."

While Mather offered scriptural references for most of these offenses, establishing that the sad history of human proclivities stretched back well into biblical times, other sins worthy of punishment seemed to him peculiar enough to the American context that he offered no precedent. Too many New Englanders, he lamented, desired to leave the close confines of towns "to live like Heathen, only so that they might have Elbow-room enough in the world." This was a symptom of a larger problem, he explained, which would become a key for understanding another set of trials soon to be endured.

"Christians in this Land," Mather lamented, "have become too like unto the Indians." He could not have known it, but an outgrowth of this fear would mark the Puritan legacy with a judgment more damning than fire.

Not long after the rebuilding of Boston had begun—with bricks this time, for arson was proving a surprisingly persistent problem in this supposedly rule-bound theocracy—there arrived by ship from the English island of Barbados a woman whose impact on the North American colonies would be greater than any disaster. Rather than divine judgment, she would be regarded first as a force sent by the devil and then as a victim of human folly.

We know her now as Tituba, though in the court records from the end of the seventeenth century, when she entered the drama of history as the first person accused of witchcraft in the Salem witch trials, she is named variously Titiba and Titibe. She may also be the young girl referred to as "Tattuba" on a deed of all "Negroes Stock Cattle and Utensils" from a plantation in Barbados a few years before her arrival. By the laws of the day, she was the property of one Samuel Parris, a young merchant with family in both the Caribbean and Massachusetts. After several years in Barbados working as an agent for sugar plantations, Parris set off for Boston to make a new life that would eventually include a change of vocation to the ministry. This future preacher arrived in the rebuilt port in the winter of 1680 with assets that included not only Tituba but a man called John Indian, who would later become her husband.

Despite Tituba's inclusion on a list of African-born slaves on a Barbados plantation, the court documents through which she has become known refer to her most often as an Indian, and recent scholarship agrees that this was most likely the case. Unlike Mustafa Zemmouri, she seems to have been born in the New World, but like him she did not arrive of her own free will in the place whose history she would shape. And she likewise did not leave behind entirely the person she had been before her arrival. Just as Esteban the Black and the other African-born men held in bondage by Spanish conquistadors carried something of their faith into the heart of America, "Titibe, an Indian Woman," as the 1692 warrant for arrest named her, carried stories from her youth in the Caribbean to the top of John Winthrop's city upon a hill.

To understand what Tituba wrought in Massachusetts, it is helpful to consider that the island of Barbados at the time was a hotbed of cultural blending. Three years before the *Arabella* had come to shore in Massachusetts, another British ship—this one carrying ten African-born slaves, along with eighty English colonists—landed at the island's port of Holetown. Through the decades that followed, shiploads of English and Africans, as well as indentured Catholics sent from Ireland, would also arrive.

At the founding of this English settlement, Barbados had no native population of any kind. Though once home to a vibrant culture similar to those described on Hispaniola and Haiti by the historians las Casas and Pané, the island's original inhabitants had been driven out of existence by the Spanish and Portuguese throughout the previous century. In an effort to help the various new populations adapt to an environment wholly unlike any they had known before, the English enticed a small group of Arawak Indians from the northeast coast of South America to come to Barbados for the purpose of instructing the colonists and their forced laborers in the fishing and farming practices best suited to the region.

Though the first Arawak in Barbados may have come willingly, these Indians and their descendants were reduced to slavery within a generation. They began to live among—and were eventually absorbed by—the much larger African population, which quickly amounted to the island's majority, outnumbering even the English while the Indians never totaled more than 1 percent of Barbados inhabitants. Throughout the early decades of the colony, it is likely more South American Arawak were regularly added to the mix; whether kidnapped or enticed, once on the island they would not leave it except as an Englishman's property.

According to Elaine Breslaw, the foremost scholar on the intersection of witchcraft and medicine in early America and author of an examination of the origins of the "reluctant witch of Salem," Tituba likely came from this small group of transplanted Arawak. In one of the great forgotten ironies of history, such origins would make this woman distant kin to the Taino, who seem to have settled the islands centuries before from Arawak strongholds on the South American mainland—the same people of whom Columbus erroneously said, "They have no religion." As the tales of devotional zemies and the prophetic visions of Taino priests remind us, this statement was far from true in 1492, and it became even less so as the diverse populations of Barbados, with their wildly different practices and beliefs, became entwined. For perhaps forty years before Tituba arrived on the island, African, Indian, and European traditions had mingled and transformed each other, creating the earliest form of Creole culture, and setting a pattern that would be followed to varying degrees throughout the islands and across the south and southwestern portions of North America.

Evidence of such blending is readily apparent in the music and languages of these regions, and religiously, too, new forms of expression were created that may have seemed to contemporary eyes mere perversions of established ceremonies but were in fact distinct traditions all their own. Not long after Tituba would have left the island, an English visitor to Barbados described hybrid African-Indian-Catholic rituals that involved using everyday items to commune with the spirit world. He claimed to have seen rituals "in which with their various instruments of horrid music howling and dancing about the graves of the dead," the multi-ethnic servants of the English colonists gave "victuals and strong liquor to the souls of the deceased" in order to ferret out the source of malevolent spiritual powers. Inhabited exclusively by people who had left behind the places where their religious lives had been formed, Barbados was an island haunted by traditions that were perhaps more susceptible to transformation because they were dislocated and half-remembered, and thus always in the process of reinvention.

This was true not only among the population of forced laborers but among the colonial occupiers as well. The Catholic Irish occupied a rung of society only slightly higher than the Africans and the Indians and so were natural participants in the blending of religious cultures, and the Protestant English seem likewise to have followed suit in taking part in the process of hybridization.

As Tituba made her way from the harbor to her first home in Massachusetts (a small house and shop Samuel Parris had rented to establish himself in the city), she would not have seen many signs that Boston, too, was a place of the blending of cultures and beliefs — at least not at first. Within the beleaguered Puritan community, the insistence on religious conformity was regarded as a matter not only of intolerance but existential concern. Remember that in the Puritan view, society itself rested on the notion of the covenant — an understanding that all relationships were a kind of contract between mutually agreeing parties. Failure to meet the demands of a contract between people could result in being cast out of the community; failure to meet the demands of a contract with God could result in even more dire consequences. As Winthrop himself had put it, to "deale falsely with our god in this worke wee have undertaken" would inevitably "cause him to withdrawe his present help from us."

For this reason, the Puritan fear of religious difference became manifest in actions ranging from the symbolic to the homicidal. Between the landing of the *Arabella* and the ship that brought Tituba, the government of the colony would pass laws banning everything from public celebration of the semi-pagan holiday of Christmas to "direct, expresse, presumptuous or high handed Blasphemie." The responses to the crimes — a fine of a few shillings in the first case, hanging in the second — were different only in degree. They were varied means toward reaching the same impossible end, which was total consensus under a singular form of the faith.

In her years in Boston, however, Tituba would have noticed that the city's uniformity was not what it seemed. Despite the religious motives that had led many of the colonists to emigrate, many of them had allowed their spiritual inclinations to travel as far from their origins as they themselves had from their birthplaces. Lamenting the difference between the first generation of Puritan settlers and those he regarded as his ministerial responsibility, Increase Mather opined, "It was not any worldly consideration that brought our Fathers into this wilderness, but Religion....Whereas now, Religion is made subservient unto worldly Interests."

With fear of straying from religious orthodoxy the animating concern of the Puritan colonies, it became common for crimes of all sorts to be associated with religious deviancy. While Tituba settled in Parris's new home, another woman brought to Boston against her will, an African-born domestic servant named Maria, burned her master's house to the ground, killing him and his family. This crime was not regarded as the inevitable outcome of a dehumanizing system in which humans were treated as property. It was instead seen as yet another religious dilemma. Convicted of "not having the fear of God before her eyes and being instigated by the devil," Maria was burned at the stake for murder, yes, but also for the far more dangerous crime of calling into question the religious basis of Puritan order.

Tituba no doubt would have heard of Maria's case, and perhaps she would have felt sympathy for her actions and her fate. To see the smoke over Maria's execution pyre wafting over the city no doubt would have served as a reminder to Tituba that she had come to a place prone to conflagrations both theological and fiery; a place that often saw people like her—who carried with them signs of religious difference that was a threat to Puritan existence—as a source of a spiritual flame that must be snuffed out.

In the Puritan mind, Satan was the true author of religious difference, and so it was deemed natural that those people who seemed most different of all must be on the closest terms with the devil. Many Puritan writers assumed that it was Native Americans who led English settlers astray.

Mather himself counted the "Sorcery" of Indians to be their greatest threat, and saw the source of their magic-making to be the Enemy himself. Not even English pets were safe: "The Indians, in their wars with us, finding sore inconvenience in our dogs, which would make a sad yelling if in the night they scent the approaches of them, they sacrificed a dog to the devil; after which no English dog would bark at an Indian for divers months ensuing." Increase Mather had likewise declared the war waged by the Indians against the English to be "devil-driven." Reverend William Hubbard, meanwhile, framed his 1677 history of the "Troubles with the Indians" entirely in terms of their "devilish idolatry." What little religion they have, he wrote, "they have learned from the Prince of Darkness." And even one who seemed to convert, he claimed, would be found out to be a "diabolical miscreant who hath put on a garb of religion...performing religious worship amongst the Indians in his way" while having "very familiar converse with the devil." The most popular literary genre of the day was the "captivity narrative," which recounted, with varying degrees of exaggeration, tales of colonists kidnapped by Indians. A common trope of these stories was the place of the devil in native cultures.

With no distance between the physical world and the realm of the spirit in such tales, the wilderness itself was often described as the source of both Satan's and the Indians' power. This was among the reasons for Tituba's arrival in Massachusetts. It was not legal to own or indenture a member of the local tribes as a servant; it was felt that such servants would still draw power from the land, bringing demonic influence into Puritan homes. Instead, Massachusetts Indians were regularly captured and sold into slavery as far away as Barbados. Natives from the south, in turn, were sent to New England. It was hoped that these "Spanish Indians" were sufficiently removed from their own sources of demonic power that they could be Christianized without risk of spiritual contamination to the households they served.

Eight years after he had arrived in Boston, the newly ordained Reverend Samuel Parris moved his family to Salem Town. His household now included not just Tituba and John Indian but a wife and three children, the second of whom—his eldest daughter, Betty—would soon cause more trouble than any preteen in American history.

To Tituba it might have been a relief to be away from the city where the smoke of execution fires still lingered in the air. Yet, as she soon would discover, greater scrutiny can also be found in a smaller town. Salem would turn to her as another in a long line of troublemaking women disturbing New England's Puritan peace.

The infamous religious troublemakers of Massachusetts are rarely mentioned in the same breath as Tituba. After all, she arrived in Boston nearly fifty years after Anne Hutchinson was driven out, Dorothy Talbye was driven mad, and Mary Dyer swung from a tree. Yet the Indian woman from Barbados was the logical extension of the question previous outliers had asked. To what extent could a community built on the myth of religious uniformity tolerate or survive spiritual difference?

While the earlier cases involved women who actively sought to assert their religious differences, Tituba may never have drawn attention to herself were it not for the real hunger for spiritual alternatives within the Puritan community. Especially in children — born in this new land, believing they were surrounded from birth by the threat of Indian attack, throughout their young lives witness to, and survivors of, epidemics that emptied households as surely as had the arsonists' fires — there was at large a rampant desire for practices not sanctioned by the divines who had exiled Hutchinson and condemned Maria and Mary Dyer to death.

Such practices were apparently so widespread that Puritan religious writers were particularly drawn to this theme. "Some young persons through a vain calamity to know their future condition, have tampered with the devil's tools," the Beverly minister John Hale wrote in 1697. He further described one such young person he knew who "did try with an egg and a glass to find her future Husbands Calling." Using a device called a Venus Glass, this credulous and unfortunate girl, Hale reported, looked into her future and saw a coffin. So upset was she by this vision that "she was afterward followed with diabolical molestation to her death." Like the preacher who used the executed woman's temptations as a warning to those who had watched her hang, Hale offered this story as "a just warning to others, to take heed of handling the devil's weapons, lest they get a wound thereby." Nor was this an isolated case. There was another girl, he writes, who suffered "sore fits and vexations of satan." She, too, he discovered, had dabbled with the Venus Glass.

These activities were not merely the pastimes of children. They were the last best hopes of a people clinging to the fringes of their own half-remembered folk traditions — practices brought from

England that were likely far older than the orthodoxies to which they formally ascribed. To the consternation of official representatives of sanctioned belief, improvised rituals were blended with established doctrine by the English in Massachusetts no less than by the Indians and Africans of Barbados.

"I knew a man in the East, who possessed the art of curing wounds, and stenching blood by a form of words," Hale writes. "I discoursed him about it, and he told me, he had been in the practice of it; and believed it to be the gift of healing given him from God, upon the use of some Scripture words he used as he had been taught by an Old woman." This man, Hale explained, had begun his career as a healer by trying such incantations out on himself. During a mishap while chopping wood, he had cut halfway through his leg with an adz. He tied up the gash with cloth, recited the magic verses the crone had taught him, and was healed within days. When he recounted the words to Hale, the shocked minister found this backwoods healer "almost as ignorant in Scriptures as an heathen." The minister informed the man that his words were in fact "a perverse addition to the Scriptures," and "that if any such healing followed upon such a form of words, it could not come from the efficacy of the words themselves or from a divine concurrence working a wonder because of those words, which were indeed a lye in the additions made; therefore if any vertue were in them, it came by the devil, and so those words a kind of Sorcerery."

Hale does not condemn those who did these things, for to do so would condemn far more of Puritan society than would be sustainable. In this spirit-haunted world, appeals to powers beyond the bounds of religious propriety were the norm. He excuses "those that ignorantly use charms, spells, writings, or forms of words, &c. being taught them by others, which are a kind of Witchcraft" because those who used them may not have realized that what they were doing stretched the limits of orthodox practice. Whether they were engaged in rituals involving pulling "fish bones out of a wound," using spells to cure tooth aches, fevers, and warts, or indulging in other such "devilish means," Hale suggests that those using such magic were "beguiled by the Serpent that lies in the grass unseen." In fact, they were merely appealing to an alternate spiritual authority, a system of practice and belief that perhaps seemed more responsive to their actual needs.

*　*　*

It is within this dual context of Puritans' frequent use as individuals of transgressive religious practices, and their inability as a community to be so broadminded, that we should consider what befell the Indian woman Tituba in the spring of 1692.

All that is known for certain about the onset of this infamous time in Salem is that two members of Reverend Parris's household began one day to behave in strange ways. It has become part of the story of the Salem witch trials that these two young girls, nine-year-old Betty Parris and her cousin, eleven-year-old Abigail Williams, had been experimenting with the kinds of practices described by John Hale before they were afflicted, yet the historical record does not provide proof of this beyond Hale's reference to two unnamed youngsters tampering with "the devil's tools."

Contrary to the usual narrative, the first and only act that one might call magic or witchcraft known to have occurred in the Parris household was performed by Tituba. In the days following the beginning of the girls' affliction, Tituba and John Indian were asked by a member of Parris's church, Mary Sibley, to make a "witchcake." Taking rye flour and a measure of the sick children's urine, the two servants then baked this mixture into an unappetizing biscuit which they fed to a dog in hopes that the animal's behavior might reveal to them the source of the girls' torment. According to a sermon Parris himself soon gave, this was the real start of Salem's troubles:

> It is altogether undeniable that our great and blessed God, for wise and holy ends, hath suffered many persons, in several families, of this little village, to be grievously vexed and tortured in body...It is also well known, that, when these calamities first began, which was in my own family, the affliction was several weeks before such hellish operations as witchcraft were suspected. Nay, it was not brought forth to any considerable light, until diabolical means were used by the making of a cake by my Indian man, who had his direction from this our sister, Mary Sibley; since which, apparitions have been plenty, and exceeding much mischief hath followed.

Though Parris did not name Tituba in his sermon, she apparently received far worse attention than merely being mentioned for her involvement in this kitchen magic. According to at least one source, the minister of Salem beat his servant in an attempt to force a confession that the witchcake was indeed her doing. While such practices were known as part of the kinds of English folk traditions described by Hale, they likewise were present among the enslaved and indentured laborers of Tituba's Barbados, where "victuals," as that early English observer called ritual food items, were regularly used to discover the source of spiritual powers. Whether the baking of a witchcake originated in England or in the Caribbean, however, what is most significant here is that it was apparently a practice recognizable across a huge cultural divide, and it was two Indians who were seen as actively responsible for introducing it to the Parris household. "By these means," Parris concluded, "the Devil hath been raised amongst us, and his rage is vehement and terrible; and, when he shall be silenced, the Lord only knows."

It was not merely the girls' distress and the accusations which followed that created witchcraft hysteria in Salem. It was also, perhaps especially, terror at the prospect that Indian sorcery had been carried out within the very heart of New England society, the godly household of a Puritan minister. It was fear of Tituba and what she represented as an Indian woman within a Christian home. She was the overwhelming metaphysical power of the wilderness suddenly brought into the one place where they imagined they were safe from its reach.

In this it is tempting to see Tituba's actions as a kind of spiritual rebellion. Despite the ambient influence of Christianity, she — enslaved though she was — believed her own skills and traditions could make a difference where conventional religious authority had not. In the days following the revelation that she had performed magic for the benefit of Betty Parris, Tituba was arrested for the crime of witchcraft.

As had been the case in the court proceedings against Anne Hutchinson, it is in the transcripts of her interrogation that Tituba's true mettle as a religious outlier is shown. She had been brought in for questioning along with Sarah Good and Sarah Osborne, two middle-aged women plainly unliked and unsupported by the townspeople of Salem. For each, an accusation of witchcraft may have seemed the inevitable end of a decades-long string of bad luck. Good's father, once a well-off innkeeper, had killed himself twenty years before, when Sarah was a teenager. When her mother remarried, she was left without her promised inheritance. She then married a former indentured servant who died in short order, leaving her without a home, deeply in debt, and with a four-year-old daughter, Dorcas, who would soon be accused of witchcraft as well. Sarah Osborne, meanwhile, was not poor but had been accused of sexual misconduct many years before. At sixty, she maintained her infamy by keeping her distance from church. Questioned over the course of three days after she had already received a beating, and now arraigned beside two people the community only needed an excuse to censure severely, Tituba no doubt feared for her life. The beginning of her testimony is understandably defensive:

"Tituba, what evil spirit have you familiarity with?" she was asked.

"None," she replied.

"Why do you hurt these children?"

"I do not hurt them."

"Who is it then?"

"The devil for ought I know."

Her first word, as Anne Hutchinson's had been in her own interrogation, was one of defiance. Given the likely consequences of admitting anything having to do with magic or other devilish behavior, she naturally hoped to distance herself from it. Even her first reference to the devil is dismissive; a pointed insistence that she had nothing to do with the children's suffering. But then something dramatic happened. Perhaps she realized, as Jacob Lumbrozo had some thirty-five years before, that in this situation simple denial would not suffice, for when she was next asked, "Did you never see the devil?" she gave an astonishing answer.

"The devil came to me and bid me serve him," she said.

Reading the transcripts, one can almost feel the air sucked out of the room. From one question to the next, Tituba moved from flat denial to descriptions of a visit from Satan himself. The effect this had on her audience — people who believed what she was saying truly happened — could only have been terrifying. What then followed, over the course of two long examinations, was a remarkably detailed account of just how Tituba served the devil and why. She recalled feeding the witchcake to the dog, and visits from spirit animals. She described flying on a stick from Salem to Boston and ultimately admitted making her mark in a "Devills Booke" that pledged her in service to a man who came to her in the night and, she said, "tell me he god."

It is a striking moment in America's religious history. For here is a woman forced into a life of labor, completely dependent on her pious master and his god-fearing congregation, and by professing religious experiences that they could only deem demonic, she managed to break free of the powerlessness expected of her. In so doing, she took control not only of her own story but of the entire community.

As her interrogation continued, a question was put before her that would later make her testimony seem meaningful to any situation in which an accused person is asked to "name names" — an open invitation to widen the net of suspicion.

"Who have you seen?"

"Four women sometimes hurt the children," Tituba said.

"Who were they?"

"Goode [Mrs.] Osborne and Sarah Good and I doe not know who the other were. Sarah Good and Osborne would have me hurt the children but I would not."

"When did you see them?"

"Last night at Boston."

"What did they say to you?"

"They said hurt the children."

"And did you hurt them?"

"No, there is four women and one man, they hurt the children," she insisted, "and then lay all upon me and they tell me if I will not hurt the children they will hurt me."

"But did you not hurt them?"

"Yes, but I will hurt them no more."

"Are you not sorry you did hurt them?"

"Yes."

"And why then doe you hurt them?"

"They say hurt children or wee will doe worse to you."

Her testimony became more fantastic by the moment. The more she embellished, the more it seemed her audience was willing to believe. And her ability to make them believe was certainly what saved her life. Of the three on trial that day, only Tituba would survive the accusation of witchcraft. Sarah Goode would hang before the year was out. Sarah Osborne would die in jail while waiting to learn her fate.

Unlike Anne Hutchinson, whose answers in court ring with the confidence of a woman of some social standing, Tituba is humbly agreeable. Yet under the surface of her testimony, she was laying claim to an alternate spiritual authority no less than Hutchinson had. While her accusers had only fears and accusations, she had answers—detailed answers—about powers beyond their imagining. As the Tituba scholar Elaine Breslaw notes, in her creative response to impossible circumstances, this "reluctant witch of Salem" reframed her role in the drama. No longer a passive player and victim, she "improvised a new idiom of resistance." The key to this, for her, was drawing on the wealth of eclectic religious ideas she seems to have brought with her into this supposed bastion of Christian conformity. "Hidden in that confession," Breslaw adds, "was not so much a Puritan concept of evil but one derived from non-Christian cultures; a set of ideas that was familiar and strange."

In the end, Tituba was one of the lucky ones in Salem. More than one hundred people would eventually be accused throughout 1692; two dozen would die as a result. Tituba, as the first arrested for the crime, seems to have escaped execution at least in part because of her audacious attempt to control the story of which she had unwittingly become a part.

Today the Salem witch trials are remembered mainly as a moment of hysteria over imagined transgressions of the established religious order. Yet while the community response certainly was hysterical, it does appear that many of these transgressions were not imagined at all. The practices we might call witchcraft today, carried out by the English and by the native peoples of the Americas before them, can be thought of as a kind of spiritual equalizer, providing religious authority outside social structures that were inevitably defined at the time by class and gender.

In this sense, the understandable feeling of outrage with which the witch trials are recalled serves inadvertently to write religious difference out of history. By insisting that these so-called witches were not what some of them clearly were—women and men who experimented outside accepted religious practices, who lived by circumstance or choice on the margins of the dominant faith—we ignore the permeability of boundaries between faiths, and the fact that individuals living in close quarters are bound to influence one another's practices and beliefs.

The occasional exile or execution of troublemakers like Anne Hutchinson or Mary Dyer might suggest that they were exceptions proving the rule of Puritan uniformity. But the documents related to the Salem witch trials, with their catalogue of the ways in which those with the least authority in the community sought spiritual solace and sanction outside the bounds of authorized religious practice, suggest that spiritual diversity was the true rule. Tituba — the South American Indian, who lived among Africans in Barbados, who baked witchcakes with an English woman, who for years served a family that seems to have had its own dabblings in non-Christian practices — was a mirror held to differences that were already present before she arrived.

In fictional depictions of Tituba's life she is often shown as a dramatic Voodoo priestess, practitioner of a religion now called, in academic circles, Voudon. Scholars of her life maintain that she was no priestess, yet the practices in which she seems to be implicated do suggest something similar: Hoodoo or conjure. While Voudon is primarily a Caribbean phenomenon, Hoodoo grew out of a blending of African American and Native American cultures. As the historian Jeffrey Anderson notes, Native Americans "did much to preserve African ideas and practices" in America, "enrich[ing] conjure with their own distinctive contributions."

Hoodoo existed well into the twentieth century. As documented most notably by Zora Neale Hurston, it was a central part of African American culture from the days of slavery until the Great Migration of southern African Americans into the Northeast and Midwest. Hurston was not only a novelist; she also trained at Barnard with the father of American anthropology, Franz Boas, and chose as the site of her fieldwork the black southern world from which she had come. Among the dozens of tales of legend and belief Hurston recounts in her classic collection of folklore *Mules and Men*, one in particular echoes Tituba's testimony both in its cast of characters and in the subtle claim it makes about the power of a good story. With the same matter-of-fact familiarity with which Tituba recounted her own dealings with the witches of Salem, a storyteller recounts a yarn about a man named Jack who played cards with the Devil and ended up losing his soul. Afraid that he will die when the Devil comes to collect, Jack decides to stop waiting for the worst and take matters into his own hands.

Hurston writes, in the voice of the storyteller, "Jack walked up to de Devil's house and knocked on de do'."

"Who's dat?" the Devil's wife asks.

"One of de Devil's friends," Jack says.

Claiming closeness with the Devil when it might do him some good, Jack not only wins back his soul, he runs off with the Devil's daughter on two horses stolen from the Devil's barn, then gets the Devil's bull to trample its master. As the storyteller wraps up the yarn, "So dat's why dey say Jack beat de Devil."

Legends involving the everyman Jack, whom Hurston called "the great human culture hero of Negro folklore...like Daniel of Jewish folklore, the wish-fulfillment hero of the race," are part of an American mythology that turned the religious tradition brought from Europe on its head. They included not only the devil but God, Jesus, and any other holy character that might be conscripted into retellings that would better serve the people against whom scripture was so often used as a cudgel justifying slavery or segregation. "Even the Bible was made over to suit our vivid imagination," Hurston once said. "The devil always outsmarted God, and our over-noble Jack...outsmarted the Devil." Such tales are part of a genealogy of American religion that has its origins in acts of religious nonconformity like Tituba's "witchcake." They were attempts by the powerless to exert control over their lives.

And they continue to be. The Anglican minister and amateur folklorist Harry Middleton Hyatt found that witchcakes were used by African Americans in Illinois as late as the 1930s. "If you think you are hoodooed," he recorded, "take one pint of salt, one pint of corn meal, one pint of your urine." After mixing this together, to rid yourself of the magical affliction, you would then "[p]ut that in a can on the stove at twelve o'clock at night and cook until it burns."

Long after the memory of Boston's great fires of divine retribution had dissipated, the smoke of Tituba's spiritual rebellion lingers. As Jeffrey Anderson has observed, "Conjurelike practices occur in some churches even today." Often these practices are masked by more orthodox beliefs, but they nonetheless remain the spiritual medium of choice for those grasping for a sense of control over their lives. And they are found not just in churches. The maintenance staffs of courthouses around the nation regularly find evidence of Hoodoo spells. In restrooms, in stairwells, before the doorways of judges' chambers, defendants and their families have been known to leave behind eggs, feathers, hair, black pepper, and blood. Sometimes they bake these ingredients into cakes, just as Tituba did shortly before her own dramatic court appearance.

In the 1990s, the physical manifestation of Hoodoo, Voodoo, and conjuration became such a problem at a Miami courthouse that officials enlisted a special cleaning squad to dispose of ritual materials. Dade County officials pointed to the city's large number of immigrants from Haiti, Cuba, and elsewhere in the Caribbean — the islands, in other words, from which Tituba and so many others were sent north into servitude three centuries before. When tasked by a newspaper with explaining this phenomenon, a local sociology professor, Teresita Pedraza, asked, "Why do people go to Lourdes? Because they believe it works. It's part of a religious belief and value system."

As the story of Salem reminds us, this is a system that has been part of the American narrative nearly from the beginning. For those who will never hold the keys to the kingdom, the idea that objects borrowed from the kitchen can be as powerful as any found in a grand temple provides a sense of hope and possibility. For Tituba, the belief that she could control the world around her nearly saw her hanged, but her ability to tell the story of that belief certainly saved her life.

A N
ACCOUNT,
OF THE
METHOD and SUCCESS
OF
INOCULATING
THE
SMALL-POX,
IN
Boſton in *New-England.*

In a LETTER *from a Gentleman there, to his Friend in* London.

LONDON:
Printed for *J. Peele* at *Lock's-Head* in *Pater-noſter Row.* M.DCC.XXII.

An account of the method and success of inoculating the small-pox, in Boston in New-England, by Cotton Mather. London: J. Peele, 1722.

CHAPTER 6

Call-and-Response

1702–1721

Late in the evening on the last day of October 1702, Cotton Mather was afraid. Puritans sanctioned no notice of Halloween, of course, and so despite the Boston minister's occult preoccupations of the previous decades, it was neither witches nor the devil he feared that night. This particular terror was not born of something that could be preached against and then exorcized by ecclesiastic tribunal. Nor apparently could it be simply and silently prayed away. He had tried as hard as anyone might to do so, but what good were pious pleas for protection when the killer in his midst had been sent by none other than God?

Mather's fear was called smallpox. The disease had lately appeared again in Boston, as it had roughly every twenty years, by the reckoning of historians of the day. In its awful wake, the city's preeminent minister had toiled for weeks, preaching from the pulpit to his ever dwindling congregation and visiting the afflicted in rooms he described as "venomous, contagious, loathsome Chambers." During this season in which funerals were "daily celebrated and multiplied," he noted, suspicion of witches and Indians had been replaced in the public consciousness with wariness of the "fevers and fluxes" that spread by the sad magic of human touch and breath.

A plague is a busy time for a man of the cloth, especially one whose family had provided spiritual solace to the city from the beginning. Yet even a preacher's faith could falter. "How often have there been Bills desiring Prayers for more than an Hundred Sick on one Day in one of our Assemblies?" Mather wondered. "In one Twelve-month, about one Thousand of our Neighbours have one way or other been carried unto their long Home." In a population that had reached little more than 7,000 by then, the loss of 1,000 in a year made the epidemic seem like a surgeon's handsaw cutting a body's legs off at the shins.

"Now the Small Pox," he noted ominously, "is on every Side of us."

To Mather, the cause for this pestilence was clear enough. It was the same cause to blame for any death that surprised with its quickness or its magnitude. Years before, he had heard of an earthquake that destroyed the city of Port Royal in Jamaica. Shortly before the ground shook and the splinters of wharf houses washed into the sea, the people of the colony had fallen into the heathen excitement of visiting fortune-tellers. Mather found it odd that, even in a place whose impiety was well known, these supposed predictors of the future had failed to expect the inevitable outcome of their sin. The first commandment—"Thou shalt have no other god but me"—applied not only to worship but to practice. As the late events at Salem had shown, even dabbling in heathenish ways could have dire consequences. Mather had also heard of fortune-tellers much closer to home, in his own Boston, and often wished "the town could be made too Hot for these Dangerous Transgressors." Lately attending a funeral every day, praying by the bedsides of neighbors whose sins he knew better than anyone, he might have wondered if he had finally gotten his wish.

At a distance, this was perhaps a subject more for sermons than for tears. But now it seemed divine wrath had come home in the most intimate way. First his wife, Abigail, afflicted with symptoms Mather diagnosed as "sore throat, and such tremor, and such dolor, and such danger of choking, and such exhaustion of strength," lay in bed calling to heaven as if pleading for death; then his children—his daughters Nibby and Nanny, and his son Increase, named for his imposing father but playfully called "Creasy"—suddenly showed signs of the sickness he had seen in so many other homes.

How quickly life turns. In what was either a cruel twist of fate or Providence's own lesson in humility, he had found cause for celebration just the day before. A gentleman had arrived by ship from New Castle, where he had purchased a copy of Mather's latest book, *The Ecclesiastical History of New England.* It was the first time Mather had seen a printed copy of his magnum opus, so he had set aside a part of the day to offer Thanksgiving to God for seeing the work to its completion. How could he have imagined that the next evening, he would sit down in the candlelight to record his terror at the thought of losing his wife and children?

"The dreadful Disease, which is raging in the Neighbourhood, is now gott into my poor Family," he wrote. "God prepare me, God prepare me, for what is coming upon me!"

Mather's study was a large yet warm chamber that housed two to three thousand books (he had lost count himself). He might have turned to any number of those scholarly volumes at that moment for the preparation he sought, but, facing the greatest distress of his life, he turned only to scripture for solace.

Naturally, he had done so many times before—but on this night, he did not search the text, or his own memory of it, for lines that might provide comfort. Instead, he decided to open his Bible at random and see if God might lead him to the appropriate words.

This was not at all a practice he often indulged in, nor would he recommend that any who came to him for guidance similarly rifle through the holy book for "divinatory" purposes. To treat scripture like a game of dice or knuckle bones smacked of superstition, perhaps even a kind of sorcery. To presume that a verse chosen by the accidental placement of a fingertip on a given page would have special significance risked making a god of chance. Truly, it was not so different from the fortune-telling that had caused the very earth to tremble on a distant island. Yet in his desperation, he performed this small blasphemy despite the risks.

"Unto my Amazement," Mather later wrote, when he placed his finger in the sacred book, he stumbled onto "the History of our Lords curing the sick Son of the Nobleman," the latter half of the fourth chapter of the Gospel according to John. The words stunned him with their relevance to his situation, as if they had been written for the sole purpose of his reading them that night:

There was a certain nobleman, whose son was sick at Capernaum. When he heard that Jesus was come out of Judaea into Galilee, he went unto him, and besought him that he would come down, and heal his son: for he was at the point of death. Then said Jesus unto him, Except ye see signs and wonders, ye will not believe. The nobleman saith unto him, Sir, come down ere my child die. Jesus saith unto him, Go thy way; thy son liveth. And the man believed the word that Jesus had spoken unto him, and he went his way. And as he was now going down, his servants met him, and told him, saying Thy son liveth. Then enquired he of them the hour when he began to amend. And they said unto him, Yesterday at the seventh hour the fever left him. So the father knew that it was at the same hour, in the which Jesus said unto him, Thy son liveth: and himself believed, and his whole house.

Had ever the father of sick children read more hopeful a "sign and wonder"? Would not any spiritual father of an afflicted city— as Mather counted himself—dare to suppose God would speak so directly to him? "I saw, that the whole Bible afforded not a more agreeable or profitable Paragraph," Mather reflected. To discover it at that moment, on that terrible night, seemed to him nothing short of miraculous. He immediately set about writing a series of sermons on the passage, hoping that his private trial might provide some public service.

As he worked, it occurred to him that those stricken in the homes surrounding his own had become so numerous he would not have time to visit them all. Though it might give further ammunition to those who claimed he had never had an unpublished thought, Mather resolved to print up a small sheet of the encouraging words he might say were he able to pay a call to every darkened room. In these printed words, he would make no mention that it was his use of sacred scripture as a fortune-telling device that had led him to the appropriate Gospel story. But then the dying might have understood better than anyone that desperate times called for unorthodox methods.

For Mather the miracles did not continue long past that one hopeful accident. Abigail—"my lovely consort...the desire of me eyes," as he achingly described her—died a hard death over the following month. At her funeral in December of 1702, the widower gave to many of the hundred or more mourners a copy of a short book he had published years before entitled *Death Made Happy and*

Easy. Into the front cover he pasted a page filled with couplets addressed to his wife of sixteen years:

> *Go then, my Dove, but now no longer mine;*
> *Leave Earth, and now in heavenly Glory shine...*
> *Dear Friends, with whom thou didst so dearly live,*
> *Feel thy one Death to them a thousand give.*
> *Thy Prayers are done; thy Alms are spent; thy Pains*
> *Are ended now, in endless Joyes and Gains.*

Mather's own pains, however, were far from ended. Never making peace with this time of particular loss ("Has not the Death of my Consort that most astonishing Sting in it?" he asked. "Truly, nothing has ever yett befallen me, that has come so near it..."), he came to feel a special antipathy toward the affliction that had troubled his community. This, he knew, put him perhaps for the first time outside the bounds of the covenantal doctrine that his father and his grandfathers had done so much to advance in New England. For as great an ill as a scourge like the pox was, as perfect a devastation as it had brought to Boston and beyond, was not sanguine acceptance of such hardships part of humanity's agreement with the divine? Was not each coming of the epidemic an act of God? The disease itself was indisputably a part of the Lord's creation, designed and employed to punish humanity for its failings or to instruct it in humility. Who then was man — even a grieving man — to question or wish to control the workings of life and death?

And yet in the year after his wife's death, Mather came to question everything. "Was ever man more tempted than the miserable Mather?" he wrote. "Should I tell, in how many Forms the Devil has assaulted me, and with what Subtilty and Energy, his Assaults have been carried on, it would strike my Friends with Horrour." An inveterate scribbler even in mourning, he made a careful catalogue of the ways in which his former surety was coming undone. "Sometimes, Temptations to Impurities; and sometimes to Blasphemy, and Atheism, and the Abandonment of all Religion, as a meer Delusion; and sometimes, to self-Destruction itself."

When it came to smallpox especially, Mather could not help inching closer to even greater impiety. If it were in man's power to counteract the sickness through the God-given gift of the intellect, would it not be wrong to squander grace by failing to do so?

Such thoughts lingered and faded through the years of Mather's grieving. And faded they might have remained were it not for another turn of fate—one that determined his internal turmoil over these matters would find an improbable resolution. It was nearly four years to the day after the funeral of "his lovely consort" that Mather sat once again at his desk and recorded the event that would change the course of his life, even as it revealed something of the early influence of religious differences in America.

"This Day, a surprising Thing befel me," Mather wrote in December 1706. "Some Gentlemen of our Church...purchased for me a very likely Slave."

When Mather received this dubious gift—a man whose life and labor he presumed to own despite not having paid a shilling for either—the practice of having an African servant living under an English colonist's roof was well established, but was not yet the "peculiar institution" American slavery would become.

It was by then eighty-seven years since the hot day in August when a Dutch ship loaded with human cargo arrived in the colony of Virginia, delivering the first African-born servants to the English colonies. Earlier that summer, in June 1619, another vessel, an English sloop called the *Triall*, had come to shore filled with corn and cattle, relieving the colonists of the always-lingering "feare of famine" and apparently allowing them to feel they had sufficient material wealth to consider an acquisition, should the right opportunity arise. Two months later, the Dutch ship brought just that. After inspection of the cargo, the Virginians settled terms of the trade—within a dozen years the going price per head would be 2,000 pounds of tobacco—and "twenty negars" came ashore to begin harvesting the crop that had been bartered for their flesh.

That same day, the chief of the local Patawomeck tribe, drawn by the sight of the ship, came to the colony to inquire about future possibilities of commerce. The English worried that the "heathen... would surprise us" by bringing violence to their transactions, yet they were oblivious of the fact that the day's earlier trade had already ensured violence for generations to come. This was not the beginning of slavery in America—as Mustafa Zemmouri and the thousands of other Africans and Indians forced into lives of servitude by the Spanish attest. Yet that day in 1619 marked the onset in the English colonies of a cancerous economic system built upon the labor of those who would not at all benefit from it. And from that first cell, the system metastasized.

The earliest Africans in Massachusetts are thought to have arrived not long after those in Virginia. The colonist Samuel Maverick, who arrived in 1624, is often cited as the first slave owner in New England, and he was certainly the first on record who attempted to breed the human beings he held in bondage like livestock. On one known occasion he even commanded the rape of one of his servants by another. By the end of the Massachusetts Bay Colony's first decade, Boston had built slaving ships of its own, gathering its supply from the usual ports in West Africa, and then from as far off as Madagascar when the local traders ran afoul of the English and Dutch monopolies on the trade. We know of the city's first recorded slave transaction from the pen of none other than Governor John Winthrop, who wrote of a ship called the *Desire* arriving in the colony with a shipment of "some cotton, and tobacco, and negroes, etc.," just eight years after he had proclaimed his settlement a city upon a hill.

This event marks the origin of the slave trade in the city that would be its northern hub for a century, but it obscures the fact that forced labor in the early colonies was not wholly based on race. Three-quarters of those who came to North America in the colonial period did so as servants laboring under some measure of coercion. Many were pressed into labor for a period of years, while others faced life sentences. Caught between these two conditions, a servant might begin his indenture with an understanding that it would one day come to an end, only to discover that he had permanently lost his freedom. As for the Africans on the *Desire*, they had been acquired through a direct trade demonstrating, as Tituba's enslavement later would affirm, that slavery was not yet entirely a matter of black and white: Indians captured in New England in the aftermath of the 1636 Pequot War were transported to Barbados, where Africans were shipped back in return.

When Massachusetts became the first colony to formally legalize slavery, it ironically did so within a document that otherwise was remarkably liberal for the time. The "Body of Liberties" adopted by the Massachusetts General Court in 1641 amounted to a bill of rights for settlers, enumerating the freedoms of the male residents

("Every man of or within this Jurisdiction shall have free libertie") while outlining protections for women ("Every marryed woeman shall be free from bodilie correction or stripes by her husband") and indentured servants ("Servants that have served deligentlie and faithfully to the benefitt of their maisters seaven yeares, shall not be sent away emptie"). Even domestic animals were offered relief ("No man shall exercise any Tirranny or Crueltie towards any bruite Creature which are usuallie kept for man's use"). Yet this same document vouchsafed the business of enslavement with a concern for justice that is difficult to find sincere: "There shall never be any bond slaverie, villinage or Captivitie amongst us unles it be lawfull Captives taken in just warres, and such strangers as willingly selle themselves or are sold to us."

With this separation of the notions of servitude and bondage, slavery took a significant step toward becoming the racially defined condition it is generally thought of as today. Thereafter, with few exceptions, Europeans would be servants able to work off their indenture; Indians and Africans would be slaves. Combined with the perceived threat of keeping captured Indians in Puritan homes during a time of intermittent war, the Body of Liberties set in motion a transition to a largely African labor force in the colonies.

At the height of slavery in colonial America, those of African descent amounted to 20 percent of the total population. In the south it was far greater — by the time the "surprising Thing befel" Mather, Africans were the majority in the Carolinas. In Mather's city, the enslaved population increased exponentially during the minister's own life: dozens at the time of his birth in 1663, around 500 when he acquired his own in 1706, more than 2,000 in 1720, when Boston was home to just 12,000 men and women.

Eventually we can see the religious influence of this population in the ritual patterns of African American churches. The call-and-response, to cite an iconic example, was noted in gatherings of the enslaved, who still spoke the languages they had spoken when they arrived. Before the practice was Christianized and took on the form most familiar today, it was part of a religious culture that endured far longer than usually supposed. Even a century later, the British-born architect of the United States Capitol, Benjamin Latrobe, made note of it while traveling in the south. Following sounds he thought must be horses galloping, he entered a public square in New Orleans and was astonished to see several hundred people gathered and performing what seemed to him a strange ceremony, moving in circles to a slow, steady rhythm.

> The music consisted of two drums and a stringed instrument....The women squalled out a burden to the playing at intervals, consisting of two notes, as the negroes, working in our cities, respond to the song of their leader. A man sang an uncouth song to the dancing which I suppose was in some African language...

Around this same time, the African-born and their descendants began to convert in large numbers, but only a small fraction of the enslaved population arrived in the colonies as Christians. Even by the end of the eighteenth century, the majority of Africans in America were neither born into nor converted to any denomination of Christianity. Indeed, in many colonies, prohibitions limiting the education of the enslaved, and the supposed scruples of Christian slave owners who did not think it right to hold a fellow Christian in bondage became de facto restrictions on the spread of Christianity as well. Likewise, laws proscribing the gathering of Africans — often passed in response to scenes like that recorded by Latrobe — determined that any kind of slave meeting, religious or otherwise, must be done in secret.

What, then, were the faiths practiced by the earliest Africans in the colonies? It is perhaps the greatest of forgotten influences on American life and culture that 20 percent or more were Muslims, about whom there is more to be said in a later chapter. Most others were followers of traditional West African belief systems, perhaps the largest number of which were followers of Yoruba, with its pantheon to rival any list of deities in Greek or Roman mythology, or indeed the thirty-seven gods Roger Williams counted among the Narragansett Indians. Other traditions included Obeah and Akan, both of which underwent hybridization in America, where formerly vital distinctions between tribal identities became far less important than fostering a shared community of the enslaved that might contribute to their survival.

This powerless population is not usually seen as having had a religious impact on those around them. But, truly, given the numbers, how can that not have been the case? While these men and women would live apart and create cultures all their own in the larger plantations in the south, in the north—in Boston, for instance—enslaved Africans lived in close quarters with white families, as was the case with Mather and his "gift."

Though most of the voices of the enslaved are lost to history, we still can find evidence of the influence exerted by their beliefs and practices. This was certainly true in that city upon a hill, where the most famous clergyman of his day had a world-expanding interaction with a religious tradition very different from his own.

The young man purchased for Mather was African-born, "a Negro of a promising Aspect and Temper."

This perk from his congregation had come to Mather "without any Application of mine to them for such a Thing," but he had certainly been in the market. It was well known, he wrote, "that I wanted a good Servant at the expence of between forty and fifty Pounds." Mather was apparently quite pleased both by the show of respect from his followers and by the addition of another set of working hands to his household. "It seems to be a mighty Smile of Heaven upon my Family," he reflected. "I putt upon him the Name of Onesimus; and I resolved with the Help of the Lord, that I would use the best Endeavours to make him a Servant of Christ."

The name he chose says a great deal about how he saw both this young man and himself. In the writings of Saint Paul, "Onesimus" was the name of an escaped slave who sought out the Apostle for protection from his master. Paul at the time was imprisoned for his preaching, and so he took the efforts of the runaway to be a sign of great devotion. After converting him to Christianity, Paul wrote a letter to Philemon, the aggrieved slave master: "I appeal to you for my child, Onesimus, whose father I became in my imprisonment." The Greek root of the name Onesimus (*onesis*) means *useful*, and so Paul puns when he says, "Formerly he was useless to you, but now he is indeed useful to you and to me."

Elsewhere in Mather's writings we can see that the story of Saint Paul and Onesimus made an impression on him. When he visited the colony prison to give solace to convicts, he preached to them from the Book of Psalms and reduced them to "floods of tears." He was himself no less moved. "Who can tell, but that I have this day found an Onesimus?" he enthused. "Who can tell, but some Wretches, by running into Prison, may run into the Arms of Christ, and His victorious Grace!"

Mather imagined himself another Paul of Tarsus, whose exploits as a preacher, he wrote, had "more true *glory* in them, than all the acts of those execrable plunderers and murderers, and irresistible banditti of the world, which have been dignified by the name of 'conquerors.'" For years he had been in search of an Onesimus of his own whom he might turn toward the faith.

Whether or not the man he renamed Onesimus became a Christian remains unknown. Mather was a proponent of the conversion of Africans, so it is likely an effort was made, but no mention of his baptism occurs in Mather's diary. He does mention the conversion of later African-born servants, so it seems likely that Onesimus held fast to whatever beliefs he had brought with him to Boston. Subsequent events would show him to be a man proud to share ideas of his own.

Once installed in the Mather home, Onesimus mainly performed daily tasks and lived in a room within the house. He thus had a front-row seat the next time tragedy visited the minister's life. Mather had remarried by then, and in 1713 his wife had twins. A measles outbreak in the city took all three.

It was likely in the aftermath of this loss that Mather spoke with Onesimus about the servant's experience with illness. Any student of New England history—or an author of it, as Mather himself was—could have done the math and guessed that smallpox might soon return to Boston. Mather asked the African-born man, who by then had lived in his home for seven years, if he had ever had the disease.

"Yes and no," Onesimus cryptically replied.

Momentarily confusing Mather, he went on to explain that there was a practice in the place of his birth by which healthy young people were exposed to fluids from the bodies of the ill in order to protect them from the disease. So treated, they became sick for a time themselves, but with a far lower rate of full-blown affliction. What he was describing, whether he used the word or not, was an early form of inoculation—more technically, variolation.

When Onesimus displayed on his arm a flash of scarred skin where the operation had been performed, it was as revelatory as those words of God on a printed page Mather had stumbled upon more than ten years before. How could he not have recalled them? Was he not a nobleman of a sort? Was he not—as Saint Paul had been—a father of sorts to this Onesimus? And here he was hearing the impossible news that a son infected with the dreaded disease had lived, that there was life to be found even in the shadow of a pestilence. This late-coming miracle would not bring any of his loved ones back to life—some signs and wonders belonged to God alone—but it did promise, as Christ had to that other nobleman, a reprieve from certain death.

Onesimus's report so excited Mather that he sought out further accounts of the novel procedure. Though it was unheard of in practice among the physicians of New England, he discovered it was not entirely unknown elsewhere in Christendom and was, in fact, widely practiced throughout what Puritans knew as the heathen world. From Turkey to West Africa to the Levant, accounts of inoculation's success reached European medical journals, where Mather himself later read of them. After studying reports printed in London about the practice, he wrote to the publisher and claimed a small portion of the glory of this discovery for himself.

> Many months before I mett with any Intimations of treating ye Small-Pox with the method of inoculation any where in Europe, I had from a servant of my own an account of its being practised in Africa. Enquiring of my Negro man, Onesimus, who is a pretty Intelligent Fellow, Whether he had ever had the Small-Pox, he answered, both Yes and No; and then told me that he had undergone an Operation, which had given him something of ye Small-Pox and would forever preserve him from it; adding that it was often used among ye Guramantese and whoever had ye Courage to use it was forever free of the fear of contagion. He described ye Operation to me, and shew'd me in his Arm ye Scar which it had left upon him.

From his letter we learn a number of things—some intended, some not. Mather regarded Onesimus as intelligent, and trusted his account of the events of his youth enough to relay it to medical professionals whom he wished to impress with his own comprehension of this surgical innovation. We also learn something about Mather's opinion of himself as not merely a preacher from the hinterlands but an intellect worthy of being heard by the better minds of London. More importantly, we learn where in Africa Onesimus came into contact with this practice. By "Guramantese," it is possible Mather was using an archaic name to refer to the Sahara tribe occupying present-day Libya and Sudan. Given the trends in the enslaved population at the time, however, it is more likely Onesimus was a member of the Coramantee, residents of the West African region known as the Gold Coast. In either case, we know that Mather, scourge of witches and heretics, had become enamored with a practice his fellow Puritans would undoubtedly consider a heathen custom.

In fact, he did not know the half of its non-Christian roots. A letter written in Arabic in 1728 refers to the practice as "ancient in the Kingdoms of Tripoli, Tunis and Algier." Historians of science also note that there is some evidence of the invention of inocula-tion in China seven hundred years before, as a mixture of medi-cine and magic performed by Taoist healers and Buddhist monks. Carried over trade routes throughout Asia into Africa, the practice found its way into the medical and religious tradition wherever it proved effective. It was not merely the custom of one set of heathens — it was the custom of nearly all of them.

In a time and place when even earthquakes were treated as unalterable divine judgment, the suggestion that one could coun-teract the obvious will of God was blasphemy at best, demonic at worst. Manipulation of the physical world went far beyond the sin of telling the future. The latter simply hoped to know what Provi-dence had in store for humanity; the former presumed to control it.

It is no surprise, then, that Mather did not immediately shout from the rooftops of Boston his opinions concerning inoculation. It was one thing to write a letter to a medical society in London, quite another to announce to his fellow ministers that he had been taking lessons in the healing arts from an unbaptized African. It would take another five years, and another outbreak of the disease, before Mather would share what he had learned from the man from the Coramantee. And when he did, smallpox would prove to be a sickness with theological implications that threatened to put him on the wrong side of the first capital law listed in the Body of Liberties: "If any man after legall conviction shall have or worship any other god, but the lord god, he shall be put to death."

In the Gold Coast of Onesimus's youth, smallpox was treated as both a religious problem and a matter of public health. The spiritual traditions of the area included paying homage to (while guarding against) a divine manifestation of the disease known as Sopona. So ubiquitous was the threat of sickness that this was also the god of the earth, who became known among Africans in America as Babalu Aye. A version of this god exists in all the West African religions, suggesting that the need to make spiritual sense of the tragedy transcended tribal and linguistic differences. In none of these traditions, moreover, was the god of smallpox thought to be so powerful that he could not be influenced through human effort. In fact, he was the god equally of sickness and healing, a dual nature that provided a framework for understanding how gathering fluids from the afflicted might also provide a cure.

Sure enough, the procedure Onesimus described to Mather seems to have been not just medical but religious. It was not only a rudimentary surgical procedure but a ritual. Another enslaved African in Boston reported that a young man would go through the ordeal of having infected blood inserted by a blade into his own flesh on the eve of making a long journey. This was undertaken at times of transition — a rite of passage. Elsewhere in Africa, a French doctor in Ethiopia later observed that "mass inoculations took on the character of a religious festival."

"Upon the approach of the disorder," another traveler noted, "the people of the country and villages collect their children and those who have not had it into one gang, for the purpose of having them inoculated...they then march together to the neighbouring town, or wherever the disorder may have made its appearance." Following this procession, they would find a priest and bid him to drain fluid from the person in town covered with the most sores. The priest collected this infected material into an eggshell and used it to anoint an X-shaped wound freshly cut into all those who wished to have protection. "After this operation," this observer goes on to say, "they all return home, singing and shouting praises."

According to other accounts, there were many approaches to inoculation: the direct sharing of blood, the sprinkling of infected material with powder (scabs ground together with roots) on skin or cloths, the use of a "magic stick" to apply pus from pox vesicles mixed with honey or butter. What these methods have in common seems to be the clearly defined religious role of those who performed the procedure. In later ethnographic accounts of inoculation in West Africa, European chroniclers have referred to those who oversee the rite in Ghana as "fetish women," the standard description of a priestess of traditional religious rites. In accounts of the same practice performed in Nigeria, it was said that the people who performed it were called *mallams*—men schooled in the Quran and other sacred texts. Among the Yoruba people, this work has been associated with blacksmiths, but even in that case inoculation involved someone with a clear religious role in the culture. Like those behiques who made the zemies among the Taino, West African blacksmiths were not merely craftsmen. As shapers of the material world, they were also conduits to divinity—specifically to Ogun, the god of removing difficulties and smoothing paths to reach a desired result. In the Obeah tradition, to which most Coramantee like Onesimus seemed to have ascribed, those who combined traditional magic and healing arts were called *obayas*. Like the priest in the Ethiopian traveler's account, *obayas* mixed human materials and natural elements into powders and potions they considered sacred, and these homegrown remedies sometimes actually worked.

Of course, no matter how effective any of these methods might have been, Puritans would have called such people witches and worse. Yet while practitioners of Yoruba or Obeah certainly indulged in a measure of magical thinking we would today call superstition, they also, at the same time, held a more flexible understanding of ways in which acts of God might be counteracted than did rigid believers in divine omnipotence and predestination. "Heathen custom" though inoculation may have been, there was an assumption of human agency in the practice that was tremendously appealing to a man like Cotton Mather—though not immediately to many who shared his faith.

Smallpox returned to Boston the same way earlier catalysts of religious change had: by ship. While Roger Williams, Anne Hutchinson, and Tituba had walked off their various vessels on their own, however, the pox came ashore along with a human carrier long since forgotten. Within days of the arrival of the HMS *Seahorse* from the West Indies, Bostonians began to report cases of the familiar illness, causing much "consternation and disorder." The disease had ravaged the city nineteen years before. Everyone over the age of thirty remembered it, and those too young to remember were not immune to the terror that spread as if by contagion.

Mather had seen three outbreaks in his lifetime and had watched the losses mount every time. By then his was a life full of this kind of ordeal. Of his fifteen children, nine died before adulthood. His father, too, was nearing death. After a long career, with the peak of his influence seemingly long behind him, Mather felt he had little to lose and much to gain by advocating a practice he knew his countrymen would dismiss as a product of "strange opinions."

In June of 1721, when he announced that he would deliver a plan to local physicians and ministers concerning what might be done about the return of the disease, his colleagues likely believed they knew what to expect. The correct view of orthodox Puritan clergy, which Mather had always upheld in the past, regarded the epidemic simply as divine will. The only explanation for it—like that long-ago earthquake in Jamaica; like each and every great fire in the city's history—was the wrath of God. Thus the only recourse they had was to determine which set of sins had unleashed it and find a way to atone. This was the default religious position on all manner of hardships at the time. Mather himself saw a direct connection between the number of miscarriages in Boston and the "great and visible decay of piety in the country." The physicians and clergymen who gathered to hear his thoughts on addressing the problem of smallpox no doubt assumed he would offer a similar diagnosis.

They did not like what they heard. The report Mather prepared unambiguously supported inoculation, even as it traced the practice to the Levant and Turkey, areas at the time firmly under Islamic Ottoman rule. Not only did the assembled ministers scoff at the notion of following such ignoble precedents, the doctors were no more interested. As far as Mather could tell, only one of the local physicians gave the least bit of respect to his suggestion. "The Rest of the Practitioners," he wrote, "treated the Proposal with an Incivility and an Inhumanity not well to be accounted for."

The lone medical man in Boston intrigued by what he heard was Zabdiel Boylston, a surgeon who had achieved some renown a decade before when he removed a stone from the bladder of a young boy; "with the blessing of God," the boy recovered in a month. Boylston seems to have been the first doctor in Boston to undertake this and similar internal surgeries on a regular basis. He was a good man for Mather to have in his corner, even if his record of success made him a touch fearless (contemporaries might have said reckless) in his approach. So taken was he by Mather's presentation on inoculation that he went to work right away, experimenting first with members of the Boylston household: two servants and his own son. When news of this spread, the doctor came under direct attack. Against his new collaborator, Mather noted, "the vilest Arts were used, and with such an Efficacy, that not only the Physician, but also the Patients under the Small-Pox inoculated were in Hazard of their very Lives from an infuriated People."

When several surrounding towns declared the practice illegal and immoral, Mather and Bolyston set about interviewing the Africans of Boston and found that most of them had received inoculation. "I have since mett with a considerable Number of these Africans," Mather later wrote, "who all agree in One story, That in their Country grandy-many dye of the Small-Pox." Trying to capture the voices of those he interviewed, he continued in what he apparently considered a folksy dialect. "But now they learn This Way: People take Juice of Small-Pox; and Cutty-skin, and Putt in a Drop; then by'nd by a little Sicky, sicky: then very few little things like Small-Pox: and no body dy of it; and no body have Small-Pox any more."

Armed with this evidence, Mather and Bolyston prepared a tract reporting their findings. In it, they issued a challenge to this last gasp of Puritan society to recognize the benefits that could be derived from paying attention to the varied knowledge cultural difference can provide. "I don't know why 'tis more unlawful to learn of Africans, how to help against the Poison of the Small Pox," they wrote, "than it is to learn of our Indians, how to help against the Poison of a Rattle-Snake."

What Mather did not report in his tract or in his frequent sermons and presentations on the subject was that those things that might be learned from either Indians or Africans were part of a larger body of knowledge that made no distinction between the scientific and the spiritual. Obviously, such information would not have helped his cause. But no matter the source of this innovation, the effect it had on the Puritan worldview could not have been more earthshaking.

Mather himself, after a lifetime of expecting to be treated as a pillar of the community, discovered the sting of ridicule. The man who emerged as his chief critic, a physician by the name of William Douglass, charged that Mather was "the hero in this farce of calumny." When the attacks went further, first questioning the inoculation advocate's faith and then his morality, Mather took to the pages of the *Boston Gazette*: "Can they not give into the method or practice without having their devotion and subjection to the All wise Providence of God Almighty called into question?"

Counterarguments did nothing to still the pens of his critics, however. Mather would have been annoyed to find in his *New England Courant* one day a long satirical piece at his expense, "A Dialogue between a Clergyman and a Layman concerning Inoculation. By an unknown Hand." The unknown hand here was likely that of the newspaper's publisher, James Franklin, younger brother of Benjamin. Founded just half a year before, Franklin's *Courant* had already made a name for itself as the first American periodical to use literary writing and scathing humor in its assessments of the news of the day. More out of a muckraker's love of controversy than personal conviction, Franklin gleefully stoked the fires of public outrage. The clergyman in this short "Dialogue" is clearly designed to be Mather. The layman — like Everyman from the morality plays of old — is a stand-in for the reader, who may yet be undecided on the question of inoculation. Quick with his tongue, the Layman befuddles the Clergyman with his wit and common sense, making the case that ministers who advocate for medical innovation are less knowledgeable than they hope to appear.

> Clergyman: The last Time I discoursed with you, you seemed to discover a bitter Aversion to the new and safe Way of Inoculation; are you yet reconciled to that successful Practice?
> Layman: I have but little reason to entertain a more favourable opinion.... I confess, I am not yet convinced that it is either a lawful or successful Practice.
> Clergyman: The Ministers of the Gospel, who are our Spiritual Guides, approve and recommend this Practice; and they are great and good Men, who would not impose on the World; and surely, you ought to fall in with their Opinion.
> Layman: I have abundant Reason to think, that they and I are equally ignorant of Inoculation, especially as to the Success of it; and if the Blind lead the Blind, both shall fall into the Ditch.

Clergyman: But why don't you believe the Ministers? They can explain the dark Passages of Scripture, and answer Cases of Conscience, better than illiterate Men.

Layman: I will believe no Man (tho he be a Minister) because he is great and good; for such may err, and have sometimes deceived themselves and others...

Clergyman: But I find, all the Rakes in Town are against Inoculation, and that induces me to believe it is a right Way.

Layman: Most of the Ministers are for it, and that induces me to think it is from the D — l, for he often makes use of good Men as instruments to obtrude his Delusions on the World.

Clergyman: You must not say it is from the D — l because of the success of it, for the D — l was never the Author of any thing for the Good of Mankind.

Layman: I think the Scripture forbids us to learn the Customs of the Heathen.

Clergyman: Inoculation is not the worse because the Heathens first practiced it; They make use of Food and Cloaths; and shall we reject those Gifts of Heaven, because they receive them? God forbid.

Layman: The Use of Food and Cloaths, which you bring for an Influence, is no ways parellel, for the Sixth Commandment requries us to use such Things for the Support of our Lives. Are you willing to imitate the Heathen in other Things besides Inoculation? The King of Calecus in the East-Indies lies not with his Queen the first Night, but one of the Priests doth, who hath a Gratuity bestowed on him for that Service. I suppose it is not a worse Sin to break the Seventh Commandment than the Sixth.

Clergyman: I should be loath to conform to the East-India Practice because it is a moral Evil, which I think Inoculation is not.

Layman: You do but think it is not a moral Evil, for you cannot prove that it is not.

This question of the supposed moral evil of inoculation rested mainly on two understandings: First, that epidemics were acts of

God; and second, that inoculation itself was a form of self-harm, a kind of suicide, really—for who but those with an unholy wish to die would voluntarily subject their bodies to infection?

There was also a third, mostly unspoken, moral objection, and it had to do with the immediate means through which Mather had learned of the practice. When Mather had Onesimus in his home and slavery was taking root in Boston, reports of practices that seemed similar to inoculation had contributed to a fear of slave rebellion. Why would the fact that inoculation had been practiced among Africans be particularly distressing in Massachusetts? Along with the general theological objection to heathen customs, there may have been particular suspicion of Onesimus and his origins. The Coramantee or its variants were—in legend and actual fact—among the enslaved Africans most prone to insurrection. Indeed, all through the eighteenth century, whenever the word "Coramantee" turns up in newspapers, it is inevitably tied to slave revolt. When Mather was becoming interested in inoculation, there were reports of slave uprisings involving Coramantee as close by as New York. Such reports would have chilled New Englanders to the bone. It is in this sense that inoculation came to be tied to slave revolt.

It was not merely the occurrence of uprisings that was so disconcerting, however, but the manner in which they sometimes took place—and the fact that they often began as inoculation seemed to, at the intersection of medicine and magic. In April of 1712, for example, when slaves revolted in New York City, they had been led by a "conjureman" known as Peter the Doctor, who initiated the uprising by anointing each of his countrymen with a special powder. As a contemporary report put it: "Some Negro Slaves here of ye Nations of Caramantee & Pappa plotted to destroy all the White in order to obtain their freedom." They "kept their Conspiracy Secret that there was not the least Suspicion of it...till it come to the Execution." To the colonists, the place of the devil in this uprising would have been found in the details:

> It was agreed to on New Years Day the Conspirators tying
> themselves to Secrecy by Sucking ye blood of each Others
> hands, and to make them invulnerable as they believed a
> free negroe who pretends Sorcery gave them a powder to
> rub on their Cloths which made them so confident that on

Sunday night Apr. 7 ab' 2 a Clock about the going down of the Moon they Set fire to a house which allarming the town they stood in the street and shot down as many as they could.

This "free negroe who pretends Sorcery," Peter the Doctor, was likely a priest or shaman of his people, and the rituals he performed to make the slaves feel "invulnerable" employed a kind of magic called *aduru*. The scholar William Rucker defines *aduru* as "medicine in the form of liquid or powder" which could take the form of "plants, herbs, human blood, graveyard dirt, and other substances that...contain a certain amount of spiritual power." While the sharing of blood described here could only have been proof of demonic influence to the colonists, to those involved it had positive religious significance.

There is no mention of the traditional, religiously influenced healing arts of West Africa in the discussions of inoculation, but in the spiritual context of the Akan tradition from which Onesimus likely had come, healing with blood was also *aduru*. Inoculation itself would have been seen as a kind of *aduru*, and *aduru* was elsewhere being used to give Africans the courage to fight, and kill, their masters.

One difference between these two instances of *aduru*, of course, is that inoculation actually worked. The magic of Peter the Doctor had a much lower success rate. Of the two dozen Coramantee slaves who took part in the revolt, six killed themselves upon being captured. The remaining men were executed—some in the Old World style reserved in Europe for witches, as befitting those who posed not just a physical but a spiritual threat.

With the news of such uprisings spreading through the colonies and becoming legend, inoculation itself carried with it a reminder of the religious risks the English colonists lived with every day: that their way of being in the world, their understanding of God's role in human lives, might prove inadequate to their surroundings; that some other way—Quakerism, witchcraft, popery, Obeah—might prove better suited to an America that was turning out to be more heterogeneous than their faith could bear.

Inoculation, in other words, called into question the basic assumptions of the society the Puritans had built. How else to explain the violent reaction to Mather's support of the practice?

This violence, it must be noted, was not merely a war of words. In November of that plague-ridden year—five months after he had first proposed inoculation—an opponent of Mather's views threw a bomb with a lit fuse through his window. Had it gone off, Mather notes, it would "have killed them that were near it, and would have certainly fired the Chamber and speedily have laid the House in Ashes."

Fortunately, the "grenado," as he calls it, seems to have hit a metal casement as it came through the glass, dislodging the lit fuse, which burned out on the floor. This assault is said to have included a written message—"Cotton Mather, you dog, dam you! I'l inoculate you with this; with a pox to you"—but truly one must question the reliability of a story in which anyone finds it useful to attach a note to a bomb.

Nevertheless, apparently the possibility of such attacks was a risk Mather was willing to take. Despite his long insistence on doctrinal purity, he had found a better way outside the bounds of his own tradition, and he was prepared to stake his reputation on arguing for the truth of it. In this sense, Boston in 1722 marks the birth of the kind of practical pluralism that would later define the American experiment.

When the tide of opinion turned and inoculation seemed to be working, it was not a universal cause for celebration. In fact, it created an existential quandary. As one pious observer worried concerning the sickness and inoculation, "Though we don't pray that it may not spread, yet by praying for a blessing on this practice, we pray against the Judgment."

Inoculation was blasphemy, but that was not all. As the scholar of American Puritanism Perry Miller has written, in New England "There was no social niche for the infidel." This was a place that had formerly preferred, like Catholic Spain, to evict its spiritual dissenters. Mather's support for a religiously suspect practice was an open questioning of the assumption of religious uniformity and shared covenant on which Puritan society was based.

Moreover, the origins of Mather's thinking on the matter showed that, Miller's comment notwithstanding, there *was* in fact a social niche for people with faiths and practices far outside the mainstream. Society at the time may have seen them as less than people, but they were there, living and dying among Christians. The fact that they had beliefs of their own is often forgotten, but those beliefs—the hidden faiths of the enslaved—helped shape the world around them, the world on which our own is built.

In the years following the display of the slave's scar that set all this in motion, the unlikely relationship between the scion of the first family of Puritanism and a man stolen in his youth from the nation of Coramantee began to fray. Without Mather's knowledge, Onesimus for years had been earning money and hiding it away, until he was finally able to buy his freedom by purchasing another African youth to replace him.

Mather seems to have had mixed feelings about this separation. "My Servant Onesimus, proves wicked, and grows useless," he noted, in reference perhaps to St. Paul's original play on the "useful" meaning of the name. Other words Mather used to describe his behavior were "Froward" and "Immorigerous," archaic expressions indicating that Onesimus was not a man to be told what to do. If he was truly one of the legendarily rebellious Coramantee, Mather might have feared having Onesimus remain within his fragile household, a possibility supported by his further reflection: "My Disposing of him, and my Supplying of my Family with a better Servant in his Room requires much Caution, much Prayer, much Humiliation before the Lord. Repenting of what may have offended Him, in the case of my servants, I would wait on Him, for his mercy."

Mather had been watchful for some time of the company Onesimus kept, and wondered if praying more for his wayward servant would make a difference. Ultimately, however, Onesimus made the choice for him. Mather prepared the necessary paperwork:

> My servant Onesimus, having advanced a Summ, toward the purchase of a Negro-lad, who may serve many occasions of my Family in his Room, I do by this Instrument, Release him so far from my Service and from the claims that any under or after me might make upon him.

Even after granting Onesimus his freedom, Mather mentions him frequently. He is concerned about the young man's future, distraught that he has not done enough praying for his soul. It is clear that Onesimus made an impression—perhaps because they had more in common than Mather admits.

Not long after Mather had lost his wife and two of his children, he made another mention of Onesimus in his diary. This time it is not to complain about the man or to record another medical innovation but simply to note that his former servant's son had also died.

While Mather makes no mention of which gods Onesimus might have appealed to in his own time of fear and mourning, they likely were those he brought from a distant shore, the same gods that had led him to transform the faith of a man who had tried — and failed — to convert him.

The Iroquois longhouse. Illustration from Emory Adams Allen's *The Prehistoric World: or, Vanished Races.* Cincinnati: Central Publishing House, 1885.

CHAPTER 7

Longhouse Nation

1744–1754

They arrived in the heat of a summer afternoon, a crowd so large it could be heard before it was seen, shaking the dry earth with the footfalls of men and horses.

Though the town's residents had known they were coming, the actual sight of the throng's advance could only have been unnerving. Anyone who unhooked shutters or inched open doors to catch a glimpse of the cause of the commotion would have seen more than two hundred well-armed men, marching like an invading army down the main path through town.

They carried French-made muskets, tomahawks of freshly sharpened iron, sapling bows and quivers of arrows. Despite this weaponry and their orderly movement, however, there was no military precision in their appearance. Some dressed in ragged match-coats, others in shirts so dirty they seemed stained with spilled ink, others with no shirts at all. They looked less like soldiers than marauders spied in the instant before the pillaging began. The only small solace to be found in what one observer called this "great concourse of people" was that among the many warriors there were also a number of women, some with young children tucked in the crooks of their arms. Their presence alone served as a reminder in case anyone in the grip of their fright had momentarily forgotten: These Indians had come not for battle but for negotiation.

Yet no sooner had these initial worries been put to rest than a chilling sound rose from the street, entering every window in town. From somewhere within the cloud of dust that moved along with the advancing crowd, a deep voice sang out a chant whose very rhythm was enough to throw off the regular beating of English hearts. Compared to the colonies to the north and east, Pennsylvania had endured relatively few Indian raids in the preceding decades—thanks in large part to the promise made forty years before by its founder, William Penn, who, in the pluralist spirit with which he had established his settlement, vowed to be "true Friends and Brothers" to "all and every" tribe in the region. Nevertheless, the residents of Lancaster knew well the stories of less happy relations with the natives. The vision of armed "savages," as the townspeople called them, marching through town to the cadence of what could only seem a war chant no doubt brought them all to mind.

Inside the courthouse, a contingent of white men had gathered in anticipation of the Indians' arrival. Their visitors had not come quite when they had been expected, however. The colonists were seated at dinner in a makeshift dining hall arranged around the judge's bench when they heard the singing voice echo in from the street, growing louder as it drew near. Pausing over their plates, most would have recognized the sounds of this once local and now foreign tongue, but few among them could understand the words.

It fell to the official interpreter of the meeting for which they all had come, a German-born New Yorker named Conrad Weiser, to explain that what they were hearing was an invitation.

The significance of Indian invitations was a subject Weiser knew personally. He had been just a boy when his father, an immigrant from the Duchy of Württemberg to New York's Schoharie Valley, had been invited by a local chief to send his eldest son to live among the Mohawk people for three seasons, including a bitter winter when food was scarce. The year then was 1712, and the elder Weiser had by then seen sixteen children born. Perhaps taking such a risk with one of the eight still living made good practical sense at the time. Throughout the century that had then barely begun, the Mohawk would remain a dominant factor in the colony's politics, trade, and security. Young Conrad's father apparently hoped that having a member of the family endure hardship to become versed in native languages and customs would be a sure investment in the future.

His gamble seemed to be paying off as Weiser, now a man of middle age, translated the chanted words giving voice to the arriving crowd. The Indians were to be treated as guests, the interpreter would have explained to the others in the courthouse, and so the negotiation sessions would take place according to their rules. The chanting—which Weiser knew came from a sachem, or chief— indicated that the elaborate protocol had already begun. Ringing through the open windows of the courthouse, carried on what little summer breeze could be found on this late June day, the song formally invited the colonists to reaffirm all prior efforts at establishing a lasting peace, and to forge a new treaty in a precarious time.

This was no local meeting between a handful of settlers and a neighboring tribe. It was a summit of the governors and representatives of the colonies of Maryland, Virginia, and Pennsylvania, and the emissaries of the Six Nations, also known as the Iroquois Confederacy. The union the Iroquois cohort represented—which first, when it was known as the Five Nations, consisted of the northern Mohawk, Oneida, Onondaga, Cayuga, and Seneca peoples, and later added the Tuscarora, who extended as far south as the Carolinas—was the oldest political body in North America, preexisting the earliest-founded colonial government by more than two hundred years. As such, these new arrivals to Lancaster had a legislative process at least as well established as the imported British system, and a polity far more certain of itself as a coalition of shared interests than the colonists had yet achieved or had even attempted.

Long before the birth of the notion of manifest destiny among Americans of European descent, the members of the Six Nations also had a clearer sense of the spiritual connection, and religious right, to the land on which they lived. This can be seen in the earliest accounts of the Iroquois creation myths, which were a key to their own understanding of how their confederacy came to be. The earliest publication of these myths was found in a short book by David Cusick, an artist and writer of the Tuscarora people, who collected and translated the oral tradition of the Six Nations early in the nineteenth century. His *Sketches of Ancient History of the Six Nations* brought a wider audience to tales that had been passed down for generations and also had been recorded in various forms by Jesuits traveling in New France.

"Among the ancients there were two worlds in existence," Cusick wrote. "The lower world was in a great darkness—the possession of the great monsters—but the upper world was inhabited by mankind." In this upper world there was once a woman preparing to give birth to twins. As her labor began, her body and mind were in such distress that she was urged to lie down and rest. So deep was the sleep she fell into, however, that she began to sink from one world to the other, from the sky world to the world of darkness. Below, the monsters of the great water that covered all of the lower realm of existence saw the woman begin to fall. They gathered together in council to determine what to do. One creature was dispatched to the depths of the ocean to find some earth to bring to the surface to make a place where the woman might land. But what would hold up the land within the water?

As Cusick wrote, "A large turtle came forward and made proposal to them to endure her lasting weight, which was accepted." Earth and muck brought up from the bottom of the primordial sea were then spread across the turtle's back—just in time for the woman to land. "While holding her, the turtle increased every moment and became a considerable island of earth, and apparently covered with small bushes." It was there, on the turtle's back, that the woman who fell from the sky gave birth to twins—a good mind and an evil mind, or a son with a gentle disposition and a son with insolent character, the warring inclinations of humanity.

This was the origin of the designation of the North American continent as "Turtle Island." It was also only the beginning of the elaborate cosmology that explained the relationship between humanity and the environment in which they lived, as well as the political circumstances that led several native peoples to unite.

Untold generations after the birth of the Sky Woman's two sons, one of these sons was said to be born again in the form of an Indian called Degawida. Also known as the Law Giver or the Great Peacemaker, he was the man—according to legend—who united the original Five Nations, teaching them to live together symbolically, under one code, and in the literal sense, through the construction of the longhouses that would provide a constant reminder of the lasting peace that had been achieved.

Though the colonists who met with the representatives of the Six Nations for the most part could not shake their feelings of cultural superiority when interacting with Indians of any sort, the spiritual confidence of the Iroquois gave them leverage in the business at hand, which was the brokering of a new and enduring accord between themselves and the American subjects of the

Crown. There were ongoing disputes involving settlers encroaching on Indian lands, and lingering questions about the allegiance of the Iroquois should England go to war with France over control of territory and trade. Like the Six Nations' unsettling arrival in Lancaster, the meeting was fraught from the start with the awareness that misunderstandings could prove calamitous.

One of the junior members of the Maryland contingent, a legislative secretary named Witham Marshe, put the Indians' number at 252. He had rushed out to witness their grand entrance to town and had seen the source of the invitation song. It came from a figure leading the procession with a royal bearing and imposing presence: a man of perhaps sixty, whom Marshe would later describe as tall and well made, with a "very full chest, and brawny limbs."

Still singing as he passed the courthouse, the Onondaga chief Canassatego led his diplomatic mission to a clearing on the outskirts of town, where the colonists had arranged poles and boards as building materials. The first rule of Iroquois treaty negotiation protocol: Under no circumstances would they sleep in structures built by white men. The deepest beliefs of the people revolved around the image of the home, the traditional longhouse, which was to them a symbol of both their political alliance and the communal nature of all life. To sleep in English dwellings even for a night while negotiating a treaty would have amounted to a kind of apostasy. Instead, they created in a matter of hours a compound that was a rough approximation of the villages from which they had come. Adding boughs gathered from the nearby woods to the supplies prepared for them, they quickly assembled a series of shelters arranged by each man's rank and his nation's current standing in the coalition, making their corner of the negotiation site a small-scale iteration of the confederacy itself.

While the Iroquois set camp, the colonists finished their dinner in the courthouse, drinking huzzahs to the health of the local hosts. Once these niceties were dispensed with, a group of young Virginians, Pennsylvanians, and Marylanders, including Marshe, made their way to the Indian village that had risen as if by magic from the earth. As they loitered among the shelters, the colonists offered snuff to the Iroquois men, threw coins to the Iroquois children, and watched in fascination as some of the visitors began to decorate themselves with white paint made of bear grease mixed with ash.

Breaking away from the curious young men, the interpreter Conrad Weiser immediately sought out Canassatego and another Six Nations leader, Tachanuntie, known as the Black Prince because one of his parents was rumored to have been of African blood. Weiser shook the men's hands and spoke to them in their native tongue, causing Canassatego to respond with a liveliness surprising for his age. The sachems knew Weiser well—so well, in fact, that they had given him an Iroquois name: Tarachawagon, "He who holds the reins." As the man through whom all negotiations would be filtered, he was in control of a process that could run wild without a steady hand.

Even as the Iroquois continued to paint themselves, becoming "frightful," in Marshe's estimation, Weiser continued to converse with the elders, as if more comfortable in native company than among his own people.

The ways of the Indians were nothing to Weiser. For one with such an essential official capacity, he was a man of unexpectedly eclectic background. Not only had he been exposed to Mohawk beliefs in his youth, he had also, as an adult, lived for a time with a breakaway religious sect, only twelve miles from this meeting site. The Ephrata Cloister, as it was known, was a utopian, occasionally apocalyptic community, where men and women slept—separately and celibately—on wooden planks, ate just a single vegetarian meal each day, and rose for two hours every night to watch for the return of Christ. Weiser remained at Ephrata for two years but soon had a falling-out with its founder, who complained that Weiser was "entrapped in the net of his own wisdom."

Weiser was what might be called today, for lack of a better term, a seeker. In the words of his nineteenth-century biographer, "We may term Conrad Weiser a sort of religious vagrant.... His spiritual activity seems to be all circumference without centre." A born diplomat, he was "all things to all men, without being anything to himself, in a religious sense—perhaps as dangerous a spiritual state as one can well occupy."

He was spiritually dangerous, apparently, because he frequently frustrated his countrymen's expectations. With his language skills in high demand, he had been enlisted briefly, following his monastic sojourn at Ephrata, in efforts to convert Native Americans. His heart was not in it, however. He had, it seems, far too much respect for the original inhabitants of America to become overzealous in attempts to change them.

"If by the word of religion people mean an assent to certain creeds, or the observance of a set of religious duties, as appointed prayers, singing, baptism, or even heathenish worship, then it may be said, the Five Nations and their neighbors have no religion," he wrote in a letter to a friend. "But if by religion we mean an attraction of the soul to God, whence proceeds a confidence in, a hunger after the knowledge of Him, then this people must be allowed to have some religion among them, notwithstanding their sometimes savage deportment. For we find among them some traces of a confidence in God alone."

As illustration of this, he recounted story after story of moments when he had learned from, or been shamed by, the religious certainty of the members of the Iroquois Confederacy. On one of his earliest diplomatic missions, for example, he was sent to the village of Onondago at the request of the governor of Virginia. He departed in February "for a journey of five hundred English miles through a wilderness where there was neither road nor path, and at such a time of the year when animals could not be met with for food." Together with a Dutchman and three Indians as companions, Weiser had traveled 150 miles of this journey when the party came to a valley one mile wide and thirty miles long, packed with snow three feet deep. As they attempted to traverse along the slope of a mountain to avoid the hard passage of the valley floor, one of the Indians slipped and "slid down the mountain as from the roof of a house."

In Weiser's estimation, he survived only by sheer luck, but the fallen man did not see it that way. "We saw that if the Indian had slipped four or five paces further, he would have fallen over a rock one hundred feet perpendicular upon craggy pieces of rocks below. The Indian was astonished, and turned quite pale; then, with outstretched arms and great earnestness, he spoke these words: 'I thank the great Lord and Governor of this world, in that he has had mercy upon me, and has been willing that I should live longer.'"

Two hundred miles along on this same journey, Weiser found himself "extremely weak....with the cold and hunger." Facing freshly fallen snow twenty inches deep and several days yet of a "frightful wilderness" to cross, he lost all hope. "My spirit failed, my body trembled and shook. I thought I should fall down and die," he wrote. "I stepped aside and sat down under a tree, expecting there to die."

His companions marched on without him, but then, "The Indians came back and found me sitting there. They remained awhile silent. At last the old Indian said: 'My dear companion, thou hast hitherto encouraged us; wilt thou now quite give up? Remember that evil days are better than good days. For when we suffer much we do not sin. Sin will be driven out of us by suffering, and God cannot extend his mercy to them; but contrary wise, when it goeth evil with us, God hath compassion on us.' These words made me ashamed. I arose up and traveled as well as I could."

On another journey he came upon a man who seemed something close to an Indian version of the famous mendicant saint, Francis of Assisi: "An Indian came to us in the evening, who had neither shoes, stockings, shirt, gun, knife nor hatchet. In a word, he had nothing but an old torn blanket and some rags. Upon enquiring whither he was going, he answered to Onondago. I knew him, and asked him how he could undertake a journey of three hundred miles so naked and impoverished, having no provisions, nor arms to kill animals for his sustenance? He told me very cheerfully that God formed everything which had life, even the rattlesnake itself, though it was a bad creature; and that God would also provide, in such a manner, that he should go thither; that it was visible, God was with the Indians in the wilderness, because they always cast their care upon Him; but that, contrary to this, the Europeans always carried their bread with them."

Perhaps most relevant to his work as an interpreter of Indian words and wishes during diplomatic negotiations, Weiser had been witness to meetings they held amongst themselves. "I have had occasion to be in council with them upon treaties for land and to adjust the terms of trade," he wrote. Whenever anyone addressed a gathering, no matter the topic they raised, "not a man of them was observed to whisper or smile—the old, grave; the young, reverent in their deportment. They spoke little, but fervently, and with elegance. I have never seen more natural sagacity."

At such times, even following heated discussions, Weiser had seen a particular ancient sachem fall peacefully back into a kind of reverie, framing with sacred ceremony even issues as mundane as property disputes. "He began to sing with an awful solemnity, but without expressing any words. The others accompanied him with their voices. After they had done, the same Indian with great earnestness of fervor spoke these words: 'Thanks, thanks be to Thee, Thou great Lord of the world, in that Thou hast again caused the sun to shine, and has dispersed the dark cloud. The Indians are Thine.'"

While the tone of Weiser's recollections perhaps suggests that these Iroquois were addressing a Christian God or otherwise imitating European styles of devotion, this was not usually the case. He likewise heard sachems speak to gatherings of Iroquois and "charge and command them to love the Christians, and particularly live in peace with me and the people under my Government....At every sentence of which they shouted and said Amen in their way."

At the start of the Lancaster meeting, it was his openness to cultural difference — as well as a well-honed diplomatic sense — that led Weiser to rebuke the colonial cohort as they stood milling around the Indian encampment. He warned them not to laugh at the often strange dress of their guests, nor even to speak of it, lest they give offense. Unlike the colonists, many of the Iroquois had no difficulty understanding the language of those on the other side of the negotiating fire.

Yet his urging largely fell on deaf ears. The assembled representatives of the colonies were far from home and could not help their gawking. Nor was their curiosity limited to the Indians. The following day, according to Witham Marshe, the Maryland contingent traveled out to a place they called the "Dunkers nunnery" — "Dunkers" being the pejorative term for those who practiced adult baptism, and "nunnery," of course, a term that smacked of the latent popery assumed of anyone diverging from Protestant norms — which happened to be the very Ephrata community of which Conrad Weiser had once been a member. With his own countrymen scornful of his prior religious commitments, and having only positive things to say about the devotions of the Iroquois, the colonial interpreter had sympathies for the nations they would face across the treaty fire that were slightly warmer than impartial.

After a weekend of conviviality — both the colonists and the Iroquois enjoyed lubricating diplomacy with wine and punch — the real work began. For most of a month, they met in marathon sessions not only to determine the fate of isolated tracts of disputed land but to consider the future of two peoples with competing claims on the resources of the continent.

The negotiations were mostly congenial—even, at times, mutually enjoyable. At certain moments, however, the radically different interpretations of history that separated the English and the Iroquois became apparent. Rarely were such differences spoken of during the meeting sessions, but when they were, the machinery of negotiation seemed to grind to a halt. One day, one of Witham Marshe's fellow representatives of the governor of Maryland laid claim to land which "Our Great King of England, and His subjects, have always possessed...free and undisturbed from any claim of the Six Nations for above one hundred years past." The following day, Canassatego rose to speak. He chose his words carefully and then listened as they were translated by his friend Conrad Weiser.

"What is one hundred years in comparison to the length of time since our claim began? Since we came out of this ground?" he asked. "For we must tell you that long before one hundred years, our Ancestors came out of this very ground, and their children have remained here ever since."

In his seventh decade, Canassatego was still regarded as a force to be reckoned with. Though he was said to possess "a good-natured smile," he did not readily offer it now. He had no desire to put the English at ease.

Again speaking through Weiser, he continued: "You came out of the ground in a country that lies beyond the Seas. There you may have a just Claim, but here you must allow us to be your elder Brethren." With a skilled debater's panache, he then casually erased the Marylander's appeal to history and offered one of his own. "The lands belonged to us before you knew anything of them," he said.

As a political body, the Six Nations had existed by this time for more than three hundred years, making it not only older than any colonial government but older than many of the kingdoms of Europe—older, in other words, than the United States of America will be in 2076. Historians have estimated that it could date from the fourteenth century. Before the English, the French, or the Dutch had come to the northern parts of the Americas, before Columbus had stumbled into a place that was not India and yet called its inhabitants Indians, the Iroquois had united diverse, often warring peoples under a common cause and a single code of law. In the not too distant past, Canassatego reminded the colonial representatives, the entirety of the land in question had been theirs.

"Above One Hundred Years ago" he said, when the first Europeans had come to Iroquois lands, they had brought with them goods including awls, knives, hatchets, and guns. "When they had taught us how to use their Things, and we saw what sort of People they were, we were so well pleased with them, that we tied their ship to the bushes on the shore; and afterwards, liking them still better the longer they staid with us, and thinking the bushes too slender, we removed the Rope, and tied it to the trees; and as the trees were liable to be blown down by the high winds, or to decay themselves, we, from the affection we bore them, again removed the rope, and tied it to a strong big rock, and not content with this for its further security, we removed the rope to the big Mountain, and there we tied it very fast, and rowll'd Wampum around about it, and to make it still more secure we stood upon the Wampum, and sat down upon it, to defend it, and to prevent any Hurt coming to it, and did our best Endeavors that it might remain uninjured forever."

Such a cozy relationship between the natives of this continent and those who hoped to remake it in their own image surely never existed in quite the way Canassatego described. Yet his parable — and it was indeed a parable, stocked with symbols drawn from his religious understanding of the land — served as a reminder to the colonists that there were two competing interpretations of history at play here. With a few choice words, he called into question the entire English experiment in the Americas, and then went on to inform them that they had not improved this land, as they supposed, but had caused it to suffer.

"By way of Reproach," he said, the English would often tell the Iroquois "that we should have perished if they had not come into the Country and furnished us with Strowds and Hatchets and Guns...but we always gave them to understand that they were mistaken, that we lived before they came amongst us, and as well, or better, if we may believe what our Forefathers have told us."

Even after he had spoken his mind, Canassatego was not quite done offering uncomfortable truths. Before the negotiations had ended, this highest-ranking member of the Iroquois Confederacy chastised the colonists for their scattershot diplomatic efforts. The fact that they—the Iroquois—had to make separate agreements with each of the colonies was a clear indication that there was too much discord among the English in America for them to ever achieve their goals.

"We heartily recommend Union and a Good Agreement between you our Brethren," he said. "Never disagree, but preserve a strict Friendship for one another, and thereby you as well as we will become the Stronger. Our wise Forefathers established Union and Amity between the Five Nations; this has made us formidable, this has given us great weight and Authority with our Neighboring Nations. We are a Powerfull confederacy, and by your observing the same Methods our wise Forefathers have taken, you will acquire fresh Strength and Power; therefore, whatever befalls you, never fall out with one another."

The turnabout here would have been jarring to any of the colonial negotiators, amounting to a cognitive dissonance long before the phrase had been coined. The colonists had arrived at the negotiations full of the usual dismissive attitudes toward their native interlocutors. Witham Marshe, for one, could not help but dwell on their weakness for alcohol, their ragged appearance, their backward ways. And yet here they were presuming to tell the king's subjects how to live and organize themselves.

No matter the immediate outcome of the negotiations, or the ultimate victory the colonists and their descendants would eventually have over native ways of life, in that moment, forced to compare their own political disorder to the accord among the Iroquois, the colonists who had earlier jeered at the Indians could only have been humbled. Conrad Weiser, meanwhile, who had actually given voice to Canassatego's rebuke, was inspired.

What accounted for such confidence on the part of the Iroquois? Though they were an ancient nation by this time, and though they occupied a strategically significant location between English and French strongholds in North America, they had nowhere near the population or the resources to truly compete with the colonists. Yet like the pilgrims who had envisioned a city upon a hill, and who drew strength from this vision despite innumerable challenges, the Iroquois sought to create a society based on religious ideas as filtered through a single enduring metaphor.

The term "Iroquois" itself seems to be a French transformation either of words neighboring tribes once used to describe them or of words they often used themselves. In the former interpretation, they were labeled with the epithet *Irinakhoiw*, "rattlesnakes," by their ancient enemy the Huron. In the latter, the name derives from a feature of their language, the tendency to end all declarations with the words *hiro koue*, which both claimed ownership of the statement and, like a prehistoric emoticon, emphasized the kind of feeling it was meant to convey.

They eventually would adopt the name applied to them by Europeans, but at the time of the Lancaster meeting they still preferred to call themselves the Haudenosaunee, which literally means "People of the Longhouse." At one time as closely associated with them as the adobe pueblos of the southwest were with the Zuni tribe encountered by Mustafa Zemmouri, the longhouse was a multiroom structure shared by as many fifty people. William Nelson Fenton describes their layout: "Typically it had from three to five fires, each of which might be shared by two nuclear families of five to six persons. Houses were on average twenty-five feet wide; the length depended on the number of families to be sheltered. Each fire added a two apartment module of about twenty-five feet to the length of the longhouse." Built this way, longhouses of two hundred feet were common, and archaeological evidence suggests they could be twice that size, creating footprints of 10,000 square feet. A large settlement within the Iroquois Confederacy might include more than one hundred of these multifamily dwellings.

For the Iroquois, to be the People of the Longhouse was not merely to describe the structure in which they lived. It was instead to affirm an image of themselves as united beyond the expected bounds of kinship. The longhouse was a physical representation of the accord that existed between the Six Nations, which was known as the Gayanashagowa, or the Great Law of Peace. No mere mortal agreement, this was regarded as a divine reality.

Whereas the English had as their American foundation myth the story of the city upon a hill, the Iroquois had the perhaps humbler image of the longhouse. The city upon the hill shines as a singular, set-apart exemplar; the longhouse, meanwhile, seeks to gather in rather than set apart; it is a founding myth of radical inclusion. Each is an extension of the respective creation stories at the root of two mythological systems: Humanity cast out of the communion with nature, on one hand; humanity rescued through communion with nature, on the other.

When the Iroquois spoke of their union and its strength, these were the stories that undergirded it. In short, they believed that their confederacy was God-given, and it was this belief that gave a small collection of tribes the confidence to tell the colonists, and through them the king of England, that peace would exist on their terms.

The Treaty of Lancaster hashed out in 1744 might have been like most other agreements between the colonists and the natives— honored in name for a time but then repealed, replaced, or simply forgotten. In this case, however, it remained relevant long after the last session had closed, not only because of what was said but because of who recorded it.

When the meeting adjourned, Conrad Weiser knew something interesting had happened, something worth publishing and sharing with his countrymen. He rode from Lancaster to Philadelphia, where he visited a printer who had in the past edited and published accounts of other treaty negotiations. As it happened, this printer was the older brother of the printer in Boston who had caused such a stir with his publications against inoculation. The older brother was forward-thinking in his openness to the possibility of change, though he too had an eye for stories that would capture the public's imagination.

According to some scholars, as he printed the Lancaster Treaty, the Philadelphia printer's thoughts ran from the Six Nations to his own thirteen colonies. Not fully free of the prejudices of the time, he nonetheless knew a good idea when he heard one. As he would later write, "It would be a very strange thing if Six Nations of Ignorant Savages should be capable of forming a scheme for such a Union and be able to execute it in such a manner, as that it has subsisted Ages, and appears indissoluble, and yet a like Union should be impracticable for ten or a dozen English colonies."

The printer's name, of course, was Benjamin Franklin, earliest architect of the union between the states. When he published the account of the Lancaster Treaty in 1744, the question he later posed would be put before the American reading public for the first time. If the nations of Indians could unite, why not the colonies? What was it that allowed the Iroquois to come together as they had?

Franklin carried these questions with him as he evolved from a printer to a writer and statesman of considerable skill and reputation. He gained much of his experience as a diplomat, which would later serve his rising nation so well when he was dispatched to win the support of France, through his role as negotiator among the various tribes of Pennsylvania and Ohio. Over time, he developed a practical understanding of how two communities whose fates were entwined for so long might influence each other. Christianizing efforts meant to replace native myths and rituals with beliefs from the Bible were not for Franklin. Instead of missionaries, for example, Franklin once proposed sending a blacksmith into every Indian village. "A smith is more likely to influence them than a Jesuit," he said.

Ten years after he printed Canassatego's words of rebuke and advice to the governors of Maryland, Virginia, and Pennsylvania, Franklin was enlisted as part of a meeting of representatives from the thirteen colonies to discuss how they might better defend themselves, as a unified body, from increasing international pressures. With war again expected against France, the colonists met with chiefs of the Six Nations in Albany in hopes that peace for the Americans would also mean peace for the People of the Longhouse.

Planning to make the first formal attempt to take action similar to Canassatego's suggestion that the colonies unite, Franklin developed on his way to Albany "a plan for the union of all the colonies under one government," as he put it in his autobiography. Such a union, he believed, "might be necessary for defense, and other important general purposes."

Perhaps uncertain about the implications of proposing such a rash change in colonial governance in the open air of a gathering of colonists and Indian chiefs, Franklin first shared it with "two gentlemen of great knowledge in public affairs," James Alexander and Archibald Kennedy. The former was a lawyer and amateur astronomer with whom Franklin had founded the American Philosophical Society; the latter, a New York colonial official who had recently caused a stir as the author of a pamphlet entitled "The

Importance of Gaining and Preserving the Friendship of the Indians to the British Interest Considered," which began by paraphras-
ing the parable Canassatego had offered at Lancaster:

> When the first ship arrived here from Europe, the Indians,
> it is said, were so pleased that they had her tied to a tree in
> order to better secure her; but as cables were subject to rot,
> they would have it an iron chain, and this to be continued
> into the Indian countries that they might be better able to
> keep their part of it clear from rust, as we were to keep our
> part. If the Indians were in distress or want, the call was, as
> it is at this day, to make clean, or renew the covenant chain;
> the Christians on their part were to do the like.

As Kennedy's pamphlet makes clear, Franklin had turned to
associates who took for granted the necessity of cooperation between
the Iroquois and the colonies. Receiving support from these two
associates (on philosophical grounds from Alexander and political
grounds from Kennedy) was apparently the affirmation Franklin
needed. "Being fortified by their approbation," he later remembered, "I ventur'd to lay it before the Congress."

As it happened, others arrived with similar thoughts, and a
number of proposals for union were offered in Albany. When the
question was asked of the assembled representatives if a union
should be established, it passed unanimously. Of the proposed
plans, Franklin's was chosen as the most preferable. It would have
established a system by which the general government of all the
colonies would be administered by a president-general, who would
be "appointed and supported by the crown." There would also be,
however, "a grand council...chosen by the representatives of the
people of the several colonies."

Despite the popularity of this scheme, the Albany Plan did not
survive. "In England it was judged to have too much of the *democratic*," Franklin wrote. Years later, even after Independence, he
would continue to wonder what might have been. "I am still of
opinion it would have been happy for both sides the water if it had
been adopted. The colonies, so united, would have been sufficiently strong to have defended themselves; there would then have
been no need of troops from England; of course, the subsequent
pretence for taxing America, and the bloody contest it occasioned,

would have been avoided. But such mistakes are not new; history is full of the errors of states and princes....The best public measures are therefore seldom adopted from previous wisdom, but forc'd by the occasion."

The "previous wisdom" cited here refers, at least in part, to Iroquois wisdom. The People of the Longhouse had accomplished a union of their various nations without bloodshed. Had the colonists followed their lead, Franklin imagined, the "bloody contest" by which they eventually won their freedom might have been avoided, replaced perhaps with a more gradual parting of the ways.

Though Franklin's Iroquois-indebted Albany Plan did not win immediate approval, some maintain that it remained a part of the Revolutionary generation's democratic DNA. As outlined most extensively by the historians Bruce E. Johansen and Donald Grinde beginning in the late 1970s, the controversial "Iroquois influence theory" posits that the Longhouse People's divinely given Great Law of Peace so inspired Franklin and others among the founding fathers that it served as the model for the Articles of Confederation, the governing document of the United States for the first decade of its existence, and the precursor of the Constitution ratified in 1787.

There is, this theory posits, a spiritual genealogy often overlooked in the establishment of a republic where there had been the colonies of a monarchy. Though most hagiography of the founders, and even the architecture of the nation's capital, usually looks to classical cultures for precedent for what the Revolutionary generation accomplished, there may have been another ancient culture much closer to home that provided inspiration as well.

Detractors of "Iroquois influence" dismiss it as wishful thinking or "shoddy-yet-trendy multiculturalism" run amok, and trace an alternate genealogy—one of inserting "fanciful" ideas into the historical record—going back through much of the twentieth century. As early as 1902, the foundational work in the ethnology of native North America, Lewis Henry Morgan's *League of the Ho-de-no-sau-see*, was enlisted in the cause of validating a notion that most historians find suspect at best. In a preface to his reprinted edition of Morgan's 1851 opus, Herbert M. Lloyd made a grand claim that was somewhat beyond the original work's intentions: "Franklin's plan of union, which was the beginning of our own federal republic, was directly inspired by the wisdom, durability, and inherent strength which he had observed in the Iroquois constitution.... Our nation gathers its people from many peoples of the Old World, its language and its free institutions it inherits from England, its civilization and art from Greece and Rome, its religion from Judea — and even these red men of the forest have wrought some of the chief stones in our national temple."

When a *New York Times* review quoted this and similar passages from the book, the "Iroquois influence theory" had its mass audience debut. Most historians remained skeptical of a direct link between the Iroquois way and the federal system through most of the twentieth century, and still are today. Yet despite scholarly reticence, the theory eventually became so thoroughly accepted in some quarters that it has even received the affirmation of the United States Congress. In 1988, the Senate passed a Resolution "To acknowledge the contribution of the Iroquois Confederacy of Nations to the development of the United States Constitution," which included affirmations that "the original framers of the Constitution, including, most notably, George Washington and Benjamin Franklin, are known to have greatly admired the concepts of the Six Nations of the Iroquois Confederacy" and "the confederation of the original Thirteen Colonies into one republic was influenced by the political system developed by the Iroquois Confederacy as were many of the democratic principles which were incorporated into the Constitution itself."

While the extent of the influence of the Iroquois Confederacy and its beliefs on the English colonists and the nation they would form remains open to debate, the consequences in the opposite direction, of the colonists' beliefs on the Iroquois, are fairly self-evident: Christianity gained ground over native beliefs just as the Iroquois political alliance began to unravel.

Despite the great show of native traditions at the start of events like the Lancaster Treaty, this was a clearly evident trajectory even then. Seeing this, Conrad Weiser — the man whose role as a translator made possible many of the notions of Iroquois influence debated centuries later — could at times barely contain his dismay over what the exposure to his people meant for the Six Nations. "The worst is that they are the worse for the Christians," Weiser wrote, "who have propagated their vices, and yielded them tradition for ill, and not for good things."

Yet the understanding that all good things came from the Iroquois and all bad came from the colonists does not do justice to the complexity of the relationships between these two communities throughout the eighteenth century. For generations, they variously were neighbors, allies, and adversaries. Beliefs passed back and forth between them as surely as goods or information. The ultimate significance of Native American influence is not limited to the similarities between the Iroquois system of governance and the Articles of Confederation.

Weiser himself is a good example of the way the complexity of the interactions between colonial and Native America has been written out of history by stalwarts on both sides of the "influence" debate. During his life, there was no one among the colonists who better understood the religious underpinning of Iroquois society — the beliefs that had allowed the Iroquois to forge a bond between nations that endured longer, ultimately, than would the British occupation of the continent. Weiser had stood inside the massive longhouses of Pennsylvania and New York and heard the stories of what it meant to the families who dwelt within to be part of a people joined by divinely inspired law.

Having died in 1760, Conrad Weiser did not live long enough to record an accounting of the debt the United States owed to the people among whom he had spent so much time. Had he lived longer, he likely would have been surprised by the way most significant elements of native culture began to fade from the new nation's collective memory, and he might have been most surprised by the role his own image would play in this great forgetting. In the following century, Conrad Weiser's name and likeness began to be used by a cigar manufacturer. He was chosen no doubt because tobacco then represented something of a domesticated native experience, affording users the opportunity to imagine themselves communing with Indians, as the long-ago colonial representatives had done in Lancaster. On the boxes in which Conrad Weiser cigars were sold, just to the right of the promise of "Highest Quality and Best Workmanship," a small illustration shows the adventurous translator making one of his visits to a native village. The Indians in the image do not stand in front of the longhouse that defined them; there is no hint of the centuries-old government the longhouse stood for; no suggestion of the great civilization once sustained by it; instead, they stand in front of a roughly sketched teepee, an entire culture diminished to a tiny square on a cigar box.

The image of the Iroquois as a people with distinct traditions that inevitably influenced those who came in contact with them has likewise been diminished to the point of fading away. With the forgotten longhouse, we have lost a powerful metaphor for what it means to be one country of many peoples, built not only upon thirteen colonies but upon Six Nations and the beliefs that held them together.

The Character of an Atheist.

AN atheist is an overgrown libertine; and if we believe his own genealogy, he is a by-blow begot by hazard, and flung into the world by necessity; he moves by wheels, and had no more soul than a windmill; he is thrust on by fate, and acts by mere compulsion; he is no more master of his deeds, than of his being, and therefore is as constant to his word as the wind in the same corner; so that an atheist, by his own principles, is a knave *per se*, and an honest man only *per accidens*. In fine he starts out of dust, and vanishes into nothing.

The Character of an Atheist. From the New York Weekly Journal, February 27, 1749.

CHAPTER 8

Awakenings

1737–1753

The Mohawk Valley, cut like a scar across the midsection of upstate New York, was named by Dutch traders for its original residents, members of the Iroquois Confederacy that joined the native nations of the region more than three hundred years before the first Europeans arrived. By the middle of the eighteenth century, the Mohawk people had already endured two centuries of Christianizing efforts by the Dutch, the French, and the English, but still some missionaries thought there was work to be done. Upstate New York would later gain a reputation as a hotbed of religious revival; it was an unlikely place for the education of one of the earliest men in America who took the once-damning accusation of being an atheist in stride.

When a boy of thirteen named William Livingston found himself in the Mohawk Valley in 1737, he was in the company of a missionary from the Society for the Propagation of the Gospel. Conrad Weiser was not yet so well known that he would have a cigar named after him, and young Will would have had no idea he was following in some illustrious footsteps. In any case, his short time among the Indians would ultimately have very different implications, both for himself and the nation he would help to found.

Up until then, his life had been one of privilege and relative comfort. His family, Scottish gentry going back generations, dominated political life near Albany from Livingston Manor, the 200-square-mile tract of land granted to Will's grandfather by royal charter. A portrait of the boy painted around this time suggests that his family indulged in the stubborn pretensions of a far-flung aristocracy. Sporting a cocked hat with a feather, a ruffled shirt, and close-fitting knee breeches, he does not seem to be someone who would choose a hardscrabble existence in the company of the natives, but a year spent among them was to prove transformative. Though his intention was to bring the Mohawks closer to the English way of life, instead he made a study of Iroquois language and beliefs. Among the things he would have learned among them was that, though his missionary endeavor sought to provide order to native society, the Mohawk were not without existing religious interpretations of the country they inhabited—and how best to organize a civilization within it. They, too, had stories about how the world came into being, and these stories conditioned the way they lived.

A century before, a Dutch missionary to the Mohawk, Johannes Megapolensis, recorded one of the earliest versions of the Turtle Island legend still told in various forms today. "They have a droll theory of the Creation," he wrote, "for they think that a pregnant woman fell down from heaven, and that a tortoise (tortoises are plenty and large here, in this country, two, three and four feet long, some with two heads, very mischievous and addicted to biting), took this pregnant woman on its back, because every place was covered with water, and that the woman sat upon the tortoise, groped with her hands in the water, and scraped together some of the earth, whence it finally happened that the earth was raised above the water."

In contradistinction to the tale of biblical origins that would have been told by this Dutch missionary and the French and English who would follow, this was a story about collaboration rather than dominion. With the woman and the turtle working together to create the places upon which the future would depend, the story served as a model for the relationship between humanity and nature, and between one individual and another. It was a myth, of course, but one with real-world implications. Its effects could be seen in this same missionary's understanding of the native approach to the structure and purpose of society: "The government among them consists of the oldest, the most intelligent, the most eloquent and most warlike men. These commonly resolve, and then the young and warlike men execute. But if the common people do not approve of the resolution, it is left entirely to the judgment of the mob. The chiefs are generally the poorest among them, for instead of their receiving from the common people as among Christians, they are obliged to give to the mob, especially when any one is killed in war, they give great presents to the next of kin of the deceased."

A century later, the basic premise implied in this description prevailed in the Iroquois Confederacy. Though sent to help the cause of their conversion, William Livingston would later write that he had learned "the genius and the manners" of the Mohawk, the people who had established the first democracy in America. Abraham Lincoln's famous "by the people, for the people" may only be a more graceful expression of Megapolensis's "judgment of the mob" that ensured chiefs would be responsible to those in need. To a boy subject to a king an ocean away, the idea would have been outlandish. That he might learn it from supposed savages allegedly in need of English salvation would have seemed extraordinary.

Will Livingston's lessons were not only about the natives, however. He also took note of the varying ways Englishmen and other newcomers to the continent dealt with the people who had lived along the same river in the shadow of the Catskill and the Adirondack mountain ranges for perhaps a thousand years. The Mohawks at the time were pawns in the chess game of North American dominance then being played by the English and the French, whose respective religious attachments were employed more to gain earthly advantage than for reasons of genuine spiritual concern. Will particularly noted the manner in which the French had tried to bring the Mohawks to the Christian faith. Even decades later he would complain of "missionaries who practise incredible arts to convert them." So thorough was their use of misinformation and guile in bringing about religious adherence for political gains, young Will noticed, that the French "persuade these people that the Virgin Mary was born at Paris" and that Jesus Christ "was crucified at London."

As he saw it, no matter the obvious skill of the French in winning converts, this was a relationship built mostly on coercion. In order to clear the way for its Jesuits, France had destroyed entire native villages and burned food supplies. Only when the French had won did the killing stop and the conversions begin. Livingston marveled at the "Jesuitical craft" that followed such mayhem. He noted the canonization of "a squaw by the name of St. Catharine," as the seventeenth-century Mohawk convert Katerina Tekakwitha was already known. (She would not be formally made a Roman Catholic saint until 2012.)

At thirteen, William Livingston felt outraged at the prospect of the French spreading their faith among the Mohawk. There was, to be sure, a good amount of anti-Catholic bias in his sentiment. But more than that, he seems to have experienced at that young age a general suspicion of the trappings of religion and its relationship to governance.

Before his time as an apprentice missionary, there was no indication that he would show interest in either government or religion. In fact, he wanted nothing so much as to be a painter. He had asked his parents to send him to Italy to study art, but they had other plans for him. As the second oldest in the third generation of New York Livingstons, he did not stand to inherit Livingston Manor, and so he would have to learn to make his way in the world.

Leaving the Mohawk Valley for New Haven at the age of fourteen, and then focusing his studies on the law, he might have practiced profitably and forgotten his youthful ardor for the problematic place of religion in politics.

Yet young William Livingston suffered from the curse of being born into interesting times. He would later command rebel troops, pen scathing jeremiads as a Revolutionary propagandist, serve as the first governor of one of thirteen states newly independent and united, and sign the U.S. Constitution. If his critics are to be believed, he was also the first vocal atheist to raise a ruckus in the public square. True or not, fifteen years after he learned his lessons among the Mohawk, he fought one of the first battles against religious establishment in America.

The "collapse of the Puritan canopy," evangelical scholar Mark Noll's memorable phrase for the end of the religious monopoly held by people like Cotton Mather in Massachusetts, is often cited as the necessary precondition for the Great Awakening, that period of fervent religious transformation that began in New England in the 1730s and spread down the East Coast in the two decades following. As Noll and others have noted, the explosion of emotional religious revivals the Great Awakening brought about, and the movement of American Christianity away from covenantal theology and toward the elevation of individual religious experience, played an undeniable role in fostering republican ideas in the colonies. "From the revivals arose new evangelical churches, activities, instincts, and ways of expounding Christian doctrine," Noll writes. "Before that rise could occur, older expectations for church and theology inherited from Europe had to give way. A process that ended with an intimate union between evangelical Protestant religion and Revolutionary politics began with disruption in the historic colonial churches."

Historians have often plotted a course of American spiritual development from the Puritans like Mather, to Great Awakening figures like Jonathan Edwards and George Whitefield, to the Revolution—as if there were no other significant religious moods that might have contributed to colonists so believing in the cause of Independence that they would risk their lives. Yet while it may be true that religious zeal can inspire armies better than most secular incentives, there was another great awakening that occurred before and during the Revolutionary era that also played a role. The other great awakening was a reevaluation of the merits of doubt. Often unspoken, religious skepticism in the colonial era was taboo even among professed radicals. Yet the spiritual awakenings of the middle of the eighteenth century signaled a transformation of "unbelief" from presumed moral failing to a reasonable theological and political position.

Among the charges leveled against the Boston inoculators in the 1720s, none was deployed with as much venom as "atheist." In the colonial world, the word was an all-purpose insult, capable of impugning one's intelligence, morality, and social status in just seven letters. While Mather might have inadvertently nudged open the door to acceptance of ideas drawn from diverse traditions, the stigma of standing outside mainstream religious assumptions did not disappear overnight—indeed, some might argue it never truly has.

Even as the inoculation controversy raged, dividing Christians over matters of practice and doctrine, one finds in Boston newspapers the specter that some in the community might be pleased with all this discord. Portraying the atheist as something of a trickster figure, the unsigned writer of a column in the *New England Courant* of 1722 suggested that those without faith were not merely blind to religious truth but scornful of it, and were ready, as a consequence, to mock the divisions between believers. Speaking of Christians mired in disagreement with their coreligionists, he writes: "While one laughs at the other's preaching, and the other laughs at his Preaching, the Atheist laughs at both, and there are very many that believe neither." With the faith of "very many" hanging in the balance, the hypothetical atheist was quick to delight in the inevitable fall that would result from such divisions.

Was this troublemaker a mere literary creation? If so, he was a busy one. In 1730, another writer imagined a local character by the name of Tom Puzzle, "one of the most eminent immethodical Disputants of any that has fallen under my Observation." To the delight of those who agree with him and the disdain of those who do not, Tom is the sort of man, the author writes, who makes himself known by insisting he be heard on every topic in public discussion. "Tom has read enough to make him very impertinent," he writes. "His Knowledge is sufficient to raise Doubts, but not to clear them."

> It is a pity that he had so much Learning, or that he had not a great deal more. With these qualifications Tom sets up for a Free thinker, finds a great many things to blame in the Constitution of his Country, and gives shrewd Intimations that he does not believe in another World. In short, Puzzle is an Atheist as much as his Parts will give him leave.

The colonial atheist was a boor, but he was also to be pitied. Compassionate souls would have nodded along to the quotations from Alexander Pope, likewise published in Boston in the 1730s: "An Atheist is but a mad ridiculous Derider of Piety." But one should try to keep their derision in perspective: "Atheists put on false Courage and Alacrity in the midst of their Darkness and Apprehensions," Pope continued, "like Children, who when they go in the dark, will sing for fear."

They should not be afforded too much sympathy, however. In the colonial worldview, the atheist was a moral hazard to the community, as were all religious outliers. ("I fear neither Atheist, nor Jew, Deist, nor Turk" another usage from the era noted.) A quarter-century after the *New England Courant* introduced Tom Puzzle, a New York paper went further in its character sketch of an unbeliever, with an opinion piece entitled "The Character of an Atheist" that catalogued the supposed deficiencies of anyone who dared to question the theological status quo:

An atheist is an overgrown libertine; and if we believe his own genealogy, he is a by-blow begot by hazard, and flung into the world by necessity; he moves by wheels, and had no more soul than a windmill; he is thrust by fate, and acts by mere compulsion; he is no more master of his deeds, than of his being, and therefor is as constant to his word as the wind in the same corner; so that an atheist, by his own principles, is a knave *per se*, and an honest man only *per accidens*. In fine he starts out of dust, and vanishes into nothing.

This captures succinctly the generally accepted colonial understanding of anyone who did not believe in God. As the unnamed author of this assessment saw it, an atheist supposed that he had no past, and so he would have no future. Having no real reason to be truthful, he could be counted on to lie. Having no real reasons for any of his actions, an atheist had no reason not to do wrong. When an atheist did right, if he ever did, it could only be *per accidens*, by chance.

The literature of atheism available to American colonists only supported these understandings. Early in the eighteenth century, tracts imported from England warned against the menace of both actual atheists and, even more sinister because they could be found anywhere, atheistical inclinations. Books with imposing titles like *The second Spira: being a fearful example of an atheist, who had apostatized from the Christian religion, and died in despair* were read and expounded upon from pulpits and were believed to be of particular use to the young. As many seventeenth-century readers would have known, the first Spira alluded to in the title was an Italian lawyer who had denied the Gospel and, as a direct result, died from a spiritual illness inflicted by God. The "second Spira" of the later book faced a similar plight. The narrative consisted of an "account of his sickness, Convictions, Discourses with Friends, and Ministers, and of his dreadful Expressions and Blasphemies when he left the World."

Such books were considered especially beneficial for adolescents—"Published for an Example to others, recommended to all Young Persons, to settle them in their Religion"—but there is no doubt their elders read them as well. There was, it seems, a titillating element to stories of those who so brazenly shrugged off faith, a kind of theological escapism. The author of "the second Spira" offered a money-back guarantee: "If anyone doubts the truth of any Particulars in the following relation, if they repair to Mr. Dunton at Raven in the Poultry [the book's publisher and place of business] they will receive full satisfaction."

Later in the same century, similar accounts of atheists and the bad ends to which they inevitably came were published on both sides of the ocean. "The atheist converted, or, The unbeliever's eyes opened" told the tale — in several hundred rhymed lines — of a professed atheist who "would not suffer his children to go to church."

> This man an Atheist, he was bred, we find,
> And so his children dear he strove to blind
> Telling them that all things by nature came
> The thoughts of heaven were all profaned.

Spared the fate of either the first or second Spira, the subject of these verses eventually is shamed by his daughter's devotion and sees the error of his ways. The atheist — and his cousins the Free Thinker, the Deist, the Jew, and the Turk — was in most eighteenth-century instances a character whose sole purpose was the enlivening of a cautionary tale.

Yet a subtle change began to occur in the meaning and use of the word in the middle of the century. With Enlightenment ideas gaining ground, the possibility of applying reason to religious belief gave "atheist" a hint of the forward-thinking intellectual. As another anonymous colonial writer proclaimed:

> If I must sacrifice my Reason, my good Nature, my Love of Society, and handsome behaviour, to what they call Christianity, I'll even continue my present Course of Life, and live and dye like a well-bred and reasonable Atheist.

Two and a half years after the *New York Weekly Journal* weighed in on the pressing concern of the "character of an atheist," the *Boston Evening Post* offered a different take on the question of the varieties of belief and their place in society. It was not lack of faith that was the true social ill; it was instead lack of sincere faith, whatever that faith may be. Atheism, on the other hand, was cast in a light that now seems prescient: "The Atheist is a man who doubts of the

King's Right to the Crown; and during the Doubt, refuses the Oath of Allegiance, or pays no Obedience to Supremacy."

Contrasting "Spurious and Genuine Devotion," the *Boston Evening Post* puts atheists on the side of the genuine. Their opinions still might be risky to espouse in polite society, but there is definite evidence that atheism was gaining ground throughout the eighteenth century. Over time, the more it became linked with political opposition to the religious authority established by the mother country, the more atheism itself began to be seen in not entirely negative terms.

As it happens, just as the meaning of atheism was changing and evolving, another publication entered the colonies' already crowded media marketplace. Not only was it more political and more pointed in its opinions, it was the first publication in America to take explicit aim at the religious alliances common to most colonial governments. It was also, according to the critics who eventually succeeded in shutting it down, a hotbed of anti-monarchical and anti-religious sentiment.

It was founded by a twenty-nine-year-old lawyer named William Livingston.

To understand the reception a religious outlier like Livingston received when he began publishing thoughts that strained the tolerance of more orthodox believers, it is first necessary to consider religious adherence—and the lack thereof—in the English colonies.

Of all the myths associated with the founding of the United States, there is none so stubborn as the notion that the colonists who rose up against the Crown did so mainly because they were a people motivated and sustained by faith. While the religious inclinations of the founding fathers provide fodder for endless contemporary political disputes, the colonial population as a whole—the more telling piece of this puzzle—is less often considered. Historians who have taken the time to tally religious adherents in the colonies have not found the first Americans to have been particularly moved by Christian commitment. One need only look at the statistics of church membership to begin to imagine an alternate scenario. The image of colonists filling chapels before and during the fight for Independence may fit a contemporary narrative—that the United States was formed with the help of the divine. However, in most cases colonists were too busy and too spread out to gather very often for prayer.

Historians Roger Finke and Rodney Stark put the percentage of religious adherence among residents of the North American English colonies at just 17 percent. It doubled, from 1776 to 1850, to 34 percent. However, religious adherence did not grow in the ways that were expected. As Finke and Stark note, fifteen years before the Revolution, Ezra Stiles (the founder of Brown University and an early president of Yale) predicted that in one hundred years the theological descendants of the Puritans, the Congregationalists, would number seven million, while the adherents of newer Christian sects would be lucky to hold even. In fact, nearly the opposite turned out to be true: Members of the churches formerly established in the colonies left in droves for the new, experimental denominations. Stiles could take heart that no less a prescient thinker than Thomas Jefferson made a prediction that was even further off base: Near the end of his life, he suggested that the whole country would soon be Unitarian. Just 0.3 percent of Americans, three per thousand, are Unitarians today.

Imagining the English colonies as profoundly unreligious is of course contrary to the usual depiction of the nation's prehistory, and to the very idea of city upon a hill exceptionalism. The always popular notion that the United States is in "moral decline" (a phrase favored in the pulpits and the press of both the nineteenth and twentieth centuries) rests on the assumption that Americans used to be far more religious and should strive to return to their former fidelity. Yet the colonial church attendance rate of less than 20 percent puts the colonists much closer to trends in twenty-first-century France than to the highly churched population of the colonists' own descendants.

Patterns of colonial geographic dispersion provide some explanation of this. The picture of life in pre-Revolutionary America most often portrayed in popular history is one of public squares and town criers announcing royal decrees until the rebellious inhabitants of urban centers like Boston and Philadelphia rose up against them. The truth is that the English colonists who would declare independence lived far afield, for the most part. Ninety percent of the population could be found in rural areas.

Leaving aside the difficulty of actually getting to a meeting-house for worship, the colonists were a people who typically had work to do and wished to be left alone — both religiously and politically. This was equally true after the Revolution. As the French chronicler of the young nation Hector St. John de Crèvecoeur would write in 1782, religious indifference, not pious fervor, was to Europeans the characteristic most remarkable about this new species called Americans:

All sects are mixed as well as all nations; thus religious indifference is imperceptibly disseminated from one end of the continent to the other; which is at present one of the strongest characteristics of the Americans. Where this will reach no one can tell, perhaps it may leave a vacuum fit to receive other systems. Persecution, religious pride, the love of contradiction, are the food of what the world commonly calls religion. These motives have ceased here: zeal in Europe is confined; here it evaporates in the great distance it has to travel; there it is a grain of powder inclosed, here it burns away in the open air, and consumes without effect.

Even among the faithful, indifference to divisions was the norm. St. John de Crèvecoeur describes the quite modern-seeming experience of passing by a number of houses, knowing that in one lives a Lutheran, in another a Calvinist, in a third a Catholic. Each "works in his fields, embellishes the earth, clears swamps." The neighbors visit, talk of local things, but "what is it to their neighbours how and in what manner they think fit to address their prayers to the Supreme Being?" In time it may come to pass that the daughter of the Catholic might marry the son of one of the Protestants and the young couple may move far from their parents. "What religious education will they give their children?" St. John de Crèvecoeur asks. "A very imperfect one. If there happens to be in the neighbourhood any place of worship...rather than not shew their fine clothes, they will go to it."

Faiths rise and fall through proximity, the Frenchman implies, but in America there is no end to distance. Religion looked in colonial times not so different than it looks now: Some Americans were true believers, but many did not give it enough thought to care. Still others doubted the whole enterprise, especially where it overlapped with politics. Though they risked the kind of opprobrium the colonial press had long heaped upon unbelievers of all stripes—"the Free Thinker, the Deist, the Jew, and the Turk"—a few of them were brave or naïve enough to say so.

Into this last camp fell William Livingston. In 1752, he founded a weekly magazine in New York called the *Independent Reflector*, which in each issue offered a single essay "on Sundry Important Subjects More Particularly Adapted to the Province of New York." Often overlooked in histories of the conflict with England, in some ways it can be seen as lighting the fuse.

When the men usually credited with crafting religious freedom in America were still boys—Thomas Jefferson just beginning his Greek; James Madison still growing in his baby teeth—Livingston was fresh out of law school and ready to begin his professional life in New York. He had given up his dream of being a painter by then but still had something of a poet's soul. Even as he settled into the bustle of the city, he wrote unpublished verses about the lure of rural life.

His first printed words, however, belie his apparent wish to remain outside the fray. Even his earliest publication—an ill-advised satirical article about his employer's wife published while he was still a teenager—showed that writing was as likely to get him in trouble as it was to earn him a living or a reputation for wit.

After law school, Livingston had settled in New York to practice. There he fell in with two other young men, each a nominal Presbyterian like him. Together they founded the Society for the Promotion of Useful Knowledge and determined the best way to promote such knowledge was through the creation of what his nineteenth-century biographer called "the first periodical in the colonies...with no professed attachment to any political party, devoted to...a close and impartial scrutiny of the existing establishments, and pursuing its course without fear or favour." The goal of the three men was "exposure of official abuse, negligence, and corruption in whatever rank they were to be found."

The *Reflector*, Livingston and his cofounders declared, "is determined to proceed inawed and alike fearless of the humble scoundrel and the eminent villain. The cause he is engaged in is a glorious cause. 'Tis the cause of truth and liberty: what he intends to oppose is superstition, bigotry, priestcraft, tyranny, servitude, public mismanagement and dishonesty in office. The things he proposes to teach are the nature and the excellence of our constitution, the inestimable value of liberty, the disastrous effects of bigotry, the shame and horror of bondage, the importance of religion unpolluted and unadulterated with superstitious additions and inventions of priests."

When it was announced, in 1753, that a new college in the city of New York would be affiliated with and controlled by the Anglican Church, this triumvirate, as they would later be called, raised their voices against it. The colony of New York was already held in the sway of the established Anglican Church. To add a college to the church's quiver of authority would, the young men feared, create a religious monopoly, a "monster tyranny" that could spread until it threatened liberty of conscience in all the colonies.

In a clear act of provocation, Livingston attempted to publish a petition against the measure with a printer thought to be a supporter of the Anglican cause, who predictably declined to provide a platform to the opposition. Displaying a propagandist's talent for creating controversy, Livingston came out swinging. The *Independent Reflector* published an issue devoted to "The Use, Abuse, and Liberty of the Press," which took direct aim at the printer and his alleged support for the Church of England at the colony's expense.

A printer ought not publish every thing offered him; but what is conducive of General Utility he should not refuse, be the author a Christian, a Jew, a Turk, or Infidel. Such refusal is an immediate abridgement of the freedom of the press. When on the other hand he prostitutes his art by the publication of anything injurious to his country, it is criminal, it is high treason...

There followed a broadening of Livingston's offensive until it included not only the printer he accused of being a stooge for the Anglican establishment but the establishment itself — and by extension the monarchy that it represented. "In absolute monarchies a vindication of the natural rights of mankind is treason," he wrote. Thereafter, he published essay upon essay against the colony's dominant religious denomination. Titles included: "Primitive Christianity, short and intelligible — Modern Christianity, voluminous and incomprehensible," and "Absurdity of the Civil Magistrates interfering in Matters of Religion." As Livingston's nineteenth-century biographer put it: "The importance attached to this journal at the time may be judged from the violence of the opposition it excited. The editor was defamed in private society, and denounced from the pulpit. The mayor recommended the grand jury to present the work as a libel; the author was charged with profanity, irreligion, and sedition, and his printer, alternately menaced and cajoled by the enemies of the paper, yielded at length to their efforts and refused to continue it."

Among the attacks leveled in print against Livingston was a two-hundred-line poem parodying his intellectual pretensions:

> *Some think him a Tindal, some think him a Chubb,*
> *Some think him a Ranter, that spouts from his tub;*
> *Some think him a Newton, some think him a Locke,*
> *Some think him a Stone, some think him a Stock—*
> *But a Stock he at least may thank Nature for giving,*
> *And if he's a Stone, I pronounce it a Living.*

The range of opinion concerning Livingston's propositions can be gleaned from the fact that he is compared not only to the major voices of the Enlightenment—Matthew Tindal, Thomas Chubb, Isaac Newton, John Locke—but also to a stone and a stock animal. He responded to such challenges to his intelligence and religious commitments with an essay entitled "Of Creeds and Systems, together with the Author's Own Creed," a scathing rebuttal to critics who had called him an immoral atheist and worse. He never claimed for himself the mantle of atheist, but given the constraints of the time and the wallop the word then delivered, he did something perhaps even more remarkable: He laughed it off, going one better than his opponents by declaring himself fit for a heretic's pyre. He well knew that among his detractors some saw him as "an Atheist, others as a Deist, and a third sort as a Presbyterian." But he said, "My creed will show that none have exactly hit it." To illustrate his point he proposed to his readers to "cheerfully lay before you the articles of my faith."

"I believe the Scriptures of the Old and New Testament, without any foreign comments or human explanations but my own: for which I should doubtless be honoured with martyrdom, did I not live in a government which restrains that fiery zeal which would

reduce a man's body to ashes for the illumination of his understanding....I believe that the word orthodox, is a hard, equivocal,
priestly term, that has caused the effusion of more blood than all
the Roman Emperors put together....I believe that to defend the
Christian religion is one thing, and to knock a man on the head for
being of a different opinion is another thing....I believe that our
faith, like our stomachs, may be overcharged, especially if we are
prohibited to chew what we are commanded to swallow."

His thirty-nine articles of faith numbered fifty-six less than
Martin Luther's 95 Theses, but they were twice as funny—and no
less revolutionary. Both before the War for Independence and after,
Loyalists later identified the culprits they deemed most responsible
for beginning the rebellion: "the wicked triumvirate of New York"
in whose publication "the established Church was abused, Monarchy derided, Episcopacy reprobated, and republicanism held up, as
the best existing form of government." Livingston in particular was
hated, for he wrote "with a rancor, a malevolence, and an acrimony, not to be equaled," earning "the applause of the mob by
propagating the doctrine that all authority is derived from the
people."

Livingston lost this particular battle. The college he had fought
to keep nonsectarian—originally called King's College, it changed
its name to Columbia after the Revolution—remained officially
Anglican, but his rhetoric and the attention it received marked an
important turning point. The understanding that politics was a
manifestation of theology had been replaced by the secular conception that rights need not be given by God to be claimed by
women and men. "The right of self defence is not a donation of law
but a primitive right prior to all political institution, resulting from
the nature of man and inhering in the people till expressly alien-
ated and transferred," he wrote. "Nor is the defence of our lives and
properties in such cases an act of judgment or the object of law; it
is a privilege of nature, not an act of jurisdiction."

His prescience in these matters was observed by historian John
Mulder, who noted that Livingston, "viciously radical in his rhetoric," had formulated "the outlines of revolutionary ideology more
than two decades before the Revolution." While Livingston was
likely not an atheist in the way we currently understand the term,
his "atheism" can be understood along these lines. The meaning of
the word has changed significantly over time. Atheism, in fact, is

more situational than is commonly understood today. In the second century, for example, the followers of the upstart faith known as Christianity were considered atheists because they refused to acknowledge the Roman gods. In Livingston's day, it was a word that could be used as a bold protest against both worldly and religious authorities that seemed too certain of themselves. Across the centuries, the core of his beliefs cannot be known, but perhaps they matter less than his actions, which showed him to be more open than most to acknowledging the influence of religious ideas far outside those expected of a man in his position. He spoke for both spiritual and political nonconformists when he expressed his refusal to remain silent in the face of resistance from the forces of the dominant belief: "Clamour is at present our best policy," he said.

Not through one voice but many, not through harmony but cacophony, Independence would be won by raising a ruckus. Whether inspired by the genius and manners of the Mohawk, or by daring to make light of the loaded charge of godlessness, Livingston and other religious outliers showed how difference, not uniformity, would set the course the nation would take.

אונדזער דעמאָקראַטישע ירושה

דזשאָרדזש װאָשינגטאָן   טאָמאַס דזשעפֿערסאָן

Cover image from *Undzer demokratishe yerushe* (Our Democratic Inheritance), a 1954 pamphlet teaching American history to Yiddish-speaking immigrants. By the time of the pamphlet's publication, the language of Eastern European Jews had been in America for more than two hundred years. (From the collection of the Yiddish Book Center, Amherst, Massachusetts)

CHAPTER 9

The Yiddish Code

1776–1787

The American Revolution is rarely described as a war of religion, but in many ways that is just what it was. It was not fought in order to establish a Christian nation, as some partisan historians would have us believe. Nonetheless, the role of ministers of various Protestant churches in lending moral weight to the republican cause cannot be denied. Each denomination had something unique to its specific interests at stake in the war's outcome, yet the general sentiment of clergy who favored separation from England was later expressed by the Baptist preacher John Leland, in words emblazoned upon his famous gift of a twelve-hundred-pound block of cheese to Thomas Jefferson: "Rebellion to tyrants is obedience to God."

The power of framing liberty in such blatantly theological terms was not lost on those advocates of Independence with no personal affection for religion or its staunchest adherents. Even notorious freethinkers like Thomas Paine — who once declared, "my mind is my own church" — recognized the potential impact of religious rhetoric and frequently drafted it into service, willfully employing any piety that promised to hasten the coming of the Revolution. Paine was no fan of scripture. Of the Old Testament, he wrote: "with a few phrases excepted," it "deserves either our abhorrence or our contempt." Of the New: "Is it not a species of blasphemy to call the New Testament revealed religion when we see in it such contradictions and absurdities?" Still, when called upon to summon the devout to the cause of dissolving the union with England, he could thump the Bible as well as anyone. With his pamphlet *Common Sense,* he built a scriptural case against monarchy and even borrowed the sermon as a literary form. "A situation, similar to present, hath not happened since the days of Noah until now," he preached. "We have it in our power to begin the world over again. The birthday of the new world is at hand." Indeed, many of his contemporaries credited Paine and George Washington equally with American victory. Derided by Theodore Roosevelt as a "dirty little atheist," Tom Paine no less than John Leland provided an example of the ways in which religious imagery was central to Independence. Christian stories served as a "disinfectant," the scholar Mark Noll writes, that made republican ideas religiously palatable.

It was not only those making radical use of Christian terms who made the Revolution a war of religion, however. Though its flames were often stoked with words fit for the pulpit, as the war dragged on, it could not have been won without the support of a group of people living on the margins of the dominant faith. Those far outside the religious assumptions of any church played a crucial role in the cause, and often paid a higher price than those in the spiritual mainstream.

By the summer of 1776, the newly declared United States of America were cut off from the rest of the world by a naval blockade. Boasting more than a hundred warships while the six-month-old Continental navy had fewer than ten, the British planned to strangle the rebels' economy, reliant as it was on trade from Europe and beyond, while pummeling its ports with cannon fire. Anyone in the former colonies who hoped to undermine the Crown's floating firewall was forced either to hazard a watery grave by charging straight through in small, fast, blockade-running schooners, or to take the more stealthy tack of sending cargo or information across the ocean by way of a zigzagging route through the European-held islands of the West Indies. This, too, had its risks, but they were considered well worth taking when the shipment was important enough.

One such important shipment left Philadelphia in July of that year, not long after Thomas Jefferson, John Adams, Benjamin

Franklin, and other members of the Continental Congress had hashed out the document that formalized the former colonists' separation from England. With the ports of New York then bracing for some of the worst fighting of the war, the parcel likely traveled overland to the southern colonies. From there, it made its way to the Dutch island of St. Eustatius, where, a full two months after it had left Philadelphia, it was loaded aboard a vessel bound for Amsterdam.

St. Eustatius at the time was the free trade zone of the Americas. Every year, thousands of ships from all trading nations made their way in and out of its ports. The Dutch were as yet officially neutral in this domestic dispute between a mother country and one of her colonial children, but they would not be for long. Already Dutch merchants were secretly supplying arms to the Continental army, and so any cargo bound for the Netherlands could not pass through the British blockade without scrutiny. When the ship carrying the parcel from Philadelphia was stopped for inspection somewhere in the Atlantic in the fall of 1776, it was subjected to a searching eye. The Royal Navy impounded all suspicious cargo, including the parcel from Philadelphia.

The exact circumstances under which the British took possession of this packet of papers is not known, but if one of the Crown's naval officers opened it, he would have found several items that were cause for alarm.

The first was a copy of the Declaration of Independence, the original of which had been written in the same month and in the very city where this package had begun its journey. Fewer than two hundred copies had been made that summer, in the print shop of John Dunlap, and so it is tempting to suppose that this intercepted document could have been taken from that first printed batch, making it one of the famous Dunlap Broadsides, of which fewer than two dozen are known to exist today. Just as likely, however, it was simply the front page of the *Pennsylvania Evening Post*, printed two days after Dunlap's efforts late on the night of July 4, which made the full text of the Declaration available throughout Philadelphia within the week. In either case, the copy discovered in this suspect parcel was almost certainly the first anyone on board the Royal Navy ship had seen of it. The crew had likely been trawling the waters of the West Indies for the better part of a year; they had undoubtedly performed too many contraband inspections to count. Now suddenly there it was: a slip of paper containing the bothersome ideas at the root of all this trouble.

Turning to the other documents, the British officer would have seen a bank draft that could be exchanged for cash in Amsterdam. This was not terribly unusual; despite the war, economic ties across the ocean inevitably found a way to endure. Nor was the amount anything to worry about—ten pounds sterling would likely not make much difference to the rebel cause.

Another item, however, was far more curious. Headed with the place and date of its composition—Philadelphia, July 28, 1776— and inked in the fine quill-lines of the day, the page's several paragraphs gave it the form of a personal letter. Its script, however, was indecipherable beyond the date at the top of the text. Filled with curls and slashes cutting backwards across the page, it might as well have been written in hieroglyphs or some language of the gods. The only clear thing about it was that it was composed in the same month and in the same city as the Declaration; how could it not be related? Perhaps it could have even been written by the same hand, making it an addendum to treason no matter what it said.

Taken together with the statement of the colonists' dissolution of their ties with the king and the bank draft for Dutch funds, the letter was assumed by the British to be some kind of cryptogram, a message of sufficient significance to the colonists' war effort to warrant transmission in a secret code.

This was in many ways a logical conclusion to be drawn from the discovery of such an incendiary document along with an unreadable missive. The year before, the Continental Congress had created a Committee of Secret Correspondence, charged not only with creating and maintaining alliances overseas but also with finding ever more innovative ways of keeping international messages and other communications out of British hands. The committee resorted to methods ranging from invisible inks to a mathematically complex substitution code that remained unbroken throughout the war. The invention of a new system of writing would not have been outside the committee's purview.

All three documents—the Declaration, the bank draft, and the enigmatic letter—were rerouted to England, where sharper minds might find a way to crack the cipher and perhaps foil a cunning revolutionary scheme.

*　　*　　*

Three months earlier, a forty-year-old merchant, Jonas Phillips, sat down in his Philadelphia mercantile shop to compose a letter to a relation and commercial associate, Gumpel Samson, in Amsterdam. After writing the date and the name of his recently adopted city in English at the top of the page, he switched languages for the body of the letter, marking it as a communiqué between two men with more important things in common than name or nation, and shielding its meaning from anyone outside the bond they shared. Contrary to the suspicions of the Royal Naval officer who would later confiscate this letter, he did not employ an encoded communication system. Instead, he simply used his first language: Yiddish, the thousand-year-old tongue of Eastern European Jews. Phillips's letter could have been read easily by hundreds of thousands on the other side of the ocean, as well as by a fair number of the roughly 2,000 Jews then living in the former English colonies.

Phillips's shop on Market Street, midway between Front and Second streets, with a view from its entrance of the Delaware River, was just four doors down from Dunlap's print shop. It was well known by the end of July 1776 that the printer had stayed up all night inking two hundred copies of the freshly penned Declaration for distribution throughout the colonies. Unlike Dunlap, the man now composing a letter at his shop counter was no revolutionary— not yet, anyway. Phillips's primary purpose in writing to his kinsman was to inquire about the welfare of his mother. Yet he had other business to attend to as well.

Born in Germany, Phillips had also lived in Holland, England, and New York but was now among the refugees transforming Philadelphia. Comprised of about 200 families, the city's Jewish community was small by European standards. Jews had begun to flee New York and Charles Town (as Charleston, South Carolina, was then known), port cities that seemed likely to fall under British control. Phillips traded in beaver pelts and fine fabrics and had worked as the *shoykhet*—the kosher butcher—for his synagogue. He was regarded as an important man, both ceremonially and financially, by all in his tight-knit community.

When he arrived in the colonies in 1756 he had owned nothing—not even his own time. He had entered South Carolina as the indentured servant of an indigo merchant, a man by the name of Moses Lindo, who was one of the earliest Jewish success stories on the continent. Lindo had brought Phillips along with him from London, where he had built a prominent indigo trading firm on Wormwood Street in the city's financial district, and had established a fortune that would make him well known during his lifetime on both sides of the Atlantic.

Before his departure from England, Lindo had announced his intention to relocate his center of business operations by publishing his assessment of the product he hoped soon to ship throughout Europe. "I have examined the major Part of the Carolina Indico entered this year," he wrote, in a letter published in the *South Carolina Gazette* in 1756, "and have the Pleasure to find a considerable Quantity equal to the BEST French." In the letter, he went on to establish his bona fides in the trade by providing directions on how most effectively to treat "indico" to remove any impurities. Three months later, he had arrived in the colonies "with an Intent to purchase Indico of the Growth and Manufacture of this Province, and to remit the same to his Constituents in London, classed, sorted and packed in a Manner proper for the foreign market." He was determined to corner the market, prepared to "employ the Sum of One Hundred and Twenty Thousand Pounds Currency" in order to set himself apart from all competition.

Lindo and Phillips's emigration came at a time when there were plentiful reasons for a Jew to abandon his own country for the unknown. For the better part of two decades before their departure, the place of Jews in England had been uncertain, seeming to improve with tolerant-seeming Acts of Parliament, only to be violently set back by latent anti-Jewish sentiment that flared up at the slightest provocation. The year Lindo and Phillips set sail, 1756, was ironically the centenary of Oliver Cromwell's readmittance of Jews to the kingdom, the end of a three-hundred-year ban on their ability to openly live, do business, and practice their faith. Since then, native Jewish Britons had secured some rights — as Lindo's success attests — but Jews not born in England still were not permitted to hold elected office or work in the government unless they were willing to convert, receive the sacraments, and swear a Christian oath. Originally envisioned as a defense against lingering Catholic elements in the kingdom, the so-called Sacrament Test required immigrants to receive the sacrament of communion in an Anglican Church in order to be naturalized, and thus caught Jews in its net as well.

In 1740, a pathway toward Jewish naturalization was opened through the Plantation Act, which allowed Jews who were willing to live in the American colonies for seven years or more the opportunity to become full British subjects with equal rights. Given that the one precondition of their taking advantage of this act was that they leave England, it should come as no surprise that it was not passed in the spirit of toleration or civil rights. Rather, it was an economic decision on the part of the Parliament.

England had until then watched jealously as the possessions of the Netherlands in the New World had prospered on a scale well beyond that of the British territories. One key to the success of these ventures, it was supposed, was the role of Dutch Jewish merchants, who enjoyed far greater freedoms of movement and property ownership than England's Jews either at home or abroad. A particular example of this Dutch success was the tiny island of St. Eustatius, where Jews had been granted full equality in 1730 and which by then, in no small part thanks to the efforts of its non-Christian inhabitants, was among the busiest and most prosperous trading posts in the Americas.

The success of St. Eustatius was something England wanted desperately to emulate, and even those who harbored anti-Semitic prejudices believed it would be for the good of the empire to seed British colonies with Jewish brokers, merchants, and other businessmen. Doing so, in the belief of the members of Parliament who had passed the Plantation Act, would allow England to benefit from established networks of Jewish commerce. As London's Member of Parliament Sir John Barnard later argued during debates regarding the naturalization of Jews, it would be a good thing to exploit connections that would endure with or without official sanction, because the Jewish people "are dispersed over the whole world, and keep up correspondence with one another."

Much of the act's support undoubtedly was based on anti-Semitic stereotypes about Jewish prowess with money, but some of the rhetoric — Jewish dispersal throughout the world; the persistence of Jewish alliances that endured despite the changing fates of the nations around them — was true. Down through the centuries of repressive laws in every kingdom in which they had lived, Jews had found a way to survive, and some had even managed to prosper. That they had done so undoubtedly had something to do with their tendency to "keep up correspondence with one another."

When the Plantation Act succeeded in convincing Jews to relocate in order to secure their rights, some in Parliament proposed that a similar path to naturalization might be opened to Jews who remained in England. The Law of Naturalization of 1753, which, like Maryland's similar law of 1826, was popularly known as "the Jew Bill," granted immigrant Jews the right to become full subjects of the Crown without renouncing their faith.

A man like Moses Lindo, who never seems to have considered conversion for reasons either practical or spiritual, would likely have been pleased to see these religious tests end, and this was precisely the point. The law was passed in part to keep wealthy merchants and their money in the British territories. However, when the popular outcry against the new law brought a fresh wave of anti-Semitism to Britain's shores — its passage was met, in the words of one historian, with "horror and execration" — the act was quickly repealed.

It was in the wake of this failed attempt to expand the rights of Jewish immigrants to England that Lindo and Phillips left London. The British-born Lindo had rights in his native country, but, faced with such a high-profile aborted effort at increased toleration, he likely began to wonder if he might have more opportunity to build his business and his reputation abroad. From the moment of his arrival in Charles Town, Lindo established an empire of commerce that spanned the ocean, creating new contacts throughout the colonies while exploiting his existing relationships with the tightly knit Jewish merchant classes of England and Holland. The governor of South Carolina soon named him inspector general of all indigo trade in the province.

For Jonas Phillips, the potential benefits of emigration were even greater. Because he had been born in Germany, in London he was sentenced essentially to statelessness. He lacked the rights to own property, establish a business, or participate in government. Thanks to the Plantation Act, however, he could secure rights equal to any British subject by accompanying Lindo to America and remaining for seven years. For a Jew in his position, even the ostensibly nonreligious choice to become an indentured servant for the purposes of emigration had a spiritual dimension. Given English law at the time, he would have had more far more latitude if he had chosen to submit himself to the Sacrament Test. The very act of emigration, then, represented a religious choice—a choice to remain a Jew rather than embrace the beliefs of the majority.

As soon as he earned his freedom from his indenture, Phillips followed in his former employer's footsteps. Like Lindo, he made no secret of his religious affiliation or of his ambitions. He established himself first as a merchant in Albany, where he filled local papers with advertisements that drew attention to the international variety of his wares. He seems to have sold everything he could get his hands on: clothing and blankets, beads and ribbons, china cups and saucers, brass and copper kettles, shoes from England and wine from France and Spain, as well as oranges, coffee, and rum from the tropics. "All city and country gentlemen, storekeepers and others, that please to favor him with their custom," he noted in one advertisement, "may depend on being well served, and on as easy terms as possible, for ready money only." Perhaps coming to terms with life near the northern frontier, he gradually became less strict about his terms of payment, soon accepting "Beaver and Deerskins, Smal fur at New York Market price" in addition to cash and credit.

After a brief setback following the French and Indian War, by the mid-1770s Phillips was again doing well enough that he was able to move south. Settling in New York City, he expanded his business and soon offered for sale real estate, Indian wampum, a horse and carriage, and, on at least one occasion, "a young negro wench of good character." As his fortunes rose, he courted the daughter of a prominent family of Portuguese Jews. At the time, the Sephardim, the Jews of southern Europe, were considered a higher class than those from Ashkenaz, as Phillips was. Crossing this cultural line, he married up, as they say. Over the course of a long marriage, his wife gave birth to twenty-one children. If Phillips had come to America with thoughts of simply putting in his seven years and returning to England with full rights, he showed no desire to leave now.

Nor did he forget where he had come from. He, too, made sure to "keep up correspondence" both with business associates from the old country and with family he had left behind. In May of 1775, for example, he had written to Gumpel Samson and asked him to deliver money to his mother. When he heard no reply, he waited long enough so that he would not seem ungrateful or impatient, and then he wrote again, choosing to write in Yiddish just in case his letter should fall before non-Jewish eyes. The letter later seized by the Royal Navy begins with the kind of overflowing sentiment that naturally precedes the asking of a favor.

"Peace to my beloved master, my kinsman, the eminent and wealthy, wise and discerning God-fearing man, whose honored, glorious name is Mr. Gumpel," Phillips wrote. "May his Rock and Redeemer protect him and all his family! Peace!"

As this missive would be sent by means not before employed between them, Phillips then explained the letter's delay and the roundabout route it took reaching its destination. "As it is not always possible to send a letter to England on account of the war in America, I must therefore write by way of St. Eustatius."

This would likely not have surprised Gumpel Samson. Like Philadelphia, St. Eustatius had by this time become an important coordinate in the Jewish geography of the New World. Despite its size, it was home to a Jewish community nearly equal to that of Philadelphia before the war, which crucially served as regular intermediaries between America and Europe now that the English colonies were hidden behind the sailcloth curtain of the British blockade. Phillips had become acquainted with the Dutch Jews of the West Indies — again through "keeping up correspondence" — after his congregation in New York had taken up the cause of supporting the St. Eustatius synagogue when it needed help rebuilding after a hurricane.

Despite the formality of the letter's greeting, Phillips and Samson seem to have enjoyed an easy way with each other, a familial willingness to speak honestly across the expanse of the sea.

"I have not yet had any answer to a letter of May, 1775, when I sent my master a bill of exchange for ten pounds sterling for my mother," Phillips wrote. "Should that letter not have arrived, then the enclosed third bill of exchange will obtain the money, and please send it to my mother, long life to her."

As he wrote, Phillips apparently considered the options open to him if the bank draft sent previously had already cleared with the money changers. It would be a waste of time and effort to ship these funds back across the ocean, especially in the roundabout way that he had been required to use. No, there was a more practical purpose to which this money might be put, though it was not without risk.

"Should the funds have already been obtained," he wrote, "you need not return the bill of exchange again." Instead, he added, "a hint to the wise will suffice" and then proposed that those same funds might be used to buy merchandise with which the two of them might run the British blockade. "As no English goods can come over at all, and much money can be earned with Holland goods if one is willing to take a chance, should you have a friend who will this winter acquaint himself with the goods mentioned below, I can assure you that four hundred per cent is to be earned thereby."

"I could write my meaning better in English than Yiddish," Phillips added, but his meaning was plain enough: There was always money to be made during a war—just as there was money to be lost. Despite the naval blockade that would soon find this letter confiscated, Phillips had no doubt who held the upper hand in the ongoing struggle. "The war will make all England bankrupt," he wrote. "The Americans have an army of 100,000 and the English only 25,000 and some ships. The Americans have already made themselves like the States of Holland"—that is, a republic. "The enclosed is the Declaration of the whole country. How it will end, the blessed God knows. The war does me no damage, thank God!"

The war was to Phillips, at the time, merely something to be endured. The Jewish people would persevere, as they always had, under whichever regime emerged victorious. This was not the statement of political indifference it might seem; rather, it was an acknowledgment, shared with one who would understand precisely what he meant, that he would be an outsider no matter who was in charge. The best they could do for now was attend to the needs of family.

"I would like to send you a bill of exchange, but it is not possible for me to get it. If my master, long life to him, will disburse for me one hundred gulden to my mother, I can assure you that just as soon as a bill of exchange on St. Eustatia can be had, I will, with thanks, honestly pay you. I have it, thank God, in my power, and I know that my mother, long life to her, needs it very much; and I beg of my master, long life to him, to write me at once an answer, addressed as herein written."

With this business attended to, Phillips ended his note with the usual niceties. "There is no further news," he wrote, "My wife and children, long life to her and them, together send you many greetings and wish you good health up to one hundred years."

When he finished his letter, he sent it to his contacts in St. Eustatius, where it was received by a young New Yorker named Samuel Curson, who forwarded the parcel containing the letter, bank draft, and the Declaration of Independence on toward its interception at sea.

On the face of it, Phillips's letter does not seem to have much to do with the success or failure of the war effort. Indeed, at the time he wrote it, he undoubtedly was more interested in his own enrichment than in the fortunes of the patriots. Yet shortly after sending this letter, Phillips seems to have had a change of heart. By 1778, he was serving in the 7th Company of the Philadelphia Militia as a middle-aged private under Captain John Linton and Colonel William Bradford. As such, he had joined the approximately one hundred Jews known to have fought in uniform against the British, as well as the vast majority of the two thousand Jews in the English colonies who supported the rebellion. For a period of two years after joining the ranks, his regular advertisements in the newspapers of Philadelphia fell away—an indication, perhaps, that he had matters other than commerce on his mind.

Phillips's letter, then, captures an intriguing moment in which a man harboring revolutionary sympathies—he had refused to stay in British-controlled New York, after all—had perhaps not yet fully committed to the cause. This temporary ambivalence aside, however, the network represented by this instance of a single Jewish merchant's efforts to "keep up correspondence" was already essential to the fight for Independence at the time he mailed the Declaration to his Dutch kinsman. Moreover, the letter provides a key to understanding the most significant role played by Jews in the war. The letter itself might be considered as a map of sorts, plotting a triangle of coordinates that shared the distinction of being home to three Jewish communities, without which American Independence may not have been achieved. The place the letter was written (Philadelphia), the place it was sent (Amsterdam), and the intermediary between the two (St. Eustatius)—each had a unique role to play in the war effort, yet they were all bound together by precisely the kind of Jewish network of commerce, communication, and family ties that the British Parliament had earlier hoped to exploit for the benefit of the empire.

Philadelphia at the time served as the center of operations to small-time Jewish businessmen like Phillips who attempted to circumvent British control, as well as to major brokers and sustainers of the war effort, who sought not merely to dodge the Crown's reach but to dismantle it. Often referred to as the financier of the Revolution, the Polish Jew Haym Solomon had been in America less than a decade when war broke out, and yet he quickly became one of the most significant benefactors of the newborn nation and many of its founding fathers, who acknowledged that they could not have persevered without Solomon's help. After he, like Phillips, had fled to Philadelphia during New York's British occupation, Solomon kept an office on Front Street, just around the corner from Phillips's shop. James Madison wrote abashedly of his frequent loans from Solomon: "The kindness of our little friend in Front Street, near the coffee house, is a fund that will preserve me from extremities; but I never resort to it without great mortification, as he obstinately rejects all recompense." Solomon was so obstinate in this rejection, apparently, that he died penniless, owed as much as $600,000 by the nation he helped birth.

Another Philadelphia Jew, meanwhile, was among the most skillful and effective blockade runners on the continent. Isaac Moses owned nearly a dozen brigs and schooners that ran regular routes from the American mainland to St. Eustatius and on to the Netherlands. Across the ocean, meanwhile, Moses's business partners in Amsterdam kept a steady stream of supplies flowing west to a war in which their nation of residence had no official stake. Moses sent flour, furs, lumber, and indigo to Amsterdam by way of St. Eustatius, and in return his partners sent munitions, rifles, blankets, and heavy cloth cloaks for use by the Continental army. Like Solomon, he also contributed to the finances of the war. The American branch of Isaac Moses & Company provided the Continental Congress with the funds it needed to fight the British in Canada, while the Dutch branch of Moses's company served as the clandestine shipping agents between Philadelphia and Amsterdam when John Adams was in the Netherlands negotiating the loan that would save his young nation from bankruptcy.

The role the merchants of St. Eustatius played was not limited to forwarding Yiddish correspondence between merchants. As the war progressed, the island became the bridge between the Americans and their European allies. Money, gunpowder, weapons, even blankets and cloth for uniforms—all of it filtered through St. Eustatius. The sympathies of those on the island were plain enough. If the British did not yet know the name of Phillips's agent in St. Eustatius before they seized his letter, they would have found it out soon enough. The agent's name, Samuel Curson, also appears throughout the correspondence of the Continental Congress, which frequently instructed him to make ever larger supplies of munitions and other necessities of war to the American cause. "We have therefore to desire you will instantly Give orders to your House in St. Eustatia to provide Fifty Tons of [gun] powder," they wrote Curson on one occasion. Also on order were "Coarse woollens, Sufficient for Five thousand pair of Overalls for the Soldiers without delay."

That St. Eustatius was more than just a neutral center of trade became clear to the British two months after they seized Phillips's letter. It was then, on November 16, 1776, that the governor of this tiny Dutch island gave instructions that ships flying the American flag should be given the international salute reserved for sovereign nations by firing its cannons in recognition.

The British would not forget this slight; nor would they forgive the role the island's Jewish community specifically had played in helping the Americans wage war on their king. When England at last had proof of Dutch involvement in the war, and declared war on the Netherlands in 1780, the British navy converged in force on St. Eustatius. Led by Admiral George Rodney, fifteen ships and a ground force of three thousand arrived—"as sudden as a clap of thunder," the admiral said—before the inhabitants of the island even knew their mother country was at war. The island's defenses included a garrison of fifty men and only a handful of ships equipped with guns. The governor of the island surrendered unconditionally.

While the victory may have been quick, the plundering of the island promised to be a more involved affair. The order was given that there was to be "a general confiscation of all the property found upon the island, public and private, Dutch and British; without discrimination, without regard to friend or foe, to the subjects of neutral powers, or to the subjects of our own state; the wealth of the opulent, the goods of the merchant, the utensils of the artisan, the necessaries of the poor." This included not only the pitiful showing of gunboats but the dozens of ships loaded with cargo that had been in port when the Royal Navy arrived. Suspecting there was still more to be gained, Rodney did not raise the Union Jack over his conquest but let the Dutch flag stay in place, inviting further merchant ships — from France, Spain, America, and the Netherlands itself — into the harbor, where they were all seized as the spoils of war.

"The riches of St. Eustatius are beyond all comprehension," the admiral wrote. "There were one hundred and thirty sail of ships in the road. All the magazines and store-houses are filled, and even the beach covered with tobacco and sugar. Upwards of fifty American vessels, loaded with tobacco, have been taken since the capture of this island. There never was a more important stroke made against any state whatever." Another witness hailed the island as "a vast magazine of military stores of all kinds" and noted that more than two thousand Americans had been captured.

And it was not just the Americans who would feel the sting of this defeat. Still in Amsterdam hoping to secure Dutch funds, John Adams noted the response to the capture of St. Eustatius in the Netherlands, where the loss of their great New World emporium meant financial ruin for many and surely made Adams's own task more difficult. As he wrote to the United States' first Secretary of Foreign Affairs, Robert Livingston (William's second cousin), "You can have no idea, sir, no man who was not upon the spot can have any idea, of the gloom and terror that was spread by this event." The damage done to the powerful Dutch merchant class was so great, he reported, that some had "expectations of popular insurrections." Should such uprisings come about, he noted wryly, the doomsayers "did Mr. Adams the honor to mention him as one that was to be hanged by the mob in such company."

Having shaken both Amsterdam and America, Admiral Rodney was feeling justifiably pleased with himself. "What blockheads have the Dutch been to quarrel with the only power that could destroy them," he wrote. Had he had a larger army with him, he mused, he might have won the whole war himself. His superior,

British Lord of the Admiralty John Montagu, was similarly impressed: "Upon every dispatch we receive from you, a new panegyric is necessary as you give us no opportunity of writing but to convey applause." All of England, in fact, celebrated Rodney's conquest as a tide-turning event in a long and costly war.

As grand a victory as this was for the British, however, it did not quite remove the sting caused by the new awareness that St. Eustatius had been secretly a vital part of the war effort for years, making a mockery of the English blockade. Admiral Rodney seems to have taken this fact personally. The entire island, he said, was "a nest of villains; they deserve scourging, and they shall be scourged....They ought to have known that the just vengeance of an injured empire, though slow, is sure."

Because of the role St. Eustatius had played in inspiring British plans to seed its own colonies with Jewish merchants, it was the island's Jews who bore the brunt of Rodney's ire now. "Commerce, commerce alone, has supported them in their rebellion," he wrote of the Americans, and his actions following the taking of the island show that he held Jewish merchants responsible for the commercial activities that had sustained the war. In a scene that revisits the Inquisitions of the past and foreshadows the worst horrors of the future, Rodney ordered all Jewish men on the island to assemble, then placed them under guard in the weighing house. Numbering more than one hundred, all of them had been taken without notice from their wives and children. They were beaten and stripped, their clothes torn to tatters in front of them as Rodney's men checked the linings of their jackets for hidden cash.

Thirty Jews were deported from the island that day; the rest were imprisoned until sales of their homes and possessions could be arranged. Their crime was simply serving as intermediaries between their landsmen in America and landsmen in Europe. Having forwarded money, munitions, and Yiddish letters across the sea in a time of war, they were guilty of putting the merchants' networks the British once hoped to exploit—the Jewish tendency to "keep up correspondence"—in the service of liberty.

After the war, the Jews of Philadelphia—Jonas Phillips among them—were well aware of the possibility that the laws of England that had made them less than full subjects might be replicated in the new nation. Just as Phillips had written in the wake of the Declaration, he wrote another letter during the debates on the Constitution in 1787. Spurred on by the concern that the United States would institute "sacramental tests" of its own, he sent this missive not to family across the ocean but to the Constitutional Convention then meeting in his city.

Identifying himself as "one of the people called Jews of the City of Philadelphia, a people scattered and despersed among all nations," Phillips voiced concern that among the provisions of the Constitution of Pennsylvania there was a clause requiring all to "acknowledge the scriptures of the old and New testement to be given by a devine inspiration" in order to hold public office. "To swear and believe that the New Testement was given by devine inspiration is absolutly against the religious principle of a Jew," he wrote, "and [it] is against his Conscience to take any such oath." Furthermore, he added, not only was this against his own conscience, it was contrary to the state's own Bill of Rights, which he quoted at length:

That all men have a natural and unalienable Right To worship almighty God according to the dectates of their own Conscience and understanding, and that no man aught or of Right can be Compelled to attend any Relegious Worship or Erect or support any place of worship or Maintain any minister contrary to or against his own free will and Consent.

It is well known among all the Citizens of the 13 united States that the Jews have been true and faithful, and during the late Contest with England they have been foremost in aiding and assisting the States with their lifes and fortunes, they have supported the Cause, have bravely faught and bleed for liberty which they Can not Enjoy.

Therefore if the honourable Convention shall in ther Wisdom think fit and alter the said oath and leave out the words 'and I do acknoweledge the scripture of the new testement to be given by devine inspiration' then the Israeletes will think them self happy to live under a government where all Relegious societys are on an Eaquel footing. I solecet this favour for my self my Childreen and posterity and for the benefit of all the Isrealetes through the 13 united States of America.

This time, of course, Phillips had written in English, not Yiddish. Yet something of the spirit of his earlier missive remained. When British naval officers seized his letter in 1776, they had taken one look at it and declared it must have a secret meaning. They were perhaps more correct than they could have known. Rather than military plans or espionage, however, hidden between the lines of both of Phillips's letters was an affirmation that those on the margins of dominant faith create bonds that transcend borders — bonds strong enough to hold a nation together, or to help one people break free of another.

Capture and burning of Washington by the British, in 1814. Illustration from *Our First Century,* by Richard Miller Devens. Springfield, MA: C.A. Nichols & Co., 1876. (Library of Congress)

CHAPTER 10

Twenty Gods or None

1814

Two weeks before a pair of Baltimore teenagers put a volley of buckshot in his chest, the British Major General Robert Ross set the capital of a young nation on fire—and inadvertently sparked a heated public debate about the influence of unpopular religious ideas in American life.

Deep in the second year of the War of 1812, General Ross led British troops through Virginia and into Maryland, with a momentous stop along the way in Washington, which was still then under construction as the first city of the nation. General Ross, a man of near fifty who was often perceived as somewhat younger (the American press figured him to be about thirty-five), was a veteran of the Napoleonic Wars, but he was new to commanding forces larger than a regiment. By all accounts, he performed beyond expectations, earning the respect even of his battlefield adversaries. His junior officers thought him at times rash, but as the scion of a military family and a former aide-de-camp to the king, he valued professionalism in his soldiers, and he kept his troops impeccably in order.

It was no doubt thanks to his usual sense of discipline that, despite being vastly outnumbered, he and his men were poised to overwhelm the Americans during their campaign along the Potomac. But on August 24, 1814, Ross's horse was shot out from under him—by a barber turned sniper, or so the war story goes—and the general, in a rare flash of rage, began ordering his men to set buildings afire. After his mount fell, Ross instantly burned to the ground the house where the barber was hiding, and then marched on as the ashes of the structure flecked the sky like hair clippings in the wind. If those ashes blew with particular force that day, it was because a reported "tremendous and unusual" hurricane made itself known as the British advanced, soon bringing driving rain and raising gusts that made it appear to one local witness that both "nature and man seemed to mark our city for destruction."

Yet the damp and darkening skies did not stop Ross from following the same fiery protocol throughout Washington. In short order he put flames to the President's House, the Treasury, and the Capitol, attacking all as if with a renewed awareness that war was fought over symbols as much as borders or shipping channels. To rob a general of his horse, to reduce him to standing in the mud like a common rifleman (he was known to harbor a special antipathy for the ragtag militias of this rebellious land), was to beg a symbolic counterattack. He chose his targets carefully, and made certain any British soldiers caught plundering private buildings during the mayhem would receive the lash. Adding self-inflicted insult to injury, Americans alone looted the burning city that day.

Torrential rain continued to fall while the disciplined English completed their arson, allowing the shells of the homes of both the executive and legislative branches to remain standing. The downpour, however, did not save the interior of the Capitol, which was gutted by a blaze fueled by the ready supply of paper within its sandstone walls. Already, governance in a nation little older than the soldiers defending it had proved to be a matter of record-keeping and research, and it was for the latter that the unfortunately combustible Congressional Library had been founded twelve years before. First proposed with the understanding that lawmakers might frequently need to reference books of law and statecraft, the collection consisted largely of legal texts and parliamentary proceedings. By the time General Ross marched into town, the library included some three thousand volumes, all of which were lost to his torch.

From Washington, Ross rode on into Maryland, where the following month he would be part of another attack rife with symbolism, though this time he found himself on the losing end. The same week that a young lawyer and amateur poet named Francis Scott Key saw "the rockets' red glare" and "bombs bursting in air" over the Chesapeake Bay, two American militiamen, little more than boys, put an end to his campaign. Concealed in woods along the road to Baltimore, they fired on a man commanding his troops from high atop a "magnificent black horse," a replacement for the one whose loss had set Washington on fire. This time the horse survived, but the rider did not. His body was shipped to the English ground of Halifax for burial, crudely preserved in a hogshead of rum.

It was a fitting turning point in the struggle between an empire and its youthful antagonist. Perhaps all wars are battles of symbols, but this one was particularly so. For the British it was a fight to redress the injury it had endured a generation prior, when the offspring had cut itself off from its motherland, as well as more recent slights, including the former colonies' impudent forays into British Canada, which likewise had seen its governmental buildings burn. For the Americans, meanwhile, in addition to the disputes over trade and borders that had precipitated the conflict, the War of 1812 was a battle over what sort of nation they would be.

During the drumbeat leading to open hostilities, the religious tenor of appeals for and against war was unmistakable. "Such a war God considers as his own cause," the Massachusetts pastor John H. Stevens wrote, "and to help in such a cause is to come to the help of the Lord." In Stevens's view, the Revolution had freed Americans from England as Israel had been freed from Egypt, and the most important liberty that had been gained was the "free enjoyment" of religion. For him, the continued English presence to the north, as well as the English threats to American sovereignty on the Atlantic and in the frontier, remained a threat to the free exercise of faith that had been so dearly won.

Anti-war preachers made exactly the opposite case. This war was not for God, they said, but against all that was holy. In a sermon immediately after President James Madison's declaration of war, the Massachusetts Congregational minister David Osgood pointedly chose as his preaching text 2 Chronicles 13:12: "O children of Israel, fight not against the Lord God of your fathers; for ye shall not prosper." In case this "ye shall not prosper" left too much to the imagination, Reverend Osgood's sermon then became achingly specific.

"At this moment," he preached, "your minds are harassed and your bosoms tortured with the idea of your sons, your husbands, your brothers reluctantly torn from all the scenes and occupations of peace, from all their domestic connexions, enjoyments and pursuits, to be exposed in the tented field, subjected to the rigors of a military life, liable to the numerous and fatal diseases of a camp, and occasionally, to stand as so many marks for the sharp shooters in the hostile army." Driving his point home, he then expressed the fears of his congregants in stark, nearly apocalyptic terms:

> You anticipate the tingling of your ears at the tidings of one, and another, and another of these your beloved friends and relatives fallen in battle, mangled with wounds, groaning and expiring on the crimsoned field, or lodged in military hospitals, there to linger in torment for a little space, till nature be exhausted, and they give up the ghost. Your bowels sound with pain and yearning at the expected accounts of garments rolled in blood, and the extensive carnage spread by contending enemies.

The "very nature" of this war, Osgood concluded, "is violence against the lives and properties of our fellow-beings, our brethren, the children of our common progenitor on earth and common Father in heaven." In a stinging rebuke of the pro-war preachers with whom he was competing for the hearts and minds of the faithful, he asked, "What Christian, under the influence of Christian principles, can dare pray for success?"

As distinct as such religious principles were, they all in fact were trying to answer some basic questions inevitable in the second generation of a new republic: What ideals should the nation embody? What were the contents of its soul?

One answer came from an unexpected source—the Olympian hilltop of Monticello—while General Ross was still floating away in his barrel of Jamaican spirits.

In early September 1814, the aging statesman Thomas Jefferson read in a Richmond newspaper of the destruction recently wrought by the British in Washington. Just a hundred miles to the north, a city reduced to ash and blackened with soot could not have seemed farther away from his busy and bucolic retreat outside of Charlottesville. A lifelong bibliophile, the former president—now five years out of office—was particularly struck by the loss of the Congressional Library. Fully aware that the contents of the nation's soul might be judged by the holdings of its bookshelves, he had in fact been the instigator of the original library, outlining its purpose twelve years earlier in a letter to Georgia senator Abraham Baldwin. Attaching a catalogue of every book he thought appropriate for legislative use, he had stressed the need for volumes on "the laws of nature and nations...because this is a branch of science often under discussion in Congress."

At the time, he had favored the idea of a library limited to reference works, for he imagined that any gentleman who might find himself in Congress would already possess the classics of literature and philosophy in his own personal library. Yet in the aftermath of the congressional collection's destruction, and perhaps with a sense that the cultural assumptions of his generation might not be those of the next, he now envisioned something grander. The Library of Congress, rather than the limited collection it had been, should instead be universal, filled with a world's worth of ideas, as his own personal library was — indeed, as his own life had been. And so from his redoubt untouched by the flames of Washington, surrounded by the greatest private collection of literature on this side of the Atlantic, Jefferson resolved to undo at least one part of the destruction wrought by General Ross.

Wasting no time once his decision had been made, Jefferson sent a three-part missive to an acquaintance in the capital city: Samuel Smith, a newspaperman likely to know who was in charge of the Library Committee in Congress. The first part of this correspondence was a casual cover sheet, a warm appeal to the friendship the two men shared and an apology in advance for any trouble he might cause him through his unusual request. The second part was a book catalogue, and the third was a longer letter he hoped Smith would share with Congress.

"I learn from the newspapers that the Vandalism of our enemy has triumphed at Washington over science as well as the arts by the destruction of the public library with the noble edifice in which it was deposited," Jefferson wrote. "I presume it will be among the early objects of Congress to recommence their collection. This will be difficult while the war continues, and intercourse with Europe is attended with so much risk."

The bulk of the original collection, Jefferson knew, had been purchased from the very people who had just reduced it to ashes. As busy as American printers were, they still could not match the output or the backlists of publishers in England or on the European mainland. Jefferson, too, had acquired most of his own collection while abroad, and was justifiably proud of the result.

"You know my collection, its condition and extent," he wrote. "I have been fifty years making it, and have spared no pains, opportunity, or expense, to make it what it is. While residing in Paris, I devoted every afternoon I was disengaged, for a summer or two, in examining all the principal book-stores, turning over every book with my own hand, and putting by everything which related to America, and indeed whatever was rare and valuable in every science."

Allowing himself a boast because it happened to be true, he added, "Such a collection was made as probably can never again be effected, because it is hardly probable that the same opportunities, the same time, industry, perseverance and expense, with some knowledge of the bibliography of the subject, would again happen to be in concurrence." Jefferson's library was unique, he knew, because throughout his life he had been the right man in the right place at the right time — and most importantly, he had always had the cash on hand to make the most of happenstance.

And like anyone who haunts used bookshops, he also knew a once-in-a-lifetime opportunity when he saw one. Now that the Capitol and its three thousand volumes were lost, Jefferson proposed starting the Library of Congress anew with his own collection. It had been his intention to do so upon his death, he explained to Smith, but now the need seemed immediate. This would not be a gift, however. Jefferson made it clear he would take whatever payment the Congress authorized to give, and left it to the scruples of his former fellow legislators, and no doubt to their feelings of indebtedness to the great man, to come up with a suitable price. Jefferson's Republican party, not incidentally, held the majority over the Federalists, so if it came to a vote over cost (a reasonable expectation, given that the nation was already approaching twenty million dollars in debt), he could have expected some debate over the legitimacy of the expense.

What he might not have expected was a fight over the library's contents. Beginning not long after Jefferson's offer in September, a months-long controversy over the nature of his library and its appropriateness as a resource for lawmakers roiled Washington, with ripples felt all over the country. The central question in the dispute — which ideas were appropriate for recognition by the government? — was an extension of the questions at the heart of the war. As controversy over the library festered and congressmen on both sides entered the fray, this disagreement showed that the "wall of separation" between church and state, which Jefferson himself had famously described twelve years before in a letter to the Baptists of Danbury, Connecticut, was not without cracks.

Indeed, if any such wall existed as the War of 1812 ended, it seemed likely to crumble under the weight of Jefferson's books — for so dangerous were the volumes he proposed to place in service to the nation that the Congress of the United States would soon discuss the merits of book burning, in a city that had only recently been engulfed in flames.

Of the more than six thousand volumes Jefferson planned to deliver to Congress (eighteen or twenty wagonloads, as he reckoned the collection to be), only about three hundred dealt with subjects we might today consider under the rubric of religion. This was a small percentage of the library, but given the uproar many of the religious opinions offered in those books would soon cause, they may be seen as the controversial core of the collection: a window into their collector's views not only of faith but of progress and human history. They are a key, ultimately, to understanding a man whose idiosyncratic thoughts on religious difference have so influenced both today's laws and our enduring national assumptions.

Jefferson was at heart a cataloguer of human experiences. An inveterate classifier and a list-maker, he famously first enumerated humankind's unalienable rights to include "life, liberty, and the pursuit of property" in his rough draft of the Declaration of Independence, before altering the final subcategory to prefer the more abstract "happiness" over "property." In his home, too, he meticulously classified and reclassified everything from seeds to living spaces to books. His library in particular was a marvel of organization, collected and arranged in an attempt to make a map of all branches of knowledge. Using a system that was "something analytical, something chronological, and sometimes a combination of both," he sought not merely to make desired books easy to find on crowded shelves but to demonstrate the relationship between them, and to suggest the connection of one set of ideas to another.

Toward this end, he divided his library into three parts, following a schema inspired by Sir Francis Bacon yet making it his own.

212 · ONE NATION, UNDER GODS

Bacon's system had been to separate fields of inquiry into the categories of Memory, Reason, and Imagination. "From these three fountains," he wrote, "flow these three emanations, History, Poesy, and Philosophy; and there can be no others."

Perhaps finding "imagination" too fanciful, and being hardwired to recognize "reason" as the governor of all, Jefferson reworked Bacon's model into a system based on the divisions of History, Philosophy, and Fine Arts, including more than a dozen subcategories in each. To the modern reader it may be odd to see that the subcategories within History include not only Ancient, Modern, and Ecclesiastical sections but also Chemistry, Zoology, and Mineralogy. Philosophy, likewise, includes the expected—Ethics comes first—but also more than a dozen other subgroups, including Mathematics, Politics, Astronomy, and Religion. In Fine Arts, a reader would find sections on Painting, Sculpture, and Gardening, as well as Comedy, Tragedy, and Architecture. As Jefferson saw it, History was objective knowledge, and Philosophy human reflection upon it, while Fine Arts reflected the application of the second upon the first. In the words of the scholar of presidential books, Arthur Bestor, it was not just through the library but the catalogue, the organization of ideas, that Jefferson has left us "a blueprint of his own mind."

And more than that, he seems to have left us a blueprint for our national approach to conflicting and competing spiritual ideas, traditions, and beliefs. The Religion section of his library provides a good example of this.

The general category of "religion" at the time was synonymous with Protestant Christianity—most non-Christians were said to adhere to "heathen religion," Jews to the "Jewish religion," and Roman Catholics to the "Romish religion"; but "religion" on its own, or "true religion," could generally mean only one thing. Yet in his classification system, Jefferson took a more expansive view. In the catalogue he created to apprise Congress of his holdings in advance of the sale, the first few books in his collection move from the Sibylline Oracles, to a tome on "heathen gods," to the Quran, to the Old and New Testaments. Reflective of human experience in its wide variety, as he understood it, Jefferson's religion collection includes works in five languages.

Somewhat poignantly, this great thinker avoided arranging books alphabetically by title or author as he reached his elder years, "because of the medley it presents to the mind, the difficulty sometimes of recalling an author's name." There was also the difficulty, when the title was used for classification, of remembering which part of the title, in which language, had been used to "determine its alphabetical place." And so Jefferson organized his books on faith in a rough system that sought to replicate his understanding of how religious ideas developed over time. His thinking here was not chronological — he ordered the titles neither by composition date nor by publication — but rather genealogical. The titles with which the catalogue begins are those upon which, in Jefferson's estimation, all the others depend — a bibliographic family tree of belief.

Each of these earliest titles in the section also provides a view of the way he saw religions at work in the world. To begin with the first title: *The Sibylline Oracles* — a collection of poems supposedly uttered by ancient prophetesses — are at once a symbol of the classical cultures the Revolutionary generation held in such high esteem, and a reminder of the religious diversity that existed even at the time of their composition. The fragments gathered throughout are not limited to standard mythological tropes but also draw on Jewish and early Christian legends. They are reflective of a time not unlike Jefferson's own, which, despite recognizing one religion as "religion" and others merely as pale imitations, was also shaped by religious diversity, often as hidden as the Christian and Jewish themes are within the Sibyls' utterances.

The second and third books in his religion collection are also instructive. *An Historical Account of the Heathen Gods and Heroes*, by William King, was a popular book of classical mythology in Jefferson's day, primarily for the reason indicated by its subtitle: "Necessary for the Understanding of the Ancient Poets." Jefferson and other men of learning of his day read widely in certain areas of religion in part to comprehend arts and cultures of the past, but Jefferson's interest did not end with literary allusions. Following King on the shelf was Samuel Boyse's *A New Pantheon, Or Fabulous History of the Heathen Gods, Heroes and Goddesses*. Boyse acknowledged the reason many might turn to such a work was that "some acquaintance with the Heathen Gods and ancient Fables is a necessary Branch of polite Learning" and "generally esteemed necessary for the Improvement of Youth," yet he then goes further to consider the well-known figures of classical mythology as the living religious system of its day. Tracing the trajectory of "Pagan Theology," Boyse sought—as did Jefferson, apparently—to understand how the "Rise of Idolatry, and its Connection with the ancient Symbols, which gave Names to the Planets" could have led to "Sentiments of the Pagans with regard to the Unity of the Deity."

There is, then, in just the first few books in Jefferson's classification of religion, a clear sense that religious ideas change over time. There is also an awareness that every age has had to square unavoidable diversity of opinion on religious matters with the shared assumptions upon which any culture relies. This same awareness can be seen in the book Jefferson chose as the next in his collection, a copy of the Quran that he had purchased as a law student almost fifty years before. It is somewhat remarkable that he still had it in his possession, for his own early library, like Congress's original collection of books, had been mostly lost, in 1770, in a fire.

Like the three earlier books in the religion section, Jefferson's Quran was read not merely as primary source but as commentary. The translator of the edition (*The Koran, Commonly Called the Alcoran of Mohammed*), the Englishman George Sale, was not very sympathetic to Islam. In his opinion, "Providence has reserved the glory of its [Islam's] overthrow" to Protestant Christians. Sale presented the book not to encourage readers to accept its original author as a prophet but rather as an act of cultural and political literacy. "To be acquainted with the various laws and constitutions of civilized nations, especially of those who flourish in our own time, is, perhaps, the most useful part of knowledge," he wrote. "If the religious and civil institutions of foreign nations are worth our knowledge, those of Mohammed, the lawgiver of the Arabians, and founder of an empire which, in less than a century, spread itself over a greater part of the world than the Romans were ever masters of, must needs be so."

To put the establishment of that empire in context, Sale paints a picture of Arabs before the coming of Muhammad as a people not unlike the Greeks and Romans, who worshipped according to the mythologies listed in books on "heathen" religions in Jefferson's collection. "The idolatry of the Arabs...chiefly consisted in worshiping the fixed stars and planets, and the angels and their images, which they honoured as inferior deities, and whose intercession they begged," he writes. "It was from this gross idolatry, or the worship of inferior deities...that Mohammed reclaimed his countrymen, establishing the sole worship of the true God among them."

Though the Quran would seem a very different book from the works of classical myths or oracular utterances, Sale's translation similarly conveys the ways in which a range of religious notions can be united through human effort and understanding.

Only after these primary texts does Jefferson turn his collection to religious tomes more commonly owned in early America, not least of which are multiple versions of the Christian scriptures. Even these, however, Jefferson would eventually turn to as fodder for his own attempt at crafting a unified, if unorthodox, religious message. No conventional Bible reader, Jefferson used his various editions of the New Testament as source material for a book so heretical he would not allow it to be published in his lifetime. Pieced together from editions of the Gospels to which Jefferson put an editor's blade, his *Life and Morals of Jesus Christ* consisted of quotations literally cut and pasted from various translations. In the same spirit of spiritual progress with which he read the first volumes of his library, Jefferson sought to excise all mention of the miracles or the divinity of Jesus of Nazareth from the foundational text of Christendom. Though not included in the library Jefferson planned to send to Congress, the so-called Jefferson Bible was in a sense a distillation of the ideas present there. It is the best evidence we have of the tenets of Jefferson's idiosyncratic faith: that religion is a work in progress, that scripture was mortal rather than divine handiwork, and that one could count religion a benefit to society without necessarily adhering to a single creed.

This was, for Jefferson, the only reasonable approach to religion. Elsewhere in the catalogue's religion list, and within other subcategories of the Philosophy section, we see the logical end of Jefferson's reasonable approach to religion: a progression from many gods, to a single God known by one name, to a sense of the divine unlimited by particular revelation—the god of deism, which to many of his countrymen, he knew, seemed like no god at all.

Within this continuum of religious beliefs and practices, it was the task of humanity to organize and classify. As a naturalist might approach flora and fauna, an observer of religion ought to organize the rites and divinities across time and among the world's peoples. Jefferson's library, in other words, presented religion as one subject among many. Receiving no special treatment, it was safe from neither Jefferson's reason nor his blade.

Religious works accounted for barely a twentieth of Jefferson's collection, but this part came to stand for the whole in the public imagination. Faced with the challenge and opportunity to rebuild the nation's first city and to restock the contents of Congress's intellectual resources, opponents of heterodoxy were horrified by the notion that Jefferson's famously eclectic opinions would soon form the core of the national storehouse of knowledge. As news spread of Jefferson's proposal, the handwringing began almost immediately. Jefferson had written his letter in late September; by early October, a sarcastic editorial appeared in the *Federal Republican*:

Mr. Jefferson's Library

A resolution has been proposed in congress authorizing a purchase of the Library of the Sage of Monticello. It no doubt contains a plentiful stock of the works of Tom Paine, Rousseau, Voltaire, Condorcet, &c. &c. in which that great statesman so successfully studied, and if purchased for Congress will afford members an excellent opportunity of improving their heads and hearts by the study of those fathers of French philosophy.

A week later, the *Salem Gazette* also reported: "Congress are about purchasing Mr. Jefferson's library. It is judged the following works will be held so high that the national treasury, exhausted as it is, will not command them." There followed a list of the collection's most egregious and useless titles, in the estimation of the unnamed editorial writer. Among those with scorn heaped upon them were titles "in the original French" (even then a supposed marker of un-American ideas), which were "much worn" (presumably from Jefferson's constant immoral use). The most suspect tomes were those by Voltaire and Diderot, and a manuscript copy of "Instructions, religious and political" addressed to King James I, a fanatical but secret Catholic. The implication of highlighting these titles was clear: Jefferson's brand of religiosity was foreign at best, outright blasphemous at worst. "It is understood that altho' the above have been *much used*, they are very fair, outside." Much used but well cared for, these books were presented not only as Jefferson's treasures but as windows into his questionable character.

An article first published in Connecticut but then republished throughout the states took issue with the sheer variety of the collection. The italics are in the original, and serve to underscore the sneering attitude some took to Jefferson's offer from the start:

"We understand that Mr. Jefferson's *invaluable* collection of Books contains, among others, more than 40 Romances in French, Spanish, and Italian — 12 different treatises on music — playing the violin, fingering the harp, &c. — rising of 50 works on architecture — together with a very extense collection of Deistical writers, from Chubb, Voltaire, Spinoza, and Condorcet, down to Ethan Allen and J Palmer. We have no doubt that Mr. Jefferson has not only *some*, but *an extensive 'knowledge of the bibliography of these subjects,'* particularly infidelity and architecture. With respect to the latter, it is said he is so great an adept as to posses a complete assortment of Joiner's tools, and with regard to the former, he is considered still more accomplished — being a master-workman."

A master-workman of infidelity is not likely the title Jefferson hoped to earn through his offer of the library he had spent a lifetime assembling, but his eclectic religious interests had become the crux of the issue.

Whether or not its opponents truly had such sensitive spiritual sensibilities as to take umbrage at the well-known writings of Voltaire or Spinoza, the fight over the library quickly became the culture war of its day. And as with more recent squabbles over federal funding for arts that may challenge traditional mores, partisan publications fanned the flames of sectarian outrage in hope of gathering religious ground troops to a largely political cause. Jefferson's longtime antagonists at the *Federal Republican* stated most plainly the position of the opposition. Should the former president's offer be accepted, the Congress of the United States would purchase a library that "abounded with productions of atheistical, irreligious, and immoral character" at a time when the national debt already seemed out of control.

Much of the response in the press consisted of earnest concern over the library's cost, but it seems that the closer to Washington a newspaper was printed, the more likely it was to take genuine pleasure in hoisting Jefferson on the petard of his own heterodoxy. Playing with the notion that the books contained heretical ideas, the *Alexandria Gazette* suggested that if the purchase must occur, then a committee suggestive of an Inquisition should divide the books into those that were useful, those that were harmless, and a third group ("which bye the bye would be the largest") that should be consigned to the pyre. Only this, an unnamed correspondent suggests, would "make the most of the bad bargain."

Similarly, a merciless parody of Jefferson's letter to Congress was published in Georgetown on October 18, 1814. Framing the letter as if addressing Jefferson himself, the writer wonders how he might likewise "turn his books into cash."

To Thomas Jefferson, esquire, late President
of the United States —

Dear Sir: — I have a library of books which I should be glad to sell. It consists of about 5000 volumes, selected with care and caution. Various projects had occurred to me to effect this object, but none had appeared free of objection. One feels awkwardly to be hawking his commodities about the streets, and to send such a quantity of books to auction... seems not quite consistent with those delicate feelings which should govern high-minded men...

Observing that you have, in one of your lucky moments, (and I never knew a man who had more such moments), hit upon a project entirely new, and seeing that it is very popular, I wish to know if you cannot, in a second application to Congress, through some Republican friend, aid me...

Many of my books are rare, most of them elegant and all inestimable. A considerable part of the works are in Sanscrit, Coptic, Celtic, and Arabic tongues. These can be translated, if it is thought proper, at little expense, though I should prefer that they should remain as written, and would respectfully recommend that Congress should immediately employ a competent number of professors to teach the members of that honorable body those languages...

Being now nearly eighty years of age, and having no children, to whom my estate can descend, and not finding much time for reading, I should be much pleased to turn these books into cash... I intended to have furnished you with an elegant catalogue of my library, that it might have been open to inspection; but am now wholly occupied in furnishing a drawing

*of the Capitol and President's House, while on fire... I will,
however, mention a few of the great number of books, and give
you a sketch of the character of the whole.*

*There are entire sets of all the works of all the atheistical
writers in every age and nation and tongue, superbly bound
and lettered. Forty different editions of the Bible, thirty-nine of
which are in the Arabic, and one in the Hebrew idiom; these are
as good as when they came from the hands of the book-binder.
A very learned treatise in ten volumes quarto, on the nature,
properties, and uses of the animal called tad-pole, stiled vulgarly,
Polly-wangs, with an appendix, in three volumes, on the toad
of Caffraria. The whole of these, I have caused to be translated
into six different languages. There is also, an elaborate and
voluminous account of the terrapin, sometimes called mud-turtle,
written by the author of sundry ingenius disquisitions on gunboats and dry-docks, in modern French... Also, a new edition in
several volumes folio, on the Russian climate, and its effects on
Frenchmen, French horses and American politics... A work of
great worth, written in Persian, on the grass-hopper of the east,
delineating, with entire accuracy, the size of his legs in different
regions of that extensive country, with a copious appendix,
containing the whole learning on the subject of that highly curious
animal called the weasel. A complete system of ornithology, giving
an account of every flying creature, from the insect of a day to the
whip-poor-will, the night-hawk and the crane, in blank verse, by
Inchiquin, translated from the Italian into the Sclavonic, by a
learned foreigner, comprized in thirteen volumes folio.*

*The books are in excellent order, many of them truly
elegant. Not a syllable could be taken from them without
prejudice to the rest, as all the arts and sciences have a
certain natural connection. I cannot consent to see my library
gerry-mandered... I must sell the whole or none... If it should
be objected, that four-fifths of this library are in foreign
languages, and of course, unintelligible by nine-tenths of the
members of Congress, I would reply that such an objection
can come only from short-sighted men...*

Accept the assurance of my high consideration.

*Johannes Vonderpuff
Missouri, October 1st, 1814*

As much fun as some journalists seem to have had at Jefferson's expense, this was no mere tabloid dispute. The editorial writers of the nation's newspapers were taking their leads from the politicians who were arguing these same points on the floor of Congress. While the Senate unanimously passed a resolution to purchase the library in October 1814, the debate dragged on for months in the House of Representatives. Divided along party lines, factions rose up for and against the acquisition of the library. Tempers flared over Jefferson's books and the supposed threat posed by the ideas within. The rhetoric was largely religious, concerned — as the Spanish had once been about Muslim influence in the new world — with the supposed contamination Jefferson's eclectic religious ideas would bring.

Within a week of the Senate's resolution, just six weeks after the original library had been destroyed, the House erupted in debate over the nature of Jefferson's interests and inclinations, with particular concern voiced over the works by French infidels like Voltaire and Rousseau, as well as "English works of progress and speculative freedom."

The final showdown came on January 26, 1815. The day's first order of business involved hearing a petition from a man asking Congress to remunerate him for "a number of negroes, horses, and cattle" that he claimed Cherokee Indians had stolen from his father almost forty years before. Citing treaties requiring Indians to return any property taken from Americans, the petitioner held the U.S. government responsible. The House in its wisdom ruled that the petitioner "neither shows himself to be the heir of the person, whose property is said to have been taken, nor does he show, satisfactorily, the value of the property taken, or that any was taken."

With such weighty questions behind them, the representatives turned to the matter that had so inflamed the press of late. Of the catalogue of titles that had been sent by Jefferson, Representative Cyrus King of Massachusetts remarked that given the character of the man who had acquired the library, and the place where he had so readily admitted he had done so — France — it was likely that the library contained "many books of irreligious and immoral tendency." Moreover, he feared that by welcoming such a library, the Congress would be allowing into their presence the spirit of "French infidel philosophers" who had ignited "the volcano of the French revolution" and whose "fatal and destructive effects" the library would bring "to our once happy country." King strongly opposed accepting the entirety of Jefferson's collection "to prevent a general dissemination of this infidel philosophy."

After first suggesting that a selection of books be taken and that the rest be disposed of "at public sale," King then proposed another solution that put a finer point on his objections. As it would certainly not be appropriate to have such dangerous material made available as government surplus, he advised sending it back to a place where it would do no further damage to unsuspecting citizens.

"As soon as said Library shall be received at Washington," King said, "the joint library committee be required, and they are hereby authorised and directed, to select therefrom, all books, if any there be, of an atheistical, irreligious, and immoral tendency, and to send the same back to Mr. Jefferson, without expense to him."

This motion was attacked first by a member of the very library committee King had just enlisted in the culling of the collection, Dr. Adam Seybert of Pennsylvania. Seybert thanked King for his confidence that he and other committee members were deemed worthy of such a lofty project, but he insisted that in this indexing of forbidden books, King alone should be regarded as the sole "Inquisitor."

Nor was King's zeal shared by his fellow Massachusetts congressman, John Hulbert, who openly mocked his colleague by observing that sending the books back to Monticello would not remove their supposed danger from the world. As had so often been the case in the history of challenging religious ideas on this continent, Hulbert described fear at work in a manner usually reserved for disease: "The motive of his colleague was to prevent the contagion which might spread from them; that if he was sincerely desirous of preventing this evil, he ought to amend the section by introducing a provision for the burning of such books."

In what must have been an entertaining exchange, King informed his fellow congressmen that he "would accept with pleasure of the modification proposed by my colleague." On reconsideration, destroying the books did not sound so bad, he mused, and it would save in shipping costs. "Indeed, I had at first drawn my amendment with a provision that these books should be burnt by the library committee," he said, "but it afterwards appeared to me, to comport better with the dignity of the house, to send them back, especially as said committee might be unwilling to perform a task usually allotted to the common hangman."

Addressing Hulbert directly, King told his fellow Massachusetts representative that he need not worry about Jefferson or his friends being further contaminated by the books, as they were "certainly secured therefrom by their own depravity."

James Fisk of Vermont next joined the fray. He observed that it was formerly the practice in Massachusetts to hang witches, and asked if King intended to revive this form of theocratic punishment. King replied that Fisk was a native of Massachusetts, and wondered if he had run off for fear of being hanged as a wizard himself.

As the *Congressional Record* sums up this rollicking session: When called upon to answer the broad and zealous attacks against it, "the friends of the bill replied with fact, wit, and argument" to show that the purchase of the library would harm neither the fiscal nor the spiritual well-being of the United States. And moreover, they argued that, in keeping with a justification Jefferson himself had suggested in his letter, "there is in fact no subject to which a member of Congress may not have occasion to refer."

The House eventually voted in favor of acquiring "Mr. Jefferson's Library," but not by a very wide margin. With eighty-one congressmen in favor and seventy-one opposed, their disagreement set the stage for culture wars for centuries to come. In every case, the question has been much the same: To what end should the nation's resources be put? One newspaper editorial captured the mood of the victors in this particular skirmish: "The next generation will, we confidently predict, blush at the objections made in Congress to the purchase of Mr. Jefferson's library."

Despite coming under scathing personal attack, Jefferson sat out the battle over his library's supposedly heretical content. This should come as no surprise. He was, after all, retired from public life by then, and less willing or able, as he grew older, to engage with critics and political rivals as he once had. Moreover, he had surely grown tired of fighting this particular battle again and again.

He was no stranger to religious conflict. The presidential election of 1800 had been in many ways a referendum on his faith — or lack thereof, according to his detractors. His opponent in the contest, the incumbent John Adams, had not shied away from exploiting the widespread suspicion of Jefferson's beliefs for his own benefit. As one slogan of the time put it, the choice between the sitting president and his challenger was clear: "God and a religious president, or...Jefferson and no god." Jefferson was no more popular in the press, where one editor warned that under Jefferson, "Murder, robbery, rape, adultery, and incest will be openly taught and practiced, the air will be rent with the cries of distress, the soil will be soaked with blood, and the nation black with crimes."

As with his library, the problem Jefferson presented was not atheism per se but deism. To orthodox Christianity in the early nineteenth century, to refer to the divine as "nature's God," as deists did, was as good as saying that there was no God at all. God, to Christians, was simply and unquestionably the divinity made manifest in the revelation of the Gospels and in the person of Jesus Christ. Appeals to a god of nature who was somehow independent of salvation history were regarded—justifiably, within the Christian worldview—as theological doubletalk. As with the anti-Jefferson slogan mentioned above, one was either with God or against him, and a deist was certainly regarded as against, no matter the vague philosophical defense he might make.

Jefferson liked to think he was "of a sect by myself," but in these beliefs he was in good company. His desire to have it both ways in terms of acknowledging the cultural significance of religion while distancing himself from specific revelation was as standard in his day as well-meaning agnosticism may be today; it was an expression of doubt designed to avoid the arguments (and the political suicide) that were the likely outcome of staunchly stated unbelief.

Like many in public life, however, Jefferson seems to have had some distance between his own privately professed feelings on faith and his official positions. The former are perhaps captured most poignantly in a letter he wrote to his nephew in 1787. In it, he encourages the young man to do as he had done—to consider reason his "only oracle"—but not to be disdainful of beliefs held by many simply because they are held by many: "Divest yourself of all bias in favour of novelty and singularity of opinion," he wrote. "Indulge them in any other subject rather than that of religion."

At the same time, he stressed, one must not be so swayed by tradition or the crowd as to lose sight of one's individual responsibility to seek truth for oneself:

Shake off all the fears and servile prejudices, under which weak minds are servilely crouched. Fix reason firmly in her seat, and call to her tribunal every fact, every opinion. Do not be frightened from this inquiry by any fear of its consequences. If it ends in a belief that there is no God, you will find incitements to virtue in the comfort and pleasantness you feel in its exercise, and the love of others which it will procure you. If you find reason to believe there is a God, a consciousness that you are acting under His eye, and that He approves you, will be a vast additional incitement; if that there be a future state, the hope of a happy existence in that increases the appetite to deserve it; if that Jesus was also a God, you will be comforted by a belief of His aid and love. In fine, I repeat, you must lay aside all prejudice on both sides, and neither believe nor reject anything because any other persons, or description of persons, have rejected or believed it. Your own reason is the only oracle given you by heaven.

"You are answerable," Jefferson concludes, "not for the rightness, but uprightness of the decision."

This was the kind of practical pluralism one can see also in his formal position on religious freedom, which became the official position of the nation as well. Crafted in collaboration with James Madison, the First Amendment's notion that one could neither prescribe nor proscribe religion, in the words of constitutional scholar John Witte, echoes precisely the two points made in his more personal advice to his nephew. For all to be considered, all must be allowed.

This was not unlike the stipulation he made with regard to his library. In order to have even a single one of his books, he stressed, Congress had to accept the lot. Undoubtedly there was an element of pragmatism in this: It would be far easier for an older gentleman to have a roomful of books packed and shipped than for him to pick through the collection volume by volume. But there was also perhaps something more significant in his desire to keep his library complete: a recognition that books—like beliefs, ideas, and the people who hold them dear—mean nothing in isolation. It is only through their interaction with each other that they may prove their worth.

Among the thousands of volumes pulled by oxcart from the hilltop of Monticello to the newly restored Capitol, only one was by Jefferson himself. *Notes on the State of Virginia* stands alone as the collection of Jefferson's writings that he allowed to be published in his lifetime. In these *Notes*, first published in 1787, Jefferson divided his thoughts on his home state—which was to him something of an America in miniature—into twenty-three categories, or queries, taking each in turn to create a kind of encyclopedia of a place, its past, and its potential. The section on religion, more than any other piece of his writing, captures the purpose and possibilities of spiritual diversity as he understood it.

Jefferson is often remembered as an avatar of a kind of "live and let live" pluralism that encouraged a form of indifference about the beliefs of others. Nothing could be further from the truth. On the contrary, he saw that religious systems inevitably and necessarily interact with each other in ways at once contentious, intimate, and transformative. Assessing the function of religious difference in his young country, he wrote, "the several sects perform the office of a *Censor morum* over each other."

Censor morum: a moral censor. The medieval implications of the phrase bring to mind an Inquisition staffed with busybody Torquemadas annihilating variety and shutting down discourse in the name of the public good—precisely the kind of role Congressman King from Massachusetts proposed to play in removing objectionable material from Jefferson's library. Yet Jefferson's meaning, like his theology, was broader than that. For each sect to be a moral censor of the others around it is not a call for mere tolerance. It is a recognition that faiths do not exist in a vacuum. They exist only in relation to each other. They change and grow, live and die, through adaptation, competition, imitation, and assimilation.

Elsewhere in the query on religion found in *Notes on the State of Virginia*, Jefferson writes, "Let us reflect that the Earth is inhabited by a thousand millions of people. That these profess probably a thousand different systems of religion. That ours is but one of that thousand." Not only is this an argument that those in the religious majority might have something to learn from those living on the margins of the dominant faith, it is an argument that, in fact, all faiths are marginal. Each on its own is just one in a thousand. Yet joined together in a community of faiths, and of belief and unbelief, each can somehow become part of something grander, ennobled through moments of interaction and transformation.

"It does me no injury for my neighbor to say there are twenty gods or no gods; it neither picks my pocket nor breaks my leg," Jefferson famously said. Considered on its own, this again might seem nothing more than benign disinterest. But in the context of his full understanding of religion, he seems here to suggest that not only does it do no injury if your neighbor believes in twenty gods or none, it may in fact do you some good. Whether you look across the fence and discover the one God brought by the Puritans or the thirty-seven Native American gods encountered by Roger Williams, the hinted atheism of William Livingston or the unabashed blasphemy of Jacob Lumbrozo, these beliefs transform each other through their interaction. And those who hold them cannot help but be changed as well.

If General Ross's burning of the original Congressional Library was necessary to have such heretical ideas enshrined within the Capitol, it may have been worth the price. However, it would be a mistake to overpraise Jefferson's notion of religious liberty without remembering an unfortunate truth. Though he championed loosening the spiritual strictures that bound all humanity, he believed physical freedom was unalienable only for some.

Omar ibn Said. (University of North
Carolina Libraries)

CHAPTER 11

O People of America!

1810–1865

In a faded photograph of the nineteenth-century Cumberland County jail, the squat assemblage of thick walls and barred windows stands like a child beside the more imposing courthouse that dominated the public square of Fayetteville, North Carolina. On the day in 1810 when an escaped slave found himself standing in front of these two buildings, the local authorities pushed him toward the former without hesitation. As far as his captors were concerned, runaways had no right to expect due process or legal protection. Even if he had been given the chance to plead his case, he would have found it impossible. Inside a courtroom, he would have understood neither the words spoken by the judge nor those within the book upon which he might have placed an oath-swearing hand. He was no stranger to laws, but his were found in another scripture, formed of another tongue.

His home for the foreseeable future, he soon discovered, was a dirty cell, its floor blackened with the dust of charcoal shards that fueled the sooty fires that in the colder months provided prisoners with their only source of warmth. As he awaited his fate—most likely an unwelcome reunion with Mr. Johnson of Charleston, from whose cruel treatment he had fled four weeks before—he passed the days as he had throughout his life: with prayer.

Decades earlier he had learned the proper way to express submission to God: Five times through the day a man should fall to his knees, press his forehead to the ground, and speak words in the language of the Prophet.

It was his devotion, in fact, that had caused him to be captured. After his escape from Johnson's farm, he had wandered in fright across much of the Carolinas, sleeping where he could, living on whatever found sustenance tobacco country could provide. He was somewhere on the northern side of the border between the two states, almost three hundred miles from where he had started, when he looked to the evening sky and noted it was a new moon. According to his faith, this was a sight that marked the beginning of things, a period of reflection and thankfulness, no matter one's present circumstances. As he walked, he had spotted what seemed to him a few "great houses," as he would later call them, in which it seemed no one lived. They were clearly gathering places, possibly sites of worship not too dissimilar from those he had known in his youth. He approached one of them with the hope that he had found shelter for his prayers.

At the time he had been taken from his homeland, three years before, he was already a man of middle age. His name, then, had been Omar ibn Said. Thirty-seven years old, set in his ways, he had been well instructed in the tenets of his faith. From boyhood, he had walked each morning to the mosque, where he washed his face and neck, his hands and wrists, his feet and ankles, all in preparation for coming before the presence of the divine. Before he was forced to scurry anonymously in the Carolina darkness, he had been a pillar of his community, a man who lived in the open in the country of the Fula people, in what is now Senegal.

In that other life, he had given tithes — gold and silver, livestock and grains — to support the less fortunate, and at the time he had never imagined he would one day count himself among them. A man of means and of family, he had five sisters and five brothers, one of whom was a learned scholar who had taught him to read and write in the manner of their holy book. So instructed, he himself had become a teacher of religion to the youth of his village.

"Then there came to our country a big army. It killed many people," he later recalled. "It took me, and walked me to the big sea, and sold me into the hand of a Christian man, who bought me and walked me to the big ship in the big sea. We sailed in the big sea a month and a half until we came to a place called Charleston. And in a Christian language, they sold me."

It had taken years, but finally he had managed to free himself from the one who had bought him. The "weak, small, evil man called Johnson," he remembered, was "an unbeliever who did not fear God at all." With the distance between himself and the man he called a *kafir*, an infidel, growing with every step, he was not without reason to be grateful. Aware of the new moon through its seeming absence, just as he was aware of Allah, he knew the prayers fitting for the occasion, which could not have seemed more appropriate to a man stolen from the country of his birth, unimaginably reduced from his former stature.

"I have faith in Him who lights up the darkness through thee, illuminates jet-black shadows by thee," the new moon prayers declare to the moon itself, "and humbled thee through increase and decrease, rising and setting, illumination and eclipse."

Omar ibn Said slipped into one of the great houses under the cover of the dark new moon night. He might have merely rested and passed a few hours there unnoticed before moving on, but a boy who lived nearby saw him and rode off to report to his family that an escaped slave—the bogeyman of southern fantasies—was hiding in their church. The boy and his father returned on horseback with dogs and reinforcements, a miniature militia that seized Omar ibn Said and marched him twelve miles to the jail in Fayetteville.

Despite the bitter disappointment of capture, and the inevitable terror at the prospect of being sent back to the evil place from which he had escaped, Omar ibn Said endured his latest imprisonment with apparent equanimity. He fell back on the solace of prayer, and turned to the walls around him as another venue for his devotion. Among the ashy cinders that littered the floor, he found a piece of coal large enough to hold between his fingers like a calligrapher's pen. With it, he began to inscribe the walls with thoughts and verses in a language he had not spoken to any person since before he had been taken. The words he wrote were, to him, as sacred as any that might be found in Fayetteville's Bibles.

As he decorated his walls with Arabic script—most likely snippets of prayer and Quranic chapters, or suras, given the type of religious education he had received—it fell to his jailer, Cumberland County sheriff Robert Mumford, to find a way to dispose of this unusual fugitive. Word had begun to spread of the dignified man redecorating the jail cell with coal-black strokes that might have looked to the locals like sketches of fish hooks strung with cat gut lines. Gawkers came to get a closer look, to see the spectacle of an African writing words his supposed betters could not understand. The small lockup was becoming more of a gallery than a jail, and Sheriff Mumford had to do something about it.

It was common practice at the time to post notices in the local press of runaway slaves, both those who remained at large and those who had been caught and held awaiting their masters' claims of lost property. If Mumford had checked the local papers, he would have read dozens of advertisements either in search of wayward humans or reporting their capture, each cataloguing the appearance and effects of desperate men and women like an immoral lost and found. On one page of an 1810 edition of the Raleigh weekly *The Star*, for example, Mumford would have seen these notices a few inches apart:

> Run-Away: A Negro man named Prince, about five feet eleven inches high, twenty-one years of age; had on when he went away a white furred hat, a light mixed cotton coat, cotton shirt, white & striped over-alls, and walks with a halt which is occasioned by his having had his right thigh broke, and is shorter than the other.

> Runaway: A Negro man named Emanuel…He is about 5 feet 8 or 9 inches high, stout made, is of a dark copper colour, has lost two of his fore teeth, has a bold look, speaks quick with great confidence.

Capture of either Prince or Emanuel, the paper reported, offered a twenty-dollar reward.

Interspersed with such runaway announcements were other notices, usually printed at the request of jailers like Mumford, providing information about African Americans who had been apprehended as probable escapees. With phrases such as "Passing himself as a free man," these reports fostered suspicion even of those who had managed to win their release from bondage, sometimes resulting in the reenslavement of recently liberated men and women who had believed their new freedom irreversible.

In the case of either type of advertisement, a crude depiction of a man was frequently shown beside the descriptive text. If the fugitive's whereabouts remained unknown, the image showed a silhouette of a body in motion, one arm forward, one leg back, a stick-and-parcel sack on his shoulder, a jaunty hat on his head, as if the image of a slave unrestrained and moving with apparent speed through the countryside would be enough to stir the citizenry to action. If the runaway had been caught, this same figure was shown shorn of his hat, stick, and parcel—all those symbols of his illicit and frightening autonomy. In these images, the recaptured fugitive is reduced to little more than an inked slash on the page, his bowed head barely a serif on a narrow line.

Placing such an ad in the *Raleigh Star* or the *Fayetteville Observer* surely would have been the protocol for Omar ibn Said, as with any other black man the sheriff had found unable or unwilling to account for his freedom. Yet Mumford had not been able to glean anything about who this fugitive was, where he had come from, or whose supposed property he might be. With no way to communicate, no mention of him in the press, and no one arriving at the jailhouse to claim him as their own, little could be known about him. He apparently knew no English and, except for the foreign warbling of his prayers, seemed disinclined to speak.

He was not without obvious talents, however, as the growing numbers of visitors to the jail attested. The markings he made in his cell perhaps held an unexpected, exotic beauty for the residents of Fayetteville. Because the practice of importing slaves directly from Africa had been outlawed three years before, he was the last of his kind that many in Fayetteville were likely see, which only heightened his mystery.

When the crowd at the jail got to be too much, Sheriff Mumford decided he had waited long enough. He knew what to do with his prisoner. With an impatient mob outside, the sheriff made a rash decision to take matters into his own hands, and allowed a hurried removal of the accused black man from his cell.

Such a scene has played out with horrific consequences throughout the nation's history, often ending with a stout tree branch and a deadly stretch of rope. After he had led Omar ibn Said from his cell, however, Mumford did what no white small-town sheriff in the mythology of the South had ever done: He brought him home.

Unlike the overwhelming majority of the half-million men, women, and children of African descent who were brought against their will to North America from the sixteenth to the nineteenth century, the escaped slave who found his way to Sheriff Mumford's jail left a record of his life, composed at the request of his eventual owners. His brief autobiography—*The Life of Omar ibn Said, Written by Himself*—allows us a window into the inhumanity of slavery. It also reveals the estrangement of those marginalized by race and faith in a nation that often used religion to justify the practice of treating human beings as property.

Yet while Omar ibn Said's autobiography is singular—the only extant personal history written in Arabic by an American slave—his life was not. He was but one of the perhaps 20 percent of African-born men and women who were followers of Islam before losing their faith and their history when transported as captives first to the English colonies and later to the young United States. Their presence is affirmed in documents dated more than one hundred years before Omar ibn Said's arrival, as in a Virginia law of 1682 which referred to "negroes, moores, molatoes, and others, born of and in heathenish, idollatrous, pagan, and Mahometan parentage and country" who "heretofore and hereafter may be purchased, procured, or otherwise obteigned, as slaves."

In an era of fracturing traditional affiliations and endless schisms among the newly established churches, the number of Muslims brought to this predominantly Christian land would have rivaled the populations of many Christian denominations in eighteenth-century America. In fact, to compare several groups that have historically faced discrimination at the hands of the majority religious culture, the number of Muslims in the newly independent United States would likely have dwarfed the number of Roman Catholics or Jews through the early years of Omar ibn Said's life. Considered another way: While Muslims accounted for less than 1 percent of the total population of the United States in 2010, enslaved Africans with a connection to Islam likely made up more than 5 percent of the population two hundred years before.

The presence of Muslims in early America has been largely forgotten in part because the complicated role of religion in the origins of slavery has been written out of history in favor of the distinctions made according to race. Some of the original laws regarding the importation of enslaved men and women were more concerned with the content of forced laborers' beliefs than with the color of their skin. The reason for this, from the perspective of Europeans of the time, was clear: Belief could spread in a way that color could not. As a Spanish law of 1685 stated, "The introduction of Mohammedan slaves into America is forbidden on account of the danger which lies in their intercourse with the Indians." As in so many moments in American history, religious difference was regarded as highly contagious, and thus dangerous.

Having a less fraught history with Islam than the Spanish, the English colonists paid less attention to the religious commitments of the people they enslaved, but they too were not blind to religion's role in the creation and maintenance of a colonial economy built on forced labor. In the beginning of slavery in the English colonies of North America, it was assumed that Christians should not be slaves. Christian servants might work for a predetermined period under strictures of indenture that were often barely distinguishable from slavery, and their indenture could be bought and sold as if they were slaves, but the duration of their servitude was limited by definition. Non-Christians, on the other hand, could be trapped in bondage for life.

This arrangement proved untenable, however. If slavery was defined in relation to belief, then conversion would become a potential path to freedom. This possibility put Christian slaveholders in the uncomfortable position of accepting the theory that the Gospel should be spread to all people in all lands, but recognizing that conversion of the enslaved would have ruinous financial effects. Another law reflected this concern: "The conferring of baptisme doth not alter the condition of the person as to his bondage or freedom," a Virginia statute of 1667 states, "divers masters, freed from this doubt, may more carefully endeavor the propagation of Christianity."

The development of this approach to the religious lives of the enslaved suggests another reason for the disappearance of Islam from popular understandings of slavery: the belief that Africans brought to America could be spiritually transformed by the will and at the word of Europeans. As the Virginia law continues, all enslaved men and women "brought or imported into this country, either by sea or land, whether Negroes, Moors, Mollattoes or Indians, who and whose parentage and native country are not Christian...they shall be converted to the Christian faith."

The legal possibility of keeping Christians as slaves did not immediately translate into widespread conversion of the enslaved, however. Throughout the colonial period, most slaveholders remained reluctant to offer salvation to the people they considered their property. To begin with, conversion was seen as needlessly expensive—the hours spent in religious instruction and then in worship were hours in which a valuable resource was not being properly invested. Allowing Christianized slaves to honor the Sabbath with a day of rest, for example, would mean a loss of one-seventh of their productivity. Moreover, many slave owners did not care enough about religion themselves to even entertain the notion of converting their slaves. A common understanding of plantation owners in the eighteenth century was that they had "No other God but Money, nor Religion but Profit." One newspaper wit of the day suggested, "Talk to a Planter of the Soul of a Negro, and he'll be apt to tell ye that the Body of one of them may be worth twenty Pounds, but the Souls of an hundred of them would not yield him one Farthing." The traveler Peter Kalm, who provided a view of colonial America similar to that of the new nation offered ninety years later by Alexis de Tocqueville, wrote in 1745 that it was "greatly to be pitied that the masters of the Negroes in most of the English Colonies take little care of their Spiritual welfare and let them live on in their pagan darkness." The reason for this, Kalm noted, was that even the pious among the slave owners feared what would happen if the people they kept in bondage came to see themselves as spiritual equals.

As the majority of the enslaved population became natives of this country—that is, born in the newly birthed United States of America rather than transported across the ocean in chains—the tendency to avoid or even prevent the conversion of slaves began to change. By the time of Omar ibn Said's enslavement in the early nineteenth century, the position of many slave owners was that, contrary to previous generations' assumptions about Christianity's potentially destabilizing influence, conversion could be good for all concerned, provided it was properly deployed. Slave owners frequently gave voice to the religious justification that it was their Christian obligation to educate their servants in the tenets of their faith. As the attendees of an 1845 meeting on "the religious instruction of the negroes" suggested, "the duty of imparting a Revelation which Divine Providence has placed in our hands, to those whom the same Providence has made dependent on us, we trust may be assumed."

The motivation for this duty, however, was of course not purely spiritual. It was also a matter of control. "I am perfectly satisfied, from long observation, of the beneficial effects of religious instruction on the minds and hearts of the blacks," one slaveholder wrote. "Those who have grown up under such instruction are more honest, truthful, moral, and well-behaved, more neat and clean in their dress, more improved in their manners, and devoted to their owners' interests than those who have not enjoyed the same advantages." With less pretense of piety or the niceties of good manners, another slave owner put it plainly, "plantations under religious instruction are more easily governed, than those that are not."

Such understandings transformed the faith that had been seen as an obstacle to slavery into a virtual requirement, as exposure to Christianity became part of the experience of bondage. Haven Percy, the mid-twentieth-century historian of American Christianity, summed up the religious assumptions of slaveholders as follows: "The Negro, like other men, is innately religious, and he will get his religion in distorted form through leaders of his own race if deprived of white guidance. Since the Christian life consists in grateful acceptance of the station to which one has been called, and faithful performance of the duties of that station, conversion will produce the most obedient slaves."

The basic assumption that Christianity was an unqualified benefit to the enslaved was not only a matter of self-justification on the part of those who profited from the arrangement, however. It was shared also by those who opposed slavery. Abolitionists told stories of men and women who won their freedom by becoming Christians and making their lives into living versions of Exodus. Such tales of emancipation were often approached through the model of religious conversion narratives, in which Christian terms were applied to both the condition of slavery and the desire to overcome it.

The *Narrative of the Life of Frederick Douglass*, for example, described the moment at which Douglass, born a slave on a Maryland plantation, first was moved to resist mistreatment by his master, a "nigger-breaker" called Covey. When he found the courage to raise his fists against this cruel man, it was, he wrote, akin to spiritual conversion. "My long-crushed spirit rose, cowardice departed, bold defiance took its place; and I now resolved that, however long I might remain a slave in form, the day had passed forever when I could be a slave in fact." Thereafter, he experienced "a glorious resurrection, from the tomb of slavery, to the heaven of freedom."

Another example can be found in the controversial leader of an unsuccessful slave uprising in 1831, Nat Turner, who is often remembered for the biblical tropes of his message. Exposed to the Christian faith by the Methodist minister who was his first owner, Turner infamously was inspired by otherworldly visions to lift a hatchet against a later master's family, and then to lead a revolt against other plantations nearby. As he later described his visions in the "Confession" he gave before his execution: "I saw white spirits and black spirits engaged in battle, and the sun was darkened — the thunder rolled in the Heavens, and blood flowed in streams — and I heard a voice saying, 'Such is your luck, such you are called to see, and let it come rough or smooth, you must surely bare it.'" Moved by what he took to be an experience akin to those of biblical prophets, he was baptized in a river, as Jesus himself was when he began his mission, and then, Turner said, "I heard a loud noise in the heavens, and the Spirit was loosened, and Christ had laid down the yoke he had borne for the sins of men." In the model of Christ, he would "fight against the Serpent, for the time was fast approaching when the first should be last and the last should be first."

Both Douglass and Turner describe their experiences in terms clearly drawn from Christian scripture, but neither man was informed exclusively by Christianity. In Douglass's case, before the showdown with Covey that left him so elated, he had been urged by a friend, in accordance with traditional African beliefs, to find a particular plant and keep it in his pocket. "He told me, with great solemnity, I must go back to Covey," Douglass wrote, "but that before I went, I must go with him into another part of the woods, where there was a certain root, which, if I would take some of it with me, carrying it always on my right side, would render it impossible for Mr. Covey, or any other white man, to whip me. He said he had carried it for years; and since he had done so, he had never received a blow, and never expected to while he carried it." Douglass expressed incredulity that this practice would have any benefit, despite American precedents dating back to the *aduru* magic used during colonial slave revolts, and even to the Hoodoo of Tituba. Still, he recognized that it was an expression of belief from which many of the enslaved drew strength. The decidedly non-Christian practice of carrying the root, then, was part of his explicitly Christian "resurrection."

Turner, too, was shaped not only by the biblical lessons he had first learned from the Methodist minister who had owned him in his youth but by traditional beliefs his mother and grandmother had brought with them across the Middle Passage. Such traditions knew the "Spirit" Turner had heard speak not as the Holy Spirit of the Gospels but as a Yoruba figure known variously as Eshu or Legbo, the god of messages, known for communicating with elements of the natural world. "Laboring in the field, I discovered drops of blood on the corn as though it were dew from heaven," Turner recalled, "and I then found on the leaves in the woods hieroglyphic characters, and numbers, with the forms of men in different attitudes, portrayed in blood, and representing the figures I had seen before in the heavens." These messages, together with the prophetic model of the Bible, formed the revelation that led to his rebellion.

In the stories of Douglass and Turner, and others like them, focus on the Christian elements at the expense of perhaps less-respected religious influences has served to create a kind of conversion narrative of the entire experience of slavery and its eventual end, making it seem as if becoming Christian was a necessary step in the struggle for freedom. Certainly a shift among the enslaved from beliefs brought to beliefs imposed did eventually occur on a communal level, giving rise to the distinctly syncretic tradition of African American Christianity, also known as the black church; but this evolution often elides the complexity of the individual lives and the struggles of those caught between one faith and the next.

This was particularly true in the case of Islam, the one set of beliefs brought by the enslaved that stressed its singularity as fervently as did Christianity. The seventeenth-century laws mentioned above allude to enslaved followers of Islam as a group, but the experiences of individuals can also be found throughout the historical record. The historian Allan Austin has catalogued and described the captivity endured by seventy-five Muslim men in both the English colonies and the young United States, many of whom left written evidence of their enduring religious affiliation with Islam. Indeed, among those who became known outside the households or plantations by which they were enslaved, literacy was not only a common bond but the trait that set them apart. The ability to read and write commanded respect in a society that did not yet take these skills for granted. Moreover, such skills represented a potential danger to a well-ordered plantation, suggesting the possibility of slaves communicating across distances and in the silence of the written word. These two implications of literacy— respect and risk—occasionally conspired to win enslaved Muslims their freedom.

Such was the case for the earliest recorded individual Muslim enslaved in North America, Ayuba Suleiman Diallo, who became known in both England and the colonies as Job ben Solomon Jallo in the 1730s. The story of Diallo's capture and enslavement— published by the Annapolis judge Thomas Bluett in London in 1734—serves as a reminder that while slavery may have become our nation's "peculiar institution," it was not particular or unique to the United States. Diallo, born in Catumbo, in present-day Angola, had assisted his father as an imam, or Islamic teacher, in their community. From his father he learned to read the Quran as well as to read and speak Arabic in addition to the local Wolof language.

Just as Christian ministers in the colonies were as likely as anyone to purchase slaves (or, like Cotton Mather, to receive them as a gift), in his native land Diallo's family of religious leaders had been wealthy enough that they had slaves of their own. As he later recounted the tale of how he came to be enslaved, in February of 1730 he had been sent by his father to sell two men, members of a neighboring non-Muslim nation, either for cash or in exchange for paper, a prize commodity in a family of scholars. When he could not reach an agreement with the English shipping captain acting as slave merchant, Diallo traded the two men for livestock and then prepared to rest for the night. After he had put down the sword he had carried with him for the journey, he was ambushed and brought back to the same Englishman with whom he had dealt the day before—this time not as a seller negotiating a price but as the one being sold.

Diallo was transported to the Americas in chains and was soon purchased at the harbor in Annapolis, the same site at which Alex Haley's ancestor Kunta Kinte would be sold to a Virginia plantation owner twenty-seven years later. Put to work on Kent Island across the Chesapeake Bay—not far from the scene of Jacob Lumbrozo's trial for blasphemy—he harvested tobacco until the work proved too physically demanding for a man of slight frame unused to long stretches of manual labor. In a bitter turnabout given the exchange he had made for two men before his capture, he was put to the task of tending livestock.

He might have passed the rest of his days as a cowherd. Like Omar ibn Said eighty years later, however, Diallo's future would be determined by his frequent seeking of solace in the prayers of his youth. While in the pastures of Kent Island, Thomas Bluett notes, "Job would often leave the Cattle, and withdraw into the Woods to pray; but a white Boy frequently watched him, and whilst he was at his Devotion would mock him, and throw Dirt in his Face. This very much disturbed Job, and added to his other Misfortunes; all which were increased by his Ignorance of the English Language, which prevented his complaining, or telling his Case to any Person about him." And once again like Omar ibn Said, he soon decided to take his chances as a runaway. He headed off to the woods as if to pray but then kept going, and did not stop running until he reached the Delaware Bay.

It was not long before he was captured. When Judge Bluett heard of a strange man locked in his jail, he brought a contingent of curious gentlemen to see him. They found that he "could not speak one Word of English," but "Upon our Talking and making Signs to him, he wrote a Line or two before us, and when he read it, pronounced the Words Allah and Mahommed; by which, and his refusing a Glass of Wine we offered him, we perceived he was a Mahometan, but could not imagine of what Country he was, or how he got thither; for by his affable Carriage, and the easy Composure of his Countenance, we could perceive he was no common Slave."

In time, they found ways to communicate. "As to his Religion, 'tis known he was a Mahometan," Bluett writes, "but more moderate in his Sentiments than most of that Religion are. He did not believe a sensual Paradise, nor many other ridiculous and vain Traditions, which pass current among the Generality of the Turks. He was very constant in his Devotion to God; but said, he never pray'd to Mahommed, nor did he think it lawful to address any but God himself in Prayer. He was so fixed in the Belief of one God, that it was not possible, at least during the Time he was here, to give him any Notion of the Trinity; so that having had a New Testament given him in his own Language, when he had read it, he told me he had perused it with a great deal of Care, but could not find one Word in it of three Gods, as some People talk: I did not care to puzzle him, and therefore answered in general, that the English believed only in one God. He shewed upon all Occasions a singular Veneration for the Name of God, and never pronounced the Word

Allah without a peculiar Accent, and a remarkable Pause: And indeed his Notions of God, Providence, and a future State, were in the main very just and reasonable."

With his captors convinced he was a man not fit for slavery, Diallo's freedom was soon purchased. He was returned home by way of England, where some well-heeled supporters first introduced him to the royal family before sending him back to Catumbo to be reunited with his own.

All told, Ayuba Suleiman Diallo remained in America less than two years, and so it is perhaps not surprising that he managed to maintain and even publicly affirm his faith. Perhaps more unexpected is the case of the man considered by Allan Austin to be the most famous African in antebellum America. Nearly a century after Diallo used his religious education to prove his humanity and escape the suffering of enslavement, a slave in Mississippi was discovered to be a prince after forty years of forced labor. He, too, revealed the extent of his education in Islam, and became a cause célèbre as a result.

Abd al-Rahman, as a contemporary newspaper account reported, was a man who "though sixty-five years of age" had "the vigour of the meridian of life." After he was recognized by an Irish doctor who had spent time in what is now Mali four decades earlier, Rahman attracted intense interest particularly among the members of the American Colonization Society, also known as the Society for the Colonization of Free People of Color of America, which advocated sending free blacks to the newly founded colony of Liberia on the west coast of Africa. ACS members, including Secretary of State Henry Clay, believed Rahman might serve as an intermediary to Muslim nations. When the sultan of Morocco heard of the slave's plight through Clay and announced that he would pay for the prince's return to his homeland, Rahman's freedom was obtained by order of President John Quincy Adams.

"Prince was educated and perhaps is still nominally at least a Mahomedian," the newspaper reporter remarked. "I have conversed with him much upon this subject, and find him friendly disposed to the Christian religion. He is extremely anxious for an Arabic Testament. He has heard it read in English, and admires its precepts. His principal objections are that Christians do not follow them. His reasoning upon this subject is pertinent, and, to our shame, is almost unanswerable."

While Omar ibn Said, Ayuba Suleiman Diallo, and Abd al-Rahman each found themselves the accidental beneficiaries of their non-Christian religious backgrounds, most other enslaved Muslims allowed their faith to slip under the surface. Understandably, many who received religious instruction from those who enslaved them or from traveling preachers repeated back the terms of Christian devotion they had been compelled to learn but kept their true religious inclinations hidden. The emergence at this time of a fully blended Muslim Christianity on southern plantations was noticed far more often in the middle of the nineteenth century than is remembered today. Describing what he would have viewed as the poor progress of slaves learning the true religion, the missionary Charles Colock Jones lamented that the "Mohammedan Africans remaining of the old stock of importations, although accustomed to hear the Gospel preached, have been known to accommodate Christianity to Mohammedanism. God, say they, is *Allah*, and Jesus Christ is *Mohammed* — the religion is the same, but different countries have different *names*."

Jones and others of his ilk saw this as a general inability on the part of enslaved Muslims to understand Christian revelation, but it more likely reflects an unwillingness to fully reject beliefs and practices smuggled aboard slave ships, even while nominally and pragmatically accepting the terms of the dominant creed. Ignoring the lessons of those who claimed to own them, enslaved men and women clung to what Jones called "*dreams, visions, trances, voices* — all bearing a perfect or striking resemblance to some form or type which has been handed down for generations." Jones, whose 1842 book *The Religious Instruction of the Negroes in the United States* was both a history of plantation-based proselytization and a how-to guide for pious slave owners, regarded the continued spiritual connection of slaves to their old ways as mere obstinance. For others, however, such acknowledgment that enslaved Africans had their own enduring traditions of belief, practice, and learning was the beginning of the realization that they were also entitled to basic human rights.

Though there was a connection between awareness of the traditions maintained by enslaved Muslims and growing wariness of slavery among some Christians, it would be an overstatement to say that Sheriff Mumford bringing Omar ibn Said to his home

244 • ONE NATION, UNDER GODS

suggests he had abolitionist sympathies of his own. He may have simply been an opportunist, or the worst kind of public servant. Omar ibn Said had come into his sphere of influence through his role as an officer of the law, but in short order the escaped slave seems to have become his property. He did not stay long with Mumford, however, but soon came under the authority of one James Porterfield Owen, a general in the War of 1812 and scion of a prominent political family that included a future governor, his brother John.

Making the best of a bad situation, Omar ibn Said remained with the family of General Owen for the rest of his life. When asked if he would like to leave the Owen plantation, he is said to have responded emphatically, "No no no no no no no." We know this and other details of his life only because, twenty years after he found himself locked in the Fayetteville jail, twenty years during which his reputation grew and he entered the service of this well-known North Carolina household, he was asked to write the story of his life.

Composed in Arabic in 1831 but not translated until 1848, *The Life of Omar ibn Said, Written by Himself* is, like many other slave memoirs of the time, framed as a conversion narrative. Yet to read between the lines is to discover a different story—a story about the surprisingly flexible meaning of religious conversion in American history.

Instructed to write the story of how he was brought to America and there found the Christian faith, he did so dutifully. The account he produced, however, is not exactly what his Christian patrons must have had in mind. Perhaps pragmatically, he mentioned more than once his newfound belief in Jesus Christ, but before any such affirmation of the tradition he had been compelled to join, he took the opportunity to make his own life story a testimony of and memorial to the way of life from which he had been torn. He had known liberty and autonomy in another language, and so writing in Arabic now, he expressed both the longing to be free, and his judgment against those who had captured him, with a fervor he apparently never expressed off the written page.

"In the name of God, the merciful, the compassionate," he wrote, beginning his life story with the *Basmala*, the phrase that begins the Quran itself, as well as 113 of its 114 suras. On the pages that follow, before a single mention of his place of birth, his family, or any other information about his life, he transcribed from memory most of the sixty-seventh sura, *Sura al-Mulk*, the identifying word of which, *mulk*, is often translated as "ownership," "dominion," or "control." As the most recent translator of Omar ibn Said's words, the scholar Ala Alryyes, points out, this meaning makes the sura the "perfect allusion to slavery." It is fitting, then, that the verses that follow are concerned primarily with divine judgment and wrath directed at those who do not know the true God—the "Christian men" who stole Omar ibn Said and the *kafir*, infidel, who purchased and abused him.

"Blessed be He in whose hand is the *mulk*," he writes, identifying the source of true ownership or control, no matter the laws that allow one man to presume to own another. This holder of *mulk* alone "has power over all things." And as for those others who defile God's dominion with delusions of their own: "We have adorned the lowest heaven with lamps, missiles to pelt the devils with," he writes. "We have prepared the scourge of fire for these, and the scourge of Hell for those who deny their Lord: an evil fate! When they are flung into the flames, they shall hear it roaring."

Only after establishing through scriptural evidence the punishment due to those who usurp the power of the divine by presuming to own others does Omar ibn Said recount the tale of how he came to be captured, brought to America, and eventually introduced to the Christian faith by the Owen family. He sings their praises as slaveholders who are kinder than most, but presents his conversion with little fanfare—as more of a practical than a heartfelt reshaping of his spirit.

When he lived in a Muslim land as a follower of Muhammad, he explained, "To pray, I said: Praise be to Allah, Lord of all Worlds, the Compassionate, the Merciful; Sovereign of the Day of Judgment; It is you we worship, and to you we turn for help; Guide us to the straight path; The path of those whom you have favored with grace; Not those who have incurred your wrath; Nor of those who have strayed. Amen."

Now that he was in a land of Christians, however, other prayers were required: "And now I pray in the words of our Lord Jesus the Messiah: Our Father, who art in heaven, hallowed be thy name, thy Kingdom come, thy Will be done, on earth as it is in Heaven. Give us this day our daily bread and forgive us our trespasses as we forgive those who trespass against us, and lead us not into temptation but deliver us from the evil one for thine is the Kingdom, the power, and the glory for ever and ever. Amen."

By entwining the story of his life with verses from the Quran and an acknowledgment of the new Christian terms to which he must adapt, Omar ibn Said created less a tale of conversion than a syncretic narrative: Like that of so many others, his is a story not of the religious remaking of a people but of a people remaking religious traditions to serve their altered circumstances. Viewed through the lens that understands conversion not merely as a change of heart or the adoption of new beliefs but rather as a negotiation that takes place on the margins of a dominant faith, Omar ibn Said's entire autobiography becomes an invocation of judgment on those who deserve it. To read of cruelty perpetrated with religious justification is to see the spiritual unsustainability of slavery laid bare. From the start of his story, when he explains that he was sold in "the Christian tongue," Omar ibn Said stubbornly asserts, to any Christian who might read his tale, that a supposedly Christian nation has been built on the most un-Christian system imaginable.

Commenting on Omar ibn Said's handwritten words in the early twentieth century, the historian John Franklin Jameson proposed that the "earlier pages of the manuscript are occupied with quotations from the Koran which Omar remembered, and these might be omitted as not autobiographical." Yet it could be argued that the judgment alluded to by these quotations was perhaps the truest expression of Omar ibn Said's thoughts on the source of the traumas of his later life. His quoted verses serve as reminders of what should have been obvious: that the men and women who had been taken in shackles from Africa brought with them their own religious assumptions, their own religious learning, their own sense of the forces, despite their current circumstances, that controlled the world.

It was perhaps the very stubbornness of Islam among its adherents that led to its broader impact on American culture. The fact that Muslims who had received religious training, as Omar ibn Said had, could recall elaborate texts and prayers decades after they had last heard or seen the Arabic language challenged Christian preconceptions about the kinds of places their enslaved population had come from, and exactly what kinds of lives they had seen stolen away.

Reflecting this, there was a noticeable shift in the purposes to which Muslim stories were put in American culture during Omar's lifetime. Mention of Islam or "Mohammedanism" in the press in the late eighteenth and early nineteenth centuries was largely limited to accounts of captivity—white captivity—among the supposedly barbarous Moors. In the year of Omar ibn Said's capture and transport to the Carolinas, for example, a popular account of one such supposed enslavement of an American in North Africa reworked the traditional tropes of kidnap and spiritual infection that had made tales of whites trapped among the Indians so popular in the previous century. The *History of the captivity and sufferings of Mrs. Maria Martin* (subtitle: *who was six years a slave in Algiers, two of which she was confined in a dark and dismal dungeon, loaded with irons for refusing to comply with the brutal request of a Turkish officer*) offered readers a salacious story couched within an overview of the history and religion of the people of Algeria. "Among these are the Moors or Morescos, who were driven out of Spain about the end of the sixteenth century," the preamble to the book's action explains, "and the Arabians who trace their descent from those disciples of Mahomet who formerly subdued this country." The role of Muslims in this and other narratives was to serve mainly as fearful villains in far-off places: dark counterpoints—in complexion and morals—to the virtue of white Americans.

Yet a half-century before the Civil War, some early abolitionists began to propose that Islam might have something to teach Christianity. This inversion of expectations can be seen in the remarkable trend that emerged in which Muslims who were slave owners in other countries began to be described by Christian opponents of slavery as being fair and just to those they enslaved. The point of such stories, at first, was to shame Christian slaveholders into acting likewise. Shouldn't followers of Jesus show themselves to be even more magnanimous than the supposedly perfidious Moor?

An 1810 edition of the *New Hampshire Patriot* recounted a tale it called "Mohammedan Forbearance," in which a Muslim is presented as a model of religious devotion and moral uprightness. "With whatever contempt a Christian may regard the faith of Mohammed," the unsigned writer states, "certain it is, that the strictness with which the observance of religious ceremonies is enforced, the alacrity with which the performance of moral duties is distinguished, and the reverence paid to the Koran by most of his followers, might be usefully imitated by the professors of purer doctrines." The case in point for this writer was, not accidentally, the treatment of slaves.

> A singular instance of forbearance, arising from the powerful influence of religious principles, is recorded in the history of the Caliphs. A slave one day during a repast, was so unfortunate as to let fall a dish which he was handing to the Caliph Hassan, who was severely scalded by the accident. The trembling wretch instantly fell on his knees, and quoting the Koran, exclaimed: "Paradise is promised to those who restrain their anger." "I am not angry with thee," replied the Caliph, with a meekness as exemplary as it was rare. "And for those who forgive offences," continued the slave. "I forgive thee thine," answered the Caliph. "But above all, for those who return good for evil," adds the slave. "I set thee at liberty," rejoins the Caliph, "and give thee ten dinars."

At a time when the abolitionist cause was in its infancy in New England, Islam was used as a parable — a moral instruction that seeks at once to enlighten, and perhaps to embarrass its audience. Not only should slaves be freed, this story suggests, they should be paid reparations. Fifty-five years before some freed slaves were granted "forty acres and a mule" in the last days of the Civil War, it was unheard-of for even the staunchest abolitionists to call openly for such a plan. Yet couched in a story of another place and another faith, such dangerous notions could be put before the conscience of the public. If a Muslim Caliph could heed his supposedly lesser religion's call to free slaves and improve their lives, how could Christians, even if they held the religion of Muhammad in contempt, not be moved to do likewise? That this was the intended message of the *New Hampshire Patriot* is reinforced by the newspaper's slogan, a well-chosen line from James Madison: "Indulging no passion which trespass on the rights of others, it shall be our true glory to cultivate peace by observing justice."

Nor was this message always so subtle. Seven years later, the *Connecticut Courant* published a lengthy report called "Treatment of Negro slaves in Morocco," calling for Christians to learn moral virtues from those who professed Islam. The abolitionists responsible for the report did not deny that Muslims were implicated in the slave trade—often as owners, sometimes as merchants—but they made the argument that followers of Muhammad treated their captives more humanely than did the followers of Christ.

> The Moors, or Moselmen, purchase their slaves from Tombuctoo....These slaves are treated very differently from the unhappy victims who used to be transported from the coasts of Guinea, and our settlements on the Gambia, to the West-India islands....After being exhibited in the souk, or public market-place, they are sold to the highest bidder, who carries them to his home, where, if found faithful, they are considered as members of the family.

Problematic though it may be as a variant on the infantilizing treatment Africans endured under the Christian yoke, the alternative model of Islamic slavery championed by the abolitionists was based on spiritual principles that would have been familiar to a Christian audience. Leading the enslaved to faith was regarded in both religious environments as a benefit to all.

> Being in the daily habit of hearing the Arabic language spoken, they soon acquire partial knowledge of it; and the Mohammedan religion teaching the unity of God, they readily reject paganism, and embrace Mohammedanism.
>   The more intelligent learn to read and write, and afterwards acquire a partial knowledge of the Koran: and such as can read and understand one chapter, from that time procure their emancipation from slavery; and the master exults in having converted an infidel, and in full faith expects favour from heaven for the action, and for having liberated a slave.

Even for those who were not so quick to learn to read Arabic and recite the Quran, slavery was considered, in the Muslim context (at least as far as the abolitionists believed), a temporary condition. The enslaved within Islam, the article claims, "generally obtain their freedom after eight to ten years of servitude; for the more conscientious Mooselmin consider them as servants, and purchase them for about the same sum that they would pay in wages to a servant during the above period; at the expiration of which term, by giving them their liberty, they, according to their religious opinions, acquire a blessing from God." Granting freedom to the enslaved was not an act of charity by which property was sacrificed. It was an opportunity to accumulate merit through an act considered more holy "than the sacrifice of a goat, or even a camel." Lest this notion fully undermine the social fabric of a nation built on slavery, the article's author rushes to suggest, "I have known some slaves so attached to their owners from good treatment, that when they have been offered their liberty, they have actually refused it, preferring to continue in servitude."

As to the conclusions that Christians should draw from this, the author pulls no punches. "While we contrast the account given above...with the manner in which the negroes have been treated for three centuries past by people calling themselves by the hallowed name of *Christian*," he writes, "what can we say other than that, the one with his heart believeth in the religion he professes, and the religion of the other lies only in his lips." Muslims, in other words, were the true people of faith — at least as far as bringing their beliefs to bear on the practice of slavery was concerned.

> Now that the abominable slave trade is no longer legalized; now that it is abolished and strictly prohibited by the general laws of Christendom, excepting Spain and Portugal: even now there are apostate Americans, who, sailing under Spanish and Portuguese colours, are robbing Africa of her sons and daughters and transporting them in fetters under every afflicting and appalling circumstance, to hopeless and most cruel servitude — even *now* there are American merchants, sitting in their counting room and coolly casting up their probable gains from such nefarious voyages, who, peradventure, on Sunday, appear at church with devout faces, and bow their heads at the name of Jesus!

A scathing attack on religious hypocrisy, but also an affirmation of a set of beliefs previously regarded as barbarous, if not demonic, this passage proposed the unthinkable: Not only could Islam provide moral instruction to Christianity, perhaps Christians themselves had something to learn from the enslaved Muslims in their midst.

*   *   *

After the story of Omar ibn Said became known—first in newspaper reports published in the 1830s, and then again when his *Life* was published in the English translation in 1848—the former fugitive slave became even more famous than he had been for filling the Fayetteville jail with Arabic graffiti.

Now a frail old man who had spent decades in the United States, he happily met those who came to see him—journalists, missionaries, scholars, and the simply curious. He claimed that though he had lived half of his life as a Muslim, those days, and those beliefs, were long behind him. An 1837 article in the *Boston Reporter* hailed him as "A Convert from Mohammedanism" and devoted two columns to an exhaustive catalogue of his Christian virtues. A magazine reporter suggested in 1854 that anyone hoping to steal a glimpse of the "venerable coloured man" could find him in the local Presbyterian congregation, where he was "a consistent and worthy member." Though he had been discovered in a church on the night he was returned to slavery forty-four years before, he now apparently sought out such "great houses" for comfort. "There are few Sabbaths in the year in which he is absent from the house of God," the magazine writer noted.

Perhaps unwittingly, Omar ibn Said was presented in the press as a "safe" Muslim to the Christian nation. It was surely not a coincidence that his story became known in the aftermath of a slave revolt in the Brazilian city of Bahia that focused the fears of slaveholders in the South and captured the imagination of the country as a whole. A report typical of the dozens that appeared throughout the winter and spring of 1835 was published in Gloucester, Massachusetts. Though far removed from the immediate threat of slave revolt, the piece described the events in Brazil in breathless detail: "On the morning of the 25th of January the whole city of Bahia was thrown into a state of the greatest excitement in consequence of an insurrection of the slaves of the Nagoa tribe, one of the bravest and most warlike of African slave nations. It was by far the best planned and most extensive rising ever contemplated by those unfortunate beings…"

According to the estimates of the day, 800 to 1,000 African-born slaves, inspired by the teachings of local Muslim teachers, had armed themselves with swords and pikes and launched an organized assault directed not just at individual slaveholders but at the government and military support that made slavery possible. According to the *Gloucester Telegraph*, the targets of the attack included "the Barracks of the Municipal Guard, the Arsenal and lastly the Palace of the President...."

Later called the Malê rebellion—from the Yoruba word for Muslim—this slave uprising was Islamic not only in the sense that most of those who fought and died were followers of Muhammad (the Nagoa tribe mentioned—now known as Nagu—accounted for the majority of Muslims in Brazil); it was also regarded as a religious battle waged against Christian slavery. Many of the nearly two hundred dead were found to be wearing protective amulets made of leather pouches containing slips of paper upon which were inscribed Quranic verses much like those Omar ibn Said had written on his jailhouse walls. Armed with this spiritual protection, the Malês "displayed the greatest intrepidity and fearlessness," the *Telegraph* continued, "many of them rushing on the bayonets when they found their project defeated, thus preferring death to continuance of slavery."

It was, in other words, every Christian slaveholder's worst nightmare—a potential holy war on every plantation. Though the revolt was ultimately quashed, news of its religious motivation spread all over the United States. The terror it caused revealed that the desire to see Muslim slaves either freed and deported (as in the cases of Ayuba Suleiman Diallo and Abd al-Rahman) or converted and brought under the control of the slaveholders' faith (as in the case of Omar ibn Said) were two means toward the same end: the eradication of Islam among the enslaved.

In the shadow of the Brazilian revolt, Omar ibn Said was cast as a formerly Muslim slave now made harmless both physically and spiritually. He was given the folksy nickname "Uncle Moro":

> Being of feeble constitution, Moro's duties have been of the lightest kind, and he has been treated rather as a friend than a servant. The garden has been to him a place of recreation rather than toil, and the concern is not that he should labor more but less. The anxious effort made to instruct him in the doctrines and precepts of our Divine Religion have not been in vain. He has thrown aside the bloodstained Koran and now worships at the feet of the Prince of Peace.

He was portrayed, in short, as everything the Muslim slaves of Bahia were not, and offered as living assurance to American slaveholders that such unpleasantness could not happen here.

"Mohammedanism has been supplanted in his heart by the better faith in Christ Jesus," his magazine biographer wrote. No longer a fugitive, he lived now "in the midst of a Christian family, where he is kindly watched over." "Since his residence with General Owen," another observer noted, "he has worn no bonds but those of gratitude and affection."

Of course, the Christian family who owned him never attempted to test this claim by setting him free.

Omar ibn Said was ninety-three years old when the Emancipation Proclamation formally liberated the enslaved African Americans of the rebelling slave states. Yet because its effects were not immediately felt across the South, he did not live long enough to again live in submission only to God and the holy book of the Prophet. His words survived him, however, and soon came to seem prophetic.

Within a year of his death in 1864, the city in which he had been jailed as a runaway slave fifty-four years earlier fell to General William Tecumseh Sherman as part of the Union army's infamous scorched-earth campaign through the Carolinas. Fayetteville had grown considerably by then, and was home to an arsenal and rifle machining facility that was one of the Confederacy's major sources of ammunition and small arms. "Since I cannot leave a guard to hold it," Sherman wrote to General Ulysses S. Grant concerning the arsenal, "I therefore shall burn it, blow it up with gunpowder, and then with rams knock down its walls." In recompense for the city's reputation as a rebel stronghold, he also ordered the destruction of "railroad trestles, depots, mills, and factories," calling for the "utter demolition" of entire neighborhoods and the wholesale pillage of the town for food and supplies. As one witness later remembered, before Sherman moved on, "the nights were made hideous with smoke."

Through this dark cloud of war, the flag of the United States again rose over the courthouse in which Omar ibn Said had never had a chance to plead his case. The Arabic verses he had written on the jail cell walls by then had been gone for more than half a century. Assuming the words he wrote then were similar to those he later committed to paper, he did not predict the destruction of this society built on the suffering of slaves. Nor did he plainly express hope that such destruction would come to pass. He did, however, ask questions fraught with the portent of prophecy:

> *O people of America, O people of North Carolina...*
> *do you have a good generation that fears Allah so much?*

Turning the terms of his religious upbringing against the institution of slavery, just as Nat Turner and Frederick Douglass had done with theirs, he directed his most chilling challenge toward the nation that had become his own:

> *Are you confident that He who is in heaven*
> *will not cause the earth to cave in beneath you,*
> *so that it will shake to pieces and overwhelm you?*

As Fayetteville shook with falling buildings and gunpowder blasts, and the peculiar institution of slavery crumbled on its cracked foundation, it was as if the city walls had finally succumbed to the weight of his prayers.

The Hindu god Vishnu and his consort Lakshmi resting on Anata, the serpent without end. Illustration from *Iconographic Encyclopaedia of Science, Literature, and Art,* by Johann G. Heck. New York: Rudolph Garrigue, 1851.

CHAPTER 12

Krishna's Sisters

1822–1893

The Reverend Elijah Parish's parsonage, in the village of Byfield, Massachusetts, was a wood-shingled embodiment of the religious legacy of New England. While it stood for more than two centuries as an undeniable monument to the influence and continuity of Puritanism in the American experience, it was also home to an accidental meeting of religious perspectives that shaped the radically pluralistic sensibility of the nation.

Built in 1703, the parsonage housed the Congregational ministers of the village for generations. It played host to major religious figures of the colonial era (the spark of the First Great Awakening, the English preacher George Whitefield, was a friend of Rev. Moses Parsons, the village's minister from 1744 to 1783) and even saw the birth of a drafter of the state constitution and chief justice of the Massachusetts Supreme Judicial Court (Moses's son Theophilus). The stubborn relevance of this humble pastor's lodging — from the era of Cotton Mather, through the ages of religious revival and revolution, and into the nineteenth century when the separation of church and state was in theory the law of the land — suggests something of the spiritual inheritance of the young democracy. The descendants of men who had ruled in an openly theocratic society often rose to prominence in the secular framework that succeeded it.

In the first quarter of the nineteenth century, everyone in the vicinity of Byfield would have known that the parsonage had a deep and significant history. To some it seemed haunted by it. As the poet Thomas Buchanan Read described it in verse (*A modest building, somewhat gray / Escaped from time, from storm, disaster; / The very threshold worn away / With feet of those who sought the pastor...*), the parsonage was a place that wore its past on its sleeve, evident for all to see. The three-story clapboard house stood behind a grove of ancient trees, which gave it the appearance of a ruin. It was said that when the branches of these trees were not fully spread with leaves, the stars shone through them like spirits staring down on the living souls who passed beneath.

Even these spirits might have been surprised by the meeting that occurred between a pair of visitors to the parsonage in the spring of 1822. The first of these guests, a forty-six-year-old woman named Mary Moody Emerson, seemed initially not at all out of place, at least not in her appearance or her background. She had in fact stayed at Byfield before ("never was solitude better personified," she said of the place). Moreover, she came from a long line of ministers, so she felt at home under Reverend Parish's roof. Yet as she was stubbornly unmarried (having sworn fifteen years before "never to put that ring on"), and traveling alone on what she called a pilgrimage, she had an autonomy that seemed suspicious to many at the time. If questions arose concerning the propriety of her solo excursions around the region, she might have pointed out that she had been present in her infancy at the first skirmishes that won the nation its independence (her father, it was said, had carried her swaddled across the battlefield at Concord), and so she expected nothing less than independence for herself.

As any who met her at the parsonage would have immediately realized, Mary Moody Emerson possessed a quick tongue, a quicker wit, and a peculiar demeanor. She stood just four foot three inches tall and kept her blonde hair cropped short, but lest anyone treat her as they might a child because of this, she became a master at challenging the expectations of others with little more than a glance. As one admirer noted, "Her blue eyes flashed like steel and stabbed like swords; she was expert in the look that demolishes." In her later years, apparently impatient for death so that she might leave behind the bothersome attentions of the living, she was known to wear a long black veil, as if she did not trust her kin to fit her with a proper burial shroud. When her death finally did come, in 1863, a Boston newspaper remarked, "She was thought to have the power of saying more disagreeable things in a half hour than any person living."

A prototypical American eccentric, she was also, many of her contemporaries said, an undeniable genius. In her youth she had been formed by works ranging from the poet of the Enlightenment John Milton to the preacher of the Great Awakening Jonathan Edwards, as well as from the classical philosophy of Plato to the classical liberalism of John Locke, and of course her Bible. A devout Christian, she nonetheless inherited the tradition of "strange opinions" that had served as counterpoint to majority religious belief in New England from the first decades of the Massachusetts Bay Colony. In another era she might have joined Anne Hutchinson in exile, or Mary Dyer on the gallows. Yet by the early nineteenth century, she was free to pursue her strange opinions with only the sniffing of polite society to fear—and she did not fear it in the slightest.

All of this made Mary Moody Emerson particularly receptive to the second unusual guest to arrive at Reverend Parish's parsonage that season. He arrived about a month after she did—fortuitously, as Mary was beginning to find that her host's orthodoxies were wearing thin. Though this second visitor's name is lost to history, we know that he had recently come from India. "Our Stranger," Mary would later call him.

The Reverend Parish had traveled the globe as a missionary. He counted himself not only a preacher but a historian of world cultures, even something of a geographer, providing his less well-informed neighbors with descriptions of the terrain and organization of far-flung lands. In his sermons he regularly expressed his thoughts on the great variety of nations and beliefs that had not yet had the good fortune, as he and his congregants of the Byfield church would have seen it, to embrace the Gospel. If any home in New England should play host to such an exotic figure as a man from the region then sometimes called Hindustan, it would have been Parish's parsonage.

In all of the reverend's recorded thoughts on the subject of "the Hindoos," however, he does not give the impression that he would welcome one of them into his home. "If you sail to India, you may see sixty millions of people bowing to thirty millions of gods," he once preached. "You may see a system of morals which strike the mind with horror; you may see infants murdered by their parents; you may see their sick friends deserted to die alone; you may see the widows burning in the same fires with their husbands."

According to the theory Reverend Parish had cited in his book *Sacred Geography*, a "gazetteer" of all the places mentioned or alluded to in the Bible, India was a land settled by Ham, a son of Noah, following the biblical flood.

"Noah foretold that the children of Ham would be servants of servants," he reported. As a result, "this country has been inhabited from the earliest antiquity by a people who have no resemblance, either in their figure or manners with any of the nations contiguous to them; though different conquerors have established themselves at different times, and in various parts of India; yet the aboriginal inhabitants have lost very little of their original character." It was, he notes, a place "where the primitive religion and languages of the Hindoos prevail at this day."

This of course was the reason Christian missionaries like himself traveled there, secure in their belief that bringing the light of Jesus Christ to a people still in darkness was a glory all its own. Yet to an extent rarely realized at the time, mission work was often a two-way street. Parish expressed some surprise at the areas of overlap between the supposedly heathen beliefs he had hoped to expunge from the earth and those with which he hoped to replace them. Of the biblical story of the ancient grudge between the serpent and humanity, in which it was said that the two species were doomed to an endless cycle of animosity in which man would crush the serpent's head and the serpent would bite the son of man's heel, Parish's gazetteer proposed: "Much the same notion, we are informed, is prevalent in the mythology of the Hindoos. Two sculptured figures are yet extant, in one of their oldest pagodas, the former of which represents Chreeshna, an incarnation of their mediatorial God, Vishnu, trampling on the crushed head of the serpent; while in the latter, it is seen encircling the deity in its folds, and biting his heel."

There was, the preacher grudgingly admitted, some connection between this backward people and those he considered by God's grace to possess the true faith. It was precisely on this subject that "Our Stranger" was invited to discourse at the parsonage.

With a former missionary and the pugnacious daughter of a long line of unyielding Puritans looking on, the guest from India presented his audience with images of the god Vishnu in various forms. The collection of icons he showed them is usually called the Dashavatara, in which a sky-blue deity is depicted alternately with the swinging tail of a fish or a whale, with the bared teeth of a ferocious jungle cat, with the shell of a tortoise, and with the tusks of a boar. In other images he is represented as Rama, as Krishna, as Buddha, and as a dwarf. The Dashavatara is a visual representation of the core truth of Hinduism: that divinity exists in all manner of manifestations.

There is no record of what Reverend Parish thought of this display. Yet something in these images apparently touched Mary Emerson deeply. Her faith as a Christian was not shaken by the Dashavatara or the accompanying explanations of devotion in a radically different context. On the contrary, she saw in this diversity of faith an affirmation of her own, not at the expense of the other but as its complement. She recognized in it something akin to the classical mythology that was then part of every well-rounded education; but more than this, Our Stranger's display seemed to point to something beyond the flawed deities sung about by the poets of the Romans and the Greeks. To her surprise, this story of Vishnu presented aspects of God she counted among her own beliefs.

If the visitor's explication of Hinduism was very different from descriptions of Indian religion offered by missionaries like Reverend Parish, it was perhaps because he was a follower of a Bengali reformer named Rammohan Roy, who early in the nineteenth century had begun to rid traditional devotions of widow-burning and other practices he believed impeded social progress. This, too, appealed to Mary Emerson. A feminist by circumstance long before the word existed, she lived her life as an expression of women's rights, even if she would not have spoken of it in those terms.

Given her prickly temperament, she was not close to many people, but she did have a nephew—then newly graduated from Harvard—whom she had taken under her wing as confidante and protégé. She had lived several years with the young man's family after his father had died, and found herself in the unlikely role of mentor and spiritual guide to a crowd of brothers at various stages of adolescence. Following the visitor's lecture on Hindu mythology, she excitedly wrote a letter, in her tidy hand, to the favorite of her four nephews:

My Dear Waldo,

*I have been fortunate this week to find a Visitor here from India,
well versed in its literature and theology. He showed us some fine
representations of the incarnation of Vishnoo. They are much
akin to Greecian fable—and from his representation I believe the
incarnations to be much like the doctrine of transmigration. At
bottom of the histories of the incarnation is often the doctrine of
the universal presence & agency of the One God...*

Our Stranger had made a gift to her of several of these images,
she added, and in each illustration—whether it showed the deity as
a fish, as a lion, as a whale, or as a dwarf—there was something
that reminded her of her own Christian faith as she understood it.
In all the strange new beliefs the visitor described to her, "there
was a strong resemblance" to Christianity—or, as she noted in her
informal shorthand, "to the xtian facts." Eager to share the Hindu
devotional pictures she had received, Mary wrote to her nephew, "I
will send some of those he gave to me, if you have not met them."

The education of this promising young man, she had decided,
would be her life's work. Given a new view of the world and its
gods by this visitor from India, she saw it as her responsibility to
share it with her nephew first of all.

Mary's nephew was Ralph Waldo Emerson, founder of the Transcendentalist movement, which would give the United States its
first poetic and philosophical vernacular. Emerson was the earliest
man of letters in America to take a sustained interest in the region
of the world broadly called "the East."

Genius though many of her contemporaries claimed Mary
Emerson to be, we likely know her name only because of her connection to this great man in the making. In this she joins uncountable other women of talent and intellect who were not allowed
either by family life or social constraints to meet their potential.
Yet in Mary's case we might find some solace in the possibility that
we know Ralph Waldo's name only because of the inspiration she
offered, and the challenges she put to him, throughout his life.
From an early age she urged one of the nation's first great public
intellectuals to look beyond his own provincial experiences, leading him eventually, though not intentionally, to shrug off his

family's expectations that he would join the long line of Christian ministers from which he came. She was, to the say the least and the best of her, an unsettling force in the lives of those around her, perhaps most of all in the life of her bright nephew. "If Aunt Mary finds out anything is dear or sacred to you, she instantly flings broken crockery·at that," Ralph Waldo later said of his aunt. She was the stone against which he sharpened the edge of his mind.

She was also the originating source of much of what seemed to make him original in his day. Before he became synonymous with the virtue of "Self Reliance," as his most famous essay is called, she was the self upon whom he relied. Even the "nonconformity" he claimed as a spiritual path he learned by her example. The frequent employment of tropes and images of Asia for which Emerson became known, for instance, came to him covered with his aunt's fingerprints.

Their correspondence concerning the arrival of Our Stranger at Byfield was not a singular moment but rather part of an ongoing conversation. It was a conversation that led Waldo to begin writing poems using the spiritual paradigms of India to explore an alternative to the religious orthodoxies of his own time and place. Initially he suspected that these traditions might contain too much superstition to withstand intellectual scrutiny, but his Aunt Mary's interest, and the new model of Hindu devotion advocated by the visitor's teacher Rammohan Roy, convinced him otherwise.

In time, the religious philosophy of India would become one of Emerson's great subjects, giving the faith of Reverend Parish's "sixty millions of people bowing to thirty millions of gods" a permanent place in the American canon, and in the process remaking the spiritual imagination of the nation.

Insofar as it is discussed at all, the history of Hinduism in America is often told as if it began nearly seven decades after Mary Emerson's meeting with the Vishnu-devoted stranger. It was then, during a much more high-profile meeting of religious perspectives, that another visitor from India, the Calcutta-born Hindu holy man Swami Vivekananda, made an attention-grabbing appearance at the 1893 Chicago Parliament of the World's Religions. Appearing on stage with a number of other exotic gurus of the east, Vivekananda treated the assembled luminaries—for the most part white Protestants not too many years away from the missionizing perspective of Reverend Parish—to words perhaps similar in spirit to those Mary Emerson had heard in the parsonage.

"I am proud to belong to a religion which has taught the world both tolerance and universal acceptance," Vivekananda said. "We believe not only in universal toleration, but we accept all religions as true." Well received though those words were, the words that meant the most to his audience were apparently his first, the greeting that by all accounts brought the house down: "Sisters and brothers of America."

The forward-thinking American attendees of the Parliament were naturally predisposed to respond favorably to the Indian's suggestion that there was a familial connection between his tradition and their own. Yet one wonders if the largely male audience even noticed the order of his greeting: sisters first, then brothers. Perhaps this was simply a nod to Western chivalry, but it would have been appropriate if he had intended to give women pride of place in his address. The outsized role they had played in the introduction of Eastern religions to America was largely responsible for his attendance.

It was not just Mary Emerson who had held open the door to the East for her male acquaintances. Another woman in the Transcendentalist orbit, Ralph Waldo's former Latin student Elizabeth Palmer Peabody, became the first publisher and translator of a Buddhist text in America. Her edition of the Lotus Sutra, translated from an earlier French rendition and published and sold in her own bookshop on West Street in Boston, has been mistakenly attributed to Henry David Thoreau (about whom we'll hear more in a moment), but in truth the work was hers alone.

Still another woman without whom Vivekananda might not have received such a warm reception was Margaret Fuller, who hosted a series of conversations in Boston, beginning in the spring of 1841, during which the city's self-styled intellectual elite attempted to describe connections between all the world's philosophies. Though the room was packed with the sharpest wits and biggest egos in New England, Fuller first held court, giving a genealogy of mythology as it developed from one culture to another. Her audience would have taken for granted the primacy of the Greek and Roman pantheons, but Fuller proposed that all attempts to capture the mysteries of the universe in narrative form actually began in India.

"The Hindus dwelt in the All, the Infinite, which the Greeks analyzed and to some degree humanized," she said. The earliest attempts to make sense of the two sides of existence could be found in the scriptures of the Bhagavad Gita, the Vedas, and the Upanishads. "All things sprang from Coelus and Terra," she added, "from Heaven and Earth, or spirit and matter."

In the generation after Fuller and Peabody, other women were the driving force behind the newly birthed Theosophy movement, which borrowed liberally from both Hinduism and Buddhism. Thanks to their well-heeled sponsors, Theosophists began bringing Indian religious teachers like Vivekananda to the United States for speaking tours that packed music halls and libraries in cities large and small. Such guests were not welcome everywhere, it must be noted. Vivekananda, for one, was denied a room at a number of hotels in Baltimore. No matter what kind of wisdom he offered, in some parts of the country he was seen as a brown man first of all.

So common were these exotic visitors in the Northeast, however, that by the 1890s, a few months after the Parliament of the World's Religions, even before Vivekananda had made his way to New England, a Massachusetts Sunday paper remarked, "Boston finds India a fascinating topic, and its swarthy representatives are always well received." Among those mentioned in the article that followed were Pandita Ramabai, an Indian social reformer who had become well known in her native Bengal as one of India's few female Sanskrit scholars. In Boston she spoke to the learned people of the city on the education of child widows, who were often as young as five years old, in the western Indian state of Maharashtra, where Ramabai had founded an organization called Arya Mahila Samaj, the "Noble Women's Society."

Other Indians gaining attention in America at this time included the Pune-born teenager Anandi Gopal Joshi, who wrote a letter at the age of fifteen to an American missionary expressing her desire to study medicine in the United States. The year before, she had given birth to her first child, but owing to a lack of medical care, the baby had died in infancy. When the missionary published Joshi's letter along with his opinion that no unconverted Hindu should come to America, the young woman's cause was taken up by a benefactor in New Jersey, who began a lengthy correspondence and soon sponsored a trip to Philadelphia. In 1886, Dr. Joshi became one of the first Hindu doctors trained in the United States,

266 • ONE NATION, UNDER GODS

and certainly the first Hindu woman to earn an American degree. Unlike many of the marquee celebrities "from the East" then filling concert halls up and down the East Coast, Dr. Joshi did not remain for a speaking tour but returned to India, where she received a hero's welcome.

Regular public appearances were also made by well-traveled American women who had been to India, including Dr. Alice Bunker Stockham (referred to in the Boston press as "physician, editor, traveler, lecturer, mother and housekeeper"), who brought back from India information about tantric sexual techniques. Dr. Stockham later became famous for secularizing these ritual practices as *maithuna*, the withholding of seminal emission during intercourse. As she wrote in her book *The Ethics of Marriage*, she had learned of this approach to marital relations when visiting "a peculiar people" on India's west coast. The peculiarity of this people, she explained, lay in the fact that among them, "women are the lords of creation."

"They are called the free women of India," she writes. "They seek their husbands, control business interests, and through them only is the descent of property. The family and the whole fabric of society is founded upon the mother. She is the key-stone of the arch, for she chooses who shall be the father of her child and bestows her worldly goods according to her desires and discretion. She marries the man of her choice. If for any reason, however, she deems him unfit to be a husband or a father of her child, it requires no ceremony of church or state to free her from him. Her wish and word are law."

The reason for this, she notes, is *maithuna* (often referred to by its alternate name *kareeza* in her work), which, practically speaking, amounted to a form of birth control and a limit on the size of families. Stockham would later become a suffragist and early advocate of women's rights not just for the "peculiar people" of India but in America as well. Similarly, references to India generally and Hinduism specifically in early feminist writing suggest that the subcontinent provided the nascent movement with a testing ground for its ideas. Among the writers thus influenced were Matilda Joslyn Gage and Elizabeth Cady Stanton, who, together with Susan B. Anthony, founded the National Woman Suffrage Association in 1869. Matilda Gage found much to admire in the treatment of women described by Indian religious texts. In her monumental work *Woman, Church and State,* Gage sifted through thousands of years of history to find examples of women both respected and abused by religion. Gage suggested that in this comparison, Hinduism fared better than most other traditions—and far better than the faith practiced closest to home.

"In Sanskrit mythology, the feminine is represented by Swrya, the Sun, the source of life, while the masculine is described as Soma, a body....The marriage of the man to the woman was symbolized as his union with the gods....In the same manner, woman representing spirit, by her marriage to man became united with a body."

In the India of bygone days, she explained, "marriage was entirely optional with woman and when entered into frequently meant no more than spiritual companionship." This companionship, according to Gage, was based foremost on religious equality. "Woman equally with man was entitled to the Brahminical thread; she also possessed the right to study and preach the Vedas, which was in itself a proof of her high position in this race. The Vedas, believed to be the oldest literature extant, were for many ages taught orally requiring years of close application upon part of both teacher and student. The word 'Veda' signifies to-know; the latter from 'Vidya' meaning wise. The English term 'widow' is traceable to both forms of the word, meaning a wise woman."

Contrasting the equality she saw in the long-ago time of a distant shore with the dominant tradition of her own time and nation, she could only find the latter wanting. Closer to home, she wrote, "woman is told that her present position in society is entirely due to Christianity...Church and State both maintaining that she has ever been inferior and dependent, man superior and ruler."

Gage provided a list of "maxims from the sacred books" that "show the regard in which the Hindoo woman is held":

"He who despises woman despises his mother."
"Who is cursed by woman is cursed by God."
"The tears of a woman call down the fire of heaven on those who make them flow."
"Evil to him who laughs at woman's sufferings; God shall laugh at his prayers."
"It was at the prayer of a woman that the Creator pardoned man; cursed be he who forgets it."

"Who shall forget the sufferings of his mother at his birth shall be reborn in the body of an owl during three successive transmigrations."

"There is no crime more odious than to persecute woman."

"When women are honored the divinities are content; but when they are not honored all undertakings fail."

And perhaps most ominous, in its combination of specificity and threat:

"The households cursed by women to whom they have not rendered the homage due them find themselves weighed down with ruin and destroyed as if they had been struck by some secret power."

In contrast to Gage's cross-cultural optimism about the role of women in India, Elizabeth Cady Stanton argued that there was also much to learn from the female oppression in Hinduism, which she felt mirrored Christian society in harsher ways. When Stanton looked East she saw only more to rail against, particularly *suttee*, or widow burning.

"Man has ever manifested a wish that the world should indeed be a blank to the companion whom he leaves behind him," Stanton said in an address to the New York State Legislature in 1860. "The Hindu makes that wish a law, and burns the widow on the funeral pile of her husband; but the civilized man, impressed with a different view of the sacredness of life, takes a less summary mode of drawing his beloved partner after him; he does it by the deprivation and starvation of the flesh, and the humiliation and mortification of the spirit."

These contrasting views reflected two approaches to the question of rights generally. While Stanton dismissed the entirety of Indian culture as uncivilized, Gage took the time to argue against disputed practices such as widow burning on the religious terms of those who stubbornly championed them: "The comparatively modern custom of *suttee* originated with the priests, whose avaricious desires created this system in order thereby to secure the property of the widow," she wrote. "The Vedas do not countenance either *suttee* or the widow's relinquishment of her property, the law specifically declaring if a widow should give all her property and estate to the Brahmins for religious purposes, the gift indeed is valid, but the act is improper."

As Gage points out, even this ability on the part of Hindu women to make a gift of their own property was an improvement over laws of some supposedly more civilized nations. "During long centuries while under Christian law the Christian wife was not allowed even the control of property her own at the time of marriage, or of that which might afterwards be given her, and her right of the disposition of property at the time of her death was not recognized in Christian lands, the Hindoo wife, under immemorial custom could receive property by gift alike from her parents, or from strangers, or acquire it by her own industry, and property thus gained was at her own disposal..."

Hinduism, then, represented an alternate cultural framework to suffragettes like Gage, one that, if implemented in its ideal form, would provide women with more rights than they enjoyed in nineteenth-century America. As a conceptual substitute for the spiritual status quo, it was a faith that seemed to Gage to make a place for the feminine in both theory and practice. As she wrote hopefully, "An ancient scripture declares that 'All the wisdom of the Vedas, and all that has been written in books, is to be found concealed in the heart of a woman.'"

Like Dr. Stockham's importation of tantra, much of this late-nineteenth-century interest in India had sexual overtones. The revered Pandita Ramabai is frequently described as "slender" and "large-eyed," clad in "her native costume of soft white draperies." The guru tours sponsored by the Theosophical Society had an undeniable sexual edge and at times were advertised with a carnival barker's sense of peep show appeal. With the promise of Swami Vivekananda revealing "his gorgeous Oriental turban," the press took pleasure in reporting, his lectures were always "crowded with ladies."

There is much that could be said about the transformation of traditions thousands of years old into the hobby of affluent Americans. Indeed, upon Vivekananda's death in 1901, the press collectively lamented that an unassailably moral teacher of wisdom had been made "faddish," and that he had fallen in with such "flighty" women as the opera star Emma Calvé.

Yet it would be too easy to dismiss the rising interest in Indian religion throughout the nineteenth century as a brief fixation with a mere spiritual bauble. To begin with, there was perhaps some karmic justice in the role of all these stubbornly independent women playing a part in a burgeoning equal rights movement of a religious tradition that included widow burning. It is no accident that the versions of Hinduism that found the most favor with American women and their Transcendentalist brethren were the same versions that in India are credited with the birth of nationalism and the eventual end of British rule.

Moreover, in their promotion of Indian ideas as an attractive alternative to local traditions, these proponents of Hinduism and its representatives answered a curiosity that existed even before Mary Emerson's time. The earliest references to "Hindoos" or "Hindooism" in the American press go back deep into the eighteenth century. Many of these references are concerned only with the odd ways of the "pagans" or "heathens," as they were variously called, but beginning not long after the birth of the new nation, there were noticeable positive developments in the way Americans talked about India.

Out of the shadow of the era of exploration, with trade between the East and West now commonplace, there arose an increased awareness (or at least the beginning of awareness) that non-Christian lands were not places suffering from a lack of belief but full of beliefs of their own.

This shift in tone in the discussion of the subcontinent, its people, and its religious ideas came about due mainly to two influences. The first was the Eastern-curious romanticism of English writers whose work was then drifting across the ocean. The Orientalist poems of William Jones (whose name and verse appear frequently in Mary Emerson's letters to Waldo) were delivered to enraptured audiences, including the one assembled on a May evening in 1787, when his Excellency George Washington was treated to a recitation of Jones's "Hymn to the Hindu God of Love." The Scottish writer Elizabeth Hamilton's *Translation of the Letters of a Hindoo Rajah*—written by Hamilton in the voice of a fictional Indian royal—became an international publishing sensation, and the measure against which similar efforts of cultural ventriloquism would be judged.

This desire to understand Indian culture from the inside can be seen with particular clarity in a proposal to publish "The Ordinances of Menu" made in 1800. A pre-publication advertisement described the ancient collection of Hindu law and custom in terms that strained to make its arcane contents relevant to an age of Enlightenment and revolution. "The work here offered to the American public contains abundance of curious matter for every intelligent reader," the publisher wrote. "A spirit of sublime devotion, of benevolence to mankind, and of amiable tenderness to all sentient creatures, pervades the whole work; the style of it has a certain austere majesty that sounds like the language of legislation, and extorts a respectful awe; the sentiments of independence, on all beings but God, and the harsh admonitions even to kings are truly noble."

Interest in India was not all so earnest, however. In a widely syndicated newspaper column claiming to be "Letters of a Hindu Philosopher Residing in Philadelphia," a writer using the name "Shah Coolen" regularly remarked on American culture in the voice of a sage of the East, sometimes to great comedic effect.

"Often, when reclining on a sofa, by the side of a fair American, I have thought that her white bosom, scarcely veiled at all from my sight, and her finely proportioned limbs, which the extreme thinness and narrowness of her apparel rendered quite evident to the eye, would have excited impure emotions in any heart less subject to reason than that of a Hindu philosopher."

Shah Coolen goes on in subsequent dispatches to compare the biblical love verses of the Song of Songs to the twelfth-century Indian devotional poem known as the Gita Govinda, which describes in great detail the god Krishna's trysts with a group of young women in the forest ("note how Krishna wantoned in the wood / Now with this one, now that"). This coupling of Hebrew and Sanskrit poetry would make a fascinating work in the study of comparative religious texts were the author not wholly concerned with the naughty bits.

Shah Coolen's "Letters" appeared in dozens of newspapers and were later compiled as a book, which the *Boston Review* dismissed as a knockoff of Elizabeth Hamilton's earlier and better effort. In the eyes of proper society, however, the real problem with Shah Coolen was not his literary ability but the apparently immoral company he kept. As one critic sniffed, "We believe the profanity mentioned in the fourth letter applicable to no sect of females but that with which Shah Coolen seems to be so intimately acquainted."

Immoral or no, all of these entries in the canon of Western Orientalism pivot around another influence that brought interest in India to the fore in America at the turn of the nineteenth century. The war — or rather, the series of wars — then being fought on the subcontinent had made it a place not unlike North America. The Polygar Wars, waged from 1799 to 1805 against the British in the area of southern India that now comprises the state of Tamil Nadu, were the first attempts to win Indian independence by force. Likewise, the Vellore Mutiny of 1806 found Indians fighting governing outsiders for the survival of their culture and beliefs. When restrictions were placed on both Hindus and Muslims making outward displays of their faith — via *tilak* forehead markings for the former and beards for the latter — the ensuing uprising killed more than a hundred British troops. Though neither the mutiny nor the wars were ultimately successful, these skirmishes recast longtime rivals in familiar roles on a novel stage, with the English attempting to put down rebellion while the French covertly funded and supported it. Becoming another New World that served as a battleground for Old World grudges, India offered the young United States, for the first time, a mirror that was not Europe. Seen in this looking glass, Americans saw the "land of the Hindoos" as a country that could not be more different from their own. Yet it, too, was being formed by an ongoing clash of beliefs.

If there was a single Hindu to whom Americans looked most often to make meaning of this reflection, it was Rammohan Roy, who was at the time becoming a subject of considerable interest in America, particularly among the Unitarians of New England.

Born in Bengal in 1772, Roy appealed to the liberal and literary classes in the United States as one who, just barely older than their own young nation, put a relatively youthful face on an ancient culture. Reports of his reform efforts in India, and occasional erroneous claims of his conversion to Christianity, appeared regularly in Boston's *Christian Register,* which was regular reading for Unitarians, including the Emerson clan. The secular press, too, hailed him as a one-man civilizing force among the heathen masses of a non-Christian land. Taking some perverse pleasure in providing detailed accounts of grieving widows throwing themselves (or being thrown) onto their husbands' funeral pyres, American journalists introduced Roy as the only hope of a backward people.

As early as 1817, the *Otsego Herald* in Cooperstown, New York, gave Roy credit for attempting to convince would-be suicides that their understanding of the practice of following their husbands into the funerary flames was not found in any sacred text. "We also have reason to believe that the Bengalee writings of Ram Mahon Roy, have made a deep, though at present not very obvious, impression on the Hindoos of Calcutta and its neighborhood, which may actually lead to the entire extinction of this, as well as many other practices, alike abhorrent to reason and humanity." As the report continued, "It was suggested. . . . by Ram Mahon Roy, that in the actual mode by which females are burnt on the funeral pyre of their husbands, there had been a wide departure from the method described in the holy books of the Hindoos." Within five years, the *Newburyport Herald* referred to him as "the celebrated Hindoo reformer Ran Mahun Roy," and praised his efforts for bringing about such widespread change that many of the "superstitions" against which he had fought were no longer common in Calcutta.

The support Roy received among Unitarians no doubt had something to do with the fact that the reforms he proposed amounted to a kind of Unitarian Hinduism. In his struggle over an exotic multiplicity of local gods and practices in favor of a more unified national religion, Unitarians saw their own struggle over the concept of the Trinity, which they took to be unnecessarily complicated and idolatrous by nature. Thanks in large part to this cross-cultural resonance, Roy's version of Hinduism would ultimately become even more dominant in the West than in India itself. His modernized faith was to some extent a vast religious system simplified and shorn of its problematic history and local customs to achieve greater uniformity and broader appeal. To some of his admirers, it seemed positively American.

Simplified though it may have been, Roy's version of Hinduism was tremendously influential, both in India and abroad. It became a philosophy that might be discussed anywhere — even in the sitting rooms and lecture halls of Boston intellectuals. In the first part of the eighteenth century, in other words, Hindus became another "people of the book," and their beliefs became something not practiced in far-off temples but thought to be containable between covers on a library shelf.

That is precisely where Ralph Waldo Emerson's friend Henry David Thoreau found them. He borrowed books from Emerson's library when he was composing his first published works. Emerson may not have known that his younger friend planned to rough it with his own precious tomes in tow, but Thoreau brought a few of these purloined texts with him to Walden Pond. The volume of writings he produced there, *Walden* — the book that many would say birthed American environmental consciousness — is in fact a marriage of Hindu religious ideas with the burgeoning romantic attachment to the American wilderness, a mapping of India within the borders of the United States: "In the morning I bathe my intellect in the stupendous and cosmogonal philosophy of the Bhagvat-Geeta, since whose composition years of the gods have elapsed, and in comparison with which our modern world and its literature seem puny and trivial; and I doubt if that philosophy is not to be referred to a previous state of existence, so remote is its sublimity from our conceptions. I lay down the book and go to my well for water, and lo! there I meet the servant of the Bramin, priest of Brahma and Vishnu and Indra, who still sits in his temple on the Ganges reading the Vedas, or dwells at the root of a tree with his crust and water jug. I meet his servant come to draw water for his master, and our buckets as it were grate together in the same well. The pure Walden water is mingled with the sacred water of the Ganges."

So moved was Thoreau by Emerson's books on Hinduism — a collection begun, it seems, with Mary Moody Emerson's gift to him of the materials she had received from Our Stranger — that he soon heard echoes of Indian religious texts as he traveled through crowded New England in search of moments of solitude. As he wrote in *On the Concord and Merrimack Rivers:* "A strain of music reminds me of a passage of the Vedas, and I associate with it the idea of infinite remoteness, as well as beauty and serenity, for to the senses that is furthest from us which addresses the greatest depth within us. It teaches us again and again to trust the remotest and finest as the divinest instinct, and makes a dream our only real experience."

Nor were the Transcendentalists the only nineteenth-century American writers drawn to this exotic literary soil. Following Emerson's lead in finding poetic inspiration in Indian texts, the far more conventional (and at the time far more popular) poet Henry Wadsworth Longfellow turned to the Ramayana for the source of one of his most beguiling poems. Longfellow used a tale well known among Hindus to tell a story of man suspended between worlds, King Trishanku, a ruler who wanted to be transported to the realm of the gods but instead became caught for eternity between the mortal and the divine: "Thus by aspirations lifted / By misgivings downward driven / Human hearts are tossed and drifted / Midway between earth and heaven."

Unlike the writers who borrowed Indian characters and tropes earlier in the century for their exotic allure, those writing after Emerson popularized Eastern philosophy sought to highlight the universal stories that could be told in Hindu terms. Walt Whitman went so far as to use the metaphor of the "Passage to India," as he called one poem, to suggest a journey to the varied kinds of knowledge that might be found among the diverse peoples of the earth. It was only through a personal "passage to India," he wrote, that the soul could approach "the far-darting beams of the spirit! — the unloos'd dreams!," "the deep diving bibles and legends," and "the daring plots of the poets," all those things that were to be found in "the elder religions."

Even Herman Melville, who at times was a scathing critic of Emerson (upon hearing him lecture, Melville once derided the "sage of Concord" as "a Plato who talks thro' his nose"), drew inspiration from the Transcendentalists' eastward turn. Unlike the other celebrated writers of his day, Melville had actually seen many of the places where worship of exotic gods could be found. For nearly four years he traveled the Pacific, becoming well acquainted with the beliefs of a number of non-Christian peoples. While his travels did not take him as far as India, his return to American shores in the late 1840s corresponded precisely with the moment at which the Transcendentalists were publishing their Indian-influenced essays and verse.

In 1849, he attended a lecture given by Emerson in Boston and, despite previous quips at his elder's expense, wrote of the experience, "I think Emerson is more than a brilliant fellow....I love all men who *dive*. Any fish can swim near the surface, but it takes a great whale to go down stairs five miles or more; & if he dont attain the bottom, why, all the lead in Galena can't fashion the plummet that will." He was talking not only of Emerson, he stressed, "but of the whole corps of thought-divers, that have been diving & coming up again with blood-shot eyes since the world began."

With *Moby-Dick* well begun, Melville's comparison of those, like Emerson, who seek out the depths of existence to "a great whale" is intriguing on its own, and it becomes all the more so when one considers how often he described the whale of his own creation in explicitly Hindu terms.

Much like Emerson's aunt, Melville was drawn to the devotional symbols of India that considered the great creature of the deep among ten forms taken on by the divine. The chase at the heart of the book is not merely after an image of God or death but "the Hindoo whale...depicting the incarnation of Vishnu in the form of leviathan." Later in the book, even the whale itself—its flesh, its form—comes to stand in for the religion of India. The smell of its burning blubber, our narrator Ishmael relates, "has an unspeakable, wild, Hindoo odor about it," adding, in a nod to one of the pressing social concerns of the day, that it was "such as may lurk in the vicinity of funereal pyres." As local and specific as that reference is, however, when Melville's whale-obsessed captain speaks of Indian religion it is far more expansive, comprising one part of the duality of existence: "Oh, thou dark Hindoo half of nature," Ahab prays, "rock me with a prouder, if a darker faith."

Most interesting, given his earlier skepticism of the Transcendentalists as self-important blowhards, Melville seems at the heart of the book to recall the praise of "men who dive" with which he responded to Emerson's lecture. As the doomed *Pequod* floats toward its reckoning (perhaps "swim[ming] near the surface" like "any fish"), Ishmael recounts a tale about another figure who dared to dive: "the dread Vishnoo, one of the three persons in the godhead of the Hindoos...who, by the first of his ten earthly incarnations, has for ever set apart and sanctified the whale."

When Brahma, or the God of Gods...resolved to recreate the world after one of its periodical dissolutions, he gave birth to Vishnoo, to preside over the work; but the Vedas, or mystical books, whose perusal would seem to have been indispensable to Vishnoo before beginning the creation, and which therefore must have contained something in the shape of practical hints to young architects, these Vedas were lying at the bottom of the waters; so Vishnoo became incarnate in a whale, and sounding down in him to the uttermost depths, rescued the sacred volumes. Was not this Vishnoo a whaleman, then?

With his white whale established as an incarnation of Vishnu, Melville crafted a great American novel with unmistakably Hindu depths. And more than that, he also paid homage to those "who *dive*," all those like Emerson—and perhaps too, unbeknownst to Melville, Emerson's aunt—who brought Indian beliefs to the surface far from where they had been submerged.

Of course, the desire of some writers to explore Hindu themes did not automatically translate into widespread interest or understanding of traditions that seemed unbridgeably foreign to most Americans. Writing in response to Emerson's celebrated poem "Brahma," for example, the poet and critic Oliver Wendell Holmes Sr. scoffed, "[T]o the average Western mind it is the nearest approach to a Torricellian vacuum of intelligibility that language can pump out of itself." Holmes was himself a former student of Margaret Fuller, Emerson's protégé and occasional promoter of Hindu ideas, yet the pluralism of Emerson's imagination was to him meaningless, or worse. "The oriental side of Emerson's nature delighted itself in these narcotic dreams, born in the land of the poppy and of hashish." At best, Holmes suggested, "they lend a peculiar charm to his poems, but it is not worth while to try to construct a philosophy out of them."

Such dismissive opinions perhaps slowed the spread of Hindu ideas throughout American culture, but they by no means stopped it. By the time Swami Vivekananda arrived and intoned the words "sisters and brothers," he spoke them to a people that had been prepared to hear them. He offered them to a nation that—in the manner of the Emersons, Margaret Fuller, Matilda Gage, Henry David Thoreau, Henry Wadsworth Longfellow, and Herman Melville—had been shaping itself in response to India, as both distant trading partner and an ever more proximate idea, for more than a century.

*   *   *

It perhaps goes without saying that Mary Moody Emerson did not become a Hindu after her encounter with Our Stranger. Far from it. No matter her level of interest, such a transformation would never have been possible in her world. Moreover, as she aged, even as her other eccentricities ran wild, she become more traditional and strident in her Christian faith. She may have even come to regret the seeds she had planted in impressionable young Waldo. She feared that his faith lay in shiny splinters, and when he left his family's well-worn path to a life spent in the pulpit, she worried his soul was lost. Yet even in this she was, as her nephew would call her, a "representative life." Americans have never been a people of fixed faith; they are, instead, a people whose spiritual lives are works in progress, open to the influences of the world at some points of their lives, as unchangeable as a closed book at others. Conversions come and go for reasons pragmatic as well as divine.

In this, Mary's life — singular though she was thought at the time — is quite like others of her age, each of whom might remind us that American history is a parlor game of unlikely contemporaries. Men and women whose experiences have nothing to do with each other may seem to have hidden resonances based on the simple fact that they walked the earth at the same time, within the borders of this improbable nation. As far as possible from the experience of Omar ibn Said wandering as a Muslim runaway in a Christian land, the New England matron Mary Moody Emerson lived through precisely the same era and was herself a kind of fugitive. Because she was a woman and an intellectual at a time when those two categories were thought rarely to overlap, she was the kind of outlier who looks beyond expected explanations to form an understanding of the world. As she pursued her interest in what seemed to her a new way of thinking of divinity, she became, in Waldo's words, an oracle speaking "the arcana of the gods" in a "frivolous and skeptical time." More than he could have known, she was also an example of the ways those on the margins of faith can influence widespread cultural change, just as a rock dropped in the Ganges might send ripples across Walden Pond.

The angel Moroni delivering the plates of the Book of Mormon to Joseph Smith, 1886. (Library of Congress)

CHAPTER 13

A Tale of Two Prophets

1800–1856

Nine years after they had arrived in the valley of the Great Salt Lake, the people who called themselves Saints gathered beneath the tree-branch roof and rough-hewn beams of a bowery to hear the preaching of their leader. The founder of their community had been dead now a dozen years, and his revelation had been made known long before many of these pioneers had been born. As they struggled to build a safe haven for their faith and a settlement that would prove a foothold for the expanding nation on the frontier, more than ever they hungered to hear an affirmation of their beliefs from one who had been there since the beginning. Brigham Young was the man to give it.

"I appear before you to bear my testimony to the truth of 'Mormonism,'" he declared to his followers in 1856, "that Joseph Smith Jr. was a Prophet called of God, and that he did translate the Book of Mormon by the gift and power of the Holy Ghost."

Young was at the time fifty-five years old, a man of the same generation as his martyred prophet, though he was more skilled at managing a burgeoning empire than attracting murderous mobs. A suitable stand-in to the many youthful Mormons around him, he had come to the faith upon reading the newly published scripture in 1830, and soon was recognized as one of Smith's original followers, known as the Twelve Apostles. Preaching in the bowery, the worship area the Saints had built at Salt Lake even before their homes, Young stressed that though he was there near the start of this great movement, the truth of Mormonism was equally available to anyone who heard him. "This same testimony all can bear who have received and continue to retain the Spirit of the Gospel," he said.

Most in attendance knew Young's testimony well. They, too, believed that some forty years before, a young man in western New York had discovered golden plates buried in the ground of a hill called Cumorah. Given the gift of two "seer stones" by an angel, Joseph Smith placed them over his eyes as if wearing a pair of spectacles and through them was able to comprehend the ancient writing on the plates. What he found there was a remarkable story. According to this new scripture, which Smith dictated in translation to his wife, Jesus Christ had visited earth far from the Holy Land of the Bible. After his resurrection, the son of God had walked in the forests of America, appearing to the only people who lived there at the time, the lost descendants of one of the tribes of Israel, known by Mormons as the Lamanites.

When Smith published this saga as the Book of Mormon in 1830, it offered both a vision of the ancient past and a prophecy of the future that foretold Jesus's eventual return to the heart of the continent. Smith and his Twelve Apostles soon brought together believers by the thousands, first in New York, then at various sites of "gathering," the term they used to refer to the process by which Smith's followers and the Lamanites, also known as Native Americans, would be joined as a renewed Israel.

Great Salt Lake was then the center of a Mormon-controlled territory that comprised a full tenth of what would become the continental United States. The provisional State of Deseret, as it was known, included parts of the territories that would yield not just Utah but Arizona, California, Colorado, Idaho, New Mexico, Nevada, Oregon, and Wyoming. It was the latest and most ambitious attempt at achieving their scriptural "gathering" of believers, and it would prove their most successful. Following earlier settlements at Kirtland, Ohio; Independence, Missouri; and Nauvoo, Illinois; the Saints had ventured into the unsettled West largely because of Joseph Smith's murder at the hands of an anti-Mormon mob in 1844. Faced with the loss of the man who had been both their prophet and the head of every local government they had established, the Saints followed Young as Smith's heir, to a place where they hoped they could be free of the persecution of nonbelieving "gentiles."

Yet they did not face the dangers of mass emigration merely to escape one group of people who did not yet accept their message; they did so to be nearer to another.

"I did not devise the great scheme of the Lord's opening the way to send this people to these mountains," Young continued in the bowery. "Joseph contemplated the move for years before it took place." As Young recounted the creation myth of what would become the state of Utah, Smith had hoped to find the ultimate gathering place on the frontier primarily because of his fervor to preach his vision that Jesus Christ had appeared in America to the descendants of those who had originally met him, those lost children of Israel whom the rest of the United States called Indians. As Smith himself had written, "One of the most important points in the faith of the Church of the Latter-day Saints, through the fullness of the everlasting Gospel, is the gathering of Israel, of whom the Lamanites constitute a part."

So taken was the prophet with this part of his mission, Young explained, that for a time "there was a watch placed upon him continually to see that he had no communication with the Indians." Young and others recognized that they had a church to build, a system of self-governance to create, and huge numbers of people to organize and protect, all of which depended upon on a certain amount of stability. Prophets, however, are rarely good administrators; Smith wanted at every juncture to push on to the next potential Zion, the models for which he found in visions of a past only he could remember.

Smith's own mother, who also was one of his earliest followers, recalled that this had always been the case. "During our evening conversations, Joseph would occasionally give us some of the most amusing recitals that could be imagined," she once said. "He would describe the ancient inhabitants of this continent, their dress, mode of traveling, and the animals upon which they rode; their cities, their buildings, with every particular; their mode of warfare; and also their religious worship. This he would do with as much ease, seemingly, as if he had spent his whole life among them."

It was an obsession that colored even his interpretation of the political controversies of the day. In the same year that he published the Book of Mormon, he greeted announcement of the Indian Removal Act of 1830 — which allowed President Andrew Jackson to enforce relocation of the Cherokee, Chickasaw, Choctaw, Creek, and Seminole tribes west of the Mississippi—as a step toward the great "gathering" that was to come. As Smith saw it, if the Lamanites were being driven beyond the Rockies and into the deserts of the West, that was where he would bring his revelation.

Writing just three months after Jackson signed the law that initiated the Trail of Tears, Smith codified his entwined desire to occupy the frontier and convert Native Americans in the secondary text of the Mormon movement. This was a collection of elaborations and interpretations on his original scripture known as the Doctrine and Covenants:

> And now, behold, I say unto you that you shall go unto the Lamanites and preach my gospel unto them; and inasmuch as they receive thy teachings thou shalt cause my church to be established among them; and thou shalt have revelations, but write them not by way of commandment.
>
> And now, behold, I say unto you that it is not revealed, and no man knoweth where the city Zion shall be built, but it shall be given hereafter. Behold, I say unto you that it shall be on the borders by the Lamanites.

Now that they were finally surrounded by "Lamanites" on all sides in the valley of the Great Salt Lake, Young acknowledged the debt his community owed to the people his late leader had hoped to convert, while also making it seem that it was not his doing but divine will that both Mormons and Indians had been forced ever further west. "Was it by any act of ours that this people were driven into their midst?" he asked. "We are now their neighbors, we are on their land, for it belongs to them as much as any soil ever belonged to any man on earth; we are drinking their water, using their fuel and timber, and raising our food from their ground."

Preaching in a rustic wooden structure near the site where the great Mormon Tabernacle would one day be built, Young did not yet know that he was part of a movement that would produce the most successful homegrown religious group in the history of the United States. Nonetheless, it was only right that this group of prototypical American spiritual originals acknowledged the debt to those they displaced. Yet there was one further debt the Mormons owed to the natives of this land that went wholly unacknowledged, perhaps because they owed to Native Americans even more than Brigham Young himself knew.

To understand the connection between Mormonism and the indigenous peoples supplanted by the moving borders of the United States, and the nation-expanding implications of this connection, we should not merely ask why Joseph Smith wanted to convert the Indians. After all, uncountable priests, pilgrims, and Puritans through the preceding three centuries had wanted to do much the same. We might ask, however, how the untrained and unordained Smith, unique among all those would-be saviors of heathen souls, came to look upon Native Americans not merely as an evangelical challenge but as a key to understanding the Christian scriptures that the English, the Spanish, the Dutch, and the French had brought from Europe. Why did Smith alone see the New World as a missing piece in the story the Old World told about itself?

To answer this question, we should begin where Smith began — not with his own story but with one that came just before. Not far from the site where he claimed to have had his original revelations, and just five years prior to Smith's birth, another man was beset with religious visions that would transform the lives of all around him — perhaps including Joseph Smith himself, and through him Brigham Young, the Saints he led to the frontier, and the nation that followed in their wake.

In the last years of the eighteenth century, the once proud Iroquois Confederacy had fallen on hard times. In the aftermath of the American Revolution, the population of the Iroquois had been reduced by half. Ten percent of all Iroquois men had died in battle, some fighting for the English, some for the Americans and the French, while dysentery and smallpox had killed more than four times that number without regard to political affiliation in the years since the war's end. The surviving inhabitants of what had been the heart of the Six Nations had been pushed from their villages. One faction crossed into the Province of Quebec, while those who remained in the United States were corralled onto reservations far from the homes of their ancestors. With living conditions deteriorating and despair rampant, many formerly powerful sachems, hunters, and warriors had begun to poison themselves with the spirits they had learned to drink from those who took their land.

A man called Handsome Lake was among them. Though he

was one of fifty hereditary chiefs of the Seneca, there was nothing that bespoke authority about him as he lay near death in the winter of 1799. For weeks he had been wasting away in a bunk in his brother's cabin, writhing in the grip of a fever dream while he waited for the end. The other inhabitants of the village of Jenuchshadego expected he would leave them, and many were not sorry to see him go. Though he had lurched in and out of illness for years, when Handsome Lake had returned to the village a month before, he apparently still had strength enough to cause a great deal of trouble.

Jenuchshadego was, in the memorable phrasing of historian Anthony Wallace, "a slum in the wilderness"—like most other newly established Indian settlements. Consisting of forty dirt-floor cabins housing more than four hundred Seneca, the village was tucked away between the Allegheny River and the steep cliffs of a ridge that would be submerged one hundred sixty years later, when the surrounding valley was flooded by the construction of the Kinzua Dam. The same traits that made this area an ideal choice for a man-made lake made it, at the turn of the nineteenth century, one of the last redoubts of Seneca autonomy. Its narrow passes, seasonally made impenetrable by winter storms, served as a natural bulwark against intruders.

Traditionally, white men were not allowed to enter this stretch of the Allegheny Mountains except by invitation. History had proven the wisdom of this within the living memory of every adult in Jenuchshadego. Though it had once been home to a thriving cultural and agricultural center for the Seneca, it had been all but wiped off the map during the Revolution, when George Washington himself had given instructions that the villages in the area should be "not be merely overrun, but destroyed." After learning that raids on rebel forces had originated nearby, Washington gave the order to Major General John Sullivan that no matter what complaints he heard from the local tribes, he should "not by any means listen to any overture of peace before the total ruinment of their settlements is effected." A generation later, Washington still was known as "Town Destroyer" by the Seneca, and the only rebuilt settlement in the area was given a name that means "There a house was burned."

While the village struggled back to life, the Seneca frequently had to venture far beyond its immediate vicinity on trade missions and game-hunting expeditions. It was one of the latter that had taken Handsome Lake away for a time, and now brought about his dire condition.

His family had last seen him when he left with a hunting party the previous autumn. They had gone downriver with the intention of harvesting deer from the bountiful Pennsylvania forests so that the village would have a surplus for the frozen months ahead. Handsome Lake and the other hunters had been gone scarcely half a season when they came to a small town the white men called Pittsburgh. Though there were doubtless many provisions available there that would have been gratefully received back in Jenuchsha-dego, Handsome Lake and his cohort made the disastrous decision to trade their cache of dried meat and deerskins for a barrel of whisky. Whether or not they initially planned to carry this prize back to Jenuchshadego, the expedition thereafter devolved into a winter-long drinking binge.

For the return trip home, the hunters had lashed their canoes together into a single barge and managed to make their way upriver as the liquor continued to flow. The most inebriated stayed in the center of the flotilla, while those less likely to topple overboard manned the paddles on either side.

When finally they reached Jenuchshadego, the empty-handed hunters became quarrelsome, perhaps channeling their embarrassment at having nothing to show for three months' supposed labor. It was later remembered that the fast-depleting barrel of fire water caused them first to "yell and sing like demented people," and then to go on a rampage. The story of their degradation later served as a cautionary tale passed down through the generations: "Now they are beastlike," it was said of Handsome Lake and the others, "and run about without clothing and all have weapons to injure those whom they meet. Now there are no doors left in the houses for they have all been kicked off."

The hunting party's behavior was frightening enough that the women and children ran from their homes, keeping to the relative safety of the woods while the drunken men scratched through cold fireplaces in search of scraps of food. Left in the care of such masters, the village dogs yelped with hunger.

Handsome Lake's half-brother, Cornplanter, watched with dismay as the ruffians added chaos to the plight of his long-suffering village. The ranking sachem of the region, Cornplanter was a chief whose power came not only from his long career as a warrior and protector of his people but from his status among the leaders of the former colonies—most of whom knew Jenuchshadego simply as Cornplanter's Town, for it had only recently been established on a tract of land given to him by the new American government.

Already faced with the daunting challenge of holding together what remained of his people, Cornplanter was so incensed by his brother's behavior that he may have pursued the harshest possible penalty against him, as he often did for the purpose of keeping peace in the village. Only weeks before, when Cornplanter suspected a woman of being a witch responsible for the death of an infant, he had ordered her stabbed to death in broad daylight. Instead of taking similar measures now, however, he looked for a solution to what he had come to see as a bigger problem than a few drunks making mischief.

Though he had fought on the side of the British during the war, Cornplanter had since become an advocate of improving relations between his ancient people and the nascent nation rising around them. He was in many ways a natural bridge between the Seneca and the Americans. His own father had been a Dutchman, and though he was raised among his mother's people, he maintained enough of a sense of connection that he used his Dutch family name—recorded alternately as Abeal or O'beal—throughout his life. He passed the name on to his sons.

In his eagerness to improve relations between the United States and the remnants of the Six Nations, he had gone so far as to invite Quaker missionaries to live in the village, even allowing them to use a section of his own cabin for the purpose of teaching English to the Seneca children. It was a decision that would have implications reaching far beyond language—beginning with the immediate fate of Handsome Lake, but not ending there.

The Quakers who had taken up residence in Jenuchshadego had been working in Iroquois country for years. Upon his arrival in the village, thirty-year-old Henry Simmons had felt comfortable enough with the beliefs and traditions of the Seneca that, when challenged to give an account of the origins of the world, he offered a version of Genesis that seemed to his interrogators nearly indistinguishable from their own stories of divine creation. With Adam and Eve standing in for the Sky Woman from whom all humanity sprang, he told of the birth of two brothers, one good and one evil, and explained that in his religion it was understood that the inclinations of these embattled siblings continued to rule human behavior. By the time Simmons was finished, it seemed to Cornplanter and the rest of his audience that Cain and Abel were simply other names for the twin sons of the Sky Woman—Flint, the bad son, and Sapling, the good—and that the Garden of Eden would fit quite naturally on the primordial turtle's back.

The Quakers had been invited to Jenuchshadego to teach the skills of "letters, pen, and tilling the field," but of course they offered religious and moral instruction as well, often hidden within the pages of the books of spelling and grammar they brought with them from Philadelphia. The textbooks these missionary teachers distributed to the Seneca wasted no ink on reading lessons that did not also convey dire moral warnings. Whatever satisfaction children might have gained from learning to read, the first lesson from a Quaker primer of this period colored the accomplishment with dread:

My son, do no ill.
Go not in the way of bad men.
For bad men go to the pit.

When children could be persuaded to remain still long enough for their lessons (and this was no easy feat—Quaker teachers complained that young Seneca would often come and go from school as they pleased), they repeated such lines until they became part of the very air of the village, ringing out like mantras from Cornplanter's cabin. Such rote learning was the norm in all early American schools, as was the moralistic approach to literacy. Whatever one thinks of this style of pedagogy, however, or of the ethics of using language instruction as a Trojan horse for faith, the Quaker teachers seem to have succeeded in introducing Christian elements to Iroquois culture in a way generations of previous missionary attempts had not.

The Quakers' success in Cornplanter's Town may have been due to the influence of another of the missionaries. Halliday Jackson, Simmons's junior by three years, was less experienced among the Iroquois, but he had a more influential career ahead. A quarter-century later, he would play a prominent role in an acrimonious split within the Society of Friends over its openness to individual interpretations of faith. His predisposition to personal religious sentiments was already apparent and would turn out to shape the outcome of the missionary endeavor.

The movement Jackson would eventually join was sparked by the writings of Elias Hicks, a Rhode Island farmer turned preacher who stressed the importance of "immediate divine revelation" in the formation of religious life. This notion would have been uncontroversial to the earliest Quakers in America, who, after all, had risked the noose with their insistence that religion rested on an inner light available to all. Yet by the end of the eighteenth century, many Quakers had become respectable citizens. There arose a divide between the largely affluent urban Quakers and much less well-off rural Quakers, who took up Hicks's call as a necessary reinvigoration of the faith. While the "Hicksite" revival would not formally split the Friends until 1826, already there were rumblings about the true nature of divine revelation, and to whom it should be considered available.

However divisive Jackson would later be among his co-religionists, there was no dissent among the Quakers at Cornplanter's Town. They were united by a common practical purpose that included an admirable restraint when it came to the question of conversion. As a result, the changes they brought were more subtle than the blanket Christianization of native cultures to which other missionaries aspired. As in Jackson's later advocacy for a movement stressing immediate divine revelation, the personal nature of religious experience was proclaimed as paramount. And like Simmons's own remaking of Genesis in the image of the Iroquois creation myth, the faith that began to grow in Jenuchshadego was not a replacement but a hybrid.

The significance of this hybrid faith began to show itself when Cornplanter ruled on how best to deal with the drunken hunting party's return. After consultation with the sobriety-preaching Quakers, he moved to forbid whisky and other spirits from the village.

Never very healthy, and now well past the prime of life at the age of sixty-four, the rebuked Handsome Lake soon fell into a sickness that had all the markings of alcohol withdrawal. He became so tortured by a constant craving for drink that he soon was unable to walk. He fell into a bed in a room within the same large cabin Cornplanter had allowed the Quakers to use for their lessons, and he remained there for days. When his grown daughter came to his side to care for him, she saw that he had been reduced to "yellow skin and dried bones."

Beyond his physical symptoms, it was believed that he was suffering a spiritual malady. As his ordeal was remembered in the tribe's oral tradition, "some strong power" held him and would not allow him to recover. He called to the Great Ruler to give him strength, but even as he prayed, he considered "how evil and loathsome" he had become. In his delirium, he intoned the chants of his people—the Death Chant, the Women's Song, the Harvest Song—and as he sang, he wondered if whisky was the cause not only of his own illness but of the straits in which his people now found themselves. As the days passed, he meditated on the rising and setting of the sun, the stars he could see when staring up through the chimney beside his bed, and the birds he could hear singing in the morning.

One such morning, as Handsome Lake's daughter and her husband were working outside the cabin, they heard a shout from within. "Niio!" the sick man called. "So be it!" When they ran inside to check on him, it seemed the inevitable end of a ruined man's days had finally come.

Cornplanter, along with other family members, friends, and Henry Simmons, soon arrived at the cabin to mark Handsome Lake's passing. When they touched his body, however, they detected some heat in it. As they moved their hands over his skin, the warmth seemed to spread from his core to his limbs. Silently, they all sat at the feet of the dead man, watching and praying for his breath to return.

It was near noon when his eyes opened, the sun high above the village on the day in June that marked the yearly Strawberry Harvest Festival.

Handsome Lake's nephew asked, "My uncle, are you feeling well?"

At first the born-again man's lips moved without making a sound, but then he found his voice.

"Never have I seen such wondrous visions!" he said.

The visions Handsome Lake went on to describe served as the basis for a new religious movement—not Mormonism; not yet.

As they were recorded in the journals of Henry Simmons and Halliday Jackson, and later passed down by Seneca oral tradition, they were in many ways an elaboration of the blending of conventional Quaker morality, Hicksite openness to individual revelation, and Iroquois mythology that had already begun to be developed in the village. Now, however, this compound faith had found a story, and a prophet, all its own.

As the suddenly revived sachem recounted, during his illness he had seen himself step into a "clear swept space," and there he met three otherworldly men "clothed in fine clean raiment." Both familiar and exotic, they were dressed as if they had been sent on an important mission, and carried blooming branches, symbols of the rebirth for which all the Iroquois hoped.

"Their cheeks were painted red and it seemed that they had been painted the day before," Handsome Lake said. "Only a few feathers were in their bonnets. All three were alike and all seemed middle aged. Never before have I seen such handsome command-ing men and they had in one hand bows and arrows as canes. Now in their other hands were huckleberry bushes and the berries were of every color."

The angelic figures approached him, and one of them spoke. "He who created the world at the beginning employed us to come to earth. Our visit now is not the only one we have made. He com-manded us saying, 'Go once more down upon the earth and this time visit him who thinks of me. He is grateful for my creations, moreover he wishes to rise from sickness and walk in health upon the earth. Go you and help him to recover.' "

Following this initial recitation of his visionary experience, Handsome Lake remained physically weak, but he had what seems to have been a miraculous spiritual recovery. Though a hereditary chief of his people, he had before this never been very influential, always overshadowed by his brother Cornplanter. Now, however, it seemed Handsome Lake's time had come. Throughout the seven-teen years that followed, until his death in 1816, he had a series of visions, in which his own resurrection came to stand for that of his people as a whole. He traveled out of Jenuchshadego, now not to hunt or drink but to preach his message back in the homeland of the Seneca, to the Indians living on reservations in western New York.

Some speculated that this new prophet was a secret Christian, surreptitiously recasting the Bible in native terms. Another possi-ble inspiration for his revelation might have been the Quakers' religiously themed reading lessons, repeated endlessly from the makeshift school that occupied another section of the cabin in which he had convalesced. No matter their source, the visions he described spoke deeply to those who heard them.

While Handsome Lake's experience became the conduit for the promise of a broader redemption, the new religion was not limited to his own apparent death and resurrection. As a subsequent vision later recorded, he also offered a thoroughly reimagined creation myth, riffing on Christian stories to create new connections and meanings, much as the Quaker missionary Simmons had done, but in reverse. His Genesis was less concerned with the creation of the earth, however, than with the origins of the circumstances that had brought the Iroquois to this low point in their history.

The first published version of the Code of Handsome Lake included a section bluntly named: "How the White Race came to America." It tells the story of a pious man who discovers a hidden text that reveals long-forgotten religious secrets. In this book, Handsome Lake's scripture relates,

> He read of a great man who had been a prophet and the son of the Great Ruler. He had been born on the earth and the white men to whom he preached killed him. Now moreover the prophet had promised to return and become the King. In three days he was to come and then in forty to start his kingdom. This did not happen as his followers had expected and so they despaired. Then said one chief follower, "Surely he will come again sometime, we must watch for him."

It is, at first, a rough refashioning of the Christian Gospel, complete with the three days of Christ's death and resurrection and the forty days between his appearance to the apostles and his ascension to heaven. As the story progresses, however, it becomes entwined with another story. The man who discovered the hidden text seeks out this son of the Great Ruler, and is convinced he has found him when he arrives at a golden castle. Inside, a figure he believes to be the one he is looking for proposes to send him on a quest.

> "Across the ocean that lies toward the sunset is another world and a great country and a people whom you have never seen," he says. "Those people are virtuous, they have

no unnatural evil habits and they are honest. A great reward is yours if you will help me. Here are five things that men and women enjoy; take them to these people and make them as white men are."

It is only as he departs that the seeker realizes the man in the castle was not the son of the Great Ruler but an impostor—a twin, perhaps. When he opens the bundle of five objects he has been given and finds enticements to drunkenness, idleness, sickness, and greed ("a flask of rum, a pack of playing cards, a handful of coins, a violin and a decayed leg bone"), he concludes that the man in the castle does not want to help those people on the other side of the ocean but to destroy them. Unwilling to complete this task himself, he passes the objects along to one who is prepared to do so. In the religion of Handsome Lake, Christopher Columbus himself becomes the serpent bringing forbidden fruit to the garden.

Primarily intended as a moral refocusing of his people, Handsome Lake's vision was also a rebuke, in religious terms, of the entire European endeavor in America. By incorporating elements of biblical imagery into a story of his own, he suggests that the God Christians worshipped, the one whose objects and ideas Columbus and those that followed carried with them across the ocean, was an impostor—the evil twin of Iroquois lore. Simultaneously, the vision was also a brazen appropriation of Christian self-understanding. Handsome Lake not only introduced new elements to Iroquois belief, he reaffirmed the traditional religion of the longhouse, complete with its savior Dekanawida. In Handsome Lake's teachings, this savior now seemed all the more like a Christ that belonged exclusively to the native peoples of America.

During his lifetime, Handsome Lake's movement seemed at first to grow slowly. He was, for years, as ridiculed as many an aspiring prophet before him had been. Nevertheless, by the time of his death in 1816, he had seen the small spark of his vision spread like a fire. Formed of a hybrid of Christian morality and Seneca stories that may have been as old as or older than the Gospel the Quaker missionaries preached, the Code of Handsome Lake inspired a spiritual revival among the Iroquois at just the moment when it seemed their way of life was destined to disappear from the earth. Though undeniably influenced by missionaries, Handsome Lake went on to become, for a time, their greatest rival for the souls of Native Americans. He supplanted Cornplanter as the voice of their people and even earned the praise of the American president, Thomas Jefferson, who called him "brother" and urged all Indians to follow his example.

"I am happy to learn you have been so far favored by the Divine spirit as to be made sensible of those things which are for your good and that of your people," Jefferson wrote to Handsome Lake in 1802, "and particularly that you and they see the ruinous effects which the abuse of spirituous liquors have produced upon them." Jefferson made this new prophet seem not just the Iroquois leader but their Luther:

> Go on then, brother, in the great reformation you have undertaken. Persuade our red brethren then to be sober, and to cultivate their lands; and their women to spin and weave for their families. You will soon see your women and children well fed and clothed, your men living happily in peace and plenty, and your numbers increasing from year to year. It will be a great glory to you to have been the instrument of so happy a change, and your children's children, from generation to generation, will repeat your name with love and gratitude forever.

That a new religious movement should have arisen in this time and place within the remnants of the Iroquois Confederacy is not surprising. Not only was there great need for rejuvenation among the people, there was also, perhaps, something in the air.

The mass of Handsome Lake's followers lived primarily in western New York. For centuries, this had been the Seneca heartland, but today it is more often remembered as the "Burned-Over District" — so called by the revivalist Charles Finney in 1876 because, in his estimation, so many in the region had been converted to new forms of evangelical Christianity that there was no one left for the fires of conversion to consume. While rarely considered a part of this groundswell in popular devotion, the Handsome Lake phenomenon in fact ought to be viewed as the Native American branch of the Second Great Awakening, the period from roughly 1790 to 1830 when membership in a variety of newly birthed sects and denominations exploded, spread, and took root across the country.

It was a time when it seemed the entire young nation was peopled by prophets and doomsday cults—and New York was ground zero for the coming apocalypse. Among the earliest religious movements that gave voice to the fervent end-times yearnings for which American religion would ever after be known, the Shakers established themselves in the central part of the state on the eve of the Revolution. They were devotees of Mother Ann Lee, who, like so many others, had come to America in hope of finding religious freedom but found instead further persecution for her heretical visions and strange ways, which included lifelong celibacy and a pacifism that came to seem treasonous as the war raged. The Shakers—so called because they physically shook in their devotions when moved by the spirit—were formally known as the United Society of Believers in Christ's Second Appearing. After their leader's death in 1784, they came to believe that this "second appearing" had already occurred in the person of Ann Lee herself. Through the century that followed, this unlikely movement spread through the Burned-Over District and beyond, establishing Shaker communities in Ohio, Kentucky, Indiana, and New England, where the last active Shaker village—two believers strong at the time of this writing—remains today.

While the Shakers saw the Second Coming of Christ and the apocalyptic era it would usher in as an ongoing concern, other groups in the Burned-Over District looked into the future and prepared for the worst. One such group was the Millerites, followers of William Miller, who, like the Quaker Elias Hicks, was a farmer turned preacher whose religious visions became deeply unsettling to those around him. Miller advocated maintaining an ever-watchful state for Christ's return, and so believed that drinking alcohol would make his followers ill-prepared for the Second Coming. He was not such a literalist that he let the biblical notion that "no one knows the time or place" deter him from calculating that Christ would return precisely on October 22, 1844. When the day came and went, the Millerites proclaimed the date ever after to be "The Great Disappointment."

At the other end of the sexual and apocalyptic spectrum from the Shakers and the Millerites, John Humphrey Noyes's Oneida Community proposed that Jesus Christ had already returned, and so it was up to communities of believers to strive toward perfection in this life rather than wait for the hereafter. Noyes's proposition for how this might take place involved "complex marriage," which consisted of—as one observer called it—a "combination of polygamy and polyandry." The participants in this experiment had less luck than the Shakers, at least as far as continuity of the religious purposes of the community were concerned. While the Shakers still have a few stubborn followers, all that remains of Oneida is the thriving flatware business started by Noyes's son.

But of all the movements that were born and flourished in the Burned-Over District during the Second Great Awakening, the most successful by far was the one founded on a hilltop in Palmyra, New York, by Joseph Smith, a twenty-four-year-old farmer's son.

According to Mormon history, Smith was still a teenager when he had the first of the series of visions that would provide the Church of Latter-day Saints with endless opportunity for interpretation. Pride of place is often reserved for this First Vision, yet in some ways the second was more important. It was this Second Vision that led him to discover the golden plates and the seer stones with which he read and translated them.

Mormon scholar Lori Taylor points out the interesting coincidence that weeks before, emissaries from the Six Nations of the Iroquois made a momentous stop in Palmyra. The principal speaker was none other than Handsome Lake's nephew, now a famous chief called Red Jacket. A detailed report was published by the *Palmyra Gazette*:

We were last week visited by the famous chief, Red Jacket, together with other chiefs belonging to the Six Nations, to wit—Blue Sky, William Sky, Peter Smoke, and Twenty Canoes, who arrived there on Monday about sun-set.

To answer the solicitations of our inhabitants, Red Jacket delivered a speech in the evening, at the academy, which was almost instantly filled with an attentive auditory. His speech, if it had been properly interpreted, no doubt would have been both eloquent and interesting. But as it was, merely enough could be understood to know his object, while his native eloquence and rhetorical powers could only be guessed at, from his manners and appearance.

He commenced by representing the whole human race as the creatures of God, or the Great Spirit, and that both white men and red men were brethren of the same great family. He then mentioned the emigration of our forefathers from towards the rising sun, and their landing among their red brethren in this new discovered world. He next hinted at the success of our armies under the great Washington; — our prosperity as a nation since the declaration of our independence; mentioned Gen Washington's advice to the red men, to plough, and plant and cultivate their lands. — This, he said, they wished to do, but the white men took away their lands, and drove them further and further toward the setting sun: — and, what was worse than all, had sent Missionaries to preach and hold meetings among them: — that the whites who instituted and attended these meetings, stole their horses, drove off their cattle, and taxed their land. These things he considered their greatest calamity — too grievous to be borne.

The principal object of this visit by these Chiefs, was, we understand, to intercede with the Friends, in whose honesty they appear to place the most implicit confidence, to use their influence to free them from the Missionaries now in their borders.

It is impossible to know for certain if Joseph Smith attended this lecture, but given what we know of him — mainly that he was a boy of sixteen apparently obsessed with the history and culture of the Indians — it is difficult to believe that he would not have been present when the most famous Iroquois in America showed up in his small town with an entourage of chiefs, and spoke at length "to answer the solicitations of our inhabitants." Red Jacket's speech in Palmyra was reported as far away as Boston, Hartford, and Alexandria, as well as, of course, in the local *Gazette* — so even if he was not there in person, the teenage Joe Smith certainly would have heard something of the event after the fact.

What Joseph Smith would have heard was basically an abbreviated version of Handsome Lake's vision: a tale of white and Indian unity interrupted by evils brought across the sea. Red Jacket's appeal to the Friends for protection from other missionaries acknowledges the practical debt the Iroquois owed to the Quakers for their assistance with cultivation and education, even as he took a stand for native spiritual autonomy.

Just as Handsome Lake had absorbed the Quaker teachings then permeating his village, Smith was a sponge of diverse religious influences. He shared the Millerite belief that the Second Coming would occur in America as well as the Oneida belief that Jesus had already returned, though in his version of these beliefs, Christ had visited the continent's inhabitants long before the coming of Columbus. Yet while the birth of Mormonism is often considered in relation to those other Second Great Awakening movements of the Burned-Over District, in fact the similarities pale in comparison to all that Smith's religious visions had in common with those of Handsome Lake.

To begin with the most obvious, Smith's movement stressed sobriety. In a further revelation of the Doctrine and Covenants, Smith instructed, "That inasmuch as any man drinketh wine or strong drink among you, behold it is not good...Strong drinks are not for the belly, but for the washing of your bodies." This rule of Mormon life was given "not by commandment or constraint, but by revelation and the word of wisdom, showing forth the order and will of God in the temporal salvation of all saints in the last days." Likewise, the revelation of Handsome Lake sought to protect the dwindling settlements of the Iroquois from the evils that had crept in among them, the evils Handsome Lake himself had once represented when he rampaged drunk through his own town.

Like Handsome Lake, Joseph Smith was a man visited by angelic figures, and his visions led to the discovery of secret texts that told a forgotten history of faith. And when one looks closely at his visions, one cannot help but see the shadow of the Iroquois prophet who died in western New York in the very year the Mormon prophet's family arrived there. Not only does Smith's account of Jesus in early America seem to echo the Iroquois tradition of the son of the Great Spirit, Dekanawida, but he too sought to explain the intersection of European and American populations in religious terms. Handsome Lake's vision can be seen as an answer, of sorts, to Henry Simmon's syncretisms, which recast Eden with figures borrowed from local mythology. Smith seems to respond to Handsome Lake's account of how the white men brought evil to the native peoples with a proposal for how white men such as himself might undo the damage done.

In this sense, Smith attempted to offer a positive counterpoint to Handsome Lake's negative theological interpretation of history.

Smith's belief—that Native Americans were in fact related to the tribes of Israel—was commonly held at the time: Both Roger Williams, in the seventeenth century, and Conrad Weiser, in the eighteenth, had believed much the same. What that belief had lacked before was the full weight of narrative. Who were the heroes and villains of this offshoot of the biblical saga? Where did it begin? How would it end? The Book of Mormon provided these answers and more. While Handsome Lake's visions told of a hidden scripture that described the religious origins of the conflict between two peoples, Smith provided an epic of two cultures, separated by an ocean and millennia, rejoined by the "gathering" he would lead.

Like the arrival of Iroquois chiefs in Palmyra a month before Smith claimed to have found the golden plates, the resonances between the Code of Handsome Lake and the Book of Mormon may merely be coincidence. Recent scholarship in the history of the Latter-day Saints and the Iroquois explores the possibility that Joseph Smith knew of Handsome Lake's visionary experiences, but no direct connection has been found. Lori Taylor, the first to note Red Jacket's visit, has also examined a tradition among Native Americans that Smith heard of Handsome Lake's revelation from three of the prophet's followers, who explained to him that a renewed spirituality had taken hold of their people. At a time when all spiritual answers seemed up for grabs in the religious upheaval of the Burned-Over District, this would have been tremendously appealing—perhaps so much so that it inspired a young man to offer to his people what Handsome Lake had offered to his own.

Not surprisingly, there is also an interpretation offering an opposite conclusion: that Joseph did not borrow from Handsome Lake, but that Iroquois religion provides proof of the Book of Mormon as not just scripture but history. In this interpretation, the Iroquois legend of the divine messenger Dekanawida is reduced to a faint echo of the supposedly historical account found on Smith's golden plates. With the assumption that the Mormon story was primary, Handsome Lake himself becomes significant mainly for his interaction with figures from the lore of the Latter-day Saints.

Mormon folk tradition maintains that three of the original witnesses of Jesus's coming to America remained on earth to witness his return. Beginning among Brigham Young's pioneers, these three figures served as a lens through which to view the Saints' struggles on the frontier, as well as the history that had brought them there. As the folklorist A. E. Fife observed in the 1930s and 1940s, "In localities of Utah, Idaho, and other states where the Mormon faith is prevalent, one frequently hears accounts of the miraculous appearance and disappearance of kindly, white-bearded old men who bring messages of the greatest spiritual or personal importance, give blessings in exchange for hospitality, lead lost people to safety, and perform various other miraculous deeds. These old men are said by the people to be the 'Three Nephites,' ancient apostles of the Christ on the American continent, appointed as His special emissaries to live upon this continent until His second coming, and to go among all people as special witnesses of the truthfulness of Christ's church." The Book of Mormon explains that these three old men were "given power over death so as to remain on the earth until Jesus comes again....They are as the angels of God, and...can show themselves unto whatsoever man it seemeth them good. Therefore, great and marvelous works shall be wrought by them, before the great and coming day [of judgment]."

The Three Nephites were said to appear in times of personal distress as well as throughout American history. According to various legends, they were spotted by a member of Columbus's crew, heard cheering Independence in Philadelphia in 1776, and seen visiting the tribes of Utah in advance of Mormon settlers. To those who embraced the legend in Deseret and elsewhere, it was only natural that these three wandering miracle workers would have visited the Iroquois as they struggled with the evils of alcohol and the dissolution of the Six Nations. Today, the Three Nephite tradition has been largely reduced to the stuff of stories for children, but at the height of its nineteenth-century popularity, it was argued that the three angelic figures who visited Handsome Lake were none other than these three immortal saints, who wandered through Cornplanter's Town while awaiting both the return of Jesus and the birth of his prophet Joseph Smith.

Each of these interpretations of the Iroquois-Mormon connection relies on one or the other being a derivative tradition, but their true relationship is at once more simple and more complicated than that. Both traditions were born in a place and at a time when the boundaries between spiritual movements were far more porous than they are generally considered today.

Joseph Smith is often portrayed as the preeminent exemplar of the American myth of the self-made man, yet what he may be instead is one of the best examples of the collaborative nature of American belief. Depending on one's religious sensibilities, and perhaps on one's corresponding level of cynicism, Smith was either a religious savant so dauntless in the courage of his convictions that he attracted millions around the world with his message, or he was one of the most successful fabulists in history.

In either case, there is no denying that he offered nineteenth-century Americans something that had been sought in the New World since Columbus arrived and believed he had found the Garden of Eden: a religious interpretation of the convergence of cultures that attempted to take the full reality and history of each into account. In the process, Smith inevitably incorporated the diverse religious influences around him. Indeed, it may have been precisely his ability to synthesize competing spiritual claims that made his vision so popular.

The same can be said of the man Thomas Jefferson called "Brother Handsome Lake." Though from the distance of centuries his success seems to be on a much smaller scale than that of a man who started the fastest-growing church in history, it is impossible to say exactly how far his influence reached, and whether or not it was ultimately good for his people. The fire of religious revelation spreads where it will, sometimes even from one prophet to another, from the Burned-Over District of New York to the Great Salt Lake of Utah, and across the nation in between.

In front of the Joss House, Chinatown,
San Francisco. Arnold Genthe, c. 1900.
(Library of Congress)

CHAPTER 14

"The Heathen Chinee"

1852–1906

Telegraph Hill, overlooking the northeast corner of San Francisco, was originally home to a signal station that alerted the city below to the number, make, and freight of ships arriving in the bay. Before Samuel Morse's invention made its way west (the first coast-to-coast electromagnetic telegraph line was completed in 1861), the raised arms of the semaphore telegraph tower that gave the hill its name were the only means of immediate communication at a distance. For a city that exported more than forty million dollars in gold dust a year at the height of the prospecting boom, the comings and goings of merchandise and manpower were a daily preoccupation.

One morning in the early autumn of 1852, down the western slope from the semaphore tower's hill, another kind of signal went up that would prove far more significant than any single maritime arrival, not only to the city but to the country of which it only recently had become a part. At sunrise that day, a group of newcomers unfurled a striking crimson banner and hoisted it to the top of their newly constructed temple.

A few hours later, the crowds began to gather for a dedication ceremony. First dozens, then hundreds, they came to light firecrackers and squibs, to fill the air with the smoke and smell of gunpowder. Many of these men — and they were almost exclusively men — worked much of the year in the gold camps of the Sierras and the Trinity Mountains, where they mingled with workers of a dozen nations and learned enough English to argue for their wages and sometimes gamble them away. Yet at the newly opened temple—the first in the city—they stood among others with whom they had everything in common. Here, they were all members of the Yeong Wo community association, not just Chinese but speakers of the Zhongshan dialect, former residents of the Dongguan, Zengcheng, and Xin'an districts, near the present-day industrial behemoth of Shenzhen. Here, in the shadow of the telegraph tower, they listened together to the raucous music of their homeland, and offered prayers to gods unlike any their new neighbors had seen before—gods they had brought with them across the vast Pacific to the place they called Gold Mountain.

Just three years after the first ship came to port with passengers from China, the people then known as "the Celestials"—for their supposedly otherworldly ways—had established themselves as a significant part of the fastest-growing city in America. The primary reason was the sheer numbers in which they arrived. Contemporary reports place the Chinese population of California in 1849 at just fifty-four men and one woman. A year later the number had increased tenfold, and by the start of 1851 more than seven thousand had arrived in the state. In the year of the temple dedication, twenty thousand Chinese immigrants came ashore, and that rate of entry only increased in the years that followed.

Another reason for the immediate impact made by the Chinese, with an influence perhaps broader but more difficult to trace, was the event that autumn morning on the western side of Telegraph Hill. Wherever they landed, the Chinese soon built centers of community and religious life, outposts around which to organize their collective efforts in a new land that was not always welcoming. Called "joss houses" by outsiders (a derivation of the Portuguese word for deity, *deus*, perhaps first applied by Jesuit missionaries in Macau three hundred years before), they were temples where Chinese immigrants could practice the many religious devotions they had brought with them: Taoist, Confucian, and Buddhist, and most often a blend of these, along with a variety of practices local to the places they had come from. These latter practices, sometimes called Chinese folk religion or Shenism, are an indication of why regionally associated temples were so important to these recent arrivals. While it is common now to speak of "Chinese religion" as if it is a closed set of practices, neither the Chinese people nor their culture was anything close to monolithic in the nineteenth century. Re-creating precisely some small experience of their homeland—as the temple dedication sought to do—was the best way for immigrants to ensure that the same deities who watched over their families six thousand miles away would continue to protect them when and if they became Americans.

The man responsible for the temple dedication, known to English-speaking residents of San Francisco as Norman Assing but to the Chinese as Yuan Sheng, had been in America since 1820, longer than most. California had only joined the Union two years before, and the city was fast filling with newcomers fresh off boats not just from China but Europe. One of the earliest Chinese in the United States, Assing had spent his first years in South Carolina. When gold fever hit the East Coast eighteen years later, he, like thousands of others, had made the journey west. Soon thereafter, he founded the Yeong Wo community association to welcome others who hailed from his region in China.

If Assing felt lonely as the first from his nation in the boomtowns of gold country, it would not be for long. By the time of the temple dedication in 1852, there were four thousand Chinese immigrants settled in San Francisco alone. Unlike Assing, they had come east to reach their destination, making a journey by sea that took several weeks at best. As one contemporary writer noted enthusiastically of the clipper ship *Challenge*, "This splendid vessel has performed the quickest passage between the coast of China and North West America yet recorded in our annals of modern voyages," transporting 553 passengers in "33 days time!" By the hundreds, they arrived mostly without restriction in a city that a few decades later became home to Angel Island, "the Ellis Island of the West." This was where tens of thousands of immigrants from Asia would be detained for months before being admitted to the country or turned away. Also unlike Assing, most of these early immigrants did not come with the expectation that this would be a permanent relocation. The majority were brought by arrangement through mining companies, builders, and later the railroad. They were expected to work and then to return home.

As a temporary solution to a labor shortage, the Chinese were at first warmly welcomed. "They were a novelty, a wonder, and a study, to which peculiar interest was attached," the missionary Otis Gibson wrote, in *The Chinese in America* (1877). "Their coming to this country was regarded as the opening up of intercourse and commercial relations between our country and the Orient, which, in the near future, would be of incalculable benefit both to them and to us."

No less a San Francisco icon than Henry Huntly Haight said much the same. Though perhaps more famous now as one-half of an intersection that bears his name, he was governor of California from 1861 to 1867, and praised the arrival of "our elder brethren — the people of China" when he was still just a young lawyer with political ambitions. Without apparent concern that such a position would hurt his future prospects, he publicly declared in 1853, "We regard with pleasure the presence of great numbers of these people among us, as affording the best opportunity of doing them good, and through them, of exerting our influence upon their native land."

What Haight and Gibson perhaps failed to consider, however, was that the exertion of influence is almost always a two-way street. While the Chinese would be changed by their experiences in America, the American experience would also be transformed by their presence — and the religious transformation they brought would prove to some the most jarring of all.

"The Chinese have opened their heathen temples, and set up their heathen idols and altars in this Christian land," the missionary Gibson lamented, "and instead of our converting their temples into Christian churches, they have absolutely changed one of the first Protestant churches of this city into a habitation for heathen. One of these heathen temples, or an apology for one, is to be found in almost every place where any number of Chinamen have taken up their abode."

When it became clear that the Chinese intended not only to remain in the city but to remake it in their own image, their fellow Californians — many only recently arrived from other countries where news of the gold boom had also spread — grew more hostile. Chinese laborers generally worked for half the price of American and European workers, and when the boom times of the gold rush began to wane in the middle of the decade, the frustrations of many failed prospectors fell upon those displaying the most obvious differences. Just a year after Haight offered his warm words of welcome, the 1854 "Annals of San Francisco" noted: "There is a strong feeling, prejudice it may be, existing in California against all Chinamen, and they are nicknamed, cuffed about, and treated very unceremoniously by every other class." In subsequent years, the California legislature followed the lead of this popular sentiment. To begin with, a fifty-dollar charge was levied on each Chinese immigrant who arrived by ship. A foreign miner's tax was set at six dollars a month in 1855, and then increased by two dollars each month in 1856 and 1857. The unambiguous goal was to tax the Chinese population out of the gold business, out of the state, and ultimately back across the Pacific.

As one of San Francisco's most influential Chinese residents, Norman Assing did all he could to change public opinion in the face of these measures. Throughout 1852, he led contingents of Chinese to march in the city's parades, including those commemorating George Washington's birthday and the Fourth of July. ("Their display of numerous fanciful flags and banners of the finest workmanship of their people was the occasion of much favorable comment," Gibson admitted.) Two years before, Assing had been the head of another group of his countrymen, marching to celebrate California's newly proclaimed statehood beneath a banner that read "China Boys." This was, apparently, the preferred designation within the community—at least among those who followed Assing's lead.

As early as 1850, Assing had sent a letter to San Francisco mayor John W. Geary "in behalf of the China Boys," thanking him for including the newcomers in municipal events. "The China Boys feel proud of the distinction you have shown them," he wrote, "and will always endeavor to merit your good opinion and the good opinion of the citizens of their adopted country....Strangers as they are among you, they kindly appreciate the many kindnesses received at your hands."

Despite his promotion of patriotic activities and his efforts to ingratiate his community with the local government, Assing did not believe in assimilation at all costs. He wanted his new fellow Americans to know that there were elements of the old ways he and other Chinese immigrants were unlikely to leave behind. And so, he made the very American move of inviting the press to events like the temple dedication. Thanks to Assing's hospitality and media savvy, a correspondent from the short-lived *San Francisco Whig* was in attendance to record his impressions.

The dedication began, the *Whig* reporter wrote, when priests dressed in "the most gorgeous robes of embroidered satin and silk that can be imagined" placed three large tablets with bold Chinese lettering outside the door, so that all passersby might know whose temple this was. Two carved "josses," as he called "the presiding deities of the place," were then positioned on either side of the entrance.

When all was in place outside the temple, explosions of firecrackers and "a most horrible discord from gongs, trumpets, cymbals, fiddles and screaming pipes" invited the devotees inside, where all watched as an assembly of priests delivered prayers before another carved divine image. This one was, in the reporter's words, "a little doll, as we supposed, a young joss, indicative of the infant state of the new building." The priests and the devotees danced around it, "waving their fans and shaking their horse-tail beards, the band in the meantime in full blast, while crackers were exploding outside the house." After "an ear-splitting blast from the broken trumpet," the *Whig* correspondent noted, "It seemed as if the Goddess of Discord had sent her favorite imps to blow this sorry strain as a grand finale of the winding up of the discordant sounds of the late political strife."

That "political strife" was in fact the first labor strike in San Francisco, which occurred when the Chinese workers constructing an all-granite building for the shipping magnate John Parrott—built out of stone cut and shipped from China—demanded higher wages. When the striking workers came out on top in this dispute in the summer of 1852, it was a signal to all that the clout of the Chinese was on the rise.

Innocuous though it may seem at the distance of one hundred and sixty years, the temple dedication was the pressing of an advantage. If Chinese laborers could raise a building on their own terms with their own materials in the heart of San Francisco, there was no reason to think they could not also construct a permanent home of their own. While the labor dispute was a hopeful sign that Chinese workers might be treated as fairly as any others, the Yeong Wo temple was a sign that the religious traditions of the workers' homeland would find a place in the city they were helping to build. As such, the temple was also potentially the cause for some alarm— a literal red flag: The crimson banner Assing and his associates hoisted to the top of their temple on the western slope of Telegraph Hill was a physical manifestation of the power the Chinese community seemed destined to attain in the city and perhaps beyond.

Inevitably, it was seen by many as a spiritual threat in need of an answer.

"These ceremonies were exceedingly novel and interesting," the *Whig* correspondent wrote, "and we could not help thinking while there, if some of the zealous friends of the missionaries could have been present, they would have found that we have as ample a field for missionary labor in our midst, as to send them to the Sandwich Islands, and distant regions in the South Seas."

The *Whig* report was reprinted as far away as Ralph Waldo Emerson's New England. However, though the Transcendentalists experimented with notions borrowed from the East, and occasionally played host to holy men for whom Christianity was the exotic faith of a peculiar people, here in California the East had arrived — not only in person by the thousands but in brick and granite, with gongs, trumpets, fiddles, and screaming pipes. Together with all this the Chinese brought their beliefs, which soon would spread to the rest of the nation.

While contemporary news reports like that of the *San Francisco Whig* provide a full-color glimpse into the past, what may be most remarkable about this particular correspondent's observations is the fact that, interesting though some of the details he recorded may be, he really had no idea what he was seeing. Not merely an isolated exotic location made interesting for a day with its fireworks and music, the Yeong Wo temple on Telegraph Hill was an example of an imported Chinese institution known as the *huiguan*, which even then was playing a significant role in shaping the future of nations on both sides of the Pacific.

In traditional Chinese culture, the connection to one's native place, as the former home and usually the burial place of one's revered ancestors, trumped all other affiliations. Because many ritual actions mandated visits to family gravesites and the shrines of deities with whom the family had a long personal history, not only all politics but all religion was local. When Chinese found themselves far from the land of their birth, they banded together in community associations so that those from the same district who spoke the same dialect and worshipped the same local gods could feel that they had never left home. This system was seen in Beijing and Shanghai as early as the seventeenth century and was replicated in major cities across the country, mainly by the traveling merchant class. As Bryna Goodman, scholar of nineteenth-century China, has noted, "Immigrants separated from their native place were not merely nostalgic, they believed they suffered physically and spiritually from the separation." The regionally affiliated temple known as the huiguan began as a kind of spiritual embassy, a homeland accessible wherever work or fate might take you. In the United States, huiguans like Yeong Wo would come to seem like native religious soil grafted to the top of Gold Mountain.

While at first the word *huiguan* meant only "meeting hall," it quickly came to have broader relevance. In neither China nor the United States did huiguans serve an exclusively spiritual purpose. As their use and prestige increased in cities like Shanghai, the system took on political significance. Following Confucian ideas of the proper organization of society, regional associations came to seem part of the system of concentric circles of affiliation and support outlined in "The Great Learning," one of the principal texts of classical Chinese philosophy: "The ancients who wished to illustrate illustrious virtue throughout the world, first ordered well their own States. Wishing to order well their States, they first regulated their families. Wishing to regulate their families, they first cultivated their persons. Wishing to cultivate their persons, they first rectified their hearts." So too, according to one Shanghai huiguan's founding document, could a nation be protected through the creation of associations encouraging regional solidarity:

> China is made up of prefectures and counties and these are made up of native villages, and the people of each make a concerted effort to cooperate, providing mutual help and protection. This gives solidarity to village, prefecture and province and orders the country....Thus people from the same village, county and prefecture gather together in other areas, making them like their own native place. This is the reason for the establishment of huiguan.

The growing sense of relationship between the local community and the country as a whole gave rise in the late nineteenth century to a nascent Chinese nationalism that often pitted huiguans against those who stood outside this system of belonging. Shanghai, which came under partial French control in 1849, particularly felt the effects of an outside presence, and the huiguans began to see themselves as the first line of defense. When French authorities attempted to appropriate huiguan-owned burial lands for the purpose of building a road, the outcry was immediate. Not only was this an assault on Chinese autonomy, but disturbing a cemetery in a culture in which the living regarded themselves as being in communication with the dead was an unimaginable religious insult. A riot soon broke out pitting dozens of French police against more than one thousand huiguan members. After two Chinese were killed, forty French buildings were burned to the ground. Such disputes between huiguans and foreign governments suspicious of their power raged through the second half of the nineteenth century. A Shanghai newspaper editorial summed up the situation following another such uprising:

> If we do not resist, the will of the [Chinese] people will appear weak and Westerners will make unlimited demands. In the future, if the people's hearts…are as steadfast as this, this will show that even though the country might be weak and the officials might be controlled, the people cannot be bullied.

Through the patriotic efforts of immigrants like Norman Assing, the California huiguans at first made every effort to show themselves to be part of American life. Yet when faced with pressures similar to those endured by their counterparts in Shanghai, they too could respond forcefully.

The earliest huiguans in San Francisco banded together to form the Chinese Six Companies, which functioned as an association of immigrant assistance programs, each with membership based around shared dialect, district of origin, and ethnic affiliation. The Six Companies, which later became the Chinese Consolidated Benevolent Association, quickly became a bridge between government and business interests in California and the explosively growing Chinese community. Throughout the latter half of the nineteenth century, the Six Companies was regarded by many outsiders as a necessary evil: a corrupt institution that nonetheless local authorities and employers relied upon to communicate with a community living behind otherwise unbreachable walls of language and culture. The Six Companies organization was viewed with suspicion, often dismissed as a criminal syndicate (a charge that was not entirely unjustified). Yet such suspicions paid no regard to the fact that its most critical function was religious.

As in Shanghai and Beijing, huiguans in San Francisco provided a place where those from the same region could worship the gods they shared, and assisted in the burial of these worshippers when they died. So central was the idea of native place to Chinese spiritual understanding that many immigrants planned to have their remains shipped back to China despite the expense. To make certain this happened, they relied on the Six Companies. If the remains of the dead could not be shipped back home (the Six Companies provided logistical support, but the expense was still shouldered by the family of the deceased), huiguans for the living established huiguans for the dead, creating burial areas where one could be laid to rest among those who had made a similar journey. In some cases, there were even huiguans for the gods. The necessity of returning to one's native place, if only symbolically, was more than a mortal concern. Huiguans were essential in the maintenance of practices that might otherwise have been lost.

The Six Companies also safeguarded immigrants from the religious milieu in which they found themselves. While Chinese culture generally is welcoming of a variety of beliefs and practices within the walls of its temples, the authorities of the huiguans were not so casual about certain kinds of religious difference. It was taken for granted in most huiguans that the beliefs and practices they would allow, no matter how diverse, would be Chinese beliefs and practices. The San Francisco huiguans actively opposed and prevented conversion to Christianity, using whatever forms of coercion that might prove effective. For example: It was a fairly common practice for workers to labor for a season in the gold fields and then, if they had earned enough, to return home. So common was this practice, in fact, that the Six Companies were given control over issuing return tickets to the Chinese. Taking full advantage of this, and not wanting to export any unwanted spiritual influences back home, the Six Companies began charging more to Chinese who had converted to Christianity than to those who had stayed true to the system of beliefs and practices offered by the huiguans.

Through such defensive efforts to maintain their culture and beliefs, the huiguans in San Francisco began to respond to external pressures in America in a way parallel to their Shanghai counterparts' engagements with the French. As in Shanghai, the more outside pressure the huiguans faced, the greater their willingness to speak out became. Legislative actions against the Chinese soon expanded beyond mine taxes, targeting explicitly Chinese norms and practices. Bans on the long braids traditionally worn by Chinese men, and even against carrying parcels with poles, as was Chinese custom, were enacted in 1870s. Perhaps most insulting to a people for whom sending the remains of the dead home was a religious duty, the state legislature even instituted a ten-dollar tax on the shipment of corpses from its ports. Such legal attacks on Chinese rights contributed to an environment in which they were openly attacked on the streets of the city. In April 1876, the leadership of the Six Companies wrote to H. H. Ellis, Chief of Police of the City and County of San Francisco:

> Sir: — We wish to call your attention to the fact, that at the present time frequent and unprovoked assaults are made upon our Chinese people while walking peacefully the streets of this city. The assaulting party is seldom arrested by your officers, but if a Chinaman resist the assault, he is frequently arrested and punished by fine or by imprisonment. Inflammatory and incendiary addresses against the Chinese, delivered on the public streets to the idle and irresponsible element of this great city, have already produced unprovoked and unpunished assaults upon some of our people, and we fear, that if such things are permitted to go on unchecked, a bloody riot against the Chinese may be the result. Regretting that the Chinese are so obnoxious to the citizens of this country... we simply ask to be protected in our treaty rights.
>
> Respectfully submitted,
> The Six Companies

The treaty to which the Six Companies leadership referred, the Burlingame Treaty of 1868, protected both American citizens living in China and Chinese living in the United States, and made explicit mention that people "of every religious persuasion...shall enjoy entire liberty of conscience and shall be exempt from all disability or persecution on account of their religious faith or worship in either country." It was against the violation of these rights of conscience that the Six Companies most strongly protested.

When the U.S. government took the ultimate steps of first restricting Chinese immigration through the Chinese Exclusion Act of 1882, and then through the Geary Act of 1892 (calling for all Chinese already within the United States to carry certificates of residence at all times), the Six Companies encouraged nonviolent civil disobedience along the lines of what would later be seen in the Civil Rights Movement. In response to the Geary Act, the Six Companies called upon Chinese in California not only to refuse to carry the certificates but to contribute their wages to the fund that would fight the act in the courts. It was in response to the Chinese Exclusion Act, however, that the Six Companies engaged in its most brazen act of civil disobedience, by actively smuggling Chinese into the country across the Canadian and Mexican borders. Faced with being cut off from their homeland, the Six Companies simply flouted the law in order to maintain their connection to the community's source of spiritual sustenance.

As a founder of one of these original San Francisco huiguans, Norman Assing was there at the beginning of the movement for Chinese civil and religious rights in America. He, too, was suspected of various extralegal activities, and was in fact a near-constant presence in the San Francisco courts. His role in most proceedings, however, was not as defendant but—like the Six Companies personified—as a go-between and a fixer; he was someone well known as a member of the Chinese community who could make problems go away. A typical entry in a local newspaper's court report:

> A-he, a Chinaman, was brought up on a charge of larceny, having stolen ten dollars. Norman Assing testified that he was a crazy man, and that he had had him locked up in one of his rooms for several days, and that he broke out and escaped. The money was taken from a gaming table in the New World saloon on Long Wharf. He was discharged, Norman Assing promising to send him to China.

Not only was Norman Assing trusted to send his countryman home, it was apparently accepted without explanation that he would take it upon himself to lock up a thief in one of "his" rooms. He was at once a promoter of Chinatown's religious life and an enforcer of its own moral code. Even as the state and federal authorities cracked down on the Chinese in California, they relied on men like Assing and the huiguan he represented to keep order in a community in which the usual mechanisms of government held little sway.

Through subtle and not so subtle influence, the huiguan system slowed the rate of assimilation of the Chinese in San Francisco and elsewhere. Yet in the process it created what has become a crucial part of the American experience: the urban enclave of new arrivals and their descendants, a hothouse where the culture brought across the ocean could not only survive but flourish. This was a process replicated across America as the Six Companies opened affiliates in New York City (1883), Seattle (1892), Boston (1923), and eventually in twenty other cities throughout the United States.

Paradoxically, it was thanks in part to the restrictive laws passed against them that the Chinese in America were able to establish themselves wherever they went according to their own religious vision, building their own unique version of the city on a hill. And, as with the Puritans, theirs was a vision that would have unexpected influence on all those around them.

The correspondent for the *San Francisco Whig* need not have worried that Christian proselytizers were missing out on a ripe field of potential converts in Chinatown. The missionaries were in fact already there. In the Presbyterian and Methodist churches, especially, it was not uncommon by the mid-nineteenth century for evangelists to spend some time in China, and then, after they had returned to the United States, to look for a mission field where they could make use of their newly acquired cultural and linguistic knowledge closer to home. For obvious reasons, San Francisco was the prime destination. As they had from their Far East outposts, the missionaries to California wrote detailed travelogues of their expeditions. Yet whereas the earlier evangelical literature had related tales of impossibly distant places, this new generation of missionary writers began to tell stories of the exotic Orient in locales that were becoming more accessible by the day.

Both the Methodist Otis Gibson and the Presbyterian William Speer were in San Francisco during the boom years of Chinese immigration, and both left remarkable records of their time there. Gibson walked his readers attentively through the sights, sounds, and smells—he was particularly taken by the smells—of China-town, which provided, he wrote, an experience of "China, as it is." Following a description of the people one might see ("Chinamen and a few Chinese women dressed in Chinese fashion, the men with shaven crown and braided cue, walking with a Chinese shuf-fle or a Chinese swagger"), Gibson provided a lengthy discourse on the meaning of the signs hanging in the windows of various businesses: "It is not customary with the Chinese to give the names of the parties composing the firm as the firm name, but some fan-ciful, high-sounding phrase is selected. Here, for instance, is this butcher-shop called 'Man Wo, Ten Thousand Harmonies.' Such phrases are peculiarly pleasing to the Chinese mind, and are sug-gestive of good luck."

Speer meanwhile saw the arrival of the Chinese in both reli-gious and practical terms. "The Creator has prepared a treasury of labor in that empire from which those lands and islands can draw without danger of exhaustion. This only we can now foretell, that the handful of Chinese now on this continent is but the trickling of the rivulet which will swell into a river that will spread over all the New World." As he understood it, God intended the Chinese to cross the Pacific for the purpose of building America—with their tireless labor and their unimaginable numbers—into the great Christian nation it was meant to be. "The stream which begins to set in from China to the New World does not remain in Califor-nia," he wrote. "It flows wherever a channel is open for it by the discovery of new mines, by the opening of new opportunities of trade or by the requirements for human labor. It is supposed that fifty thousand Chinese are distributed over other Pacific States and Territories. Half of these are in Montana and Idaho; a fourth of them are in Oregon and Nevada; the remainder are distributed along the lines of railroad eastward and in Colorado and Utah.... As the number increases, they will press on into all the States."

All of this would be for the good, Speer supposed, if this river was converted as it flowed. Representatives of the mainline Protes-tant churches became unlikely supporters of the rights of the Chinese in America, but it was understood by all sides that this support came with strings attached. Christian Chinese should be welcomed, the missionaries asserted, but those who frequented temples such as the one dedicated on Telegraph Hill would be seen primarily as potential converts.

Although Speer and others undoubtedly had some success in their conversion efforts, the missionary influence in Chinatown also had unexpected consequences. Once again this was a moment when religious influence proved to be not a stream moving in only one direction but an estuary in which a number of different sources combined, each challenging and changing the composition of the other. Combined with the huiguan system's establishment and support of the religious life of Chinatowns, the new crop of missionaries telling intriguing tales of the Chinese brought about an unexpected side-effect that would have surprisingly broad influence: spiritual tourism.

Huiguan temples in China had been strictly members-only affairs. But in America an unexpected thing began happening. Mainly thanks to the efforts of community spokesmen like Norman Assing, Chinese temples—and Chinatowns generally—became the subject of intense interest among non-Chinese. In Sacramento, for example, one could stop into the shop known as Tobin & Duncan's and purchase all manner of Chinese exotica. Postcards depicting the inside of Chinese worship houses showed well-dressed Anglos looking quite out of place: the nation's first religious sightseers. Newspapers began to fill with offers of entertainments that promised entry into exotic "Oriental" worlds.

In the short term, many more Westerners began to frequent Chinese temples. Gibson clucks disapprovingly about the abodes of "gods many and lords many" visited by former churchgoers. "One of the principal Chinese 'joss-houses' is called the Eastern Glorious Temple," he writes. "This temple is largely owned and controlled by Dr. Lai Po Tai, a Chinese quack doctor, who is said to have accumulated a large fortune practicing medicine among a class of weak-minded, easily duped Americans, both men and women." Gibson had come to Chinatown eager to bring souls over to his side of the spiritual divide, only to find, with some discomfort, that many of his fellow citizens were going there for the purpose of moving in the opposite direction: not away from "heathen" practices but toward them.

In the longer term, journalistic explorations into the spiritual lives of the Chinese followed in the missionaries' wake. The temple dedication report that appeared in the *San Francisco Whig* was but the first entry in a genre that would regularly feature the religious gatherings of Chinatown well into the twentieth century.

To combat the work of evangelists like Speer and Gibson, the Six Companies in 1876 brought the Confucian revivalist Fung Chee Pang from China to deliver a series of lectures on traditional Chinese ethics, ritual, and religion. Dr. Pang, as Gibson deigned to call him, was interviewed at length in the *San Francisco Chronicle*, which used the lectures as an opportunity to reflect on the culture then making itself at home in the city. When "John Chinaman" arrived in America, the *Chronicle* wrote, "he brought his rice, his chopsticks, his language, his peculiar and disgusting habits, and now, to make the thing complete, he imports his religion and literature, and whisks them fairly in the faces of our men of letters with the remark that it is more authentic and as old as the everlasting hills."

To give its readers "some idea of what they might expect from the advent of this new and yet old religion," a reporter from the *Chronicle* had a "literary pow-wow" with the Chinese scholar. When asked to explain the content of his teachings, Fung Chee Pang expounded upon "The Great Learning" — the text cited by the Shanghai temple as the reason for the creation of the huiguan system. Shrewdly, in inviting Dr. Pang, the leaders of the Six Companies were fighting fire with fire, using missionary techniques not to convert their people but to prevent them from converting — to remind them, in other words, that they, too, were a people of the book. This strategy was not lost on the reporter from the *Chronicle*: "For a long time our celestial residents have been keeping a suspicious eye on the inroads the Christian religion has been making in their ranks," he wrote. "They noted with alarm the capture of some of their brightest young men by the irrepressible missionaries, and to stay the progress of Christianity, and at the same time fix the love of country firmly in the mind of the heathen horde, the Six Companies have inaugurated a series of protracted meetings of the most approved fashion; but, instead of the Bible, the law and gospel as laid down is taken direct from the musty volumes of the great Confucius." In this, the reporter grudgingly notes, Dr. Pang was "stirring up quite a revival among the almond-eyed horde."

While much of the coverage of Chinese religion was dismissive, other times it showed signs of a surprising pluralism, as in a short item titled "Religious Freedom" that appeared in the *Los Angeles Herald* in 1875:

> Nowhere in the civilized world is there such perfect religious freedom as on the Pacific Coast. The worshippers at every shrine, the champions of every creed known among civilized men, reside together in the most perfect harmony. Whether the citizen of California be a follower of Confucius, or a disciple of Jesus Christ, his rights are respected, and the fullest liberty accorded him. Jew or Gentile, Christian or Infidel, Catholic or Protestant, worship according to the promptings of their own hearts, and there are none so hardy as to gainsay their privilege. While Europe is still struggling under the curse of religious persecutions either open or silent, while Canada is intolerant, and religious hatred still bitter over most of the United States east of the Rocky mountains, absolute freedom prevails in California. The general spirit of tolerance everywhere visible in this section is witnessed nowhere else in the world. Nor does it spring from irreligion, for our people are individually as zealous in their worship as their more bigoted brethren in other parts of the world. The church steeple rises in every valley and upon every hill and every Sabbath the sun looks down upon the eager thousands wending their way to the houses of prayer.

Still other engagements between the American press and the growing Chinese community displayed an ambivalence indicative of the simultaneous suspicion and curiosity the residents of Chinatown inspired. Perhaps the best example of this is a poem by the American writer and editor Bret Harte. Harte had arrived in San Francisco as a teenager not long after the dedication of Norman Assing's temple, and so he came of age around the sights and sounds of Chinatown. As the editor of the *Overland Monthly* magazine, he regularly published sympathetic explorations of Chinese culture, including a long essay on the benign role of the Six Companies in 1894.

Harte's greatest success as a writer, however, also became his greatest regret. In 1870, just as an economic downturn created more competition for jobs than ever before in California, Harte published a satiric poem — "Plain Language from Truthful James" — that lampooned the racism of white laborers who blamed the

Chinese for their woes. The poem follows two dishonest gamblers, the narrator James and his belligerent friend Bill Nye, as they attempt to cheat a "heathen Chinee," an immigrant laborer called Ah Sin, out of his wages in a game of cards. As the verses progress, Harte shows the two card sharks at first confident they will easily fool the man with a "smile that was childlike and bland," but they are in for a surprise.

> *The hands that were played*
> *By that heathen Chinee,*
> *And the points that he made*
> *Were quite frightful to see.*

When Ah Sin wins the next hand, an enraged Bill Nye cries, "[W]e are ruined by cheap Chinese labor," and then attacks. The reader does not directly learn of Ah Sin's fate, but Harte describes the cards strewn portentously on the floor "like leaves on the strand."

Harte's point was clear enough: The gamblers had lost at their own game and so resorted to racist justifications for their violent response. Yet when the poem began to be reprinted far and wide, retitled as "The Heathen Chinee," much of Harte's wit was lost. Underscoring the fact that the prejudice faced by the Chinese was both racial and religious, "Heathen Chinee" became a popular slur for Chinese immigrants across America—and a rallying cry for those who identified with the bumbling thugs in the poem. Since the earliest days of Chinese immigration, nativist politicians and newspaper editors had warned of the "yellow peril" that Asian newcomers represented to the United States; now the exclusionists had their own unlikely poet laureate. To Harte's chagrin, his words were reprinted in offensively illustrated editions far outside the highbrow context of the *Overland Monthly*, which had initially made his intentions obvious. Years later he would declare, "Plain Language from Truthful James" was "the worst poem I ever wrote, possibly the worst poem anyone ever wrote.... I was almost ashamed to offer it," though as historians including Ronald Takaki have noted, he never publicly protested the almost universal misreading of his work as it was making him famous.

While Harte would later lament his most significant, and unfortunate, contribution to American race relations, the sympathetic interest he and other writers of the day showed to the people and practices of Chinatown would have other, more positive, effects. Harte was, for example, a founding member of the Bohemian Club, a San Francisco association of journalists, artists, and businessmen. In 1882, the same year the Exclusion Act was passed, members of the Bohemian Club constructed a seventy-foot-tall Buddha at Bohemian Grove, their camp outside the city. Given that the benefactors of Bohemian Grove were well-heeled San Francisco businessmen of just the sort seen in postcards depicting the rise of spiritual tourism in San Francisco, there can be little doubt where they had seen their first images of the Buddha. Bohemian Grove later would become the storied home to gatherings of political and cultural leaders, but it drew some of its early inspiration from the margins of San Francisco society.

The Bohemian Grove Buddha may be dismissed as mere esoterica with little long-term influence, but Chinatowns around the United States only grew in their cultural impact as the nineteenth century gave way to the twentieth. By then Chinese communities had been established, as the missionary Speer predicted, in dozens of states, gradually introducing images and ideas first imported from Asia into the mainstream of American culture. Just as the Transcendentalists had prepared the way for the arrival of Hinduism in the person of Swami Vivekananda, the presence of Chinatowns in major American cities prepared the American public for the arrival of ambassadors of Taoism and Buddhism. Indeed, at the same Parliament of the World's Religions where Vivekananda received his rapturous welcome, contingents of Japanese and Sri Lankan monks offered thoughts that perhaps would not have been so warmly received were it not for the role Chinese immigrants had played in making familiar the variety of spiritual expressions that could be found in Asia.

It was not just self-styled intellectuals who were exposed to new religious ideas in this way. Beginning in the late 1890s, images of Buddhas, robed monks, and Chinese temples began to filter into public consciousness through dime store detective novels that were the mass-market entertainment of the day. The *Secret Service* series of novels, for example, jumped between Chinatowns in California and New York, and even featured a wisecracking missionary's daughter who was likely the first Mandarin-fluent Western woman in American literature. When the plot of more than one involved the intrepid father and son private eyes and their Chinese-speaking gal Friday sneaking into a "joss house" or Chinese secret society, it was proof that the huiguan system that had begun among merchants in seventeenth-century Beijing had become fully a part not only of the cities Chinese immigrants had helped build but of popular culture as well.

As surely as a semaphore tower spread news of the arrival of ships at port to even those who could not see the bay, the construction of a network of temples on U.S. soil safeguarded the religious ideas of the local community they served and allowed those ideas to be broadcast into the distance. Two further scenes of life in San Francisco's Chinatown illustrate just how far those signals could travel, and how great the interference was that they overcame.

The first scene occurred a little more than fifty years after the dedication of the temple on Telegraph Hill. It was then, during the earthquake of 1906, that nearly everything the Chinese had built over the preceding five decades was reduced to rubble. Yet even in that moment of utter disaster, the Chinese of San Francisco found ways to continue the practices they had preserved against all odds.

On a spring morning in the aftermath of the earthquake, twenty Chinese men and women arrived at the ruins of what had been the most prominent temple in the city. Military guards had formed a wide ring around the devastation that extended beyond the formerly crowded confines of Chinatown to the wrecked mansions of Nob Hill. Yet the Chinese, emboldened by their rising status in the city and determined to salvage what they could, found a city police officer to escort them as they sought permission to approach the spot where their temple had stood.

After the last tremors, a fire had raged through the neighborhood, reducing the fallen walls to timbers and ash. It was only after some digging that the Chinese contingent found what it was looking for. At the sight of a charred wooden image, they dropped to their knees in the soot. As the smoke from their burning incense sticks mingled with the still smoldering embers of a scene the local press referred to as a "holocaust," the faithful knelt and offered silent prayers. Lying before them was the carved image of the temple's presiding deity, blackened by fire but still sacred. The temple members performed their usual rites with careful attention to detail, undaunted by the catastrophe. The twenty Chinese left San Francisco that evening, sent by circumstances across the bay to

Oakland as they had once been sent across the sea; but they would return to rebuild. This American place had become their own native holy ground.

Some fifty years later still, exactly a century after the dedication of the temple on Telegraph Hill, the groundwork laid by Norman Assing and other organizers of the Chinese Six Companies continued to serve as a foundation for Chinese immigrant life, which began anew to spread its influence through the curiosity of outsiders. Following in the footsteps of earlier chroniclers drawn to the fully American yet foreign-seeming streets of San Francisco's Chinatown, the writers of the Beat Generation in the middle of the twentieth century knew nothing of the politics that had made the place what it was—but still they came to experience the exotic close to home. In his autobiographical novel *The Dharma Bums*, Jack Kerouac recounts meeting up in Chinatown with his friend the poet Gary Snyder. Snyder was usually credited as the member of the Beat Generation most responsible for introducing Kerouac and the poet Allen Ginsberg to Buddhism. At the time of Kerouac's arrival on the West Coast, Snyder was studying Asian languages at Berkeley, preparing himself for a trip to Japan to deepen his knowledge of Zen meditation.

After wandering around the streets where Assing and his China Boys had marched to prove their patriotism, the two young writers sat together "in the Sunday morning grass" of a Chinatown park.

"Across the street was the new Buddhist temple some young Chamber of Commerce Chinatown Chinese were trying to build, by themselves," Kerouac wrote. No longer immigrants, these were the children and grandchildren of immigrants, building temples in what was now their native land. "They were young Sinclair Lewis idealistic forward-looking kids who lived in nice homes but put on jeans to come down and work on the church," Kerouac went on, "like you might expect in some midwest town, some midwest lads with a bright-faced Richard Nixon leader, the prairie all around. Here in the heart of the tremendously sophisticated little city called San Francisco Chinatown they were doing the same thing, but their church was the church of Buddha."

Kerouac does not mention the name of this temple, but it is now known as the Buddha's Universal Church—the largest Buddhist temple in the United States, built from the rubble of the 1906 earthquake that destroyed Norman Assing's huiguan.

For all his curiosity about the East, Kerouac noted, Snyder was strangely uninterested in the Buddhism of San Francisco's Chinatown—"because it was traditional Buddhism, not the Zen intellectual artistic Buddhism he loved." But for Kerouac it was all the same, all of it part of a culture and system of beliefs he felt strongly enough about to help build that church of Buddha himself. "One night I'd come by there," he said, "and, drunk, pitched in with them with a wheelbarrow, hauling sand from outside in."

"From outside in" was precisely how the religious life of the nation had been formed. Kerouac and Snyder are often credited with introducing the religious ideas of Asia to the American counterculture of the decade that followed. From there, they became mainstream enough that Buddha statues can now be found in the gardening section of your local big box hardware store. This was a process that did not begin in the rucksacks of beatniks, however. It began with the courage of a few immigrants who dared to raise a red flag to the top of their temple, sending a signal to all that they and their gods were here to stay.

Bhagat Singh Thind, Sikh veteran of
the U.S. Army, 1917.

CHAPTER 15

"Go Ahead, Keep Your Whiskers"

1907–1923

Even as they saw their door kicked in, they did not draw their knives. It would have been so easy: Each man among the small group gathered around a single rice pot in the dirt-floor shack was armed with a small dagger kept discreetly within his clothing. The blades were not very sharp, but curved and pointed, like the horn of a bull — certainly adequate, if brandished in sufficient number, to the task of keeping a mob at bay.

They had not come to this country to fight, however. They had come to work. Two days after seeing the other residents of Bellingham, Washington, celebrate Labor Day, they might have wondered if laborers were as valued as the holiday declared.

They wore their kirpans, as they called the bejeweled ceremonial knives tucked at their waists, not for self-defense but to remind themselves that they were engaged in a larger struggle, one that could not be won with brute force. The kirpan was one of the so-called Five Ks — *panj kakaar* — of their faith, the five external markers every male Sikh was expected to carry with him at all times. According to the code of conduct known as the Rehat Maryada, the others markers were *kesh*, their own uncut hair, symbol of the divine requirement to do no harm to the body; *kachhehra*, the ritual undergarment that stood for self-control; *kanga*, the wooden comb that spoke of the virtues of hygiene and discipline; and the steel bracelet they called the *kara*, worn as a constant reminder that one's very hands were a gift from God. To do wrong with them was to wrong the giver of all things, and so to wrong oneself.

It was perhaps this knowledge that kept the Sikhs from fighting as the white men burst into the weather-beaten shack and kicked their simple dinner to the ground. It stayed their hands when excited schoolboys, following their fathers' cruel example, pulled the foreigners by their beards, knocked the turbans from their heads, and went wide-eyed at the great lengths of raven hair concealed beneath. This was the knowledge, the belief, that ensured that even when their pockets were emptied and they were shoved toward the street to be beaten in full view of a crowd of hundreds squalling approval—even then the Sikhs did not unsheathe their blades.

Like the kirpan itself, refusing to misuse it was a symbol of the need to stand for righteousness in the face of injustice. Faith, too, could have a cutting edge. As a prayer of the seventeenth-century Sikh spiritual leader Guru Gobind Singh expressed it: "I bow with heart and mind to the Holy Sword....The sword cuts sharply, destroys the host of the wicked...is very sharp and its flash pales the radiance of the sun. The sword brings peace to the saints, fear to the evil minded, destruction to sin, so it is my refuge."

If any among the attacked men had spoken these words aloud on the night of September 4, 1907, they might have been struck by the sad fact that hope of refuge was precisely what had brought them to this land.

The city of Bellingham, hard upon the Canadian border in Washington State, then less than twenty years a member of the Union, was a hardscrabble lumber and mining town tucked between Lake Whatcom and Bellingham Bay, which by way of the Strait of Georgia made Vancouver just a day's journey by steamship. Thanks to an influx of European immigrants eager to work the mills and the docks, the population more than doubled from 1900 to 1910, when it stood just shy of twenty-five thousand.

It was right in the middle of this boom—in January of 1906— that groups of men born in South Asia began to trickle down from British Columbia. Mostly from the Punjab, along the line of demarcation that would separate India from Pakistan forty years later, they were almost entirely followers of the Sikh religion. Sikhism is organized around belief in one God yet reveres ten historical gurus who led the community in succession from the fifteenth to the eighteenth century, as well as one "living guru," which is not a person but a collection of hymns describing the nature of the divine. Often confused with both Hinduism and Islam, it arose during one of the many periods of conflict between the two, emerging as a third way among a people caught in the middle of warring faiths. By necessity, Sikhs were known as warriors from their earliest days, yet as the tradition developed, the symbols of combat such as the kirpan, which once perhaps served a practical purpose, came to be interpreted in spiritual terms.

As the locals of Bellingham understood it, the first two Sikhs in their city had walked down the Great Northern Railway line to escape the harassment and threats of violence they had faced across the border in Canada. Perhaps they had hoped that America, with all its promises of freedom, was a place where they might carry out the struggle of their faith in peace. They also hoped to find a place where they could earn money to send to the families they had left behind. When it was determined that these first two Sikhs, whose names were recorded in the local press as Linah Singh and Pola Singh, had not passed through required immigration examinations, they were arrested and deported, to the relief of the white Christian immigrant workers in town.

Within two months, however, others began to arrive—most also called Singh, the traditional surname of all male Sikhs. Coming through proper immigration channels, and now inside railcars instead of walking along the tracks, the next group of Sikhs took jobs as ditch diggers before finding work in the lumber mills that filled the town with the screech of band saws late into the evening. Unlike many of the other available workers, apparently, these newcomers had little interest in the saloons that both catered to mill employees and hurt their employers' bottom line. The lumber mill owners proclaimed they would rather have other laborers, but this group of men whose faith prohibited drink proved more reliable. "We cannot get white men who will remain steadily at their work," one owner lamented. "A large number are transient and work only for 'whisky money' leaving the company in the lurch just at the time that their services are most desired."

The need was so great for workers with no interest in "whisky money" that soon there were hundreds of Sikhs in Bellingham. Locals, many of them immigrants themselves, greeted them on the street with shouts of "Hindus go home!" That they were not actually Hindus did not seem to matter — not to the white workers who believed they had been put out of a job by cheaper labor, which was not apparently the case, and not to the editors of the city's several daily newspapers.

By September of 1906, readers of the *Puget Sound American* were greeted with an ominous headline: "Have We a Dusky Peril?" Beneath it, an illustration of bearded men in turbans — one playing a flute to charm a cobra emerging from a basket — bore the caption "Hindu Hordes Invading the State." The story itself warned, "Hordes of Hindus have fastened their eyes on Bellingham and the northwestern part of the United States in general, and the vanguard of the invasion which in the minds of many discerning people, threatens to overshadow the 'yellow peril,' has reached this city." Describing them as "swarthy sons of Hinduism," the article went on to suggest that "thousands of worshippers of Brahma, Buddha and other strange deities of India may soon press the soil of Washington."

That the unsigned writer of this news report knew nothing about the spiritual tradition that had actually arrived in Bellingham did not prevent the article from going on in great detail about the religious complexities of India:

> The land of the Hindus harbors 300,000,000 souls, and it has been called "an epitome of the whole earth," so varied is its physical characteristics. There the bull, the cow and the monkey are held sacred. In all there are about fifty tribes, which can be traced back to two or three original races. The Hindus form the largest part of the population, and their religion, Brahmanism, is therefore, chief. Of the other principal religions, Mohammedanism has 60,000,000 followers and Buddhism 8,000,000 believers.
>
> Brahmanism was originally a philosophical religion, mingled with the worship of the powers of nature....In practice, in the course of years, the religion became a system of idolatry, with cruel rites and hideous images. The caste system, a part of the religion, became a grievous burden, and still is. In the first class are the priests. Warriors are next, followed by traders, and they by the common types.

If the vast populations cited in the article were not enough to alarm the residents of this small town who believed a horde of thousands would soon descend upon them, the paper put the supposed threat in unambiguous terms through a letter to the editor featured as a sidebar. Written by an Englishman named George Pertinet, who obviously had no problem with immigration per se, the letter painted the group as armed and dangerous guerrillas:

Bellingham, Sept. 15, 1906
Editor, American.

Having resided in India nine years and closely observed the habits of the Hindus, I consider their advent in this country very undesirable. They are strictly non-progressive and adhere to their old established customs with far more tenacity than either the Japanese or Chinese. Their code of morals is bad (from our point of view), and if allowed the freedom, which they naturally expect in America, they will eventually become troublesome. The most of them have been soldiers under the British government and are well-versed in the use of fire-arms. In conclusion, they have the habit of running amuck, when annoyed, in which case a number of innocent people get butchered. By all means keep them out.

The combination of these sentiments — obvious religious otherness combined with an alleged violent history — suggested that the newcomers posed both spiritual and physical danger to the community. As a sermon published in the *Bellingham Herald* and reprinted around the region put it, "At the present rate at which they are coming, we can no more Christianize them than we can put out hell by throwing snowballs into it."

The Bible says that if one careth not for his own household he is no better than an infidel. This is true also of nations. Charity begins at home. While the people of the United States have gladly offered asylum and refuge to the millions of tempest-tossed and persecuted of the earth, yet we have no right before God to carry this hospitality one step beyond the point where we endanger and imperil our integrity as a Christian nation. Christ's injunction, "Go ye into all the world and preach the gospel to every creature," does not imply that we should invite those people here in such hordes that we shall be swamped, inundated, despiritualized, and un-Americanized.

The headline under which this sermon ran put the matter succinctly, if with less of the pulpit's brimstone: "Unrestricted Immigration Means Total Annihilation of the American State." Only this nearly apocalyptic fear in the face of religious difference can explain what occurred on the evening of September 4, 1907. There were by then several hundred Sikhs residing peacefully within Bellingham's city limits. Most lived in bunkhouses constructed near the lumber mills where they worked. Others stayed in small clusters in the lodging house district. Wherever they were, the mob found them.

The word *pogrom* is most often associated with czarist Russia; it usually refers to a violent attack against Jews — in cities like Kiev and Kishinev — by rampaging mobs of Christians, who, in flare-ups of anti-Semitism frequently fomented and encouraged by civil authorities and the press, murdered their neighbors and ransacked homes and businesses on hundreds of separate occasions. The era of pogroms lasted in Russia from medieval times well into the twentieth century, and is generally regarded as a precursor to the genocidal ambitions of Stalin and Hitler. Pogrom is not a word often associated with the Pacific Northwest of the United States, but it is difficult to find a more appropriate description for what occurred in the aftermath of a Labor Day celebration gone awry. On September 2, during a parade and other festivities, curious Sikhs who had come to watch found themselves jeered at and harassed at every turn. Two days later, apparently after negative feelings had time to be organized and directed, more than five hundred white men, trailed by boys apparently skipping school to watch the spectacle, moved methodically through town, stopping at every shack and lodging where "Hindus" were known to live. Papers as far away as the *New York Times* reported what happened next:

> The long-expected cry "Drive out the Hindus!" was heard throughout the city and along the waterfront last night. The police were helpless. All authority was paralyzed, and for five hours a mob of a half-thousand white men raided the

mills where the foreigners were working, battered down doors of lodging houses, and, dragging the Asiatics from their beds, escorted them to the city limits with order to keep going.

After a sweep of the lodging house district near the docks, the mob's last stop was the Lake Whatcom Logging Company, the scale of which gives some indication of what it would take to organize hundreds into hours of violence spread across a city, and the enormity of the hatred that must have fueled the effort. A full five miles from the waterfront where the riot began, the largest mill in the area occupied eighty acres and produced 45,000,000 board feet of cut lumber in the year the Sikhs arrived in Bellingham. Consisting of dozens of laborers' cottages, it was a village unto itself — a village that was stormed as midnight passed on September 5. Hundreds of men with torches descended on the company compound. Battering down doors, they pulled sleeping Sikhs from their bunks and marched them back to town.

Far from "helpless," as the *New York Times* report suggested, the police at this point — and only at this point — saw fit to respond. The chief of police made his way to "two crumbling shacks" where a crowd he numbered at close to two thousand had enclosed and surrounded the Sikhs. As reported by *Collier's* magazine a month later, the chief of police, named Thomas, "a great, calm, ungrammatical man of unbounded tact," approached with an ease of manner that does not suggest a town official concerned about the welfare of people it was his job to protect.

"What are you doing, boys?" he asked members of the crowd.

There were men among the mob throwing rocks at the two makeshift jailhouses, pausing only to shove back inside any "Hindu" who dared to show himself. They broke from this pastime just long enough to answer.

"Running 'em out of town," they said.

Chief Thomas replied, "That's right. But say, if you fellows keep 'em in them shacks, some bad man may start a riot. Why don't you take 'em down to the police station? They'll be safer there, and in the morning we'll all chuck 'em out together."

Though he would later be faulted for how he handled the situation, that night the police chief earned a cheer.

Bellingham's Sikhs carried nothing with them as the deputized mob marched them through town. As another local report put it, "The Hindus have a love for jewelry, and hundreds of dollars' worth of it was taken by the members of the mob. The places were also turned topsy-turvy, and much valuable clothing and articles owned by the Orientals was destroyed that was not carried off." In a photograph of the group taken after they were locked in the basement of the city hall—Chief Thomas's jail could only hold so many—they do not look like men who had been hoarding jewelry. Half in turbans, half in western-style hats, all wore the sad expression of men half a world away from their families. Men who had just been snatched from their meals or their beds, they do indeed look like people who have had something precious taken from them. Yet most likely the jewelry mentioned was nothing but a few of the more ornate examples of the Five Ks their code of conduct instructed them to carry: fine wooden combs, steel bracelets, bejeweled ritual blades. Even these markers of their faith they had seen snatched away, a sure sign that neither they nor their beliefs were welcome in America.

The following day, the jailed men crowded the train station by the hundreds. Even in the light of morning, some remained so frightened they walked north along the tracks before the first departure's whistle was heard. Within a week, not one Sikh remained.

The aftermath of the attacks that later became known as the Bellingham Riots was not what might be expected today. There was little handwringing within the community that things had gotten out of hand. On the contrary, the remaining residents, including the mayor, the police chief, and other officials, were glad to see the Sikhs go. The San Francisco–based Korean and Japanese Exclusion League, which had no fewer than eight hundred members in Bellingham, felt so emboldened by the riot and its success that they renamed themselves the more inclusive Asiatic Exclusion League. Within two months, copycat crimes occurred in the nearby cities of Vancouver, Aberdeen, Everett, and Boring, Oregon. Nor was this merely a story of local interest. In addition to the far-off press coverage, the violence in Bellingham was brought to the attention of the federal government by parties on both sides. A letter from the Seattle Exclusion League warned President Roosevelt that "in view of the Bellingham riots," he must "take immediate action in checking the Oriental immigration into the Northwest." The State

Department, meanwhile, braced for inquiries from the British ambassador, demanding an explanation why these visitors to the United States, who remained British subjects, would be treated so poorly. Speculating on how the U.S. government might respond, the *Times* reported that this state of affairs was becoming the new normal: "All that the State Department can do in such a case as that at Bellingham is to follow the well-worn precedents established in Wyoming, Louisiana, California, and elsewhere, where foreigners have been mobbed or killed," the paper of record said. "That is, the department, in the name of the President, may address the Governor of Washington, transmitting perhaps the complaint of the British Embassy…and requesting him to take action to prevent a recurrence of the trouble."

Perhaps not as quickly as the various exclusion leagues would have liked, the mounting attacks did eventually result in action by the federal government. Washington did not act to protect the Sikhs and those endangered immigrants who might come after them, however. Instead, with nativist sentiment exploding as the First World War raged, Congress passed the first of a series of laws preventing anyone born in Asia to enter and remain in the United States. These laws were adopted mainly due to the rising influence of the Pacific states, which in official reports now referred to the threat of "the Hindu" far more often than "the heathen Chinee"; in most cases, this actually referred to Sikhs. Of the more than seven thousand Indians who emigrated to the Pacific coast between 1899 and 1917, nearly all were from Punjab; around 90 percent were Sikhs, and most of the rest were Muslim. No "Hindu" threat in fact existed, and yet the combined threats of foreign customs and alien religion spread by that name. "The Hindu is the most undesirable immigrant in the state," a report from the California State Board of Control stated in 1920. "His lack of personal cleanliness, his low morals, and his blind adherence to theories and teachings, so entirely repugnant to American principles make him unfit for association with American people."

With the passage of the Immigrant Act of 1917, the same restrictions faced by the Chinese since 1882 now applied to those within the Asiatic Barred Zone, which included all those from Turkey to the Polynesian Islands, nearly half of the world's population—not incidentally, the non-Christian half. U.S. immigration policy became even more strident in the years following with the passage of the

338 • ONE NATION, UNDER GODS

Emergency Quota Act in 1921 and the Johnson-Reed Act of 1924, both of which hoped to stem the tide of unwanted immigrants through the creation of a quota system. Encouraging religious as well as ethnic homogeneity, the act established a formula based on the national origins of citizens of the United States as numbered in the census of 1890. The goal was maintenance of the racial composition of the population – in other words, no more diversity than existed thirty years before would be allowed.

Of course, before these laws were passed, many supposedly "undesirable" immigrants had been making lives for themselves throughout the United States. Among these, no minority religious group did more for the ultimate acceptance of themselves and others than the spiritual kin of the men who had been chased out of Bellingham in 1907. Though derided in the press as "timid sons of India" in the days after the riot, Sikhs elsewhere in America became known as embodiments of their warrior heritage – not by answering violence with violence but by showing their grit in places as varied as farmers' fields, sports arenas, and the courts.

In the decade following the attacks in Bellingham, Sikhs became among the most productive agricultural workers on the West Coast. In the Imperial Valley, extending from the Mexican border to the Salton Sea, they first picked cotton as migrant laborers and then began growing it themselves. With very few women joining them in emigration from Punjab, many Sikh men married Mexican women – a cross-cultural experiment ironically aided by California's anti-miscegenation laws, which regarded these two groups from far sides of the earth as equally "brown." Many of the children born from these unions adopted their mothers' Catholic beliefs, but throughout the state Sikh religious devotion remained strong enough that incorporation papers for a Sikh temple in Berkeley were granted in 1912. Continued adherence to the beliefs they had brought with them did not prevent them from becoming well versed in areas of civic life many natives failed to understand. According to Karen Leonard, the leading scholar on Punjabi-Mexican culture, Sikhs in the Imperial Valley were adept at using the legal system of their new land to address grievances both within their community and between themselves and their non-immigrant neighbors. They were so adept, in fact, that within their first decade they initiated nearly twice as much litigation in the county courts as one would expect from a population their size.

Further up the coastline, Sikhs gained a reputation as wrestlers of the first order. Importing the ancient art of Punjabi judo known as *kabaddi* to lumberjack camps of the Cascades and the Sierras, grapplers such as Dodan Singh and Kapoor Singh established themselves as men who would not be pushed around. The latter (described in the press as "the burly Hindu...a magnificent specimen of brawn and muscle") also bore the dubious distinction of being the first "Hindu" sent to San Quentin State Prison, while the former fought one Eddie O'Connell for the welterweight title in Astoria, Oregon, in 1910. Before the bout, O'Connell trash-talked his opponent, indicating that he expected no timidity from him in the ring. "The turbaned wonder from the trans-Pacific shores will not last," he taunted. Emerging victorious, "Dodan Singh: The Hindu" was declared the new welterweight champion of the Pacific coast. A rematch between the Sikh and the Irishman was canceled when judges announced they had evidence that O'Connell was not planning to fight fair.

If acceptance in the United States was at times a matter of endurance in the face of rules that seemed constantly to change to an immigrant's disadvantage, none had more right to call himself an American than another new resident of Dodan Singh's adopted hometown of Astoria. After the dissolution of Bellingham's Sikh community, this Oregon lumber town became briefly the hub of the South Asian community in the Northwest. Born like most Sikhs at the time in Punjab, Bhagat Singh Thind made his way to Astoria in 1913, settling for a time in the part of town known by all as "Hindu Alley." Like so many before him, he worked turning the region's timber into milled lumber, earning enough in this profession that he regularly sent money home. In letters to his father he sounds very much like the Philadelphia Jewish merchant Jonas Phillips writing to Amsterdam to arrange payments to his mother 140 years before. In each man's letters there is religious sentiment mixed with practical concern, as well as notes of an immigrant's impatience for news from his homeland. "My dear old and saintly father," Thind wrote:

> ...May The Wonderful Teacher bless you with good health for a long time! Please accept my greetings. Everything is fine here. I pray to the Immortal for your well-being day

and night...In the month of December, I had sent 280 rupees to you, but do not know whether you received the same or not. Please do favor me with a reply.

It was said that immigrants from India were slow to assimilate. Thind adamantly refused to change his appearance or otherwise accommodate the public in this regard. Later describing his first years in the country, he wrote, "America got everything except my whiskers and my turban, and I want to keep my head Indian." It would have been a simple thing, he added, to change his appearance — "to shave and cut everything off in five minutes" — and so better to go unnoticed among all the other newcomers. "But why should I do that?" he asked. "Some people will think I am an Italian, a Jew, a Rabbi, a Greek. Now, nobody thinks who I am. They know it. They know I am from India, a Sikh teacher and philosopher."

He was in fact trained in philosophy, and later would go on to become a well-known lecturer on the subject, but for his first few years he took on odd jobs, including washing dishes, before he began at the Astoria lumber mill, where his religious otherness came as a surprising boon. When asked if he was willing to work Sundays, he replied, "Thank God, I am not a Christian; I can work on Sundays, too." Willing to clean saw blades on the Sabbath in advance of the working week ahead, he was paid overtime.

When not working in the mills, he worked toward a degree at the University of California in Berkeley, and soon set about establishing a career as a writer and spiritual teacher. Like a page torn from a Horatio Alger story, his journey began with a mixture of immigrant naïveté and improbable optimism. He booked a hall for himself and determined that if he filled it every day for a series of sixty lectures he would be able to pay the rent. Taking to the street with a stack of printed handbills, he worked like a carnival barker to find an audience. As he recalled his strategy: "If people looked spiritual, I asked them: 'Are you interested in lectures on divine realization?' If they looked business-like, I asked: 'Are you interested in lectures on applied psychology?'" He tried in vain to get attention from the local press, but never lost his sense of humor about the kinds of stories most often published about men like him. "Sometimes I even felt tempted to go and punch the editor on the nose," he wrote, "and thus get a front page story—'Hindu lecturer knocks down editor.' I would get lots of publicity."

Thind's insistence that his Sikh identity and residence in the United States were not incompatible showed itself most when he was drafted into the U.S. military at the tail end of the First World War. "I made my mark during the World War and that in spite of my whiskers," he said. "I was a good soldier. When I joined the army I forgot I was a philosopher and my only idea was that I should shoot and shoot quick. You can't keep a good man down even in the United States Army."

Told by his commander that had he been an American citizen he would have been recommended for a commission, Thind applied for naturalization before his discharge and received a certificate of citizenship while still in uniform at Camp Lewis, just south of Tacoma, Washington. However, when his pending naturalization came to the attention of immigration officials in the state, it was revoked just four days later. Six months after that, now honorably discharged from the army after the war's end, he applied again in Oregon. This time denied by an immigration examiner, he brought the matter to the Federal District Court in Oregon and was again granted a certificate of citizenship. The Oregon Bureau of Naturalization appealed the ruling on the grounds that the Immigration Act of 1917 required that naturalized citizens be "free white persons" or aliens of "African descent." Thind's case eventually reached the U.S. Supreme Court.

The question that *United States v. Bhagat Singh Thind* put before the top justices of the land in 1923 was twofold: First, should "a high caste Hindu of full Indian blood" be considered "a white person"? And second, did the 1917 Immigration Act "disqualify from naturalization as citizens those Hindus...who had lawfully entered the United States" before the act had been passed?

In other words, as the court's decision framed the issue at hand, "If the applicant is a white person...he is entitled to naturalization; otherwise not." Rather than a protest against the obvious racism of the existing law, Thind's claim to citizenship rested on the assertion that people of India should be considered, in the terms of existing law, "white"—or, to use the term his lawyer favored, "Caucasian." Based on the theory that an early people then known as Aryans had been responsible for the settlement of both Europe and India, Thind's argument positioned Asian civilizations as distant kin of Christendom.

The justices were having none of it. As Justice Sutherland wrote in his decision against Thind, "The Aryan theory as a racial basis seems to be discredited by most, if not all, modern writers on the subject of ethnology." Moreover, Sutherland continued, it did not really matter whether the theory was valid or not. The real issue was not heritage but the perceived possibility of assimilation. "The children of English, French, German, Italian, Scandinavian, and other European parentage, quickly merge into the mass of our population and lose the distinctive hallmarks of their European origin," the decision states. "On the other hand, it cannot be doubted that the children born in this country of Hindu parents would retain indefinitely the clear evidence of their ancestry."

While primarily racially motivated, the court's ruling against Thind also demonstrated that reasons for objection to Asian immigration were not limited to skin color. They were also matters of custom and belief, the fear—announced shrilly in the Bellingham press and echoed more mutely in Washington, D.C.—that more worshippers of the "strange deities of India" might soon wash up on white Christian shores. Perhaps imagining the rebuke of history, Justice Sutherland backed away from the judgment's obvious implications, but even then he expressed terror at the prospect of a group of people living in the United States whose very nature prevented them from ever becoming true Americans. "It is very far from our thought to suggest the slightest question of racial superiority or inferiority," he wrote. "What we suggest is merely racial difference, and it is of such character and extent that the great body of our people instinctively recognize it and reject the thought of assimilation."

Though Thind ultimately was denied citizenship by the Supreme Court, several years later he quietly applied for and was granted naturalization as a beneficiary of the Nye-Lea Act of 1935, which allowed "certain resident alien World War veterans" to be naturalized "notwithstanding the racial limitations" of existing laws. Significantly, despite the countrywide application of the new act, Thind applied for citizenship this time in New York, perhaps supposing that on the East Coast neither the public nor immigration officials would harbor lingering concern about the coming "Hindu hordes" and the strange gods they might bring.

As an American citizen, Thind would live to see the passage of a number of revisions to the xenophobic immigration policies of the 1910s and 1920s. Thanks entirely to the Chinese American alliance during the Second World War, 1943 brought the repeal of the Chinese Exclusion Act. The Magnuson Act of 1943 permitted Chinese nationals already living in the United States to become naturalized citizens, and allowed a quota of 105 new Chinese immigrants per year. Three years later, the Luce-Celler Act ended the era of official animosity toward "Hindus," both those who truly were of the Hindu faith and those who merely had been painted with the same broad brush before the courts or the majority of Americans bothered to understand the difference. The new law was only a minor victory. Allowing immigrants from India at last into the quota system, it assigned a nation growing toward a billion people an annual limit of only one hundred immigrants per year, but it did allow Indians already in the country to become citizens at last.

The Immigration and Nationality Act of 1952, also called the McCarran-Walter Act, claimed to remove all racial barriers to naturalization even as it maintained, in the words of its sponsor, Senator Patrick McCarran of Nevada, "fixed limitations...to prevent an influx of more orientals than can be assimilated." However, it did signal the coming end of the era in which immigration laws were shaped by successive panics over various invading ethnic "hordes." This evolution did not come altogether for progressive reasons. It came simply because the fear of "Hindus" so prevalent early in the century had been replaced by a fear of Communists. The language in which this new fear was expressed sounds much the same as the headlines from Bellingham in 1907. On the floor of Congress, Senator McCarran railed against "indigestible blocs which have not become integrated into the American way of life" and warned specifically about the supposed threat posed by the ineffectual Communist Party USA: "Nurtured by the Soviet Union, it strives incessantly to make the United States a Soviet America." When McCarran went further and said opponents of his act "contributed more to promote this nation's downfall than any other group since we achieved our independence as a nation," it was clear that the yellow and the dusky perils had given way to the Red Scare.

The final corrective to the immigration policies that had hindered Bhagat Singh Thind's claims to citizenship in the 1920s came with the Immigration and Nationality Act of 1965. Also known as the Hart-Celler Act, it brought an end to a quota system that had been devised to limit ethnic and religious diversity in perpetuity. In place of the former racially defined limitations, the new law, which continues to govern immigration to the United States, established policies favoring immigrants who brought specific skills and talents. Signed into law two years before Thind died in 1967, the Hart-Celler Act could have been written specifically for him, an educated immigrant with an apparently inexhaustible entrepreneurial spirit.

One ironic consequence of the radical change in immigration policy adopted in the 1960s was that Sikhs, who early in the century accounted for the majority of immigrants from India, quickly became a minority within a minority. With the door now open to all varieties of immigrants from the subcontinent, the population of actual Hindus, not merely those mislabeled as such, skyrocketed, while that of Sikhs in America grew at a slower rate. According to the Pew Forum's 2012 statistics on religion in the United States, there are now approximately two hundred thousand Sikhs, while the number of Hindus is over two million. Following such a drastic demographic shift, history looks back and often misremembers those who bore the brunt of both prejudicial legislation and violent attacks.

Yet precisely because they are now perhaps among the most marginal in relation to the faith held by the majority of their fellow citizens, the story of Sikhs in America provides the best example of the ability of even tiny religious groups to make themselves known in a vast nation now filled with too many gods to count. Bhagat Singh Thind no doubt would have understood why the Sikhs of Bellingham refused to draw their kirpan blades when they were attacked. It was likely the same reason why he had refused to cut his hair or shave his beard. He knew that the faith and traditions he had brought with him would make his country more, not less, of what it claimed to be.

Recalling his time at Camp Lewis in 1918, Thind described his insistence that he would serve as his people always had in time of struggle. "When my commander told me that there was a law that no whiskers were allowed, I told him: 'My people are Sikhs; they are fighters, the finest soldiers in the world. Even the British have admitted it.' " Faced with a choice between his identity and his loyalty, he contended that he should not have to choose. "I don't mind fighting for you," he said. "But I must fight as a Sikh."

With war still raging in Europe and fighters of all kinds needed, the Sikh sergeant's commanding officer apparently took this in stride.

"Thind, I will let you have a chance," he said. "Go ahead, keep your whiskers; it makes no difference."

Japanese Americans behind a barbed-wire fence say good-bye to others departing for relocation camps around the country, 1942. Photograph by Julian F. Fowlkes. U.S. Signal Corps, Wartime Civil Control Administration. (Library of Congress)

CHAPTER 16

War Prayers

1941–1950

As the priest rose to speak to his grieving congregation, nothing about his manner suggested that he had recently been arrested as a spy.

Certainly, he appeared as worn-down as any of the women and men arranged on the benches before him, as cautious as anyone might become living under guard and far from home. Just thirty-four years old, the priest had lately taken on an air of aged wisdom in his thinning face. So slight that he was sometimes called *pakkai* — "spareribs," in his native tongue — he looked in danger of disappearing into his flowing robes. Nonetheless, given the circumstances, he seemed remarkably in control. Offering prayers at a time of need was, after all, what he had been training to do since adolescence. With no hint of the anxiety one might expect in the falsely accused, nor any outward sign of his own private grief, he was the image of a man made confident by his faith.

On this late August evening in southwestern Arizona, in the hot summer of 1944, the Reverend Bunyu Fujimura of the Buddhist Mission of North America had not yet been cleared of the charges of espionage that had started his journey through four federal detention centers more than two years before, but at the moment he had more immediate concerns. Tonight he was to deliver a sermon in memory of two Japanese Americans even more grievously affected by the war: Privates Yamamoto and Shiomichi, U.S. servicemen recently killed in action while fighting in Italy. Their families sat before Fujimura now — all of them, like him, doing their best to respond as the Buddha might to tragedy both personal and political. In this improvised liturgical setting of a tar paper and plywood mess hall of a desert internment camp, the priest's seemingly impossible task was to provide a comforting religious context in which to consider lives given in defense of a nation that had already taken everything else away.

A young man incarcerated because his beliefs were thought to make him a threat to the United States, and two even younger men now dead because they had fought for it—their intersection on this wartime evening represented the paradox of Buddhism in America during the Second World War. The supposedly foreign religion to which they stubbornly clung had made them easy targets for accusations that they might be willing to work against the interests of their adopted country, and yet their desire to maintain the traditions and language of that religion had contributed in a singular way to the American military effort on both fronts.

Fighting in Europe, the unit to which the two soldiers had belonged—the 442nd Combat Regiment—was not only entirely Japanese, it was predominantly Buddhist. By V-E Day, it would also be the most decorated infantry regiment of the war. In the Pacific theater, meanwhile, six thousand more American servicemen of Japanese descent worked as linguists and codebreakers. While many of their contributions would remain classified for more than twenty years—even to the point of having their names withheld from memorials to the war dead—it later became known that the Japanese Americans recruited into the Military Intelligence Service (MIS) had served in battles including Guadalcanal and Bataan, had gone deep behind enemy lines, and by the end of the war had handled between two and three million intelligence documents, most significantly Imperial Navy plans that led to the defeat of the Japanese fleet in the Philippines. It was largely thanks to them that General Douglas MacArthur could later say, "Never in military history did any army know so much about the enemy prior to an actual engagement."

A more personal view of the experiences of Buddhists during the war can be seen in the lives of these three men—the privates and the priest. Their stories came together in the Poston Relocation Center, which was home to nearly eighteen thousand imprisoned Japanese Americans from 1942 to 1945. Made up of seventy-one thousand dusty acres near Arizona's border with California, it was the largest of ten long-term internment camps spread out through the western United States. Poston consisted of three compounds of several dozen buildings each, each a mile square, all enclosed within a "man-proof" perimeter fence that made those inside feel, according to a poem circulated among the confined, "like rats in a wired cage."

Though machine guns pointed into the camp from one of the fence's guard towers, a schoolhouse within betrayed the fact that it was not enemy combatants held here but families and children. That the schoolhouse was made of the adobe favored by the natives of the region might have reminded those who saw it that this was not the first the surrounding desert had seen of forced relocation. The part of the vast Colorado River Valley in which the camp stood was now an Indian reservation; the chaparral to the northeast had once hosted Mormons chased across the country to one of the harshest landscapes America had to offer.

The newest inhabitants of the valley had also come on orders of the U.S. government. On February 19, 1942, President Roosevelt had signed Executive Order 9066, authorizing the evacuation of all of those of Japanese descent from the West Coast to war relocation centers — often called "concentration camps" before that term came to have other connotations.

Like the anti-Sikh, anti-Hindu, and anti-Chinese sentiments at large through much of the preceding hundred years, the anti-Japanese feelings that led to the relocation of Japanese-born immigrants (known as Issei) and their American-born children (Nisei) were justified on racial rather than religious grounds. Those forced to leave behind homes, farms, and businesses in states bordering the Pacific were not of a single faith. There were Buddhists among them, and many maintained Shinto rituals that spiritually connected the Issei to their homeland, but there were also Christians of various denominations, as well as those with no particular affiliation. Despite this seeming diversity, however, and again like the "yellow peril" and the "dusky peril" before it, the treatment of Japanese Americans during the war also had a religious dimension.

When the FBI first set about compiling its list of suspect individuals after the attack on Pearl Harbor and the formal entry of the United States into World War II, they had naturally included members of various American Nazi parties and groups with political ties to Japan. Yet they also paid particular attention to Buddhist priests. The Custodial Detention List initiated by FBI director J. Edgar Hoover used a classification system designating the supposed risk of individuals and groups on an A-B-C scale, with an "A" ranking assigned to those deserving greatest scrutiny. While immigrants from other Axis powers were also arrested and brought in for questioning, the number of each group in custody as of December 9, 1941 — 497 Germans, 83 Italians, and 1,221 Japanese — is a reflection of those believed to have posed the greatest immediate threat to national security.

Within Hoover's A-B-C system, ordained Buddhist ministers like Reverend Fujimura were designated "A-1," those whose apprehension was considered a matter of urgent concern. Even before Executive Order 9066, leaders of various Buddhist organizations were rounded up as "dangerous enemy aliens." The motives for government policy toward Japanese priests, as well as the suspicions of the public, were captured in Alan Hynd's best-selling *Betrayal from the East* (later turned into a film of the same name), a jingoistic potboiler, ambiguously sold as nonfiction but often described as a novel in the press, that claimed to recount "the inside story" of a network of 1,300 spies active in America since well before the attack on Pearl Harbor. "Buddhist and Shinto missions, officiated by Japanese priests, dotted the whole of southern California," Hynd wrote. "If these supposedly religious sanctuaries were going to be integrated into the Japanese spy machine on the Pacific Coast, the work of the O.N.I. [Office of Naval Intelligence], the F.B.I. and other investigative bodies was going to be just that much more difficult."

Caught in the snare of such suspicions, the priests became the first of a relocation effort that would soon detain more than 110,000. Many within this larger group, having heard of the sudden arrests and harsh interrogations endured by Buddhist community leaders, sought refuge in Christianity, hoping — in vain, it turned out — that church membership might shield them from such treatment. Others had made similar calculations upon their arrival in the United States. Fewer than 10 percent of the Issei had been Christians when they left Japan, but by the time of the war, they were converted to the faith they believed moved them well along the path to assimilation. Regardless of their particular religious affiliation, then, the Nisei born in America were for the most part just one generation removed from the traditional beliefs and practices of Japan. The most famous member of the 442nd Combat Regiment, for example, the late senator Daniel Inouye, recalled that his father had been a Buddhist, as had his grandparents on both sides. Only when his mother's parents died and she was adopted into the home of American Christians did the predominant faith of her new nation determine the faith of subsequent generations of her family.

Those who did not go this route but maintained their traditional beliefs despite social pressures were called "Buddhaheads," an epithet often applied to the Japanese Americans of Hawaii. Even before the war, Japanese Buddhists were thought to be less "Americanized" than their countrymen who had converted to Christianity, and in some ways this was true. Within the Japanese community, Buddhists were more likely than Christians to maintain their native language, as well as their facility with customs and rituals performed in that language. They were also more likely than Japanese Christians to read publications concerned with Japanese political affairs. Subscription rolls of such publications provided the FBI with a natural starting point for building its "A" list of suspects. Finally and obviously, they were more likely than Christians to attend Buddhist temples, which were not merely places of religious observance but served as social hubs, education centers, and function halls. In short, in their design and adornment, temples seemed to help erase the distance the immigrants had traveled from their homeland.

Because of the connections and the traditional knowledge Buddhist temples and similar organizations helped maintain, to be a Japanese Buddhist in America was to be considered at once a greater risk to the nation and a potentially valuable asset to the war effort. Buddhist priests, the FBI presumed, could thus serve as a bellwether for the loyalty of the entire Japanese American population.

While many of the priests seized in the early days of 1942 were kept apart from other internees for the duration of the war, some were eventually allowed to join their families and communities in order to resume their former roles presiding over rituals of celebration and loss, all now held in temples improvised behind barbed wire.

* * *

Behind the fence at Poston, Reverend Fujimura began his memorial service for the two fighting men of the 442nd with a poem recited from memory:

> *The cherry blossoms on Mount Yoshino—*
> *All right if they fall,*
> *All right if they remain.*
> *How like a warrior's life.*

"That Privates Yamamoto and Shiomichi died for their country in a hail of bullets while in the prime of their life is something their families can take pride in," he said. "Theirs is truly the Bodhisattva Way in the Buddhist teaching."

In the "Pure Land" tradition of Fujimura's Jodo-Shinshu school of Buddhism, to be a Bodhisattva is the most revered of paths one can pursue. Those who attain this level of spiritual achievement are thought to have had the chance to become enlightened Buddhas themselves, and thus to be released from the wheel of life and death that governs all existence. But they have foregone personal salvation in order that all others may first be saved. Bestowing such a title upon these young men—boys, really—was no small matter. Fujimura no doubt intended it as a great honor and solace to their families.

Not content to leave his reflection on the young men's lives at the level of the palliative, however, the priest then questioned his own straightforward religious interpretation of the meaning of the soldiers' deaths. "But the above feeling is only the joy of reason, the satisfaction of logic," he said. "In the world of human beings... we must know that the opposite sentiment, that of sadness, also exists."

Fujimura had no firsthand knowledge of the "warrior's life" he had invoked through his opening poem, but sadness was something he understood. Though he had never been in battle himself, the last few years had often felt like one. It had been early in the morning almost three years before, in a dark hour even before the milkman had arrived, that he had heard a knock on the door of his bedroom at the Nishi Hongwanji Buddhist temple of Salinas, California. While his wife lay sleeping, he had opened the door and found two white American men identifying themselves in well-practiced Japanese.

"We are from the FBI," one of the agents said.

Fujimura was not entirely surprised. For weeks, the priest had been hearing rumors that leaders of other Buddhist communities had been questioned and arrested. Some had been taken quietly from their families under cover of darkness—or they were, as Fujimura himself soon was, caught in the flash of newspaper photographers eager for images of "enemy aliens" in handcuffs on U.S. soil. The next day's edition of the local *Index Journal* displayed his image beneath a damning front-page headline: "Wholesale Jap Raids Staged by Agents in Salinas." Shown the picture at the police station, he was dismayed to discover that he had reflexively smiled into the photographer's lens.

Along with thirty members of his congregation, he spent several nights in the Salinas jail under constant interrogation.

"Are you a spy?" the Japanese-speaking agent asked him.

"No," he replied.

"Did you come to the United States because of orders from the Emperor of Japan?"

"No."

"Have you ever met the Japanese Emperor?"

"No."

"Are you a Japanese Naval officer?"

"How can a skinny person like myself be a Japanese Naval officer?"

Then came the transport train. As Fujimura would later write, he and several other Buddhist priests, along with dozens of people who called him *sensei*, teacher, were shipped "like livestock." They were not told where they were going or when they would arrive. The sight of children crying and calling to fathers now locked behind barred windows was the last he saw of the outside world for days. Heavy curtains had been installed in the railroad cars, keeping the passengers in semi-darkness.

When the train finally ground to a halt some seventy-two hours later, the doors opened to reveal a frozen white landscape, empty but for a number of green army vehicles. In California it had been a pleasant sixty degrees; wherever they were now, the temperature was well below freezing. Like fenceposts rising from the snow, soldiers in fur-lined hats stood at ten-foot intervals around the trucks, rifles at the ready.

As they soon discovered, the priests' ultimate destination was

Fort Lincoln, a decommissioned army base five miles south of Bismarck, North Dakota. Confined to brick barracks through the winter, they did what they could to keep warm and to carry on something like normal lives. On Buddha's birthday in April, with the temperature still near freezing though it was time for their traditional springtime festival, Fujimura and the rest of the Bismarck Buddhists crafted flowers from tissue paper, and carved an image of the Buddha out of a large carrot stick.

After five months at Fort Lincoln, just long enough for them to see spring finally arrive in the form of a few dandelions poking through the snow, Fujimura was put back on a train, shipped south and east for internments of varying lengths at Camp McCoy in Wisconsin and Camp Livingston in Louisiana, and then west to Camp Santa Fe in New Mexico, and finally to Poston, where his wife had been sent not long after his arrest.

He had not seen her in more than two years; they had been kept apart for nearly half their marriage. Making up for lost time, and uncertain when they might win their freedom, the Fujimuras set about starting a family.

Eight and half months after their reunion, his wife gave birth to a baby boy. It was a cause for great excitement not only for father and mother, but for a camp full of people eager for any portent of new beginnings. Because of conditions at Poston, however, the usual physician was not available to attend the delivery. The only medical professionals present had been a veterinarian and an inexperienced nurse. On the infant's death certificate, written just an hour and twenty minutes after he was born, an animal doctor wrote "asphyxiation" as the cause of death.

Everything about Fujimura's experience of internment thus far had seemed designed to reinforce the truth of a basic Buddhist idea: impermanence. The understanding of the contingent, dependent nature of all things and the consequent inevitability of their loss was regarded as the key to attaining enlightenment. "This impermanent world," the founder of his Jodo-Shinshu Buddhist tradition had written, "is like a burning house." Awareness of impermanence was not an excuse for complacency or despair, however, but a call to action. As the same sage had said: The compassion of the Buddha, which benefits all creatures, "must be repaid, though I be crushed."

And now came the memorial for the young men killed in the

war — an opportunity to meditate on the subject of impermanence in its most searing form.

As he stood before the dead men's families, the priest recited verses from a second poem, this one as true of their experience as of his own:

Though I know
How transient this world is
Still, I cannot give him up.

Gesturing to the parents, he added, "For over twenty years, their sons were always at the forefront of their minds. After learning to crawl, then to stand, and finally learning to walk, the sons were in a position to repay their parents. But the beloved child they finally raised to adulthood has now been transformed into a single telegram informing the parents of his death." Along with these telegrams, he explained, the Yamamoto and Shiomichi families had also received their sons' last letters home.

The final words Pfc. John T. Yamamoto had sent to Poston had been as matter-of-fact as he had always been. "I guess I might as well tell you that we're in action now," he wrote. Not a man for embroidery, he was an American archetype of strong and silent farmboy, raised picking his father's strawberries in the shadow of oil derricks on the southern California coast. The "T" in his name was for Tsuyoshi, meaning "strength." The "John" was added because his parents had known no American names, and the doctor who delivered him thought John "was as good as any."

Plainspokenness was a trait he shared with his sister, Hisaye, who would become a celebrated journalist and short story writer, a crafter of deceptively simple tales of immigrants and their children — none more powerful than those inspired by her time at Poston, "that unlikely place of wind, sand, and heat," she called it, and her younger brother's too brief life. In a short essay she wrote at the war's end, "After Johnny Died," Hisaye Yamamoto described his nineteen years in a heartbreaking accumulation of detail: the joy he found in the color of his first bicycle (blue), his touching fondness for the baby brother "who had died soon after he learned to walk and sing and dance a little," the automobile accident that had left a small scar giving him a permanently crooked grin.

He was in junior high, his sister noted, when their mother died; he was a safety monitor in his school at the time, and even in those days of mourning he came home wearing a blue satin ribbon reading "hall guard" across his chest. In high school, he went out for football but "fumed when talking about the coach because he had spent the season on the bench." He felt better later when he switched to basketball and earned a letterman's sweater — "green with two white stripes on the left sleeve" — paid for with money picking tomatoes for other farming families in need of an extra hand.

Though he was known primarily as a Japanese Nisei by both his country and his community, Johnny's life had been first of all thoroughly American — cut short, as so many others were, by an exploding 88-millimeter shell. It had also been a thoroughly Buddhist life. The Yamamotos had moved often as farmers who owned no land, but the family had attended temples often enough to know well the chanting and bowing of the priests, the sweet smell of the incense, and the huge feasts that followed weddings and funerals. His faith was perhaps not as intensely lived as that of Reverend Fujimura, but he took pride in not having taken the Christian path toward assimilation. "What would I know about God?" he wrote to his sister. "I've never even been to church." So, too, he had come to know personally the Buddhist truth of impermanence through the war, and even to acknowledge that not all transformations were improvements. "I've changed," he wrote from the front. "Don't expect me to be the same guy I was."

The other Poston soldier killed in action that summer also showed himself to be something of an American archetype: a striver and a true believer in the possibility of assimilating into the melting pot while maintaining a particular cultural and religious identity. Unlike Johnny Yamamoto, Joe Shiomichi had already finished school by the time of his relocation to Poston. A graduate of the University of California at Berkeley, he became a chemistry teacher at the camp school, and from the beginning knew that the lessons he wanted to convey to his classes were not limited to science. Faced with students burning with resentment at what the only country they had ever known had done to them, he would say, "All this is a temporary aberration. We don't belong in a camp. But don't be bitter. Don't let this get you down. America is the best country in the world. There will be flukes and aberrations along the way. But get past it. This is temporary."

His life, too, had been fully American and fully Buddhist. A Boy Scout in elementary school, a track star in high school, Shiomichi was a natural for the service when it was announced Nisei would be allowed to volunteer. "I've become more and more convinced that we must take a firm stand now in asserting our beliefs in regards to being Americans," he wrote. "We may have just causes for some of our grievances but I certainly don't feel that those grievances should be kept so long and harbored with us to the point of distorting our views for the future." Particularly dismayed by pro-Axis sentiments expressed by his more disgruntled peers, he saw enlisting as having benefits that would long outlast the fighting on either front. "By volunteering for the Army," he said, "I feel that the Niseis are building up something concrete with which to fight discrimination after the war is over."

During the memorial, Reverend Fujimura read aloud an expression of faith found in a letter written home. "Okaa-san, mother, this will probably be the last letter I write to you in my poor Japanese. I am finally being sent to the front lines. You have taken good care of me for a long time, and I would like to thank you from the bottom of my heart. Even if, unfortunately, I fall in battle, I will go to the Buddha's land that I heard about from sensei from the time I was a child, so there is nothing for you to worry about...."

This same spiritual optimism had led Joe Shiomichi, as it had led Reverend Fujimura, to start a family while still confined to Poston. Before enlisting with the 442nd, he had married a fellow Berkeley student; they were expecting their first child by the time he shipped out. Allowed to accompany her new husband out of the camp for the start of the journey that would take him first to Basic Training at Camp Shelby, Mississippi, and then to war, his pregnant wife waved from the platform as his train left the station.

"A child's death has been said to be the death of the parents," the priest said. "And that is why tears flow. Why I sorrow. When Saigo Takemori, the great warrior and statesman, learned that his younger brother had died in battle, he is said to have clung to the dead body, and wailed long and hard." Even the Buddha, he added, "raised his voice and cried in sorrow at the sight of the dead."

"Trying to discard sorrow is a lie," the Reverend Fujimura said. "Telling someone not to cry is unreasonable. To sorrow when we should sorrow is what makes us human. To cry when we should cry is what the parents of a child should do. The tears that flow at the most miserable periods of life, the tears unknown to others that soak our pillow, that is where the light of the Buddha's Great Compassion is always found."

Speaking to his own hopes and those of the parents who had lost sons, the siblings who had lost brothers, and the child born a month after her father died, he added, "When we accept the Buddha's teaching, those who pass on first, and those who are left behind become one. We enter the world where we can meet again, the Pure Land. That is how we are 'saved.' "

The Pure Land of which he spoke is a key concept of Buddhist thought. As the realm where the Buddha awaits all those who near enlightenment, it is often described as a world of overwhelming beauty, opulence, and happiness. The sutras describe it as a place where "heavenly music is played continually. The ground is made of gold. Six times during the day and night mandarava flowers rain down from the sky." The Pure Land has another meaning: the higher state of consciousness achieved through meditative practices that has the potential, Buddhists believe, to bring enlightenment to individuals as well as nations.

"This is what I believe," the priest concluded. "I believe the great land has been soaked bright red with Yamamoto and Shiomichi's blood and the heartrending tears of their bereaved family." This blood and these tears, he suggested, were symbols of the Japanese American experience during the war, a "sacred sacrifice that will in the near future sound the bell of the dawn of peace in the entire world."

By the time the war ended, exactly a year later, in August 1945, there could be little doubt that the experiences of Japanese Americans had indeed helped sound the bell of peace. Some 15,000 men served in the 442nd, earning 9,486 Purple Hearts, 21 Medals of Honor, and eight Presidential Unit Citations—a full fifth of all such citations awarded during the war. They are credited with being instrumental in breaking the last defenses of the Axis Powers known as the Gothic Line, the breach of which helped end the war in Italy, making ultimate Nazi surrender inevitable. Elsewhere in Europe, Nisei soldiers detached from the 442nd as the 522nd Field

Artillery Battalion were sent to support the Seventh Army in Germany, where men with families still confined to places like Poston participated in the liberation of Dachau. In the Pacific, MacArthur's chief of intelligence, Major General Charles Willoughby, described the contributions of the Nisei servicemen as having "shortened the Pacific war by two years and saved possibly a million American lives."

More than half of the soldiers of the 442nd and the Military Intelligence Service (MIS), which had trained Nisei linguists and codebreakers, were Buddhists. They were using the knowledge that their families had maintained through temple activities to benefit the national interest. It was on the home front, however, that they had their most significant impact on American culture, through the unlikely medium of the U.S. military itself.

When Hisaye Yamamoto visited her brother's grave in Italy many years after his death, she found that though their family had been set apart for particular scrutiny back home, in the U.S. military cemetery outside Florence, Johnny had been treated like any other G.I. She was dismayed, however, to see "only crosses and stars" over the American graves. There were "no Buddhist wheels," she wrote, "which would have been more appropriate."

At the time of his burial, the *dharmachakra*, the eight-spoked wheel of life and death signifying the impermanence and interdependence of all things, had not been sanctioned by the U.S. military as a symbol appropriate for the grave markers of those killed in action. Subscribing to the view of acceptable religious diversity common in the middle of the twentieth century, the army's official recognition was reserved for those who fit into the triad soon to be defined by the sociologist Will Herberg as "Protestant-Catholic-Jew." Herberg saw American life divided along Judeo-Christian lines and no further, and this division found expression not only on the graves of the dead but on the dog tags of the living. On the lower right corner of the small metallic rectangle used to identify a soldier by name, rank, serial number, and blood type, Catholic soldiers had a "C", Protestants a "P," and Jews had an "H," for Hebrew. All the rest were "O," for "Other." Acknowledgment of diversity beyond that, it was argued at the time, would only cause confusion.

In the wake of Japanese American accomplishments during the war, Buddhist groups petitioned for the military throughout the late 1940s to add a "B" to their dog tags. Such requests were repeatedly denied, but a turning point in their quest for formal acknowledgement of their right to express religious affiliation eventually came with a dispute concerning the use of crosses over the graves of the war dead.

The National Memorial Cemetery of the Pacific, located in a volcanic depression known as the Punchbowl Crater, overlooking Honolulu, was designated as the final resting place for the service members killed in the Pacific theater in 1948. When burials began, each grave was marked with a white wooden cross. Within two years these crosses numbered fifteen thousand.

The crosses were intended to be temporary; they were to be replaced with flat marble stones as the cemetery was developed into what one congressional patron of the effort called "one of the great patriotic shrines in the nation." However, when the crosses came down in 1950, there was outrage. Members of Congress led by Joseph Rider Farrington, the nonvoting representative from the Territory of Hawaii, and Edith Nourse Rogers of Massachusetts, sought funds to erect permanent crosses. The Subcommittee on Public Lands hearings devoted to debating these funds became a dramatic portrayal of differing notions of the meaning of religious liberty in America.

After Representative Farrington lamented that the loss of the crosses had made the cemetery look like a "vacant lot," Fred Crawford of Michigan objected that the replacement of the temporary markers with stones set into the earth was part of a larger design including a chapel and an amphitheater, the completion of which would be threatened by undoing work that had already been done. "It takes a lot of money to run this government," he said, "and I am not in favor of taking $3,000 or $750,000 to put these crosses back, and thus further deprive funds that we might use to go ahead and complete this plan with."

Speaking in defense of the bill she had introduced the previous October (H.J. 338, for "the installation of crosses to replace the white wooden crosses which until recently marked the graves at the National Memorial Cemetery"), Congresswoman Rogers delivered something of a sermon on the singular significance of Christian symbolism to the men whose remains now lay in the Punchbowl. While she allowed that those who followed other creeds might prefer different symbols, she left little doubt that the cross alone deserved pride of place in this "great patriotic shrine."

"The resolution which we have under consideration here at this moment has a fundamental significance to our American way of life," she said. "Ours is a Christian nation, inspired in its establishment by strong, courageous, determined men and women in their decision to worship their God in their own way. Freedom of religion constitutes and assembles the strength of America. The graves which are the subject of our hearing this morning hold for all time the fighting hearts of these Americans who, among other things, gave their lives to preserve the precious right of freedom of religious worship.

"I believe every one of our soldiers, sailors, marines, and airmen, would feel stronger in their hearts if they knew that when they fell, their sacrifice would have the honor of the cross....I know that the men who live, after the shock of battle has cleared away, are pleased to know and are satisfied in the knowledge that their comrades who fell in the fury of the struggle have the distinction and honor and the glory of the cross standing at the head of their own graves....The cross stands for the Christian way of life. It stands for all that is right. It stands for belief in the right, and stands for the courage to sacrifice for the right. It stands for life everlasting. I believe this powerful symbol of our Savior is a fighting symbol for those who gave all for what they believed to be right.

"Yes, gentlemen," the congresswoman said to the members of the committee, "I believe that Our Savior, Jesus Christ, is pleased to have the symbol of the cross on the graves of those who believed in him, and sacrificed their lives for the right. Who are we as government officials to dispute this fact? Who are we to contest the power and the meaning of the cross? Every fighting man, as he goes into battle, has a prayer on his lips. Do we as government officials have the right to take from him the last visible symbol of the meaning of Christ, his Savior, and his salvation?"

Apparently awed by this pious performance, it took Representative Lloyd Bentsen, the committee chair and future senator and vice-presidential candidate, several minutes to return the hearing to the subject at hand, which was the cost—nearly three quarters of a million dollars—rather than the symbolism of replacing crosses that had just been removed. "Mrs. Rogers, I would like to ask," he ventured, "do you dispute the evidence or the opinion that has been given to us in the report, that if you go to a permanent cross, that it would cost $740,000?"

"Perfectly frankly," Rogers said, "I am rather shocked at the government's raising the matter of cost in this matter."

"I know we don't like to put a dollar value on these symbols," Bentsen said, "but it seems to me...that some of these funds can be expended toward taking care of veterans who are still alive, and that sort of thing, and saving the economy of our country, if it would be possible, perhaps, to put up one symbolic cross in the center of the cemetery and one symbolic Star of David, and whatever other religious faiths are represented, in order to make it easier to maintain the cemetery and to limit the cost to some extent."

After shrugging off a few more questions concerning budgetary matters, and about the memorial practices at various American military cemeteries around the world, Rogers deployed an argument that she may have suspected would be her most persuasive in the political climate of the day. She had received a great many letters, she explained, from constituents who "state they feel that the removal of the crosses is a move toward Communism."

At this point the most fiscally cautious member of the subcommittee, Representative Crawford of Michigan, spoke up: "Let me ask you this question: Which do you think is the greatest contribution to the progress of the Communists: the destruction of our economic powers here in the United States, or the preservation of a sound fiscal policy?"

Rogers insisted that theology, not the economy was what separated Americans from their Russian rivals. "I think the most important thing for us here in the U.S. is to state our belief in God and religion," she said. Saving money was not the point, in other words; the salvation of the nation was.

At the height of the Red Scare, the push to maintain the Christian atmosphere of a "great patriotic shrine" grew out of the same politicized religiosity that led to efforts to insert the words "under God" into the Pledge of Allegiance that began a year later. Explaining the motivation of that later bill, its original sponsor, Representative Louis Rabaut of Michigan, echoed Rogers's sentiments about how public displays of American religiosity could be used as weapons of the Cold War: "You may argue from dawn to dusk about differing political, economic, and social systems, but the fundamental issue which is the unbridgeable gap between America and Communist Russia is a belief in Almighty God. From the root of atheism stems the evil weed of communism and its branches of materialism and political dictatorship. Unless we are willing to affirm our belief in the existence of God and His creator-creature relation to man, we drop man himself to the significance of a grain of sand and open the floodgates to tyranny and oppression." This basic understanding was elaborated in a report submitted to the Judiciary Committee in May 1954:

"The inclusion of God in our pledge therefore would further acknowledge the dependence of our people and our Government upon the moral directions of the Creator. At the same time it would serve to deny the atheistic and materialistic concepts of communism with its attendant subservience of the individual.... From the time of our earliest history our peoples and our institutions have reflected the traditional concept that our Nation was founded on a fundamental belief in God."

While her colleague from Michigan soon would make a battleground of the Pledge, Rogers believed that the Cold War should be fought even with the memories of those lost to the hot war of recent memory. Rogers, it should be noted, was a vocal supporter of the House Un-American Activities Committee, which made the Communist hunter Senator Joseph McCarthy a fan of her legislative efforts. "We probably owe it to her and the grace of God," McCarthy once said of Rogers, "that American boys are not being killed today by American-trained Reds."

Yet even as members of Congress were pushing for various official proclamations of religious uniformity—demonstrations that the "one nation" was indeed under one God—the U.S. military, newly aware of the number of war dead who did not fit neatly into the Protestant-Catholic-Jew understanding of American religious life, was simultaneously reinforcing the right of service members to have their remains buried under the signs not of one god but many.

In the hearing room, just as the tide seemed to turn in favor of replacing the crosses in the Punchbowl, Colonel James B. Clearwater, chief of the Memorial Division of the army's Office of the Quartermaster General, was called to testify on behalf of the Department of Defense. Clearwater explained that his efforts as administrator of the nation's military gravesites and other memorials were informed by a directive issued by the Secretary of Defense in 1947 that there would thereafter be no discrimination in national cemeteries based on race, rank, creed, or religion. Though this directive had been issued explicitly to end the shameful practice of segregation of the remains of white from black service members, at the Honolulu site it was proving to have unexpected implications.

"Many of the Hawaiian war dead were of the Buddhist faith," Colonel Clearwater explained to the committee. As a consequence, for the first time military funerals were held not only with Protestant ministers, Catholic clergy, and rabbis but with Buddhist priests — the very class of people who had been classified as A-1 suspects during the war.

The one Japanese American called to testify, Mike Masaoka, the National Secretary of the Japanese American Citizens League, corroborated Clearwater's sense of the number and influence of Buddhist troops. "I think it should be pointed out for the record that aside from the Christian and Jewish faith, probably more persons of Buddhist faith have served in and are serving in the armed forces of the United States than any other group," Masaoka said in his testimony. "I think today, when the world is in such a state of flux, that attention to the religious recognition of a great faith of Asia is very important in terms of our national policy."

If the crosses were to be put back in place, Clearwater insisted, they should be erected in the company of Stars of David and Buddhist Wheels of Righteousness. As a compromise to the call to replace specifically Christian markers with a stone of the same rectangular shape for all, the Department of Defense would inscribe the appropriate symbol on the face of the gravestones already in place. Crosses would return to the Punchbowl, but they would not be set above the messages of other religions.

In response to the colonel's testimony, Congressman Arthur Miller of Nebraska made it clear that he wanted no sign of religious difference in the national cemetery. Crosses, he argued, would be fine for all. "I have always felt it was unfortunate that someone decided to remove the crosses," he said, "because a cross in a military cemetery is such an essential part of that cemetery, you might as well have a garden without flowers or a church without Bibles or an altar as to have a cemetery without crosses."

Then Miller challenged Clearwater directly: "You said no discrimination, but you do propose to mark the cemeteries in Hawaii as to whether they are Christian, Jew or Buddhist. Why don't you put white or black or yellow? It's the same thing, why put on Christian, Jew or Buddhist, if you are not going to have discrimination?"

"That is according to the wishes of the family which they indicate on the application for the headstone," Clearwater said. "Or, in those cases where there is no next of kin, according to the religion indicated on the man's service record."

Becoming increasingly combative, Miller chided, "You don't put on his color. Why put on his religion?"

Clearwater was unfazed. "One of the freedoms of this country is the freedom of religion, sir," he said. "One of the things that caused the directive to be issued in 1947 was the question of color."

Congressman Crawford, who was generally opposed to replacing the crosses on fiscal grounds, jumped in with concern that if you started identifying Buddhists as well as Christians and Jews, where would it end?

"To carry that further," he said, "chances are within the very near future we are going to have Christians, Jews, Buddhists, Mohammodists, Confucianists, Taoists and Hindus mixed into this very picture. This is before you, and you can't escape it…and you are not going to restrict this country to three religions."

"That is correct, sir," Clearwater said. "It just happens, Congressman Crawford, that, so far, outside of the Christian faith, the Buddhist religion is the only one that has brought up the question."

"But certainly there will be further additions."

"We anticipate that," the colonel said.

In the end, the white crosses were not replaced at the Punchbowl. Instead, the existing graves and those to come each received an inset stone featuring a medallion etched with the appropriate religious symbol. With the new grave markers at the National Memorial Cemetery of the Pacific, the "Buddhist wheel," as Hisaye Yamamoto had called it when she wished such a symbol had been available for her brother, became the third religious icon sanctioned by the Department of Defense.

Small matter though this may seem, its implications were less so. The symbols of other religious traditions followed, and now number close to fifty. As Private Shiomichi had predicted, Nisei veterans continued to fight discrimination after the war was over, and not just for themselves. The deaths of Buddhist soldiers led the way for members of all faiths to join the symbols of their belief to the memory of their service. In all these cases, the enduring significance was not merely the inscription of a further symbol of faith in stone. It was also the entwining of forms of belief formerly supposed to be distinct: the American and the spiritually marginal. On an island that would become part of the fiftieth state, for the first time in U.S. history, military funerals were held not only with Protestant ministers, Catholic clergy, and Jewish rabbis but with Buddhist priests.

Even Reverend Fujimura soon found himself putting his skills to work in the military's service. When the Poston Relocation Center shut down for good a month after the war's end, its former inhabitants were, for the most part, allowed to return to the lives they had left behind three years before. Fujimura, however, was not permitted to return to California immediately upon his release. With the taint of his espionage charge still lingering, and still considered an "enemy alien," he was told he would remain on probation for a year, during which time he would be legally prohibited from living on the Pacific coast. Making the best of an impossible situation, he moved to Chicago, where he resumed his ministry. He could come and go as he pleased from his home but had to receive prior approval from the FBI in order to leave the city. The terms of his probation also required him to check in once a week with a government-appointed supervisor, as if he had committed a crime other than being a largely Buddhist priest during a war with a Buddhist nation.

When finally Fujimura was permitted to return to Salinas, four years after he had been transported out of town on a darkened train, he found that his temple had not been able to fully recover from the forced relocation of all its members. Only twenty-six of the three hundred families who once attended the temple had returned, and those who did complained of a chilly reception from the locals. Many of his former congregants, however, had settled in nearby Monterey, where a sardine packing factory helped reintegrate the recently returned evacuees by hiring Japanese American workers immediately after the war. Despite the flagging numbers in Salinas, Fujimura did not consider abandoning his temple. Instead, he opened another.

At his new temple in Monterey, he was soon providing services for the families who had come to work in the sardine factory and for young men in uniform. The Military Intelligence Service had moved its language school from a bare-bones aircraft hangar at the army's Crissy Field in San Francisco to Camp Savage in Minnesota during the war, and moved it now to the Presidio, which at the time was a satellite of nearby Fort Ord. There were seven different chapels for various religions to use on the base, but not one for Buddhists, and so once a week, a bus full of soldiers would appear in their dress uniforms to hear Reverend Fujimura speak on the dharma, the teachings of the Buddha. At first most of these soldiers were of Japanese descent, either Nisei who had been too young to serve during the war or the next generation — the Sansei — for whom the Japanese homeland was but a grandparent's memory. As the weeks passed, however, when Fujimura looked out over his military congregation, he saw that they were no longer all Japanese. There were soldiers with English and Norwegian names, as well as African Americans and Filipinos. Some were there, he soon learned, to practice the language they were learning in order to serve in the U.S. occupation force in Japan. Others had genuine interest in learning about Buddhism. Many came for the food. Sushi, udon noodles, and other traditional fare were regularly offered after the service.

When news began to spread of how popular Fujimura's sermons had become with the soldiers of the Presidio and Fort Ord, the head chaplain of the base grew concerned that non-Buddhist soldiers were sneaking away from other commitments to hear talk of the dharma.

"You seem to have altogether too many soldiers here for your Buddhist service," he said to Reverend Fujimura. "There must be some Christians among them. Could you ask the non-Buddhists not to attend?"

Given that he had spent many of the preceding years under armed guard, taking orders from soldiers, it was perhaps with both trepidation and delight that Reverend Fujimura told the chaplain that he would like to help but that his temple was open to all.

"Our custom is to welcome everyone who comes," he said. "How can I tell anyone not to attend?"

Poster for the Human Be-In, designed
by Michael Bowen, disciple of the guru
John Starr Cooke.

CHAPTER 17

The Immortality Racket

1967–1976

Late in the evening of January 14, 1967, a few of the people responsible for turning the seventh decade of the century into the cultural moment known as "The Sixties" were lounging in a small back room of the artist Michael Bowen's San Francisco painting studio. Though grandly called the "meditation room," it was not much bigger than a walk-in closet, and maintained its contemplative aura through an ambient haze of incense, framed pictures of gods and gurus staring down from the walls, and dark tapestries hung over every surface, including the room's lone window. Allen Ginsberg, the Beatnik writer who had lately emerged as the paterfamilias of the hippie movement (in the estimation of the *New Yorker* later that year), sat cross-legged on one of the thin mattresses that cushioned the floor, passing a bottle of wine with another Beat turned hippie, the Zen poet Gary Snyder. Timothy Leary, the former professor remade as the nation's high priest of LSD, was also there, as was the activist Jerry Rubin, who would soon join with Abbie Hoffman to start the rabble-rousing Youth International Party, better known as the Yippies. Had an earthquake toppled 1371 Haight Street that night, many of the pivotal movements and events of the following years — Flower Power, the March on the Pentagon, the demonstrations at the Democratic National Convention, the trial of the Chicago Seven that followed — might never have occurred.

Though full of luminaries, this party was a low-key affair, just a gathering of twenty or so who had come together to celebrate the success of that day's Human Be-In, the first large-scale summit of various strains of the counterculture, which, until then, had been largely divided between political and nonpolitical communities and forms of dissent. National press coverage helped lure more than one hundred thousand young adults to the Haight-Ashbury neighborhood of San Francisco throughout the following months, culminating in 1967's Summer of Love, which spread across the nation and set the stage for larger gatherings like the Woodstock festival two years later.

While usually eclipsed by that later event in popular accounts of the era, the Human Be-In was at the time seen as the start of it all. The morning after the event, the *San Francisco Chronicle* ran the headline "Hippies Run Wild," but that was not even the half of it. More than twenty thousand flower children, anti-war radicals, anarchist Diggers, Hari Krishna devotees, Hell's Angels, and assorted other cultural outliers had assembled in the Polo Fields section of Golden Gate Park to watch Ginsberg chant mantras, to dance to the music of the Grateful Dead, to hear Leary preach his acid gospel, and to heed that gospel in the form of doses of a particularly potent mixture of the drug called "white lightning" that were distributed free to all.

A few days before, the organizers now lounging in Bowen's meditation room had issued a perfectly trippy press release announcing the event to the world: "For ten years a new nation has grown inside the robot flesh of the old," it began. "Before your eyes a new free vital soul is reconnecting the living centers of the American body." As a coming-out party for this new body, the Human Be-In would bring together "Berkeley political activists" and "the love generation of the Haight-Ashbury" as two parts of "the new nation who will be coming from every state in the nation, every tribe of the young (the emerging soul of the nation)."

According to the organizers, the purpose of calling these groups together was simply "to powwow, celebrate, and prophesy the epoch of liberation, love, peace, compassion and unity of mankind." The organizers' motive, however, was left unsaid: With LSD made illegal in California the month before, they hoped to demonstrate that a whole city dosed on acid would be, as Jerry Rubin once said, "like heaven on earth." "The night of bruited fear of the American eagle-breast-body is over," the organizers' announcement continued. "Hang your fear at the door and join the future. If you do not believe, please wipe your eyes and see." At a public question-and-answer session held to explain the event's intentions, a man who called himself Buddha had passed a basket filled with marijuana cookies to members of the press.

The notices posted around San Francisco had billed it as a "gathering of the tribes," but the Human Be-In was also a gathering of big and often conflicting personalities. Ginsberg, for example, had made sure that Leary would be given no more than the seven minutes of microphone time allotted to each poet scheduled to speak throughout the day, rather than the thirty minutes that had been offered to "prophets." Other organizers threatened to cut the power to the amplifiers if Leary or any other speaker rambled on long enough to complicate the packed six-hour schedule. In the end, Leary needed only enough time to utter six words — "Turn on, tune in, drop out."

In the afterglow of an event that went off without a hitch (or a single arrest), any lingering tension between these larger-than-life personalities grew slack in the meditation room that night. Outside, sirens announced that police were beginning to crack down on hippies still wandering the streets, but all was hazy quiet on the batik-covered mattresses until the artist whose studio this was burst into the room carrying a telephone.

A twenty-nine-year-old painter and art director of the local street newspaper, the *San Francisco Oracle*, Michael Bowen was at the time considered "Mr. Haight-Ashbury" by the writer Michael McClure. He had been the main organizer of the Be-In, which he had envisioned as a New Age version of the ancient Kumbh Mela, the enormous Hindu pilgrimage that draws tens of millions to bathe in the waters of one of India's sacred rivers every three years. Not overly concerned with making distinctions between various Asian traditions, Bowen was known to say that through events like the Hindu-inspired Be-In, he and his hip fellow travelers were "building an electric Tibet in California."

The idea for the Be-In had not been Bowen's, however, but that of the man he was now trying to reach on the phone. Bowen's guru, as he called him, was John Starr Cooke, a well-traveled American living in a village near Cuernavaca, Mexico, where he and a group of followers known as the Psychedelic Rangers ingested Olympian amounts of LSD and hallucinogenic mushrooms on a daily basis, using them, like the Taino caciques in the earliest religious rituals of the Caribbean, for what they believed were the drugs' entheogenic, or God-experience-inducing, qualities. Though located roughly a thousand miles south of the border, Cuernavaca was ground zero for the "better living through chemistry" spirit then spreading through the United States. It was there that Leary and other "turned-on" researchers had had their first trips; at his guru's request, Bowen had invited many of them there throughout the preceding years. And when the leaders of acid America could not come to Cooke, Cooke sent his emissary to them. Among Bowen's claims to psychedelic fame was being present when G. Gordon Liddy, then a New York assistant district attorney, raided the Millbrook Estate, the sixty-four-room mansion loaned to Leary for his experiments with LSD.

A laughing Buddha of forty-seven who chuckled at the notion that his own image shared a wall in the meditation room with various Hindu icons, Cooke found it funny to be considered anyone's guru. Yet he nonetheless reveled in finally being at the top of a spiritual chain of command. He was himself a veteran of a dozen enlightenment schemes stretching back to the 1940s, more often on the giving than the receiving end of devotion. He was known by some as a magician, by others as a snake oil salesman, and by all as the deep-pocketed scion of an old-money former missionary family. A sickly son of wealth intent on giving it all away before he died, Cooke had long since shaken off his Christian roots, but he had often seemed in the market for a messiah, turning up wherever the latest path to enlightenment was being peddled. By 1967, that new path was a chemical compound soaked into tabs of paper and ingested like tiny communion wafers, and Cooke had become one of its most enthusiastic advocates. A few years before, he had entrusted his acolyte Bowen with the mission of bringing influential people like Leary, Rubin, and Ginsberg into his circle of influence.

During the Be-In, the Cuernavaca Psychedelic Rangers had been meditating for six hours straight in solidarity with the San Francisco gathering of the tribes. When Bowen heard this news, he thought it was too good to keep to himself. He pushed the phone into the hands of the hippie paterfamilias, who took it with some surprise.

"You mean to say you have a telephone in your meditation room?" Ginsberg asked.

"Electric Tibet, baby!" Bowen replied.

Ginsberg did not speak long with the guru that day, but he did agree that the Be-In had been "a serious religious occasion." For Bowen, that was putting it lightly. When he hung up the meditation room telephone, he did so firm in his conviction that he had been part of an epoch-shaping afternoon.

"Never before had America, or the world, witnessed such an unusual and remarkable event," he said. "The Human Be-In was designed to reverse the entire thought process of the human race."

And it had all happened, he believed, thanks to his mysterious teacher. Even the lovely day itself—uncommonly warm and bright for a January afternoon in San Francisco—was thought to have come as the result of Cooke's intercession. According to Bowen, the wizard-bearded, wheelchair-bound man whose photograph stared down from his wall of gurus and icons had arranged for the weather of southern Mexico and northern California to switch places for as long as the Psychedelic Rangers were meditating. In semi-tropical Cuernavaca on January 14, Bowen claimed, it had snowed heavily all day.

"I was on a mission from God [and] from John Cooke to do that Be-In," Bowen later said. "This extraordinary event produced shock waves of consciousness and cultural change that would reverberate over the entire world."

If the various beliefs and practices often identified as "new religious movements" born in the middle of the twentieth century were arranged on a bulletin board and connected with strings—as a police detective might chart the relationships within an organized crime family—one of the pictures in the middle would belong to John Starr Cooke. Even setting aside the obviously biased assessment of his importance made by a true-believing disciple like Bowen, one can safely say that Cooke was a Zelig figure of the alternative spiritual yearnings of the postwar years in the United States. He served as a connection between the chemically enhanced religious eclecticism of the Age of Aquarius and the far older American tradition of tarot-reading, Ouija-board-consulting, consciousness-expanding curiosity seekers that stretches back into the nineteenth century. From his birth in Hawaii in 1920 to his death in Mexico in 1976, Cooke's life provides a glimpse of the ways in which the spiritual fringe crossed into the mainstream in the twentieth century, remaking both the center and the margins in the process.

Just as the Human Be-In has become a footnote to Woodstock despite having a claim as an earlier and more influential event, Cooke has been overshadowed in the intervening decades by the likes of Timothy Leary, Leary's former colleague Richard Alpert (better known as Baba Ram Dass, author of the hippie Bible *Be Here Now*), and other members of what the religion journalist Don Lattin has called the Harvard Psychedelic Club. Leary and Alpert are usually credited with mainstreaming the idea that hallucinogenic drugs might be used for spiritual purposes, yet more so than in the case of those famous names, it is the career of this mostly forgotten midcentury mystic that best demonstrates the ways in which obscure religious ideas can have broad cultural influence.

The origins of Cooke's unlikely role in American history can be traced as far back as his great-grandfather, a Yale-educated missionary called Amos Starr Cooke. Born in Danbury, Connecticut, in 1810, he was sent by the American Board of Commissioners for Foreign Missions to the Kingdom of Hawaii at the age of twenty-six to instruct the family of King Kamehameha III in subjects both secular and divine. Fifteen years later, when funding for his school faltered, Reverend Cooke partnered with another missionary, Samuel Northrup Castle, to open a general store, which soon began to prosper by supplying sugar to the American mainland after the Civil War. By the turn of the century, the Cooke family business had grown into one of the "Big Five" companies that unofficially governed the Hawaiian archipelago until statehood was granted in 1959. Following in their progenitor's footsteps, Amos Cooke's children and grandchildren built a massive family fortune through banking, politics, and real estate ventures that at one time included owning outright the island of Molokai. By the 1960s, Castle and Cooke had expanded through acquisition of Dole Food and Standard Fruit, making it the largest food-producing company in the world.

As John Starr Cooke was known to say later in life, his family had gone to Hawaii to bring religion, and they had taken land in return. "While the natives stand confounded and amazed," his great-grandfather wrote, "the foreigners are creeping in among them, getting their largest and best lands, water privileges, building lots, etc., etc." Men from the mainland were not just forcing native Hawaiians out of their villages and onto sugar and pineapple plantations, however—they were also forcing them out of their most sacred religious practices. Most conspicuously, Amos Cooke's generation of missionaries banned the islands' iconic dance ritual, the *hula halau*, not only because it was deemed lascivious by buttoned-up New England Protestants but because its performance was traditionally preceded by prayers to the forest goddess Laka, and presented before an altar dedicated to her veneration. Now known mainly as innocuous staples of the state's tourism industry, the driving drums and grass skirts of the hula fit the definition of demonic in nineteenth-century missionaries' conception of the word. The taking of land and the transformation of beliefs thus went hand in hand in Hawaii, each serving to consolidate the political power and cultural dominance of those converting the islands to Christianity.

The eighth child of one of Reverend Cooke's many grandsons, John was born into a home of such wealth that he never had to work a day in his life. While many of his siblings and cousins used their positions of privilege to expand the island empire of their forebears, John pursued activities others regarded first as childish hobbies and then as adolescent distractions as if they were a religious vocation.

And in a way, they were. According to family lore, when he was just nine years old, John Cooke came down with a case of the measles. In those prevaccinated days, the boy's spots would have been treated with only bed rest, fluids, and a strict order to keep him apart from other children until the period of contagion had passed. Any child his age might have become bored in such a situation, and so he was allowed a quick excursion out of his bedroom to buy a pack of playing cards that would let him pass a few of the lonely hours with solitaire. When he returned from a local shop and opened the deck, however, he was in for a shock that changed his life. Inside the cardstock box, he did not find the expected diamonds, clubs, hearts, and spades, but tarot cards: a strange series of images that seemed pulled from another time.

As the creation myth of John Starr Cooke came to be told, when he first saw the tarot, he threw it aside, fearing he had stumbled upon black magic, a manifestation of malevolent forces that threatened the pious foundations upon which his clan had been built. The truth was perhaps a bit more than a nine-year-old could understand: that such tools of fortune-telling had been a part of European Christian culture all along, and even were a part of his family. He had an aunt, it was said, who dabbled in palmistry and soothsaying. There was also a native nursemaid who exposed him to the very rituals that missionaries like his great-grandfather had driven underground. John's own sister Alice, ten years his senior, felt an affinity for the esotericism of Theosophy. Studying the tarot for signs of what was to come, he soon discovered that despite the Cookes' missionary past—because of it, perhaps—the mixing of religious traditions was as much a part of the family business as sugarcane.

The future guru's next known interaction with new ways of seeing the world came when he was fifteen. To celebrate twenty-five years as president of the Bank of Hawaii, and no doubt to distract himself from the recent loss of his wife, John's father, Clarence Hyde Cooke, decided to take his youngest son on a 37,000-mile jaunt exploring the Southern Hemisphere aboard a Cunard–White Star ocean liner called the *Franconia*, which set off from Honolulu for the South Pacific in 1935.

Perhaps inevitably for a pleasure cruise in the midst of the Great Depression, the Cookes shared passage on this around-the-world journey with a cast of the rich and the famous, including European royalty and well-known American entertainers. As the society pages reported at the time, the composer Cole Porter was also on board, having gone with his writing partner Moss Hart to finish their musical *Jubilee*. The melody of one of Porter's most famous songs, "Begin the Beguine," was inspired by the sights and sounds of native rituals on the islands that now comprise Indonesia, which he and his shipmates were able to see during frequent expeditions led by two lecturers employed by Cunard–White Star to put the cruise's exotic destinations in historical context.

Young John Cooke had become friendly with Porter on board the *Franconia*, and always felt that the song was somehow written for him. True or not (Porter himself told many variations of stories concerning the genesis of the tune, and none of them included a fifteen-year-old boy), the notion of the music of the South Pacific filtering into the collective consciousness of Western culture was something the future guru carried with him long after the cruise had returned to Hawaii. From that time on, Cooke was drawn to practices that seemed to provide a mystical bridge between worlds, the physical and the spiritual, the East and the West.

In this he was perhaps the perfect target audience for the runaway supernatural fad of the day. While still a teenager, he started to use the Ouija board, which had begun as a parlor-game version of automatic writing (the nineteenth-century practice of recording on paper messages from a subconscious or a spiritual source) but soon became a controversial occult item promising a means of communicating with the dead. Having first appeared in Baltimore as a novelty in the 1890s, Ouija was lauded in the press early on as "a very popular means of entertainment in many intelligent families," and like the best of entertainments, it was simplicity itself: Consisting of just an alphabet board and heart-shaped wooden planchette used to point at letters, its workings were somewhat mysterious, which only heightened the fun.

"When the right conditions prevail," a newspaper columnist wrote in 1892, "the board seems to grow electric, and questions are answered and advice and information given with head-swimming, brain-turning dispatch."

Despite this initial reputation as a harmless diversion, the "talking board" transformed through the following two decades into a device many took seriously as a portal to realms beyond the material. By 1920, with the desire to connect to the "spirit world" spurred on by the First World War's unprecedented loss of life, the makers of the Ouija had created, as the New York Times said at the time, "a national industry which bids fair to rival that in chewing gum." Alphabet boards and planchettes had become so popular on college campuses, for example, that one university faculty member declared that "the lure of Ouija is becoming a national menace." Health professionals likewise reported that Ouija-related nervous conditions were on the rise.

After a plateau in its sales through the lean years of the 1930s, the new World War apparently brought a boom in the desire to communicate with the dead. One New York City department store sold fifty thousand Ouija boards within a five-month period in 1944. Sales peaked again during the 1960s, just as the conflict in Vietnam was beginning to escalate. After acquiring the game from its inventor's heirs in 1967, Parker Brothers sold 1.5 million units without spending a dime on marketing or promotion. For a board that offered the chance to connect with the spirit world, the uncertainty of wartime may have been advertisement enough.

John Cooke took to the Ouija board not long after his return from the voyage on the Franconia, and discovered he had great skill with it. While the game's conceit was that ghostly powers, rather than the mischievous natures of those playing, moved the planchette from letter to letter, inevitably some were more talented than others at creating messages. Likewise, some players were more likely to believe what those messages might say. Cooke was both skilled in the manipulation of the game and credulous of its results. When he asked it, as a young man, where he should go to begin his adult life, he followed the Ouija's instructions to move to California to try his luck as an actor and dancer in Hollywood. When the Ouija gave him further career advice after he had left Hawaii, he followed its directions first to New York, where he appeared in a poorly reviewed production of *King Lear* as a bit player in a Shakespeare troupe ("the performance is loose and flabby," one critic opined), and then back to California, where family connections and a job working in a hospital for paralyzed children kept him safe from the draft.

His sister was at the time an ardent follower of the dashing Indian philosopher groomed since boyhood to be the leader of the Theosophy movement, Jiddu Krishnamurti, who was then living in Ojai, California. Despite John's growing esoteric interests, the teachings of his sister's guru were not for him. "There's no hocus pocus mysticism about [Krishnamurti]," Alice Cooke later explained. "He says we all have the same abilities and anything we believe about past lives or future lives or whatever is really symbolic of a way of saying who you are, and who cares if you were in Egypt once when you were Tutankhamen or whoever you want to be?" Such belittling of reincarnation and other subjects John was beginning to take seriously caused a rift in the family. "We always disagreed on that because I was much more the thinking type and he was much more the mystic," Alice said.

Parting ways with his sister for a time, Cooke soon found an Indian teacher more in keeping with his mystical inclinations. While traveling in Europe, he met Meher Baba, whose devotees believed him to be the "avatar of the age" and "God in human form." When they met, Baba was planning a trip to America to "lay cables," he said, for the worldwide spiritual network he hoped to build. He had toured the United States once before, in 1932, and during his short stay he had become the toast of high society and young Hollywood by visiting with stars including Douglas Fairbanks, Tallulah Bankhead, and Mary Pickford. In his address to a reception of admirers at Paramount Studios, he delivered some tough love to an industry built on image management and self regard: "The root of all our difficulties, individual and social, is self-interest," he said. "But the elimination of self-interest, even granting a sincere desire on the part of the individual to accomplish it, is not so easy, and is never completely achieved except by the aid of the Perfect Master." To demonstrate his availability for this role, Meher Baba expressed his desire to find a West Coast outpost to complement the five-hundred-acre East Coast retreat his followers had recently purchased for him in South Carolina.

Naturally drawn to this charismatic teacher (not least of all because Meher Baba communicated, like a human Ouija, solely by pointing at letters on an alphabet board), Cooke helped secure 170 acres of mountain property two hours from downtown Los Angeles for the avatar's devotees. His family fortune may have been acquired by moving Hawaii toward Christianity and taking land in return, but now Cooke wanted to put that same wealth to the opposite purpose. He would spend his missionary inheritance to further complicate the religious geography of the nation.

A few years before Cooke involved himself in the purchase of the property now known as Meher Mount, he had become involved with another mystic—this time intimately so. Thanks again to the Ouija board's guidance, he had impulsively married a woman several years his senior, Wilma Dorothy Millen Vermilyea. Known as Millen, she often spoke of being visited at night by a Tibetan guru eager to impart esoteric knowledge, and would later claim to have taken Polaroid pictures of an alien spacecraft flying over her home, and to be a practitioner of a means of interplanetary communication she called "galactic telepathy." Given such claims, it is perhaps not surprising that she was also an aspiring science fiction writer, and that her literary interests were not unrelated to her husband's future endeavors.

When John met Millen, she had just begun to submit her writing to various twenty-five-cent pulp magazines. The publications she favored mostly featured short stories—ranging from juvenile space operas to the dark "social science fiction" pioneered by writers like Isaac Asimov through the 1940s—but occasionally the pulps published essays as well. No doubt keeping an eye on the competition, she happened to read a remarkable manifesto by a

fellow science fiction writer by the name of Lafayette Ronald Hubbard. "Dianetics: The Evolution of a Science" appeared in the May
1950 issue of *Astounding Science Fiction* and provided the broad
strokes for a pastime that soon came to compete with Ouija boards
for John Cooke's attention — as well as that of a significant portion
of the national consciousness.

Hubbard's *Astounding Science Fiction* essay was the first published explanation of the practice now known as Scientology.
Building on the stir caused by the initial article, a book-length
treatment of the subject, *Dianetics: The Modern Science of Mental
Health*, became an international publishing phenomenon later that
same year. The reviews it received ranged from the derisive ("a set
of fantastic theories without proof") to the concerned (the book, it
was often said, was "dangerous"), but with the public it hit a nerve.
As the *New York Times* attempted to explain the months *Dianetics*
spent on its best-seller list: "Suffering people will understandably
run to any movement which promises infallible cure of all their
psychosomatic and psychological ills."

While the particular ills that caused her to seek out the movement are now unknown, Millen Cooke not only ran but flew. When
she read about Hubbard's "modern science of the mind," she left
her husband in California to be close to one of the rising centers of
the Dianetics practice in New York City. At this point in its development, Hubbard's teachings amounted to a kind of do-it-yourself
psychotherapy. The basic notion was that every human being's
development is scarred throughout life by "engrams," traumas
recorded on the unconscious "reactive mind" that can be removed
through "auditing," a process of intentional revisiting of the moment
at which the pain was first experienced. After submitting successfully to the long process of auditing, Dianetics practitioners were
said to be "clear" and could accomplish anything to which they set
their newly unscarred and allegedly unmuddled minds.

In the beginning, Dianetics was self-help in the truest sense.
Anyone could buy the book, learn the fundamentals, and perform
audits on friends and family. It was not a religion; in fact, it was
generally opposed to religions as external forces counter to the
concept of "self-determinism" central to the process. While religion
might be a cause of repression, a "clear" "is an unrepressed person,
operating on self-determinism." Hubbard turned his idea of help-

ing readers "rehabilitate" their natural ability to control their lives into an empire by offering progressively more intense auditing sessions for ever greater fees, as well as a certification system through which one could become one of his official auditors. In a spirit similar to Michael Bowen's assertion that the Human Be-In was "designed to reverse the entire thought process of the human race," Hubbard called the creation of Dianetics "a milestone for Man comparable to his discovery of fire and superior to his inventions of the wheel and arch."

Though he was usually an easygoing fellow, content to let people come and go as the Ouija board directed, after Millen took an unannounced flight from California to New York to begin her Dianetics process, Cooke drove across the country in a rage-fueled burst, determined to bring his wife back home. When he arrived in New York and met the other practitioners of this strange new "technology," however, he was no longer so angry. In fact, he found he fit right in. The Dianetics people were visibly impressed with what they considered to be his powers, which he demonstrated by means of his trusty Ouija. The practice of letting the alphabet board and the planchette speak while those around it remained silent turned out to be particularly well suited for discovering troublesome engrams wherever they might hide. In fact, the device soon adopted by Dianeticists to add the veneer of technology to the process, the e-meter, was in some ways a Ouija board reimagined for the computer age then being born.

Particularly impressed with the newcomer was a young woman from Oregon, Mary Oser, who believed that Cooke might be able to cure her husband of what she considered his "money sickness." Peter Max Oser was the grandson of the founder of Standard Oil, John D. Rockefeller. He had nearly endless resources and only a vague sense of how they might best be used. Mary proposed that John, who was obviously not burdened with caring too much about his own wealth, travel with them in order to cure her husband of the malady another of their friends later referred to as his "havingness": the affliction of having it all.

Leaving Millen after eight years of marriage, Cooke flew off with Mary and Peter to Switzerland and followed the direction of the Ouija from there. Peter became John's eager pupil, and Mary became his muse. By the end of the threesome's adventures first through Europe and then on various expeditions in Africa, Rockefeller's grandson had not been relieved of the illness of inheritance, but he had been relieved of his wife.

Around this time, the center of the Dianetics movement had shifted across the Atlantic to England, and so that was where John and Mary, now the new Mr. and Mrs. Cooke, settled. While in London, they were known to wear flowing African robes they had acquired throughout their travels, and passed the days often in the company of L. Ron Hubbard himself. During their meetings, they discussed John's magical abilities and memories of past life experiences, and Hubbard's "science of the mind" began to take on a cosmic dimension. Hubbard in the mid-1950s was in the process of transforming the vaguely spiritual technique of auditing into the central ritual of an actual religion. An often-quoted Hubbard statement on this period of transformation ("I'd like to start a religion," several acquaintances recall him saying. "That's where the money is") may be apocryphal, but recasting Dianetics as the scripture of a new faith proved to make it even more lucrative than it had been as a "poor man's psychotherapy."

Many of the original followers of Dianetics, which began to be known as Scientology with the establishment of several official churches in the United States, were uneasy with the transition. "The news was received with mixed emotions," a 1954 newsletter popular among early practitioners declared. "Some were outspokenly antagonistic to the idea. Some who'd nursed the glories of self-determinism since Book One," as *Dianetics* came to be called, "couldn't subscribe to the new idea that the best way to win is to BECOME the enemy. Many from California feared that designating Scientology as a religion would classify it with that state's 9,857,385,237 cults."

John and Mary were less concerned. They had witnessed the development of the movement's religious dimension firsthand in London, and may have even played a part in the incorporation of some of its more esoteric elements. Like Amos Starr Cooke setting off for the islands a century before, they soon returned to Africa as missionaries of Hubbard's increasingly supernatural notions. Following a similar zeitgeist as the one that would flood Haight-Ashbury with hippies a decade and a half later, they arrived in the Moroccan city of Tangier, at the time an autonomous International Zone on the southern shore of the Strait of Gibraltar, just as it was becoming the destination of choice for a previous generation of nonconformists, recreational drug users, and others with a reason to be free of governmental attention. As one such famous drug user the Cookes soon would meet, the writer William Burroughs, once said of his adopted hometown, "Nobody in Tangier is exactly what he seems to be." A city of reinvention, it was "one of the few places left in the world where, so long as you don't proceed to robbery, violence, or some form of crude, antisocial behavior, you can do exactly what you want."

A perfect place, in other words, to plant a new religion, though how far its branches would reach remained to be seen.

When the Cookes arrived in Tangier in the mid-1950s, it was perhaps best known in the United States as the home of the writer Paul Bowles, who had become a household name with the 1949 publication of his novel *The Sheltering Sky*. Bowles himself had originally gone to Tangier with his friend the composer Aaron Copland at the suggestion of Gertrude Stein in the 1930s. After more than a decade away, he settled there for good in 1947. His presence, as well as the Moroccan setting of the book that made him famous, and the notion that, as he later wrote of Tangier, "certain areas of the earth's surface contained more magic than others" soon attracted the likes of Burroughs, Ginsberg, Kerouac, and the artist Brion Gysin.

Now a lesser-known figure of the Beat Generation, Gysin was known by his contemporaries as both a devilish prankster and a visionary saint. Timothy Leary once called him "one of the great hedonic mystic teachers"; to Burroughs, he was "certainly the greatest painter living." Among his other claims to fame, he was the original source of the recipe for the cannabis-laced confection known from the 1950s to the 1970s as "Alice B. Toklas brownies." Gysin had sent Toklas, his friend Gertrude Stein's lover and longtime companion, instructions for making what he called "hashish fudge," which she included in her best-selling memoir-with-recipes, *The Alice B. Toklas Cook Book*, in 1954. Upon preparing this dish, Gysin warned, "euphoria and brilliant storms of laughter, ecstatic reveries and extension of one's personality on several simultaneous planes are to be complacently expected."

The man responsible for the dessert now more commonly known as pot brownies also proved to be the Cookes' entree to

Tangier's vibrant expatriate community. Unlike many of the Westerners who came and went in those days, Gysin was enough a part of the life of the city that he had opened a popular, if financially struggling, café. Called 1001 Nights, it was a gathering place for the International Zone's visitors, who unfortunately came more often to gawk and be seen than to spend money. It was there one night that a mysterious couple made a grand entrance into the tangled affairs of the assembled bohemians. Burroughs later suggested that they had suddenly materialized, as if they were "holograms." As Gysin recalled, John and Mary Cooke came "floating into my restaurant...telling me that they had been on my trail for a long time." Their Ouija board, they claimed, had given them directions.

"They were the first rich hippies I had ever seen," Gysin remembered. Dressed in "sandals and saris and sarouels," and "dripping with real jewels of great price in the best possible taste," they were flush with cash and drank only champagne. They seemed to Gysin to be "Magic People," and it was obvious that the most potent spell in their store of enchanted resources was a level of wealth that surprised even the International Zone's traveling class.

From that night on, the Cookes became fixtures at 1001 Nights. They were "the stars of my late show," Gysin said. Though like the rest of the clientele they came mainly for the exotic entertainments for which the café was known — dancing boys and the trance-inducing Sufi musicians of the Jilala and the Gnawa Islamic mystical traditions — it often seemed as if John and Mary were truly the ones on stage. John especially, with his "big Buddha ears sticking out on both sides of a wide guru grin" and "big bugged-out green eyes laughing like crazy," was a subject of fascination to all. When the Sufi musicians played, he was known to leap onto tabletops in an ecstatic dervish dance, performed barefoot to display the jeweled rings on his toes. He delighted audiences with fantastical tales of his childhood in the "far out islands" and the mind-transforming practices he had discussed with Hubbard.

The Cookes so liked the venue in which they were the center of attention that they soon bought the place. Just as he had acquired a mountain retreat for Meher Baba's California devotees, Cooke now set about creating a bastion of exotic spiritual experience for the visiting bohemians of Tangier.

Though he became personally devoted to the Cookes, not least of all because buying 1001 Nights had kept it in business, Gysin was skeptical of the new religion they preached. John's tales of Scientology and its leaders were, the artist said, "enough to make me laugh myself sick, but who was I to have an opinion when my restaurant was coming apart under me like an old rotten undervest or a leaky boat in heavy weather?" Kept to himself at the time, his feelings about it remained sufficiently strong that he later wrote a scathing satirical novel about the Cookes and their "billion buck scam." In allusion to Scientology's auditing obsession, Gysin called his novel *The Process*, and used it to recount the way a couple he renamed "Thay and Mya Himmer" had deployed a spiritual practice called "Grammatology" to bilk Mya's first husband, "Peter Paul Strangeblood, the richest little boy in the world," out of a cardboard box full of cash they had arranged to have parachuted into the desert. "I'd been giving Strangeblood various occult exercises for his *havingness*," Gysin wrote in the voice of John/Thay, "and one exercise we had almost forgotten was making him send to his bank for one million dollars U.S. in cash." Driving home the fact that "Thay" was in fact a stand-in for his friend and financier John, Gysin described him as both a "Doctor of Grammatology" and, in reference to the Cooke missionary lineage, a "Hereditary Bishop of the Far Out Islands."

"Poor PP," John/Thay says of the character based on Mary's first husband, the Rockefeller heir, "there really wasn't much anyone could really do for him except take all that money away from him and he knew this. It made him nasty as hell."

Gysin saw it as a swindle from the start, but others in the orbit of 1001 Nights proved more susceptible to Scientology's pull. Burroughs especially was intrigued. Years after his first meeting with the Cookes, his writing continued to reference Hubbard by name and often concerned themes explicitly drawn from *Dianetics*, such as the erasure of traumas stored in the unconscious, discussions of which appear in his celebrated works of the 1960s. Godfather of the Beat Generation, he even attempted to bring his literary friends into the fold. He credited his experiences with auditing for inspiring new creative techniques and wrote to Ginsberg about it more than once. "The method of directed recall is the method of Scientology," he wrote the younger poet. "You will recall I wrote urging you to contact your local chapter and find an auditor. They do the job without hypnosis or drugs, simply run the tape back and forth until the trauma is wiped off. It works."

Despite this emphasis on the drug-free nature of Scientology, the apparently addictive nature of auditing, which promised to bring the one being audited (or "pre-clear") ever closer to the elusive experience of becoming "clear," was precisely what appealed to the morphine- and heroin-dependent Burroughs. Hubbard's teachings provided a new field for the writer's explorations of consciousness-expanding challenges to conventional perceptions of reality. Through his experiments with engrams and e-meters, Burroughs found fresh literary possibility in the Scientologist understanding (alluded to in his letter to Ginsberg) that memory and consciousness were like the magnetic tape of early computers. The basis for Hubbard's entire system was the notion that the mind was essentially mechanical and thus could be manipulated. Burroughs took this as an inspiration for the development of the "cut-up" technique of writing, which involved excising passages from a variety of texts and using them to build another. The purpose of this, he said, was "to make explicit a psycho-sensory process that is going all the time anyway."

"Somebody is reading a newspaper, and his eye follows the column in the proper Aristotelian manner, one idea and sentence at a time," he explained. "But subliminally he is reading the columns on either side and is aware of the person sitting next to him. That's a cut-up."

The cut-up method was Burroughs's way of dramatizing on paper the human mind's attempts to control the various stimuli it encounters through the creation of a narrative. For Hubbard, however, the idea of controlling reality in this way was not merely a literary device. While Dianetics as an approach to psychology proposed that an individual psyche could be repaired through the removal of engrams, Scientology as religion maintained that reality itself could be similarly manipulated by the "clear" mind. The physical world — which Hubbard referred to as "matter, energy, space, and time" or MEST — existed apart from the self, or the thetan, which, despite appearances, was truly in control.

The nature of this control was held to be of cosmic significance, but Hubbard often expressed it in terms that made it seem little more than the showmanship of a spoon-bending magician. In 1955, for example, he spoke with great excitement about one of his students levitating an ashtray "about three feet off of a desk." The student did so, he said, "simply by making all the particles of the ashtray receive the communication of gravity and mak[ing] earth receive the communication from all the particles of the ashtray, and gravity disappears."

Lest this be dismissed as a parlor trick, however, Hubbard was quick to point out that the power available to those who became "clear" was a matter not merely of manipulating the physical world but of controlling all aspects of existence. In the same lecture in which he rhapsodized about levitating ashtrays, Hubbard explained how his teachings had developed from mere psychology to a form of modern necromancy that allowed practitioners to master their own mortality, albeit not without risk.

"Scientology has moved up into a bracket of where one of its processes can process in reverse, right down to death or insanity just as fast as it can go the other way," he said. "This is not a frightening fact, but it happens to be a true one. A Scientologist can handle life. Well, if he can handle life he can certainly handle death."

During his fourth year in the International Zone, Cooke was stricken with a mysterious ailment. He had been spending more and more time with the Sufi trance musicians, who had begun, he later claimed, to regard him as something of a holy man or a *mejdoub*, a mystical healer. Despite this reputation, he was powerless to heal himself. At first he wondered if he had been cursed with black magic: Had the long-ago fears inspired by his first tarot deck finally been realized? He also might have blamed the particularly potent narcotic popular among denizens of 1001 Nights. Gwama musicians in particular were known for inhaling or otherwise ingesting enormous quantities of *kief*—the highly hallucinogenic pollen of the cannabis plant, commonly prepared as hashish, which left what Gysin would later remember as "blue veils of smoke" hanging over the region.

In fact, though Cooke had begun to experiment with a variety of drugs, he had been stricken by polio. In the 1950s, the incidence of polio was twenty times higher in the European and American populations of Tangier than among its native inhabitants. By the time the illness had run its course, the *mejdoub* healer had lost the use of his legs.

When news of the diagnosis—paralytic poliomyelitis—reached London, L. Ron Hubbard likely supposed that an engram must have been the true cause of Cooke's affliction. As Scientology literature from this period explains, "We don't believe in sickness, we do not address illness, we do not diagnose, we believe that freeing the human spirit also incidentally prevents sickness." The Cookes hoped the top Scientologist himself would materialize in Tangier to tend to his friend, but Hubbard instead dispatched one of his high-ranking auditors to see what "the process" could do for one of its earliest adherents.

A gaunt Australian by the name of James "Lucky Jim" Skelton soon arrived with specific instructions on how to overcome the "suppression" that had crippled the usually spry Hawaiian dervish. In a shuffling of roles that might have made the former Shakespearean ensemble actor nostalgic for a time when such things happened only on stage, now it was John who was the afflicted one, and the younger man claiming magical skills who had come to heal him. Given the way the Cookes' earlier and similar drama unfolded, it perhaps came as a surprise to no one that Lucky Jim eventually ended up not only with Mary but with custody of Mary and John's newborn son, who would grow up in the Scientologist fold. The boy, Chamba — great-great-great-grandson of the missionary Amos Starr Cooke — would later recall hearing L. Ron Hubbard recounting fantastic tales of his past life as a pirate, while his mother and stepfather listened with childlike credulity.

Unhealed by Skelton's auditing attentions, and troubled that Hubbard had not made a greater personal effort on his behalf, John Cooke left Scientology and his young family behind. He returned to California, still unable to walk, still believing he had been cursed, but eager to resume his old mission of putting his money to spiritual use. He settled in the Carmel Highlands, 120 miles south of San Francisco, and soon brought the Indonesian holy man Muhammad Subuh Sumohadiwidjojo to California, allowing practitioners of the once-popular but now mostly forgotten Subud movement to make his home their American headquarters. Having been declared "clear" by Hubbard in the early 1950s, he was "opened" through a similar process by Pak Subuh in 1958, with no apparent relief to his spiritual searching or physical ills. Cooke and a small community of his own followers also engaged in practices ranging from Huna (traditional Hawaiian beliefs made over to fit in with the New Age), Bahai, astrology, transcendental meditation, mandalas, ESP — really every spiritual fad then active in California, with one notable exception: Despite having once been a recipient of Cooke's largesse, Meher Baba told his followers to have nothing further to do with him. "God in human form" believed something had happened to Cooke that "had affected his mind."

It may have been the drugs. Along with this eclectic mingling of various esoteric disciplines, Cooke's return to California also led him back to the basic tools with which his career as a would-be guru had begun. He began channeling the voice of a being he called "One" through the medium of a homemade Ouija board and soon had a series of visions that inspired him to reimagine the cards of the tarot, which had set him on this path four decades before. Now, however, he performed his Ouija divinations and tarot readings while dosed on enough LSD to make his Carmel retreat the West Coast answer to Timothy Leary's Millbrook.

Though far removed from the jewel-toed dervish who delighted crowds at 1001 Nights, the man often stoned and slumped in his wheelchair in some ways had not changed at all. In letters written to Brion Gysin around this time, William Burroughs noted that in his recent interactions with Cooke, it was as if he had seen Thay Himmer, Gysin's fictional version of the man, "stepping right out of your pages." By writing a novel about his old friend, Gysin had captured another truth about Cooke as well, though this one he left out of the version published in 1969. Before he settled on calling his book *The Process*, Gysin had considered other titles. One possibility captured succinctly the industry in which the peddlers of both Scientology and acid trips were all involved to one degree or another: *The Immortality Racket*.

As the conflict in Vietnam helped transform the Beat Generation into the counterculture of Haight-Ashbury, Cooke's homes in Carmel and then in Cuernavaca became virtual pilgrimage sites for the discontented and the seeking. Many of his followers moved to Mexico for the purpose, they said, of preparing for their action in the world. Among the first was a young artist named Michael Bowen, who had sought out Cooke when a friend told him there was "a wizard that lives down the coast in Carmel Highlands." The artist was immediately taken with his new teacher, and in Mexico joined Cooke's hallucinogenic order through an "initiation" that involved eating so many narcotic *tolguacha* flowers that he was left comatose and hospitalized for a month. Bowen's wife, Isabella Paoli, would later describe the imagined purpose of Cooke's "brotherhood": "Like the Knights Templars of the 10th century, this militarily organized group practiced their mind control skills as a matter of duty to their order and their survival."

After Bowen's recovery, Cooke used his still substantial resources to send his protégé as a missionary of sorts in search of fellow travelers in New York (where he tripped with Leary), England (where, his wife later recalled, "he met with L. Ron Hubbard and others of the Brotherhood"), and finally back to San Francisco. There, he opened his painting studio to the hippie scene on Haight Street, making it a community hub in the mold of Gysin's 1001 Nights, a place from which they might draw in the rest of the world. When their dream seemed to become a reality with the Human Be-In, Bowen and Cooke considered the twenty thousand who had crowded the Polo Fields "initiates" and "apostles" in a cultural revolution.

In the words of political commentator Hendrik Hertzberg, who happened to be in attendance in Golden Gate Park on January 14, 1967, the San Francisco Human Be-In was "as good a marker as any for the arrival of the counter culture as a mass movement." It had been born out of John Cooke's desire to spread, far and wide, the high he had found in the wake of personal catastrophe, but its influence grew well beyond his original intentions. According to the people involved, it played an essential part in the birth of a new kind of protest movement.

When the East Coast had its own Be-In three months later, on March 26, 1967, it was modeled specifically on the original. Organizers of the Easter Sunday happening in the Sheep Meadow section of New York's Central Park attempted to emulate the success of the "gathering of the tribes" yet hoped also to avoid its failures. Jerry Rubin, the one overtly political voice at the first Human Be-In, had actually been booed when he spoke out against the Vietnam War. Because the Haight-Ashbury crowd considered politics in general to be just one more source of tension they could do without, Ginsberg found Rubin's remarks "too histrionic," and unlikely to inspire the kind of change they were looking for. After the event, Rubin decided the poet was right. "It was the first time I did see a new society," he said of the San Francisco Be-In. "I saw there was no need for a political statement. I didn't understand that until then, either."

The planners of the Central Park Be-In understood that from the start. "We wanted to be a celebration of being alive, of having that experience in the park," one of the main organizers, an actor named Jim Fouratt said. "People in New York don't look at each other, don't see each other, don't talk to each other. This is the one time they can do that without being uptight or afraid of it. It's an affirmation of not being afraid, an affirmation of love and happiness."

Despite such apolitical rhetoric, both events included a common element that was definitely political, if not obviously so. "Acid actually played a very important role in the alteration of the American psyche," Allen Ginsberg said, "in catalyzing a lot of the anti-war movement in the sense of altering the basic social conditioning and the semiotics and the terminology and the take. Acid was one of the main catalysts of the anti-war movement, to the activation of it on a grand scale.... It was the deconditioning agent that got people into another world, into the flower power, the psychedelic thing that was connected with the anti-war movement."

Yet in the aftermath of the Be-Ins, their organizers came to believe that acid alone wasn't the answer. Many of the politically minded radicals in the growing anti-war movement mocked Leary for his desire to simply disconnect from a troubled world, adding two words to his mantra to capture their disdain: "tune-in, turn-on, drop-out, jerk-off." Psychedelics for their own sake would not bring the revolution they longed for. The answer instead was acid plus action. But as Rubin had discovered at the Polo Fields, action could be a tough sell to the Love Generation. What kind of action would they buy?

The answer came, indirectly, from John Starr Cooke.

After the Be-In, Bowen had returned to Mexico to reunite with his teacher, and the two there deepened their studies, now covering ever more esoteric terrain. They worked on extrasensory perception, ancient Mayan shamanic rituals, more of the metaphysical symbology that had long informed the artist's paintings, and the possibilities of manipulating matter, energy, space, and time, which Cooke had discussed with the founder of Scientology a decade before. When the guru dispatched his student back to the United States, he sent with him an outlandish idea that soon found a surprisingly receptive audience.

One of the volunteers working with Jim Fouratt on the East Coast Be-In, Abbie Hoffman, was at the time looking for ways to harness the energy that had been successfully expended on gatherings without particular purpose to explicitly political ends. A veteran of the Civil Rights Movement through the Student Nonviolent Coordinating Committee, he found one way when he became involved with the National Mobilization Committee to End the War in Vietnam, an affiliated group of organizations also known as "the Mobe." In the latter half of 1967, the Mobe had begun planning the largest protest yet against the war: a two-day demonstration in Washington that organizers hoped would draw 100,000 people.

The Mobe had recently hired Jerry Rubin as the Washington demonstration's project director, and the first thing the Berkeley radical did was inject a little West Coast logic into the East Coast radicals' plans. The initial conception of the protest had been to occupy the Capitol, but that, Rubin suggested, might send the wrong signal to the public at large, suggesting that the marchers wanted to shut down the democratic process and thus were offering only more of the kind of political negativity that had earned him boos from the hippies in Golden Gate Park. His friends behind the Be-In, he told his Mobe colleagues, had an idea for a different stage on which to perform their dissent: the Pentagon.

Even before the Be-In, Michael Bowen had spoken to Rubin, and anyone else who would listen, about the occult significance of the pentagram, and the five-sided shape that might be inscribed around it, as representing evil forces at work in the world. More than the Capitol, Rubin now agreed, the Pentagon was a natural symbol of the war. As such, it would serve as a far more resonant target. He and his collaborator on the *San Francisco Oracle*, the editor Allen Cohen, had been particularly taken with a passage from the American philosopher and historian Lewis Mumford's *The City in History* (1961). No hippie pamphlet, Mumford's book was "one of the major works of scholarship of the twentieth century," according to the *Christian Science Monitor*. In it, the Pentagon is painted in nearly Manichaean terms. Mumford was no esotericist like Cooke, nor a radical like Hoffman, but he provided historical and intellectual justification to ground Bowen's occult reasoning.

"The Pentagon," Mumford wrote, "across the Potomac from Washington," is "an effete and worthless baroque conceit, resurrected in the nineteen-thirties by United States military engineers and magnified into an architectural catastrophe. Nuclear power has aggravated this error and turned its huge comic ineptitude into a tragic threat." It gets better (or worse) from there:

> The Bronze Age fantasies of absolute power, the Bronze Age practice of unlimited human extermination, the uncontrolled obsessions, hatreds, and suspicions of Bronze Age gods and kings, have here taken root again in a fashion that imitates — and seeks to surpass — the Kremlin of Ivan the Terrible and his latterday successors. With this relapse, in less than a decade, have come one-way communication, the priestly monopoly of sacred knowledge, the multiplication of secret agencies, the suppression of open discussion, and even the insulation of error against public criticism and exposure through "bi-partisan" military and foreign policy, which in practice nullifies public reaction and makes rational dissent the equivalent of patriotic disaffection, if not treason. The dismantling of this regressive citadel will prove a far harder task than the demolition of earlier baroque fortifications. But on its performance all more extensive plans for urban and human development must wait.

Apprised of this understanding of their target, another voice from the original Be-In, the poet Gary Snyder, contributed the idea that what was needed at the Pentagon was not just a protest but an exorcism. Like a mystical arms race, Bowen went one better than Snyder and suggested that the exorcism should include a ritual that would actually lift the Pentagon off American soil and into the air, where it would, as *Time* magazine later reported the intention of the proposed ritual, "turn orange and vibrate until all evil emissions had fled" and the war came to an immediate end.

Rubin and Hoffman had acid in common with Bowen (Rubin had first been "turned on" in the artist's studio the year before, and Hoffman by then was an old hallucinogenic hand), but they were not true believers in the reality of visions one might have while on LSD. They were, however, pragmatic and theatrical activists, open to any idea that might bring attention to their cause. As such, perhaps as much as Bowen and his Cuernavaca guru, they recognized and respected the power of symbols. So when it came time to announce plans for the protest to be held in late October 1967, Rubin declared that they would shut down the Department of Defense because the anti-war movement was "now in the business of wholesale disruption and widespread resistance and dislocation of the American society." Hoffman elaborated with a description of the exorcism rite they would perform to end the war, declaring, "We're going to raise the Pentagon three hundred feet in the air" — significantly higher, John Cooke might have been proud to note, than L. Ron Hubbard's ashtray ever dared to fly.

As organizer Keith Lampe remembered Bowen's involvement in the planning: "We didn't expect the building to actually leave terra firma, but this fellow arrived with ideas on how to make it happen." Following the artist's journey to Mexico to consult with Cooke, "he dropped in during one of our preparation meetings in New York," ready to discuss the logistics and requirements of the ritual. "What a charming moment," Lampe said. "All of us 'radicals' there suddenly became 'moderates' because Michael really expected to levitate it whereas the rest of us were into it merely as a witty media project."

"You think Abbie believed in a lot of that stuff?" the Central Park Be-In planner Fouratt once asked. "I don't think so." However, Hoffman and others were drawn to "anything that would disrupt the mindset of middle Americans, anything that attacked their value system."

The ritual conducted on the Pentagon steps on October 21 certainly fit the bill. After a gathering of more than 100,000 before the Lincoln Memorial for anti-war speeches by luminaries including the poet Robert Lowell and the nation's baby doctor Benjamin Spock, perhaps a third of the crowd began to march across the bridge to Virginia. Norman Mailer was on the scene for the entirety of the protest, and so we know that the air was as thick with marijuana smoke as Cooke's Tangier had been with *kief*. "The smell of the drug, sweet as the sweetest leaves of burning tea, floated down to the Mall," Mailer wrote, "where its sharp bite of sugar and smoldering grass pinched the nose, relaxed the neck."

Once they had assembled before the Pentagon, where military police and federal marshals were waiting to keep them in designated protest areas, organizers distributed a leaflet program for the ritual. Mailer reproduced it in his book *Armies of the Night;* other existing versions are less poetic, so there were either multiple programs available that day or Mailer has added his own literary flair:

October 21, 1967
Washington, D.C., U.S.A.
Planet Earth

We Freemen, of all colors of the spectrum, in the name of God, Ra, Jehovah, Anubis, Osiris, Tlaloc, Quetzalcoatl, Thoth, Ptah, Allah, Krishna, Chango, Chimeke, Chukwu, Olisa-Bulu-Uwa, Imales, Orisasu, Odudua, Kali, Shiva-Shakra, Great Spirit, Dionysus, Yahweh, Thor, Bacchus, Isis, Jesus Christ, Maitreya, Buddha, Rama do exorcise and cast out the EVIL which has walled and captured the pentacle of power and perverted its use to the need of the total machine and its child the hydrogen bomb and has suffered the people of the planet earth, the American people and creatures of the mountains, woods, streams and oceans grievous mental and physical torture and the constant torment of the imminent threat of utter destruction....

On the makeshift altar before the Pentagon, meanwhile, a number of competing rituals began simultaneously to unfold. Ed Sanders, of the rock band the Fugs, delivered an impromptu, sexually suggestive invocation punctuated with repeated calls of "Out, demons, out!" Unhappy with what he considered Sanders's lack of solemnity, filmmaker Kenneth Anger took matters into his own hands and performed a parallel exorcism nearby. "Ed Sanders and the Fugs are a bunch of crap," Anger later said. In his estimation, the crowd as a whole was not much better: "They were doing their omni hare krishna chant chant, peace peace, whatever." His ritual, he believed, would be far more effective. Abbie Hoffman, likewise, had his own ideas about the necessary elements of an exorcism. He busied himself pairing up couples to perform public displays of affection that would surround the Pentagon in communal love—and create great photo opportunities for the press in the process.

Elsewhere, Mayan traditional healers known as *curanderos* sprinkled cornmeal in circles of power. Ginsberg declaimed his mantras for the cause. Michael Bowen was also on the scene. He had trucked in two hundred pounds of flowers and distributed them to the crowd. When the military police and federal marshals confronted the protesters, images of gun barrels blooming with daisies became the iconic photographs of the day.

While the building never did get off the ground, the ritual inspired by Bowen and his far-off guru in some ways succeeded. As the actor and Central Park Be-In organizer Jim Fouratt noted, the theater of attempted levitation and exorcism was able to take "the hippie element and weld it together with the hard line political reality." By focusing on a symbolic target, the Pentagon march "acknowledged where the war was being fought" and "where it had to be stopped." It succeeded, too, as the "witty media project" most of the organizers believed it mainly to be. Bowen's ideas about dark metaphysical connotations of five-sided shapes goaded much of the media into the odd position of defending, on religious grounds, the architectural implications of the Department of Defense. "Actually and expectedly, the hippies are wrong," *Time* argued. "Most religions, including Judaism, Christian mysticism and occult Oriental sects, find the Pentagon to be a structure connoting good luck, high station and godliness."

Most significantly, the ritual contributed to the transformation of public perception. "The levitation of the Pentagon was a happening that demystified the authority of the military," Ginsberg said. "The Pentagon was symbolically levitated in people's minds in the sense that it lost its authority which had been unquestioned and unchallenged until then. But once that notion was circulated in the air and once the kid put his flower in the barrel of the kid looking just like himself but tense and nervous, the authority of the Pentagon psychologically was dissolved."

In the aftermath of the ritual, when the military response to the chanting hippies turned from cautiously reserved to actively belligerent, this authority took another hit. As Mailer notes, the MPs moved as a wedge through the crowd with "M-14 rifles, bayonets, clubs, and stone faces." While the protesters sang "The Star-Spangled Banner," he continues, "slowly the wedge began to move in on people. With bayonets and rifle butts, they moved first on the girls in the front line, kicking them, jabbing at them again and again with the guns, busting their heads and arms to break the chain of locked arms." Hundreds were beaten, and a thousand arrested. For many who had taken part in the ritual, farce turned

into tragedy—which historically has been a more reliable induce-
ment of religious experience than even LSD.

Though his name was not mentioned in connection with the March
on the Pentagon, echoes of John Cooke's magical thinking could
be seen in the crosscultural esoteric ramblings of the ritual invocation, in the drug-enhanced optimism that authority could be
flouted with flowers, even in the casual acceptance among the
pragmatic organizers of the Mobe that many of their fellow Americans genuinely believed that buildings and ashtrays could be willed
into the air. After peddling such beliefs around the world for
decades, Cooke's influence came to occupy some of the most well-
protected real estate in the nation.

Glimpses of his shadow could also be seen from time to time
in what remained of the era. The 1969 publication of his newly
illustrated deck of tarot cards, *T: The New Tarot for the Aquarian Age*,
"caught on like wildfire nationwide," became what current enthusi-
asts call the "quintessential hippie tarot," and even made a brief
appearance in Charlton Heston's iconically campy science fiction
thriller *Soylent Green*. When a character flips through a few tarot
cards ten minutes into the film, it is unmistakably the deck Cooke
had been inspired to create while channeling the voice of an otherworldly being he called "One."

More significantly, at the 1969–1970 trial of the Chicago 7, at
which Jerry Rubin, Abbie Hoffman, and others who had been
involved with the March on the Pentagon were charged with starting a riot at protests during the 1968 Democratic National Convention in Chicago, Allen Ginsberg, who had spoken to Cooke on the
phone after the Be-In from Bowen's meditation room, was called as
a witness to discuss the events that had brought them together.

After a bit of comedy when the prosecution, the defense, and
the judge expressed perplexity as to just what a Be-In could be,
Ginsberg explained matter-of-factly that it had been "a gathering-
together of younger people aware of the planetary fate that we are
all sitting in the middle of, imbued with a new consciousness, a
new kind of society involving prayer, music, and spiritual life
together rather than competition, acquisition and war." Warming
to his subject, he noted that it was also "what was called a 'gathering of the tribes' of all the different affinity groups, spiritual
groups, political groups, yoga groups, music groups and poetry

groups that all felt the same crisis of identity, crisis of the planet, and political crisis in America, who all came together in the largest assemblage of such younger people that had taken place..."

Ginsberg could have been describing a snapshot of what is now often remembered of the Vietnam era as whole. It was a portrait of a community that, for better or worse, perhaps would not have come together without the influence of men like Cooke, Leary, and even Hubbard, charismatic seekers who were first concerned with personal experience, and only secondarily with the effects personal experience might have on the wider world.

By the time of Cooke's death, in 1976, the man Leary once called "the great crippled wizard" had mostly been forgotten. Yet the spiritual searching of which he was both a symbol and a part had remade the nation in his image. Erratic, naïve, and often dangerous though Cooke's seeking was, his example had its own kind of power. While it would be easy to dismiss the attempt to levitate the Pentagon as the product of a mind addled by drugs and one too many enlightenment schemes, the numbers who turned out in support of this attempt are less easily explained away. Most of the thousands gathered in the nation's capital that day had known nothing of the Ouija board–following, tarot card–reading, Scientologist magician whose ideas had helped bring them there, but their presence suggested that the country as a whole had been turned on to an idea John Starr Cooke learned early: In America, even the most far-out beliefs will eventually find their way in.

El Pocito, the little hole filled with holy dirt in Chimayo, New Mexico. Photo by Richard Rieckenberg. (Santuario de Chimayo)

CHAPTER 18

City on a Hill, Revisited

Barack Obama's first inaugural address, delivered on January 20, 2009, was notable for a number of reasons. After a decisive victory, the new president gave some Americans hope of a coming post-partisan era, bringing closure to years of party-line rancor in Washington. Gathering more than a million and a half supporters in the nation's capital on a subfreezing day, the inauguration itself was viewed as a rare moment of widespread optimism during a young century that had already seen the worst terrorist attack in U.S. history, natural disasters that showed the fatal weaknesses in the infrastructure of our cities, and the dawn of two wars, which candidate Obama had promised to end. And, of course, the inaugural celebration also marked the ascension of the first African American to the highest office in the land.

January 20, 2009, was also the first time a newly elected president used the occasion sometimes called a secular sermon to the nation to give voice to the diversity of religious life among its people. "We are a nation of Christians and Muslims," Obama said, "Jews and Hindus, and nonbelievers. We are shaped by every language and culture, drawn from every end of this Earth."

Such a high-profile expression of the varieties of American religious experience was unprecedented, even if the reality it described predates the Republic itself. A spectrum of beliefs has shaped our common history since well before the first president, in his 1789 inaugural address, spoke of "that Almighty Being who rules over the universe." But Obama's choice of words served as a reminder that only recently did the range of opinions about the nature of that Being begin to receive their due in the ongoing national conversation about the appropriate place of religion in American life.

Perhaps most noteworthy about the president's acknowledgment that the United States is a country of many faiths was that it seemed noteworthy at all. His simple declaration of a catalogue of beliefs surprised many, because there persists, among believers and nonbelievers alike, an assumption that the United States is, for better or worse, a Christian nation.

Nothing has done more to keep this notion alive than the stubborn persistence of words spoken more than a century before the United States was a nation at all: John Winthrop's designation of the community he would establish in America as a "city upon a hill." For at least the past fifty years, that single unifying metaphor has dominated presidential rhetoric about the nation's self-understanding, causing an image borrowed from the Gospels to become a tenet of faith in America's civil religion. While not a direct refutation, Obama's statement of religious diversity presented a challenge to reconsider the meaning, and even the relevance, of this image in the twenty-first century.

Much as this moment of reevaluation came in an election full of firsts, the earliest effort to make Winthrop's phrase a widely accepted metaphor for the origins and purpose of the United States came at a time self-consciously declared as the dawn of a new era in American political life, when "a torch had been passed to a new generation." Ironically, it was the first Catholic president who cited the words of the man who came to Massachusetts in part to build a "bulwark" against Jesuits and their church. Less than two weeks before intoning "ask not what your country can do for you" during his own inaugural address in 1961, John F. Kennedy reminded the legislature in his home state of Winthrop's words:

> I have been guided by the standard John Winthrop set before his shipmates on the flagship *Arabella* three hundred and thirty-one years ago, as they, too, faced the task of building a new government on a perilous frontier. "We must always consider," he said, "that we shall be as a city upon a hill — the eyes of all people are upon us."
>
> Today the eyes of all people are truly upon us — and our governments, in every branch, at every level, national, state

and local, must be as a city upon a hill—constructed and inhabited by men aware of their great trust and their great responsibilities. For we are setting out upon a voyage in 1961 no less hazardous than that undertaken by the *Arabella* in 1630. We are committing ourselves to tasks of statecraft no less fantastic than that of governing the Massachusetts Bay Colony, beset as it was then by terror without and disorder within.

Concerned as he was with distancing his approach to governance with his religious affiliation, Kennedy edited out any mention of God from the original sermon. But he did accurately capture something of the uncertainty Winthrop himself must have felt casting off from a familiar shore. Moreover, by entwining the dangers faced by the *Arabella* with his own, he enlisted "city upon a hill" in the Cold War conflict that would define his presidency, making of it a "bulwark" not against Rome but Moscow. Though he could not have known how well "terror without and disorder within" would capture the decade that had just begun, the threat of the "shipwreck" Winthrop feared remains palpable in Kennedy's borrowing of the words.

Not so just thirteen years later, when Ronald Reagan began testing out the trope that would define his political future. Then governor of California, Reagan used more of Winthrop's words than Kennedy had, adding back in the theology that the Catholic president had excised: "Standing on the tiny deck of the *Arabella* in 1630 off the Massachusetts coast, John Winthrop said, 'We will be as a city upon a hill. The eyes of all people are upon us, so that if we deal falsely with our God in this work we have undertaken and so cause Him to withdraw His present help from us, we shall be made a story and a byword throughout the world.' "

Elsewhere in the speech, delivered at the first Conservative Political Action Conference in 1974, Reagan offered his own religious interpretation of this early moment in American history:

You can call it mysticism if you want to, but I have always believed that there was some divine plan that placed this great continent between two oceans to be sought out by those who were possessed of an abiding love of freedom and a special kind of courage. This was true of those who pioneered the great wilderness in the beginning of this country, as it is also true of those later immigrants who were willing to leave the land of their birth and come to a land where even the language was unknown to them. Call it chauvinistic, but our heritage does set us apart.

Reagan would go on to use his version of the city upon a hill at every major juncture in his public life, including three campaigns for the presidency, two administrations, and perhaps most significantly in the farewell address that marked his departure from the national stage. Describing his last week in the White House in January 1989, he closed his final remarks as president with an elaboration of his understanding of what Winthrop might have had in mind on the *Arabella* 359 years before:

The past few days when I've been at that window upstairs, I've thought a bit of the "shining city upon a hill." The phrase comes from John Winthrop, who wrote it to describe the America he imagined. What he imagined was important because he was an early Pilgrim, an early freedom man. He journeyed here on what today we'd call a little wooden boat; and like the other Pilgrims, he was looking for a home that would be free.

I've spoken of the shining city all my political life, but I don't know if I ever quite communicated what I saw when I said it. But in my mind it was a tall, proud city built on rocks stronger than oceans, wind-swept, God-blessed, and teeming with people of all kinds living in harmony and peace; a city with free ports that hummed with commerce and creativity. And if there had to be city walls, the walls had doors and the doors were open to anyone with the will and the heart to get here. That's how I saw it, and see it still.

And how stands the city on this winter night? More prosperous, more secure, and happier than it was 8 years ago. But more than that: After 200 years, two centuries, she still stands strong and true on the granite ridge, and her glow has held steady no matter what storm. And she's still a beacon, still a magnet for all who must have freedom, for all the pilgrims from all the lost places who are hurtling through the darkness, toward home.

Of course, Winthrop's city was never "shining," nor was it so well established as the thriving and cinematic cityscape Reagan described. It is also a remarkable feat of revisionism to praise the governor who exiled Anne Hutchinson and Roger Williams as a "freedom man." Yet the most interesting departure from history in this American creation myth may be that though Reagan spoke often of the courage it took to reach this city, there was for him little hint or risk of the possible "shipwreck" of which the Puritans were warned. His city upon a hill, "built on rocks stronger than oceans," was divinely guaranteed success in a way Winthrop's and Kennedy's were not.

In the forty years since Reagan successfully repainted the origins of the United States with this broad brush, nearly every national candidate has repeated some version of "city upon a hill" as creed and shibboleth. Even Obama, years before he delivered his affirmation of multi-religious America, made use of this well-worn Christian phrase. Invoking Winthrop's city as Kennedy did, while speaking in Massachusetts, he delivered a commencement address that at once echoed and questioned earlier allusions. He did so when he was still just the junior senator from Illinois, his presidential future still far from certain:

> It was right here, in the waters around us, where the American experiment began. As the earliest settlers arrived on the shores of Boston and Salem and Plymouth, they dreamed of building a city upon a hill. And the world watched, waiting to see if this improbable idea called America would succeed.
>
> For over two hundred years, it has. Not because our dream has progressed perfectly. It hasn't. It has been scarred by our treatment of native peoples, betrayed by slavery, clouded by the subjugation of women, wounded by racism, shaken by war and depression. Yet, the true test of our union is not whether it's perfect, but whether we work to perfect it.

Obama's city upon a hill was a return of sorts to Kennedy's; he removed it from its theological frame, treating it instead as a verse from the secular scripture of American history. Nonetheless, he did not depart as far from Reagan's interpretation as it at first might seem. After all, he still insisted that it was with the Puritan dream of a city upon a hill that the "American experiment began." He would not embrace this dream, however, without acknowledging how it had been "scarred" — a mixed metaphor, perhaps, but an arresting one: a wounded city upon a wounded hill.

Despite Obama's overwhelming victory in two presidential elections, his revised sense of the city upon a hill, taking into account as it does the many ways it has not been perfect, has not yet supplanted the fortieth president's "shining" notion. Nor is it likely to. The phrase maintains its "mysticism," to use Reagan's terms, and it remains "chauvinistic." While making no threats, its use implies, like the infamous Spanish Requerimiento, a society certain in its supremacy and the righteousness of even its questionable acts.

For this reason, it is thanks more to Reagan than anyone else — including Winthrop himself — that "city upon a hill" has come to mean what it does today. And it is thanks to the growing ubiquity of the phrase over the past several decades that even the earliest moments of our prehistory are now remembered as if they were merely scenes from this mythical city's construction. Different as they were in approach and outcome, the various settlements throughout North America — those of the Spanish in the South, and those of the English, Dutch, and French in the North — are often viewed through this single lens, as if the radically divergent forms of Christianity brought across the Atlantic were a unified monolith of faith; as if the lands soon conquered by Europe were not already full of cities upon hills of their own.

All of which made the new president's words in January 2009 all the more surprising. They represented not only a nod to minority voters who had favored him by unprecedented margins in 2008 but a rhetorical shift away from the Puritan dream of uniformity and toward the more complicated truth of difference, an acknowledgement that the nation "shaped by every language and culture, drawn from every end of this Earth" cannot be contained in a single religious idea. To speak of the United States simply as a city upon a hill as described in Christian scripture is to limit it by pretending that it is not home to many traditions, each with a scripture of its own.

While demographic changes since the transformation of immigration policy in the 1960s may have made this broadening of the national religious self-definition inevitable, the president's own life provides some insight into why this rhetorical shift came about just when it did.

Certain parts of his biography, of course, are well known: Born to a Kenyan father with Muslim roots and to a Kansan mother with family ties to mainline Protestant churches, Obama was perhaps destined from birth to be a man with a multilayered religious identity. As he described his earliest spiritual education in his memoir *Dreams from My Father*, he attended both a Muslim school and a Catholic school in Indonesia. Neither one inspired religious devotion, but he was taught a first commandment applicable to either learning environment: "Be respectful," his mother had simply said. Consideration for others' faiths mattered more than his own individual belief, or lack thereof.

Back in the United States, the future president's spiritual education took another turn, which may have seemed likely to lead to no religion at all but in fact opened up the world of global faiths in all their possibility. "I was not raised in a religious household," he writes, in *The Audacity of Hope*. "My maternal grandparents, who hailed from Kansas, had been steeped in Baptist and Methodist teachings as children, but religious faith never really took root in their hearts. My mother's own experiences as a bookish, sensitive child growing up in small towns in Kansas, Oklahoma and Texas only reinforced this inherited skepticism."

Despite this inheritance, he soon discovered that to live in America can mean having eclectic interfaith experiences as if by osmosis. "This isn't to say that she provided me with no religious instruction," Obama adds of his mother. "In her mind, a working knowledge of the world's great religions was a necessary part of any well-rounded education. In our household the Bible, the Koran, and the Bhagavad Gita sat on the shelf alongside books of Greek and Norse and African mythology. On Easter or Christmas Day my mother might drag me to church, just as she dragged me to the Buddhist temple, the Chinese New Year celebration, the Shinto shrine, and ancient Hawaiian burial sites."

On his father's side, Obama was exposed to other traditions — of faith and of doubt. The man also named Barack Obama was largely absent from his family, but his son knew that the senior Obama, too, had come from a religious background defined by change. "Although my father had been raised a Muslim," Obama

408 • ONE NATION, UNDER GODS

writes, "by the time he met my mother he was a confirmed atheist, thinking religion to be so much superstition."

Obama was not merely a product of his parents, his schools, or the homes in which he was raised, however. It was only as an adult, during his work as a community organizer in Chicago, that he ultimately embraced Christianity—specifically African American Christianity, often called the black church. "I was drawn to the power of the African American religious tradition to spur social change," he writes. "Out of necessity, the black church had to minister to the whole person. Out of necessity, the black church rarely had the luxury of separating individual salvation from collective salvation."

To the diverse international lessons of his youth, he added the call to communal action found in a particular American tradition. This combination led him to be informed by his faith, but he was never limited by it at the expense of openness to the broader community. "Given the increasing diversity of America's population, the dangers of sectarianism have never been greater," he has written. "Whatever we once were, we are no longer just a Christian nation; we are also a Jewish nation, a Muslim nation, a Buddhist nation, a Hindu nation, and a nation of nonbelievers" —precisely the sentiment that he echoed when looking out over a million and a half well-wishers packed between the Capitol and the Lincoln Memorial in January 2009.

The years since Obama's first inaugural have been in many ways the pinnacle of acceptance and influence of those formed on the margins of the demographically dominant Christian faith. Look no further than 1600 Pennsylvania Avenue for proof: The black church that remains Obama's primary inspiration was born of the experiences of African Americans going as far back as Onesimus and Omar ibn Said. It is not merely an ethnic variation of the Christianity brought from Europe, but a distinctly American tradition shaped by practices with deep African roots. And the gathering of diverse spiritual influences in the current White House does not end there. During his first campaign for the presidency, Obama famously carried a figure of the Hindu deity Hanuman and a Catholic icon of the Virgin Mary among an assortment of good luck charms he kept in his pocket. Just three months in office, the Obamas hosted the White House's first Passover seder; a celebration of an iftar dinner marking Ramadan came six months later.

Though he had been dogged through the campaign by rumors that he was secretly a Muslim, the president did not shy away from making clear that Islam was as welcome in his new home as it was in the homes across the country. "Tonight's iftar is a ritual that is also being carried out this Ramadan at kitchen tables and mosques in all fifty states," he said. "Islam, as we know, is part of America."

Yet Obama is obviously not the source of this period of increased awareness; he is rather one sign among many showing how pervasive the influence of marginal religious traditions has become. When the nation faced another presidential choice four years after Obama's 2008 election, for the first time neither major-party candidate had what would have been considered a conventional religious affiliation a century ago. As heir to the spiritual legacy of Joseph Smith, Brigham Young, and perhaps Handsome Lake, the Republican candidate, former Massachusetts governor Mitt Romney, represented the final proof of mainstream American acceptance of a movement that had once been literally chased beyond the nation's borders. If foretold in the mid-nineteenth century, Romney's candidacy would have seemed just as unlikely as Obama's.

The first dozen years of the twenty-first century have also seen the election of Keith Ellison, the first Muslim in Congress, who took the oath of office with his hand on Thomas Jefferson's Quran in January 2007. The House of Representatives later welcomed its first Hindu, Hawaii's Tulsi Gabbard, who took her oath of office on the Bhagavad Gita in January 2013. That same month, when another Hawaiian politician became the first Buddhist in the Senate, she promised she would not be the last. "There need to be many more of us in here," Mazie Hirono said. "I am going to make sure that happens."

No doubt there will continue to be increased representation of specific minority religious groups in government, and we should also expect growing numbers of those who are significantly influenced by traditions other than their own. When the then mayor of Newark, New Jersey, Cory Booker, released a video in December 2012 discussing his political future, for example, he was shown seated beside a stack of religious tomes that included a Hebrew Bible, a New Testament, a Quran, and a Bhagavad Gita. Perhaps most interesting about the display was that he did not mention it at all, instead letting the collection of books speak for itself. The eclectic spiritual interests this small library represented did not stop Booker from being elected to the U.S. Senate in 2013.

Of course, the early years of the twenty-first century have also been marked by some of the worst interreligious violence in the nation's history. In the year following the devastating terrorist attacks of September 11, 2001, hate crimes against Muslims increased by an astonishing 1,600 percent. A 2010 Gallup poll found that 43 percent of Americans readily admit feeling prejudice toward Muslims, and more than half of all adults in the United States have an unfavorable view of Islam generally. More than thirty states have reported incidents of violence or vandalism at mosques in the past five years. And clearly the perpetrators of these kinds of assaults do not harm followers of Islam alone. The first man killed in supposed retaliation after September 11 was the Arizona gas station owner Balbir Singh Sodhi, a member of that group of perennially mislabeled religious Americans, the Sikhs. Sodhi was shot outside his gas station on September 15, 2001, because his killer saw his turban and beard and assumed he was a Muslim. In the summer of 2012, Sikhs fell victim yet again to a violent attack—this time a mass shooting at a temple in Wisconsin. Responding to these attacks in a way no one did to those in Bellingham a century ago, President Obama said, "Regardless of what we look like, where we come from, or where we worship, we're all one people."

As important as it undoubtedly is to repeat this basic premise upon which the Republic stands, it may be time to ask if our dominant symbol of national unity may be part of the problem. Does the city upon a hill, that stubborn Puritan metaphor, carry with it the very images of walls and exclusion that contribute to attacks against those on the margins of the dominant faith? So long as the call to build Winthrop's city endures, will we continue to imagine ourselves under spiritual siege and in need of a "bulwark" against whichever current peril must be kept at bay?

Perhaps it is time to consider a metaphor offering a different kind of inclusion. One possibility might be found in the image with which this book began. Not a fictional city but an actual place: the small side chapel at New Mexico's El Santuario de Chimayo, in which we can read the whole history of the nation in a humble hole in the ground.

According to an account published in 1915, the tiny Catholic shrine in the foothills of the Sangre de Cristo Mountains had been built early in the previous century "on the spot where for long years wonderful cures had been performed by the strange virtue of the soil." From its earliest days, it had been a location that "every day throughout the year" attracted "men, women, and children from all directions...all inspired with full faith in the supernatural remedial power that is here manifested."

It was not uncommon to see among the crowds "in carriages, in wagons, on horses, on burros, or on foot" entire families in the company of "some little one deformed from birth or injured by accident, whose case is beyond the curative power of the most skilful physician." When they arrived, these families would approach a small hole cut in the church floor—el pocito, the "little well," as it is called—and scoop out "a small amount of the sacred earth and make a kind of tea or drink of it....Those who come long distances usually take back with them a small quantity of the earth as a safeguard for the future." In cases of illness so severe that the infirm could not be brought to Chimayo, Chimayo could be brought home a handful at a time.

Those who made use of the powers of el pocito did not concern themselves with how the miracles began ("How and when the healing virtues of the sacred earth of this favored spot were first manifested, not even tradition tells us," the 1915 account reports), but it is generally accepted that the local Tewa people visited this site for much the same purpose long before the first Spanish missionaries arrived. The church was built here, in other words, because the ground itself was already regarded as holy.

Founded by Christians on land sacred to people who had lived there for millennia, El Santuario de Chimayo might be seen as a reply to the long-ago challenge put before Native Americans to abandon their cultures or die. The answer given, centuries in the making, was that if they must be changed by the faith brought across the ocean, then that faith itself would be transformed as well.

From the intersection of these two conflicting traditions, which first squared off during that meeting of the gods on the island of San Salvador more than five hundred years ago, there arose a religious site of interest to pilgrims who might consider themselves Roman Catholic, Native American, both, or neither. As the shrine's own welcoming materials state, "Visitors to El Santuario come from all over the world and represent many diverse religious and cultural beliefs. Many are pilgrims who walk long distances, sometimes barefoot, sometimes carrying large wooden crosses. Some visitors are Jews, Hindus, Muslims or Buddhists who come initially out of simple curiosity. Some are blessed with the belief that they are at a place of God that transcends those things which tend to separate us."

It is likely only a coincidence that the shrine's description of the visitors to its crater in the sacred soil echoes precisely the same diverse people of faith President Obama had in mind when he wrote, "Whatever we once were, we are no longer just a Christian nation." Yet coincidence though it may be, it is not a meaningless one. After all, the history told by this "little well" in New Mexico belongs equally to all Americans. There is no sign here of a city upon a hill that must be breached or defended, only the very stuff of which the country is made.

This goes beyond the physical; it is not just a matter of the chunk of earth that we call the United States. The hole at the back of the church is a product of the same process of conflict, negotiation, and compromise that can be seen in the lives described and the stories told throughout the American story. Though the epic of belief and unbelief in America seems from the start to be one of weaker faiths and unpopular ideas vanquished by those strong enough to impose creeds and consequences as they see fit, the more enduring theme in this saga is resistance.

Though the particulars of their beliefs were informed and limited by the times in which they lived, a line of spiritual descent can nevertheless be traced from the Indian chief Hatuey insisting he would prefer hell to a Christian heaven, to the Muslim Zemmouri escaping Christian slavery for an uncertain future. One can see the same kind of defiance at work when Jacob Lumbrozo plainly doubted the dominant faith, when Anne Hutchinson refused to silence her "strange opinions," and when Tituba used the very fears that had condemned her to save her own life. Were these stories merely of individual actions, these moments of personal rebellion might have had no further significance. Yet they are also stories of people forced to live in community with those who have startlingly different ideas. We cannot help but learn and change through exposure to religious difference, as did Cotton Mather, William Livingston, Conrad Weiser, Thomas Jefferson, Handsome Lake, Joseph Smith, Mary Moody Emerson, and her nephew Waldo.

Collectively, they remind us that religious outliers are usually not outliers for long—as the Spanish feared about the interaction of Indians and Muslim slaves, ideas are contagious. Their stories also tell us something about those who seem very much to be religious insiders, whose families are well-churched enough to imagine that they live in an exclusively Christian nation. Like New England missionaries whose great-grandson became a wizard in California, they are never more than an experience, a marriage, or a generation away from becoming as spiritually eclectic as the people of this land have always been. They are as open to new influences and interpretations as a hole that, depending on what you are looking for, contains nothing or the world itself.

According to legend, one of the miraculous aspects of *el pocito* is that no matter how many come to fill their mouths, plastic bags, or coffee cans, the hole will never be empty. The Catholic priests in charge of the shrine smile at this suggestion, and then point discreetly behind the church, where a huge pile of freshly delivered soil awaits blessing with holy water before it is transported by shovel, sweat, and wheelbarrow inside the church. Often the priests are too busy to fill the hole themselves, and so they have been known to provide a bucket to the willing and ask volunteers to lend a hand.

If the shrine is too crowded for these deputized hole-fillers to make their way to the front of the assembled faithful, the bucket will pass from hand to hand through a room decorated with cast-off crutches and photographs of those in need of healing. When the hole is finally refilled, it is the work of many, working in concert despite all differences, for the benefit of those they may never know. It is a process few would call sacred, but it may indeed make the little well, like the vast nation of which it is both a symbol and a part, a miracle of the most unlikely kind.

Acknowledgments

One Nation, Under Gods could not have been written without the support of several institutions and many friends. Most significantly, I was fortunate to spend a year working on the book at Washington College, in Chestertown, Maryland, as a Patrick Henry Fellow at the C.V. Starr Center for the Study of the American Experience. The Starr Center's staff welcomed me into a wonderfully collegial home away from home, and I could not have asked for an environment more conducive to historical research than its eighteenth-century Custom House. During the project's earliest stages, I was simultaneously completing my dissertation at Georgetown University, where conversations with faculty members and my fellow graduate students in the doctoral program in religious pluralism helped me find many of the stories told here. I am also grateful to the National Endowment for the Arts, the Social Science Research Council, and the Smithsonian Institution, each of which provided funding that allowed me to focus on research and writing at crucial times. My sincere gratitude, too, to my agent Kathleen Anderson, who encouraged this project from the beginning, and to my editors at Little, Brown—John Parsley, Junie Dahn, Janet Byrne, Ben Allen, and Deborah Jacobs—who helped see it through to the end. The friends and family members I should thank are too many to name; the one I must thank—my best friend, my first reader—is my wife, Gwenann Seznec Manseau. The book is dedicated to our daughters, Annick and Jeannette, who will live the next chapters of this history.

Notes

To complete this work of both synthesis and original research, I have relied on the work of dozens of historians of various periods of American history, as well as primary source materials drawn mainly from two digital archives: for periodicals produced from the seventeenth through the mid-nineteenth century, I used Readex's America's Historical Newspapers database, and for publications produced during the last 160 years or so I frequently turned to the California Digital Newspaper Collection of the University of California, Riverside. While the book itself took four years to write, I have also drawn on more than a decade of traveling through, and reporting on, religious America in its many manifestations. The people of all faiths and no faith whom I met during those travels have served as the inspiration for this book; they are the spiritual descendants of the figures described throughout, as are we all.

Over the next few pages, I will highlight the most significant scholarship and other materials I read while writing *One Nation, Under Gods*. Specific sources follow this brief overview. Indebted as I am to the work of several generations of historians, any errors in the preceding chapters are of course my own.

Introduction: I first visited El Santuario de Chimayo in the spring of 2002, and since then have remained drawn to it as a vivid example of American syncretic religion in action. As noted in the conclusion, the faithful of Chimayo seem to remake the notion of what constitutes a "miracle" through their eclectic and occasionally chaotic approach to ritual observance. This is an idea I first explored in a commentary for National Public Radio's *All Things Considered* in 2004. A decade later, the dirt of Chimayo still strikes me as a fitting lens — albeit a dusty one — through which to view the great collaborative history of religion in America.

Chapter 1: For this group portrait of the religious motivations of those involved in the earliest encounter between the Old World and the New, I consulted popular histories of different eras, scholarship in a variety of fields, and primary sources concerning the conquest of the Caribbean. In the first category, popular accounts, works consulted include James Reston Jr.'s *Dogs of God: Columbus, the Inquisition, and the Defeat of the Moors* (2005), Robert Irwin's *The Alhambra* (2004), Laurence Bergreen's *Christopher Columbus: The Four Voyages, 1492–1504* (2011), and Samuel Eliot Morison's *Admiral of the Ocean Sea: A Life of Christopher Columbus* (1942). Older popular works include *Out of the Sunset Sea*, by Albion Tourgee (1893), *With the Admiral of the Ocean Sea: A Narrative of the First Voyage*, by Charles Paul MacKie (1891), and Washington Irving's 1828 biography, *The Life and Voyages of Christopher Columbus*. While these nineteenth-century works are responsible for most of the widespread misconceptions about Columbus that exist today, they remain of interest as a window into the changing cultural attitudes about what his journeys accomplished. Among the misconceptions for which these older works are *not* responsible is the Jewish Columbus thesis mentioned in this chapter. The notion that Columbus was a "secret Jew" using the voyage as an escape from anti-Jewish Europe is mainly the legacy of Simon Wiesenthal's provocative *Sails of Hope: The Secret Mission of Christopher Columbus* (1973). A good debunking of this and various other claims about Columbus's birth, religious affiliation, and nationality can be found in Fred Bronner's "Portugal and Columbus: Old Drives in New Discoveries" in the academic journal *Mediterranean Studies* 6 (1996). Works of recent scholarship consulted in this chapter include *Viking America: The First Millennium* (2001), by Geraldine Barnes; *Jews and Muslims in British Colonial America: A Genealogical History* (2012), by Elizabeth Caldwell Hirschman and Donald Neal Yates; the multi-authored volume *The World of Columbus* (1993), edited by James R. McGovern; and the independent scholar Lynne Guitar's work on the Taino and their myths. Primary sources consulted include *The Saga of the Greenlanders*, *De Orbe Novo: The Eight Decades of Peter Martyr D'Anghera*, *The relación of Fray Ramón Pane*, *A Brief Account of the Destruction of the Indies*, by Bartolomé de las Casas, and Columbus's own *Book of*

Prophecies, as well as his journal, published in an edition summarized by las Casas.

Chapter 2: The two most important texts for telling the tale of Mustafa Zemmouri and the failed Narváez Expedition are the *Narrative of Cabeza de Vaca* (also known as *Castaways* and *The Shipwrecked Men*), and Ralph Emerson Twitchell's *The Leading Facts of New Mexican History,* Volume 1 (1917), which not only narrates the events of the expedition in harrowing detail but places them in the context of existing scholarship at the time it was written, which was already extensive in the early twentieth century. Following in the footsteps of these two classic sources, several works have marked the last decade as a time of increased interest in the man more often called Esteban de Dorantes. Recent popular accounts of his life, and of the exploits of other members of the Narváez Expedition, include *Brutal Journey: The Epic Story of the First Crossing of North America* (2006), by Paul Schneider; *A Land So Strange: The Epic Journey of Cabeza de Vaca* (2007), by Andrés Reséndez; and *Crossing the Continent: 1527–1540* (2008), by Robert Goodwin. For pointing me toward considering the conquest of the Americas in light of struggles between Christians and Muslims in Spain, I am grateful to Ana Marcos Maíllo's article, "Los Arabismos Más Utilizados por los Conquistadores de Nueve España en el Sigle XVI."

Chapter 3: Despite its unambiguous place in American mythology, John Winthrop's sermon "A Model of Christian Charity" continues to puzzle scholars. To begin with, there is some question whether Winthrop delivered this sermon aboard the *Arabella,* or before its departure, in the port of Southampton, England. Others question whether it was delivered at all, but merely written as Winthrop crossed the Atlantic. See Francis J. Bremer's *John Winthrop: America's Forgotten Founding Father* (2003), p. 174, for more on this question, and on Winthrop's life and times generally. Similarly, Richard Gamble's *In Search of the City on a Hill: The Making and Unmaking of an American Myth* (2012) explores the afterlife of Winthrop's words, revealing how their current significance is a product more of twentieth-century politics than of centuries of American self-understanding. Recent reevaluations of religious dissent in early New England include *The Times and Trials of Anne Hutchinson,* by Michael Paul Winship (2005), and Eve LaPlante's *American Jezebel:*

The Uncommon Life of Anne Hutchinson, the Woman Who Defied the Puritans (2004). The trial transcripts from which dialogue between Hutchinson and Winthrop were drawn can be found through a number of online sources as well as in David Hall's *The Antinomian Controversy, 1636–1638: A Documentary History* (1990).

Chapter 4: The primary sources for this chapter are the documents related to Jacob Lumbrozo in the Maryland State Historical archives (MSA SC 3520-14037). Particularly useful is the information collected by Lois Green Carr, of the St. Mary's City Commission, MSA SC (2221-3-4-1). Lumbrozo-related documents also appear in *The Jew in the American World: A Source Book*, edited by Jacob Rader Marcus (1996), pp. 40–42, and in J. H. Hollander, "Some Unpublished Material Relating to Dr. Jacob Lumbrozo, of Maryland," *American Jewish Historical Quarterly* 1 (1905), 25–39, American Jewish Historical Society. Documents related to Peter Stuyvesant and the Jews of New Amsterdam can be found in *The Jew in the Modern World: A Documentary History*, edited by Paul R. Mendes-Flohr and Jehuda Reinharz. For background on the colony that hosted Lumbrozo's trial, I relied on Matthew Page Andrews, *History of Maryland: Province and State* (1929) and Harry Wright Newman's *The Flowering of the Maryland Palatinate* (1961).

Chapter 5: Documents related to the events in Salem in 1692 are widely available and make riveting reading on their own. The University of Virginia's Salem Witch Trials Documentary Archive and Transcription Project (http://salem.lib.virginia.edu/home.html) is a particularly user-friendly resource. Elaine Breslaw's *Tituba: Reluctant Witch of Salem* (1997) is the most recent and most compelling treatment of the various personalities and contexts that must be taken into account when considering the events in Salem in 1692. Other background and general sources consulted include *Devil in the Shape of a Woman: Witchcraft in Colonial New England* (1987), by Carol Karlsen, *Conjure in African American Society* (2005), by Jeffrey E. Anderson, and Zora Neale Hurston's *Mules and Men* (1935) for examples of practices with roots that can be traced back to colonial-era religious experience. Similarly, the works of Harry Middleton Hyatt (*Folk-lore from Adams County, Illinois; Hoodoo, Conjuration, Witchcraft, Rootwork: Beliefs Accepted by Many Negros and White People*) provide a fascinating window into eccentric American beliefs that have always existed alongside more normative traditions. Details of the fires that afflicted Boston in the seventeenth century are taken from Russell Herman Conwell's *History of the Great Fire in Boston, November 9 and 10, 1872*, Arthur Wellington Brayley, *A Complete History of the Boston Fire Department...from 1630 to 1888*, and Annie Haven Thwing's *The crooked & narrow streets of the town of Boston 1630–1822*.

Chapter 6: As the most famous Puritan in American history, Cotton Mather is often remembered as either a witch-hunter or a scold. To consider his openness to new religious and cultural influences, I consulted texts including *The Life and Times of Cotton Mather*, by Abijah Perkins Marvin (1892), and Kenneth Silverman's biography of the same name, published ninety-two years later. Except where noted, the Cotton Mather quotations used throughout are from his journals (*The Diary of Cotton Mather 1681–1724*), which he kept obsessively throughout his life, even during smallpox epidemics.

Chapter 7: To set the scene of this summit between British colonists and the Iroquois, I relied largely on Witham Marshe, who provided a play-by-play of the Lancaster Treaty as it unfolded in his *Journal of the Treaty at Lancaster in 1744, with the Six Nations*. Also useful, though it was written more than a century after the fact, is the 1876 biography of the translator Conrad Weiser, *The life of (John) Conrad Weiser, the German pioneer, patriot, and patron of two races*, by Clement Zwingli Weiser. For overviews of Native American religious ideas and their influence on the Six Nations Confederacy and governance, I turned to older sources including Cadwallader Colden's *The History of the Five Indian Nations of Canada* (1727), Elias Johnson's *Legends, Traditions and Laws, of the Iroquois, Or Six Nations, and History of the Tuscarora Indians* (1881), and David Cusick's *Sketches of Ancient History of the Six Nations Comprising First a Tale of the Foundation of the Great Island (now North America), the Two Infants Born and the Creation of the Universe* (1848), as well as more recent scholarship including *The History and Culture of Iroquois Diplomacy: An Interdisciplinary Guide to the Treaties of the Six Nations and Their League*, edited by Francis Jennings et al. (1985), and William Fenton's *The Great Law and the Longhouse: A Political History of the Iroquois Confederacy* (1998). While the scholars behind the "Iroquois influence theory" make a case for a more direct connection between the governance of the Six

Nations and the early American republic than I claim here, I am nonetheless indebted to their work for pointing me in the direction of primary sources, including Benjamin Franklin's autobiography, the Lancaster Treaty, and the writings of Conrad Weiser. Bruce E. Johansen's *Forgotten Founders: How the American Indian Helped Shape Democracy* (1982) was a particularly useful resource, as were two attempts to challenge "Iroquois influence" claims, Philip Levy's "Exemplars of Taking Liberties: The Iroquois Influence Thesis and the Problem of Evidence," *The William and Mary Quarterly*, 3rd Ser., Volume 53, Number 3 (July 1996), 588–604; and Elisabeth Tooker's "The United States Constitution and the Iroquois League," in *The Invented Indian: Cultural Fictions and Government Policies* (1990), edited by James A. Clifton, 107–128.

Chapter 8: A good overview of the relationship of the European Enlightenment to early American varieties of theism, deism, and atheism can be found in James Turner's *Without God, Without Creed: The Origins of Unbelief in America* (1985). Details concerning the Livingston family and Livingston Manor are from *The Livingstons of Livingston manor; being the history of that branch of the Scottish house of Callendar which settled in the English province of New York during the reign of Charles the Second; and also including an account of Robert Livingston of Albany, "The nephew," a settler in the same province and his principal descendants* (1910). The work of Livingston and his colleagues was discussed by Philip G. Davidson in "Whig Propagandists of the American Revolution," *The American Historical Review* 39, no. 3 (April 1934): 442–53, and their rabble-rousing writings were republished as *The Independent Reflector Or, Weekly Essays on Sundry Important Subjects More Particularly Adapted to the Province of New York* by Harvard University Press in 1963.

Chapter 9: The role of religion in the birth of the United States has been a much discussed topic in the last decade, inspiring popular books including Steven Waldman's *Founding Faith* (2008), which begins with an entertaining description of the mammoth cheese delivered to Jefferson, Thomas S. Kidd's *God of Liberty* (2010), and John Fea's *Was America Founded as a Christian Nation?* (2011). Mark Noll's *America's God: From Jonathan Edward to Abraham Lincoln* (2002) puts the role of religion in the revolution in the broader context of the "collapse" of Puritanism and the "surge" of new denominations.

While each of these recent books considers the varieties of Christianity at large on the eve of Independence, the late scholar and rabbi Jacob Rader Marcus remains the best source for the history of Jews in the colonial period and the early United States. His collection *Jews and the American Revolution: A Bicentennial Documentary* (1975) provides primary sources related to Jonas Philips, Chaim Solomon, and other Jews who contributed to the cause of liberty. Histories of the Jews of St. Eustatius consulted include Samuel Kurinsky's article "The Jews of St. Eustatius: Rescuers of the American Revolution"; Barbara Tuchman's *The First Salute* (1988); and the original teller of this tale, J. Franklin Jameson, whose short but thorough account, "St. Eustatius in the American Revolution" (*American Historical Review* 8, no. 4 [July 1903]), set a high bar for all scholarship concerning these events. An overview of the influences of Jewish struggle for rights in the British colonies can be found in *Search Out the Land*, by Sheldon and Judy Godfrey, and *The Settlement of the Jews in North America*, by Charles Daly (1893).

Chapter 10: Both the War of 1812 and the ensuing disagreement over Jefferson's library played out in the early American press in as close to real time as early nineteenth-century printing technology allowed. My primary sources for this discussion of both conflicts were the headlines of the day. William Dawson Johnston's 1904 *History of the Library of Congress* provided context for considering early disagreements over the collection in light of the essential institution it would become.

Chapter 11: This chapter could not have been completed without the efforts of Yale University's Ala Alryyes to put Omar ibn Said once again before the public through his *A Muslim American Slave: The Life of Omar Ibn Said* (2011) and the pioneering work of Allan Austin's *African Muslims in Antebellum America: Transatlantic Stories and Spiritual Struggles* (1997). Timothy Marr's *The Cultural Roots of American Islamicism* (2006) provides insights into the uses of Islam by the abolitionists in the decades leading up to the Civil War. Except where noted, all quotations from Omar ibn Said are from Alyyres's recent translation.

Chapter 12: Mary Moody Emerson's story is best told through her own writing, particularly her correspondence with Ralph Waldo

Emerson and other family members as collected in *The Selected Letters of Mary Moody Emerson*, edited by Nancy Craig Simmons (1993). See also *Mary Moody Emerson and the Origins of Transcendentalism: A Family History*, by Phyllis Cole (1998). Diana Eck's *A New Religious America* (2001) provides another view of the literary moment she calls the " 'easting' of old New England' " and of the arrival of Swami Vivekananda at the 1893 Parliament of the World's Religions in Chicago.

Chapter 13: This chapter seeks to put into conversation two histories: the decline of the culture that had produced the Six Nations, and the rise of Mormonism. For the former, Anthony Wallace's *Death and Rebirth of the Seneca* is essential reading. The recent explosion in scholarship on earlier Mormonism includes John G. Turner's *Brigham Young: Pioneer Prophet* (2012) and Richard Lyman Bushman's *Joseph Smith: Rough Stone Rolling* (2005). For connecting these strains of scholarship, I am indebted to Lori Taylor's doctoral dissertation, "Telling Stories About Mormons and Indians" (State University of New York at Buffalo, 2000), as well as to Richard Brodhead's article "Prophets in America Circa 1930: Ralph Waldo Emerson, Nat Turner, Joseph Smith" — in *Joseph Smith Jr.: Reappraisals After Two Centuries*, edited by Reid L. Neilson and Terryl L. Givens (2008) — which positions both the founder of Mormonism and the author of the Code of Handsome Lake within a broader spectrum of mid-nineteenth-century religious figures. The section on Quaker activity in Cornplanter's Village is informed by Jill Kinney's doctoral dissertation, "Letters, Pen, and Tilling the Field: Quaker Schools Among the Seneca Indians on the Allegany River, 1798–1852" (University of Rochester, 2009), as well as the journal of the Quaker missionary Henry Simmons, as presented by David Swatzler's *A Friend Among the Seneca* (2000).

Chapter 14: This chapter relies largely on contemporary press reports, which displayed a fascination with the exploding Chinese subculture in San Francisco throughout the second half of the nineteenth century. I am grateful to the Chinese in North America Research Committee for confirming that the 1852 temple dedication I discovered during an archival search is among the earliest surviving records of Chinese religious activity in the United States. Missionary literature of the time, particularly Otis Gibson's *The*

Chinese in America (1877), also provides a view of immigrant life. Such sources are unfortunately biased and must be read critically, but they nonetheless preserve details that might otherwise have been lost. For a good sampling of primary source materials related to the arrival of the Chinese and other Asian immigrants in the United States, see *Asian Religions in America: A Documentary History* (1999), edited by Thomas A. Tweed and Stephen Prothero.

Chapter 15: The Asian American Curriculum and Research Project of Western Washington University's Woodring College of Education (http://www.wce.wwu.edu/Resources/AACR/) is an excellent source of images and documents related to the mistreatment of Sikhs in Bellingham, and the lives of Indian immigrants in the Pacific Northwest generally. Materials related to Bhagat Singh Thind's life, career, and legal struggle for citizenship can also be found online, thanks to the foundation established in his name (http://www.bhagatsinghthind.com/). Thind's autobiography, *House of Happiness*, which provided the anecdotes about his life and teaching career, was republished in 2006.

Chapter 16: The primary source for the memorial service sections of this chapter was Reverend Fujimura's memoir, *Though I Be Crushed* (1985). He describes the funeral he performed for two Japanese American soldiers of the 442nd Combat Regiment on pages 97–99. While Fujimura's recollections never venture intentionally from the historical record, it is important to note that he seems to have made a mistake in recalling the names of the two service members killed in action, whom he remembered as "Privates Yamamoto and Shiomitsu." Records of both the Poston Relocation Center and the 442nd show that there was no Shiomitsu held at Poston or killed in action during the time of the internment. However, these same records show that a Joe Shiomichi (the only name close to Shiomitsu among Poston servicemen killed in action) did die at the time the memorial service suggests. Shiomichi's daughter, Ryoko Shiomichi Thomas, born after her father died in 1944, published letters he sent home from the front sixty years later in a booklet titled "A Guy Named Joe." The journalist Vanessa De La Torre wrote a short feature about those letters for the *Imperial Valley Press* in 2004 (" 'Relocated' idealist lived—and died—devoutly 'pro-American,' " July 5, 2004). Information about the other memorialized service member,

John Yamamoto, can be found in writings by his sister, Hisaye Yamamoto, including the collection *Seventeen Syllables and Other Stories*, originally published in 1988. Other general sources include Alexander Leighton's classic 1946 book on the Poston camp, *The Governing of Men: General Principles and Recommendations Based on Experience at a Japanese Relocation Center*, Robert Asahina's *Just Americans: How Japanese Americans Won a War at Home and Abroad* (2006), James C. McNaughton's *Nisei Linguists: Japanese Americans in the Intelligence Service During World War II* (2006), and a number of articles by the scholar Duncan Ryuken Williams, including "From Pearl Harbor to 9/11: Lessons from the Internment of Japanese-American Buddhists," in *A Nation of Religions: The Politics of Pluralism in Multireligious America* (2006), edited by Stephen Prothero, and "Camp Dharma: Japanese-American Buddhist Identity and the Internment Experience of World War II," in *Westward Dharma: Buddhism Beyond Asia* (2002), edited by Charles S. Prebish and Martin Baumann.

Chapter 17: For details related to Michael Bowen's studio and Haight-Ashbury in 1967, I am indebted to Jane Kramer's classic *New Yorker* profile of Allen Ginsberg ("Paterfamilias," August 24, 1968) as well as to photographs found in Gene Anthony's *The Summer of Love* (1980), and in unpublished chapters of Bowen's memoir, *My Odyssey*, made available to me by his student Mark Walker. I am grateful to John Starr Cooke's son Chamba for taking the time to talk with me about his father and his eventful family life, and to other scholars who have explored the elder Cooke's legacy, including Eliza F. Kent, who discussed the relationship of Bowen and Cooke as part of a presentation given at the American Academy of Religion Conference in 2011 ("California Hinduism: The Shiva Linga of Golden Gate Park, 1989–1994," November 23, 2011), and Camelia Elias, who has considered Cooke's relationship to Theosophy ("Gone with the Wind of Tarot: John Starr Cooke and the Esoteric Tradition in the West," unpublished at the time of this writing). I am also indebted to other writers who have noted William Burroughs's fascination with Scientology, including John Lardas Modern, who discusses the religion of various Beats in *The Bop Apocalypse* (2000), and Lee Konstantinou, who wrote of the Burroughs-Hubbard connection for the science fiction website io9. com ("William S. Burroughs' Wild Ride with Scientology," May 11, 2011). Quotes related to the attempted levitation of the Pentagon are from Norman Mailer's *The Armies of the Night,* originally published in *Harper's* and *Commentary,* and the oral history of the event assembled by Larry "Ratso" Sloman, Michael Simmons, and Jay Babcock, "OUT, DEMONS, OUT!" for *Arthur* (November 2004).

Chapter 18: The notion that presidential inaugural addresses serve as secular sermons to the nation was proposed nearly fifty years ago by the sociologist Robert Bellah, who regarded such public displays of patriotic devotion as bellwethers of the phenomenon he called "American civil religion." His seminal essay by a similar name, "Civil Religion in America," first written in 1966, was republished more recently in the collection *Beyond Belief: Essays on Religion in a Post-Traditionalist World* (1991). Writing in the long shadow of the Kennedy assassination, Bellah focused on the inaugural address of 1961 and found in it expressions of the ways in which religious language can both unite and divide the nation. The same might be said of Barack Obama's 2009 inaugural address, and many of his other uses of religious language, such as those found in his 1995 memoir *Dreams from My Father* and in *The Audacity of Hope,* published in 2006. The descriptions of El Santuario de Chimayo in the early twentieth century with which the chapter concludes can be found in Le Baron Bradford Prince's *Spanish Mission Churches of New Mexico* (1915). I witnessed firsthand—and took part in—the collaboration necessary to fill the sacred hole when I visited the church in the spring of 2002.

The specific sources for materials quoted throughout the text are as follows:

Notes to pages 9–27 [Chapter 1]

"a race of men wearing clothes": Peter Martyr D'Anghera, *De Orbe Novo: The Eight Decades of Peter Martyr D'Anghera,* translated from the Latin with Notes and Introduction by Francis Augustus MacNutt (New York: G. P. Putnam's Sons, 1912), Book 9.

"to trample the head of their enemies": Jacques Bouton, *Relation de l'establissement des francois depuis l'an 1635 en l'isle de la Martinique* (1640), quoted in Bernard Grunberg, "An Ethnohistorical Approach of the Carib through Written Sources," in Corinne Lisette Hofman et al., *Communities in Contact: Essays in Archaeology, Ethnohistory & Ethnography of the Amerindian Circum-Caribbean* (Leiden: Sidestone Press, 2011), 339.

"the death apple": For more on this dangerous tree, see, for example, *The Wilderness Medicine Newsletter,* "Toxins #1—The Manchineel Tree," online at http://wildernessmedicinenewsletter.wordpress.com/2006/12/18/toxins-1-the-manchineel-tree/.

"Moor's last sigh": An account of the Muslim evacuation of Alhambra can be found in James Reston Jr., *Dogs of God: Columbus, the Inquisition, and the Defeat of the Moors* (New York: Random House, 2006), 241–43.

"the countries of India and of a Prince, called Great Can, which in our language signifies King of Kings": *Personal narrative of the first voyage of Columbus to America: from a manuscript recently discovered in Spain* (Boston: Thomas B. Wait and Son, 1827), 9.

"murmur": Christopher Columbus, "Journal of the First Voyage of Columbus," in *The Northmen, Columbus and Cabot 985–1503: Original Narratives of Early American History,* edited by Julius E. Olson and Edward Gaylord Bourne (New York: Charles Scribner's Sons, 1906), 100.

"the image of America as a land unseen, unnamed and otherwise without mortal creator"; "transient glimpses of the new world"; "the sublime of humbuggery": Geraldine Barnes, *Viking America* (Woodbridge, Suffolk, UK: Boydell & Brewer, 2001), 48.

"There shall ye bury me…and set up crosses at my head and feet": *Saga of the Greenlanders,* available in various online editions, including https://notendur.hi.is/haukurth/utgafa/greenlanders.html.

"The going out of a Curious Man to explore the Regions of the Globe": A partial English translation of Idrisi's text can be found in *Other Routes: 1500 Years of African and Asian Travel Writing,* edited by Tabish Khair (Bloomington: Indiana University Press, 2006), 85–101. See also *The Geographical Lore of the Time of the Crusades: A Study in the History of Medieval Science and Tradition in Western Europe,* by John Kirtland Wright, PhD, Librarian (New York: American Geographical Society, 1925); and Stuart Peebles's unpublished paper "The First Braudel: The Mediterranean and Mediterranean World of al-Idrisi," May 11, 2013, available online at https://www.academia.edu/3568043/The_First_Braudel_The_Mediterannean_and_Mediterranean _World_of_al-Idrisi.

"certain intelligent men": Wright, 80.

"All grace goes back to Allah": Khair, 89.

"Gloomy Sea"; "No one knows what lies beyond it…": Peebles, 17.

"people with red skin"; "not much hair"; "extraordinarily beautiful": Quoted in Abbas Hamdani, "An Islamic Background to the Voyages of Discovery," in *The Legacy of Muslim Spain,* edited by Salma Khadra Jayyusi and Manuela Marín (Leiden: Brill, 1992), 276.

"the Earth is": Khair, 86.

"carried with them their books and sacred images and the ritual": Edward Payson Vining, *An Inglorious Columbus: Or, Evidence that Hwui Shan and a party of Buddhist monks from Afghanistan discovered America in the fifth century, a.d.* (New York: Appleton & Co., 1885), 42; see also Charles Leland, *Fusang, or The Discovery of America by Chinese Buddhist Priests in the Fifth Century* (1875).

"youthful indiscretions at which modern sinology is accustomed to blush": Joseph Needham and Gwei-Djen Lu, *Science and Civilisation in China: Physics and Physical Technology,* Volume 4 (Cambridge: Cambridge University Press, 1971), 540.

"Fourth Part of the World": The phrase first appears in Matthias Ringmann's *Cosmographiae Introductio* of 1507. For discussion of the religious implications of the medieval notions of the world divided into parts, see

Jonathan Z. Smith, "What a Difference Difference Makes," in *Relating Religion: Essays in the Study of Religion* (Chicago: University of Chicago Press, 2004).

"a wax candle rising and falling"; "Come see the men who have come from the heavens!": *Journal of the First Voyage of Columbus*, as summarized in Bartolomé de las Casas, *A Brief Account of the Destruction of the Indies Or, a faithful Narrative of the Horrid and Unexampled Massacres, Butcheries, and all manner of Cruelties, that Hell and Malice could invent, committed by the Popish Spanish Party on the inhabitants of West-India, TOGETHER With the Devastations of several Kingdoms in America by Fire and Sword, for the space of Forty and Two Years, from the time of its first Discovery by them*. Las Casas's text is available online from Project Gutenberg: https://archive.org/details/abriefaccountoft20321gut.

"It is hardly to be wondered": Albion Tourgee, *Out of the Sunset Sea* (New York: Merrill & Baker, 1893), 260.

"Come and see the men": *The Journal of Christopher Columbus* (London: Hakluyt Society, 1893) 41.

"I have already said": Kay Brigham, ed., *Libro de las Profecias de Colon* (Terrassa: Editorial Clie, 1992), 38.

"When the Spaniards landed the islanders then referred the prophecy to them": d'Anghiera, *De Orbe Novo*, Book 9.

"The Spaniards first assaulted the innocent Sheep"; "The Isle of Cuba": Las Casas, *Destruction of the Indies*, preface.

"In Honour and Reverence": Las Casas, *Destruction of the Indies*, "Of the Island Hispaniola."

"cruelly and wickedly inclined": Las Casas, *Destruction of the Indies*, "Of the Isle of Cuba."

"killing them in great numbers and reducing the others to such a state of despair": D'Anghera, *De Orbe Novo*, Book 8.

"Now will you yield good and abundant fruit?": *The relación of Fray Ramón Pane*, online at http://faculty.smu.edu/bakewell/BAKEWELL/texts/panerelacion.html.

"a profligate Christian attempted to devirginate the Maid"; "This Deep, Bloody American Tragedy is now concluded": Las Casas, *Destruction of the Indies*.

"Shalom...A salaam aleichem": The notion that Columbus's translator used Hebrew during his encounter with the New World is included in the opening chapter of a 1920 book of historical vignettes for Jewish School children (Elma Levinger, *The New Land: Stories of Jews Who Had a Part in the Making of Our Country* [New York: Bloch Publishing Co., 1920]) and in the newsletter of a Jewish American veterans association in 1938, and was used as a punch line by the comedian and performance artist Susan Mogul in the 1970s. Mel Brooks took the seeming incongruity of this early American use of a Jewish language one step further by making his *Blazing Saddles* Indians speak Yiddish.

Notes to pages 29–56 [Chapter 2]

"Mustafa Zemmourri": This chapter's main figure is more commonly known by the names Esteban or Estanbanico, as he is called in various Spanish *relaciónes*. I have chosen to refer to him primarily as "Zemmouri" because it refers to all those from Azemmour and takes into account his identity before his enslavement and the loss of the religious tradition into which he was born.

"the king sent another navy of two hundred sail": Leo Africanus, *History and Description of Africa*, Volume 2, quoted in Chouki El Hamel, *Black Morocco: A History of Slavery, Race, and Islam* (New York: Cambridge University Press, 2013), 141.

Magellan in Azemmour: Laurence Bergreeen, *Over the Edge of the World* (New York: HarperCollins, 2009), 19.

murabits within the ramparts: For a description of Muslim fortifications in Morocco, see Martin M. Elbl, "Portuguese Urban Fortifications in Morocco," in *City Walls: The Urban Enceinte in Global Perspective*, edited by James D. Tracy (New York: Cambridge University Press, 2009), 357.

"In the year 734": E. G. Ravenstein, *Martin Behaim: His Life and His Globe* (London, 1908), 77.

"He wore the mark of a saber slash across his face": For more on Dorante's appearance and biography see Andrés Reséndez, *A Land So Strange: The Epic Journey of Cabeza de Vaca* (New York: Basic Books, 2007), 50.

Requerimiento: There are several extant versions of the Spanish Requirement. The one likely used by the Narváez Expedition can be found in Ralph Emerson Twitchell, *The Leading Facts of New Mexican History*, Volume 1 (Cedar Rapids: The Torch Press, 1917), 61–63, and is also partially quoted in Paul Schneider, *Brutal Journey: Cabeza de Vaca and the Epic First Crossing of North America* (New York: Macmillan, 2007), 83–84. The original version of the text used here is quoted in John Tillotson's *The Golden Americas* (London: Ward, Lock & Tyler, 1869), 35.

"remarkable document": Twitchell, 61.

"after we had eaten the dogs": *The Journey of Alvar Nunez Cabeza de Vaca, Translated from his own Narrative*, by Fanny Bandelier (New York: Williams Barker Co., 1904), 114.

"One-third of our people were dangerously ill": Ibid, 35.

"stirrups, spurs, cross-bows": Ibid., 35.

"The rest of us, as naked as we had been born": Ibid., 57.

"The men have one of their nipples perforated": Ibid., 64.

"Upon seeing the disaster we had suffered"; "When the lament was over": Ibid., 58.

"Arabic terms have been found": Ana Marcos Maíllo, "Los Arabismos Más Utilizados por los Conquistadores de Nueve España en el Sigle XVI," *Res Diachronicae* 2 (2003): 228–35.

a la manera de albornoces moriscos"; "*muy bien vestidas*": Quoted in Mailo, 229. See also Bernal Díaz del Castillo, *Historia verdadera de la conquista de la Nueva España*, Volume 2 (Oficina tipográfica de la secretaría de fomento, 1905), 165.

"*la zambra de los moros*": Quoted by Mailo, 229. See also Francisco López de Gómara, *Historia de Mexico* (1554), 107

"married or betrothed through the rite and custom of the Moors": For an example of an Edict of Faith targeting Muslims, see Helen Rawlings, *The Spanish Inquisition* (Hoboken: John Wiley & Sons, 2008), 77.

"these Moors": Quoted in John Huxtable Elliott, *Spain, Europe and the Wider World, 1500–1800* (New Haven, CT: Yale University Press, 2009), 194.

"military and political ritual"; "The first formal step of jihad": Patricia Seed, *Ceremonies of Possession in Europe's Conquest of the New World, 1492–1640* (New York: Cambridge University Press, 1995), 69–99.

For more on Cortés's tendency to use Islamic terms, see D. A. Brading, *The First America: The Spanish Monarchy, Creole Patriots and the Liberal State, 1492–1866* (Cambridge: Cambridge University Press, 1993), 26.

mound-building cultures: The description of precolonial American cities here is informed by the prologue to Daniel K. Richter's *Facing East from Indian Country* (Cambridge, MA: Harvard University Press, 2001), 1–10.

"were there made slaves": "Joint Report" of Cabeza de Vaca, Andrés Dorantes de Carranza, and Alonso de Castillo in *Cabeza de Vaca's Adventures in the Unknown Interior of America* (Albuquerque: University of New Mexico Press, 1983), 77.

"On the Island I have spoken of": Cabeza De Vaca, 68.

"The way we treated the sick": Ibid., 70.

"It was the negro": Ibid., 158.

"at dances, or as medicine," Ibid., 129.

"land of Christians": Ibid., 135.

"A hawkbell of copper": Ralph Emerson Twitchell, *The Leading Facts of New Mexican History*, Volume 1, (Cedar Rapids: Torch Press, 1911), 97.

"pearls and great riches on the coast": Annual Report of the Bureau of American Ethnology to the Secretary of the Smithsonian Institution, Volume 14, Part 1 (U.S. Government Printing Office, 1896), 350.

"land of Christians": Cabeza de Vaca, 135.

"large and powerful villages, four and five stories high": Pedro Reyes Castañeda, *The Journey of Coronado: 1540–1542* (Washington, D.C.: U.S. Government Printing Office, 1896), 474.

"I sent Estéban de Dorantes"; "a very large cross"; and other quotes from the account of Friar Marcos: *The Journey of Fray Marcos de Niza* (Dallas: Southern Methodist University Press, 1987), 28–36.

"It seems that, after the friars": Castañeda, 474.

"Marabout are assumed to have mystical powers…": Donald Martin Carter, *States of Grace: Senegalese in Italy and the New European Immigration* (Minneapolis: University of Minnesota Press, 1997), 94.

"a black man with a beard, wearing things that sounded, rattles, bells, and plumes, on his feet and arms": Smithsonian Institution, *Annual Report of the Bureau of Ethnology*, Volume 14, Part 1 (1896).

"lived on among the Zunis for many years, finally dying an old deity"; "placed him flat on his back and worshipped him as a god": Quoted in Hsain Ilahiane, "Estevan de Dorantes, the Moor or the Slave? The Other Moroccan Explorer of New Spain," *Journal of North African Studies* 5, no. 3 (Autumn 2000): 1–14.

Beginning in 1680: For more on the Pueblo Revolt see David Roberts, *The Pueblo Revolt: The Secret Rebellion That Drove the Spaniards Out of the Southwest* (New York: Simon & Schuster, 2008). Popé's revival of the suppressed kachina dance is described on page 140.

"holy war": Robert Silverberg, *The Pueblo Revolt* (Lincoln: University of Nebraska Press, 1994), 114.

"The general in command, Francisco Vazquez Coronado rode at the head of some two hundred and fifty horsemen": Winship's introduction to Pedro Reyes Castañeda, *The Journey of Coronado: 1540–1542* (New York: A. S. Barnes & Co., 1904), vii.
"I always notice": Castañeda, 472.

Notes to pages 59–79 [Chapter 3]

"Now the only way to avoid this shipwreck": John Winthrop, "A Model of Christian Charity," online at http://religiousfreedom.lib.virginia.edu/ sacred/charity.html.
A layman and a lawyer: For more on the ambivalent influence of legal thinking on Winthrop's lay sermon and Puritan mindset, see Andrew Delbanco, *The Puritan Ordeal* (Cambridge, MA: Harvard University Press, 1991), 68–80. Delbanco notes Winthrop's sermon is often seen as a starting point, "enshrined as a kind of Ur-text of American literature" (72).
"a bulwark against the kingdom of Anti-Christ"; "God hath provided"; "this land grows weary": John Winthrop, "Arguments for the Plantation of New England," *Winthrop Papers V*, Massachusetts Historical Society.
"recent biographers have noted": See Francis J. Bremer, *John Winthrop: America's Forgotten Founding Father* (New York: Oxford University Press, 2003), 174–175.
"delighted to show forth"; "high and eminent"; "The work we have in hand"; "But if our hearts shall turn": Winthrop, "A Model of Christian Charity."
"the leader and standard-bearer of an impious and abominable kingdom": John Calvin, *Institutes of the Christian Religion*, chapter 7. Electronic edition available through the Christian Classics Ethereal Library: www.ccel.org/ ccel/calvin/institutes.
"infected both heaven and earth": Théodore de Bèze, *The Life of John Calvin* (Philadelphia: J. Wenthem, 1836), 60.
"Whoever shall now contend that it is unjust to put heretics and blasphemers to death": Quoted in "Calvin's Defence of the Death Penalty for Heretics," topic 157, in *History of the Christian Church, Volume VIII: Modern Christianity, the Swiss Reformation*, edited by Philip Schaff (Grand Rapids: Eerdmans, 1984).
"After we had escaped the cruel hands of persecuting prelates": Thomas Weld, preface to *A Short Story of the Rise, Reign, and Ruine of the Antinomians, Familists & Libertines* (1644).
"The chief occasion was...the much sickness of pox and fevers"; "The devil would never cease to disturb our peace"; "good esteem for godliness"; "the poorer sort of people": John Winthrop, *The History of New England from 1630 to 1649* (Boston: Phelps and Farnham, 1825), 284.
"a man godly and zealous": William Bradford, quoted in *Annals of New England*, Part II, Sec. 2 (Boston: Collections of the Massachusetts Historical Society, 1826), 48.
"the said opinions were adjudged by all": John Winthrop, *The History of New England from 1630 to 1649* (Boston: Phelps and Farnham, 1825), 162–63.
"From Adam and Noah that they spring": This and following Williams quotes from "To Dear and Welcome Friends and Countrymen," republished by Narragansett Club, in *Publications*, Volume 1 (Providence, 1866).

"a woman of a ready wit and bold spirit": Winthrop, *The History of New England from 1630 to 1649*, 200.

"The last and worst of all": Weld, preface to *A Short Story of the Rise, Reign, and Ruine*.

"a very proper and fair woman...notoriously infected with Mrs. Hutchinson's errors"; "a monster...a fish, a beast, and a fowl"; "It was of ordinary bigness"; "When it died in the mother's body": Winthrop, *The History of New England from 1630 to 1649*, 261–62.

"thirty monstrous births": Weld, preface to *A Short Story of the Rise, Reign, and Ruine*.

"troubled the peace of the commonwealth and the churches here," and all following dialogue between Hutchinson and her interrogators: "The Examination of Mrs. Anne Hutchinson at the Court at Newton. 1637," online at http://www.constitution.org/primarysources/hutchinson.html.

Notes to pages 81–97 [Chapter 4]

"described as 'black'": Statements found in the Maryland State Archives suggest that Lumbrozo may have been a Jew of North African descent. See, for example, the note at the bottom of the biographical sketch found online at http://msa.maryland.gov/megafile/msa/speccol/sc3500/sc3520/014000/014037/html/14037bio.html.

For details on the kinds of enticements offered to physicians to settle in colonial Maryland, see "Land Notes: 1634–1655," *Maryland Historical Magazine* 6 (1911): 65.

"customary usury"; "present indigence"; "Such hateful enemies": Peter Stuyvesant, "Petition to Expel the Jews from New Amsterdam," September 22, 1654, in *The Jew in the Modern World*, edited by Paul Mendes-Flohr and Yehuda Reinharz (New York: Oxford University Press, 1995), 452.

"We would have liked": "Reply to Stuyvesant's Petition," *The Jew in the Modern World*, 453.

"No man shall raise or bring forward any question or argument on the subject of religion": Esther Singleton, *Dutch New York* (New York: Dodd, Mead, and Co., 1909), 187.

"His Lordship requires his said Governor & Commissioners": Percy G. Skirven, *The First Parishes of the Province of Maryland* (Baltimore: Norman Remington, 1923), 7.

"the linens were lost": Harry Wright Newman, *The Flowering of the Maryland Palatinate* (Washington, 1961), 39.

"Upon the whole, they cultivate generous minds": Andrew White, *Relatio Itineris in Marilandiam; Relation of the Colony of the Lord Baron of Baltimore* (1847), 23.

"It was informed the governour": Winthop, *The History of New England from 1630 to 1649*, 136.

"The only spot on the earth where the principle of Live and Let Live was the law of the land": Hester Dorsey Richardson, *Sidelights on Maryland History* (Baltimore: Williams and Wilkins, 1903), 75.

"Bee it therefore ordayned": Maryland's Act Concerning Religion, quoted in Richard H. Clarke, "Maryland or Rhode Island...Which Was First?" *American Catholic Quarterly Review*, Volume XX (Philadelphia: Charles Hardy, 1895), 292.

"beguile or deceive": Archives of Maryland, Volume 1, edited by William Hand Browne, Clayton Colman Hall, and Bernard Christian Steine (Baltimore: Maryland Historical Society, 1883), 360–62.

"His disciples stole him away": This and other quotes from the proceedings against Jacob Lumbrozo come from court documents and biographical details collected in the Maryland state archives.

"The Lord said": Exodus 7:8–12.

"I doe hereby pardon & acquit": Quoted in J. H. Hollander, "Some Unpublished Material Relating to Dr. Jacob Lumbrozo, of Maryland," *Publications of the American Jewish Historical Society*, No. 1 (Philadelphia, 1905), 39.

"to extend to the sect of people": An image of Maryland's "Jew Bill" of 1826 appears in Lauren R. Silberman, *The Jewish Community of Baltimore* (Charleston: Arcadia Publishing, 2008), 14.

Notes to pages 99–117 [Chapter 5]

"the greatest fire that ever happened in Boston": Robert C. Winthrop, quoted in R. H. Conwell, *History of the Great Fire in Boston* (Boston: B. B. Russell, 1873), 32.

"Lost-town": Cotton Mather noted Boston was so called "for the mean and sad circumstance of it." *Magnalia Christi Americana, Or, The Ecclesiastical History of New-England: From Its First Planting, in the Year 1620, Unto the Year of Our Lord 1698.* Volume 1. (Hartford: S. Andrus and Son, 1855), 91.

"a grand triumph"; "grand climax": Arthur Wellington Brayley, *A Complete History of the Boston Fire Department* (Boston: John P. Dale, 1889), 16.

"provoked the Lord to bring His Judgments on New-England": Increase Mather, quoted in Williston Walker, *The Creeds and Platforms of Congregationalism* (Boston, 1893), 423–31.

"Ah, Boston! Thou hast seen the vanity of all worldly possessions": Cotton Mather, *Magnalia Christi Americana*, 104.

"That God hath a Controversy" and quotes following are from Increase Mather's classic jeremiad of 1679, available online at http://www.swarthmore.edu/SocSci/bdorsey1/41docs/34-jer.html.

"Tattuba"; "Negroes Stock Cattle and Utensils": quoted in Elaine Breslaw, *Tituba: Reluctant Witch of Salem* (New York: New York University Press, 1996), 24.

"in which with their various instruments"; "victuals and strong liquor": Elizabeth A. McAlister, *Rara!: Vodou, Power, and Performance in Haiti and Its Diaspora*, Volume 1 (Berkeley: University of California Press, 2002), 32.

"direct, expresse, presumptuous or high handed Blasphemie": "Body of Liberties" (1641); *American Historical Documents: 1000–1904* (New York: P. F. Collier & Son, 1910), 84.

"It was not any worldly consideration that brought our Fathers into this wilderness, but Religion": Increase Mather, quoted in Williston Walker, *The Creeds and Platforms of Congregationalism* (Boston, 1893), 423–31.

"not having the fear of God before her eyes and being instigated by the devil": *Witch-Hunting in Seventeenth-Century New England: A Documentary History, 1638–1693*, edited by David D. Hall (Durham, NC: Duke University Press, 2005), 261.

"The Indians, in their wars with us, finding sore inconvenience in our dogs": Cotton Mather, *Magnalia Christi Americana*; also quoted in William Scranton Simmons, *Spirit of the New England Tribes: History and Folklore, 1620–1984* (Lebanon, NH: University Press of New England, 1986), 54.

"devilish idolatry": William Hubbard, *A Narrative of the Indian Wars in New-England* (Stockbridge: Heman Willard: 1893), 59.

"they have learned from the Prince of Darkness": Ibid., 334.

"diabolical miscreant": Ibid, 355.

"Some young persons through a vain calamity to know their future condition": John Hale, *A Modest Inquiry into the Nature of Witchcraft* (Boston: Benjamin Eliot, 1702), 132–33.

"I knew a man in the East"; "those that ignorantly use charms": Ibid.

"It is altogether undeniable that our great and blessed God": Reverend Parris's sermon, quoted in Charles Upham, *Salem Witchcraft, with an Account of Salem Village and A History of Opinions on Witchcraft and Kindred Subjects* (Boston: Wiggin and Lunt, 1867), 95.

"Tituba, what evil spirit have you familiarity with?": This and the following dialogue can be found in the transcript of Tituba's examination online at http://salem.lib.virginia.edu/texts/tei/swp?div_id=n125.

"improvised a new idiom of resistance": Breslaw, 117.

"fictional depictions of Tituba's life": Dramatic interpretations of the events in Salem include Arthur Miller's *The Crucible* (1953) and its various screen adaptations (1957 and 1996), Maryse Condé's *I, Tituba: Black Witch of Salem* (1986), Ann Petry's *Tituba of Salem Village* (1964), and, most recently, the television drama *Salem* (2014).

"did much to preserve African ideas": Jeffrey Anderson, *Conjure in African American Society* (Baton Rouge: Louisiana State University Press, 2008), 68.

"Jack beat de Devil"; "the great human culture hero of Negro folklore": Zora Neale Hurston, *Mules and Men* (New York: Knopf, 1935), 237.

"If you think you are hoodooed": Harry Middleton Hyatt, *Folk-lore from Adams County, Illinois* (New York: Alma Egan Hyatt Foundation, 1935), 543.

"Conjurelike practices": Anderson, 158.

"Why do people go to Lourdes?": *Miami Herald*, April 9, 1995.

Notes to pages 119–142 [Chapter 6]

"Cotton Mather was afraid": This account of Mather's fears concerning the coming of smallpox to Boston relies on the *Diary of Cotton Mather, 1681–1708* (Boston: Massachusetts Historical Society, 1911).

"venomous, contagious, loathsome Chambers": Ibid., 451.

"daily celebrated and multiplied": Ibid., 365.

"How often have there been Bills desiring Prayers": Cotton Mather, *Magnalia Christi Americana, Or, The Ecclesiastical History of New England* (Hartford: S. Andrus and Son, 1855), 92.

"Now the Small Pox": *Diary of Cotton Mather*, 443.

"Thou shalt have no other god but me": Exodus 20:3.

"the town could be made too Hot for these Dangerous Transgressors": Mather, *Magnalia Christi Americana*, 99.

"sore throat, and such tremor, and such dolor, and such danger of choking, and
such exhaustion of strength": Abijah Perkins Marvin, *The Life and Times of
Cotton Mather; Or, A Boston Minister of Two Centuries Ago, 1663–1728* (Boston:
Congregational Sunday-School and Publishing Society, 1892), 228.
"The dreadful Disease, which is raging in the Neighbourhood": *Diary of
Cotton Mather,* 445.
"divinatory"; "Unto my Amazement": Ibid., 446.
"There was a certain nobleman": John 4:46.
"I saw, that the whole Bible afforded not a more agreeable or profitable Para-
graph": *Diary of Cotton Mather,* 446.
"my lovely consort...the desire of me eyes": Ibid., 447–48.
"Go then, my Dove": Ibid., 450.
"Has not the Death of my Consort": Ibid., 451.
"Was ever man more tempted"; "Sometimes, Temptations to Impurities":
Ibid., 475.
"This Day, a surprising Thing befel me": Ibid., 579.
"feare of famine"; "twenty negars"; "heathen...would surprise us": "The
General Historie of Virginia by Captain John Smith," in *Narratives of Early
Virginia, 1606–1625,* Volume 5, edited by Lyon Gardiner Tyler (New York:
Charles Scribner's Sons, 1946), 337.
"some cotton, and tobacco, and negroes, etc.": John Winthrop, *The History of New
England from 1630 to 1649* (New York: Charles Scribner's Sons, 1908), 260.
"Every man of or within this Jurisdiction": "Massachusetts Body of Liberties,"
in *American Historical Documents, 1000–1904,* 73.
"Every marryed woeman": Ibid., 61.
"Servants that have served": Ibid., 62.
"No man shall exercise any Tirranny": Ibid., 63.
"There shall never be any bond slaverie": Ibid., 62.
Boston slave population: According to a census taken in 1715, there were at that
time two thousand slaves in Massachusetts, with most living in Boston. See
Evarts Boutell Greene and Virginia Draper Harrington, *American Population
Before the Federal Census of 1790* (New York: Columbia University Council
for Research in the Social Sciences, 1932), 4. See also Douglas Harper,
"Slavery in the North" (online at http://slavenorth.com/massachusetts
.htm), and Edgar J. McManus, *Black Bondage in the North* (Syracuse: Syracuse
University Press, 1973), 14–15.
"The music consisted of two drums and a stringed instrument": Benjamin Henry
Latrobe, *The Journal of Latrobe* (New York: D. Appleton and Co., 1905), 180.
"a Negro of a promising Aspect and Temper": *Diary of Cotton Mather,* 579.
"without any Application of mine to them for such a Thing"; "that I wanted a good
Servant"; "Smile of Heaven"; "I putt upon him the Name of Onesimus": Ibid.
"I appeal to you for my child, Onesimus"; "Formerly he was useless to you":
Philemon 1:10 (Paul's Letter to Philemon).
"floods of tears"; "Who can tell, but that I have this day found an Onesimus?":
Diary of Cotton Mather, 272.
"more true *glory* in them": Mather, *Magnalia Christi Americana,* 29.
"Yes and no"; "Many months before": Quoted in George Kittredge, *Some Lost
Works of Cotton Mather* (Cambridge: Proceedings of the Massachusetts
Historical Society, 1912), 422.

"Guramantese": According to Walter Rucker, "The various terms Koromantyn, Coromantee, Corornantin, Korman-tine, Kromnantine, and Cormentine all refer to an important trading port located on the Gold Coast of Africa during the 17th and 18th centuries. The correct appellation, Kromantine, was the name of a key commercial region controlled by the Fante Kingdom of Efutu. Africans exported from this region of West Africa were principally Akan speakers." Walter Rucker, "Only Draw in Your Countrymen: Akan Culture and Community in Colonial New York City," *Afro-Americans in New York Life and History* 34 (July 2010): 76–118.

"ancient in the Kingdoms of Tripoli, Tunis and Algier": Cassem Algaida Aga, quoted in Arthur Boylston, "The Origins of Inoculation," *JLL Bulletin: Commentaries on the History of Treatment Evaluation,* 2012, online at http://www.jameslindlibrary.org/illustrating/articles/the-origins-of-inoculation.

"mixture of medicine and magic performed by Taoist healers and Buddhist monks": Ibid.

"If any man after legall conviction": "Massachusetts Body of Liberties" in *American Historical Documents, 1000–1904,* 84.

Babalu Aye: See Migene González-Wippler, *Santería: The Religion: a Legacy of Faith, Rites, and Magic* (New York: Harmony, 1989), 53.

"mass inoculations took on the character of a religious festival": Eugenia W. Herbert, "Smallpox Inoculation in Africa," *The Journal of African History* 16, no. 4 (1975): 548.

"upon the approach of the disorder"; "magic stick": quoted in Richard Pankhurst, "The History and Traditional Treatment of Smallpox in Ethiopia." *Medical History,* Volume 9, Number 04 (October 1965): 347.

"fetish woman"; "mallams": Herbert, 546.

"consternation and disorder": Zabdiel Boylston, *An historical account of the smallpox inoculated in New England upon all sorts of persons, whites, blacks, and of all ages and constitution,* 1726.

"great and visible decay of piety in the country": Mather, May 27, 1725, quoted in William Stevens Perry, ed., *Papers Relating to the History of the Church in Massachusetts, 1676–1785* (1873), 172.

"The Rest of the Practitioners": Cotton Mather, *The Angel of Bethesda,* in Otho T. Beall and Richard Harrison Shyrock, *Cotton Mather: The First Significant Figure in American Medicine* (Baltimore: Johns Hopkins University Press, 1954), 223.

"with the blessing of God": An account of Boylston's bladder stone surgery can be found in L. H. Toledo-Pereyra's "Zabdiel Boylston: First American Surgeon of the English Colonies in North America," *Journal of Investigative Surgery* 19, no. 1 (January–February 2006): 5–10.

"The vilest Arts were used": Mather, *The Angel of Bethesda,* 113.

"I have since mett with a considerable Number of these Africans": *Some Lost Works of Cotton Mather,* 431.

"I don't know why 'tis more unlawful to learn of Africans, how to help against the Poison of the Small Pox": Ibid., 430.

"the hero in this farce of calumny": William Douglas, *The abuses and scandals of some late pamphlets in favour of inoculation of the small pox, modestly obviated, and inoculation further consider'd in a letter to A- S-, M.D. & F.R.S., in London* (Boston: J. Franklin, 1722), introduction.

"Can they not give into the method or practice": *Boston Gazette*, July 31, 1721.

"A Dialogue between a Clergyman and a Layman Concerning Inoculation. By an Unknown Hand": *New-England Courant*, January 8, 1722.

"Some Negro Slaves here of ye Nations of Caramantee": Chaplain John Sharpe, quoted in Thelma Wills Foote, *Black and White Manhattan: The History of Racial Formation in Colonial New York City* (New York: Oxford University Press), 133.

"It was agreed to on New Years Day": Walter Rucker, "Only Draw in Your Countrymen: Akan Culture and Community in Colonial New York City," *Afro-Americans in New York Life and History* (July 2010); see also Rucker's *The River Flows On: Black Resistance, Culture, and Identity Formation in Early America* (Baton Rouge: Louisiana State University Press, 2006), 28.

"Cotton Mather, you dog, dam you! I'l inoculate you with this; with a pox to you": Abijah Perkins Marvin, *The Life and Times of Cotton Mather* (Boston: Congregational and Sunday-School Publishing Society, 1892), 480.

"Though we don't pray that it may not spread": Quoted in Perry Miller, *The New England Mind from Colony to Province* (Boston: Beacon Press, 1961), 363.

"There was no social niche for the infidel": Ibid., 363.

"My Servant Onesimus, proves wicked, and grows useless"; "Froward"; "Immorigerous"; "My Disposing of him": Cotton Mather, "Diary 1716," *Collections of the Massachusetts Historical Society* (Boston: Massachusetts Historical Society, 1912) 363.

"My servant Onesimus, having advanced a Summ": Ibid.

Notes to pages 145–164 [Chapter 7]

"great concourse of people": Witham Marshe, "Witham Marshe's Journal of the Treaty Held with the Six Nations," *Collections of the Massachusetts Historical Society for the Year 1800* (Boston: Charles C. Little and James Brown, 1846), 178.

"true Friends and Brothers": Society of Friends, *Some account of the conduct of the Religious Society of Friends towards the Indian tribes in the settlement of the colonies of East and West Jersey and Pennsylvania: with a brief narrative of their labours for the civilization and Christian instruction of the Indians, from the time of their settlement in America, to the year 1843*, London Yearly Meeting, Meeting for Sufferings, Aborigines' Committee, 1844.

"Among the ancients there were two worlds in existence"; "A large turtle came forward": David Cusick, *Sketches of the Ancient History of the Six Nation* (Lockport: Turner & McCollum, 1848), 13.

"very full chest, and brawny limbs": Marshe, 179.

"He who holds the reins": Henry Melchior Muhlenberg Richards, "The Weiser Family," *The Pennsylvania German Society, Proceedings and Addresses at Allentown, October 7, 1921* (Lancaster: Lancaster Press, 1924), 12.

"frightful": Marshe, 180.

"entrapped in the net of his own wisdom"; "We may term Conrad Weiser a sort of religious vagrant": Clement Zwingli Weiser, *The life of (John) Conrad Weiser, the German pioneer, patriot, and patron of two races* (Reading: Daniel Miller, 1876), 95, 142.

"If by the word of religion"; "for a journey of five hundred English miles"; We saw that if the Indian had slipped"; "extremely weak": Conrad Weiser, quoted in Robert Proud, *The History of Pennsylvania, in North America, from the Original Institution and Settlement of that Province* (Philadelphia: Z. Poulson, 1798), 316–18.

"An Indian came to us in the evening": Conrad Weiser, quoted in Israel Rupp, *History of the Counties of Berks and Lebanon* (Lancaster: G. Hills, 1844), 26.

"I have had occasion to be in council with them": Conrad Weiser, quoted in C. Z. Weiser, 140. In this letter "respecting the Indian's views on the subject of religion," Weiser seems to have borrowed from the writings of William Penn, to whom a similar quote is attributed in John Warner Barber's *The History and Antiquities of New England, New York, New Jersey, and Pennsylvania* (Hartford: Allyn S. Stillman & Son, 1856), 539.

"He began to sing with an awful solemnity": Weiser, quoted in Rupp, 207.

"charge and command them": Weiser, quoted in C. Z. Weiser, 141. These words, too, have also been attributed to William Penn.

"Dunkers nunnery": Marshe, 181.

"Our Great King of England, and His subjects": *Indian Treaties Printed by Benjamin Franklin, 1736–1762* (Philadelphia: The Historical Society of Pennsylvania, 1938), 48.

"What is one hundred years"; "You came out of the ground"; "Above One Hundred Years ago"; "By way of Reproach": Ibid., 51–52.

"We heartily recommend Union": Ibid., 78.

"Typically it had from three to five fires": William Nelson Fenton, *The Great Law and the Longhouse: A Political History of the Iroquois Confederacy* (Norman: University of Oklahoma Press, 1998), 23–24.

"It would be a very strange thing": Benjamin Franklin, "To James Parker," *The Writings of Benjamin Franklin*, Volume 3 (London: Macmillan, 1907), 42.

"A smith is more likely to influence them than a Jesuit," Ibid., 45

"a plan for the union of all the colonies under one government"; "Two gentlemen of great knowledge in public affairs": Benjamin Franklin, *The Autobiography of Benjamin Franklin* (New York: American Book Company, 1896), 147–48.

"When the first ship arrived here from Europe": Archibald Kennedy, *The Importance of Gaining and Preserving the Friendship of the Indians to the British Interest Considered* (London: E. Cave, 1752), 1.

"Being fortified by their approbation"; "appointed and supported by the crown"; "a grand council"; "In England it was judged"; "I am still of opinion": Franklin, *Autobiography*, 148–49.

Discussion of Iroquois influence theory: "shoddy-yet-trendy multiculturalism": Ed White, "The Challenge of Iroquois Influence," *American Quarterly* 52, no. 1 (March 2000); "fanciful": Gordon S. Wood, "Federalism from the Bottom Up," *The University of Chicago Law Review* 78 (2011): 705.

"Franklin's plan of union," Herbert M. Lloyd, introduction to Lewis Henry Morgan's *League of the Ho-de-no-sau-see*, quoted by Francis W. Halsey in the *New York Times*, June 7, 1902: 27.

"the original framers of the Constitution": H. Con. Res. 331, online at http://www.senate.gov/reference/resources/pdf/hconres331.pdf.

"The worst is that they are the worse for the Christians": Weiser, quoted in C. Z. Weiser, 142. Again, Weiser here uses words similar to those earlier written by William Penn.

"Highest Quality and Best Workmanship": Conrad Weiser cigar box label, online at http://www.cigarlabeljunkie.com/Html/Archives_F10.html.

Notes to pages 167–182 [Chapter 8]

"They have a droll theory of the Creation"; "The government among them": Dean R. Snow et al., *In Mohawk Country: Early Narratives About a Native People* (Syracuse: Syracuse University Press, 1996), 45–46.

"the genius and the manners": Thomas Sedgwick, *A Memoir of the Life of William Livingston* (New York: J.J. Harper, 1833), 46.

"by the people, for the people": Lincoln used this description of American government in the Gettysburg Address.

"missionaries who practise"; "persuade these people"; "Jesuitical craft"; "a squaw by the name of St. Catharine": Sedgwick, 97–98.

"he wanted nothing so much as to be a painter": P. G. Davidson, "Whig Propagandists of the American Revolution," *American Historical Review* 39 (April 1934): 442–53.

"collapse of the Puritan canopy"; "From the revivals": Mark Noll, *America's God: From Jonathan Edwards to Abraham Lincoln* (New York: Oxford University Press, 2002), 31.

"While one laughs at the other's preaching": "To the editor of the *New-England Courant*," *New-England Courant*, October 15, 1722.

"one of the most eminent"; "It is a pity": reprinted in *The Works of the Late Right Honorable Joseph Addison, Esq.*, Volume 3 (Birmingham: John Baskerville, 1761), 546.

"An atheist is but a mad ridiculous Derider of Piety"; "Atheists put on false Courage": "The Good Reception, Mr. Pope's Thoughts on Various Subjects," *Boston Evening-Post*, February 16, 1741.

"I fear neither Atheist, nor Jew, Deist, nor Turk": "A Letter to Rev. Thomas Sheridan, D.D.," *The New-York Weekly Journal*, December 4, 1738.

"An atheist is an overgrown libertine": "The Character of an Atheist," *New-York Weekly Journal*, February 27, 1749.

"account of his sickness, Convictions, Discourses"; "Published for an Example to others"; "If anyone doubts the truth": *The Second Spira* (John Dunton at the Raven in the Poultry, 1693).

"This man an Atheist, he was bred": Rev. Dr. Jones, *The Atheist Converted, or, The Unbeliever's Eyes Opened* (Bennington, VT: Collier and Stockwell, 1802), 2.

"If I must sacrifice my Reason": "And to be dull was constru'd to be good," *New England Weekly Journal*, August 28, 1727.

"The Atheist is a man who doubts of the King's Right": "Of Spurious and Genuine Devotion," *Boston Evening Post*, August 17, 1752.

"Historians Roger Finke and Rodney Stark put the percentage of religious adherence among residents of the North American English colonies at just 17%": See Finke and Stark, *The Churching of America, 1776–2005: Winners and Losers in Our Religious Economy* (New Brunswick: Rutgers

University Press, 1992), 16. This accounting of religious adherents is also cited by Noll, *America's God*, 166.

"the whole country would soon be Unitarian": Thomas Jefferson, letter to Timothy Pickering, Esq., Monticello, February 27, 1821.

"All sects are mixed as well as all nations": J. Hector St. John de Crèvecoeur, *Letters from an American Farmer* (New York: Fox, Duffield & Company, 1904), 66.

"the first periodical in the colonies"; "is determined to proceed inawed": Sedgwick, 74–75.

"monster tyranny": William Livingston, quoted Milton Klein's introduction to Livingston's collected essays, *The Independent Reflector Or, Weekly Essays on Sundry Important Subjects More Particularly Adapted to the Province of New York.* (Cambridge, MA: Harvard University Press, 1963), 26.

"A printer ought not publish every thing offered him": *The Journals of Hugh Gaine, Printer: Biography and bibliography* (New York: Dodd, Mead, & Co., 1902), 12.

"The importance attached to this journal": Sedgwick, 76.

"Some think him a Tindal": Edwin Brockholst Livingston, *The Livingstons of Livingston Manor* (New York: Knickerbock Press, 1910), 169.

"an Atheist, others as a Deist, and a third sort as a Presbyterian"; "I believe the Scriptures": Sedgwick, 86.

"the wicked triumvirate of New York": Rev. Samuel Johnson, quoted in *The Livingstons of Livingston Manor*, 168.

"with a rancor, a malevolence, and an acrimony": Thomas Jones, quoted in "Presbyterianism and the American Revolution in the Middle Colonies," Joseph S. Tiedemann, *Church History* 74, no. 2 (June 2005): 306–44.

"the applause of the mob": Cadwallader Colden, *Colden Letter Books*, Volume 9 (New York: New York Historical Society, 1877), 187.

"The right of self defence is not a donation of law": Livingston, quoted in Woodbridge Riley, *American Philosophy: The Early Schools*, Volume 1 (New York: Dodd, Mead & Co., 1907), 28.

"viciously radical in his rhetoric:" John M. Mulder, "William Livingston: Propagandist against Episcopacy," *Journal of Presbyterian History* 54 (spring 1976): 83.

"Clamour is at present our best policy": Livingston, quoted in Sedgwick, 136.

Notes to pages 185–202 [Chapter 9]

"Rebellion to tyrants is obedience to God": In common usage in the years before and after the Revolution, the phrase was taken as a slogan by both Thomas Jefferson and Benjamin Franklin, who proposed it as the motto of the nation.

"my mind is my own church": Thomas Paine, *The Age of Reason* (New York: Truth Seeker Company, 1898), 6.

"with a few phrases excepted": Thomas Paine, *The Age of Reason* (New York: G. N. Devries, 1827), 18.

"Is it not a species of blasphemy": Thomas Paine, "Examination of the Prophecies," in *Life and Writings of Thomas Paine*, Volume 7 (New York: Vincent Parke and Company), 252.

"A situation, similar to present, hath not happened since the days of Noah until now": Paine, *Common Sense*, quoted in Noll, *America's God*, 84.

"dirty little atheist": Theodore Roosevelt, *Gouverneur Morris* (New York: Houghton Mifflin, 1888), 289.

"disinfectant": Noll, *America's God*, 83.

"I have examined the major Part of the Carolina Indico entered this year": Moses Lindo, *South Carolina Gazette*, August 19, 1756, quoted in Barnat Elzas, *A Sketch of the Most Prominent Jew in Charleston in Provincial Days* (Charleston: Charleston News and Courier, 1903), 1.

"are dispersed over the whole world"; "keep up correspondence with one another": Sir John Barnard, quoted in Sheldon J. Godfrey and Judy Godfrey, *Search Out the Land: The Jews and the Growth of Equality in British Colonial America, 1740–1867* (Montreal: McGill-Queen's Press, 1995), 53.

"horror and execration": Charles Daly, *The Settlement of the Jews in North America* (New York: Philip Cohen, 1893), 153.

"All city and country gentlemen": advertisement, *New-York Mercury*, January 26, 1761.

"Beaver and Deerskins, Smal fur at New York Market price": advertisement, *The New-York Gazette*, August 17, 1761.

"a young negro wench of good character": advertisement, *The New-York Gazette*, February 9, 1767.

"Peace to my beloved master" and subsequent lines from the Phillips letter: Jacob Marcus, "Jews and American Revolution: A Bicentennial Documentary," *American Jewish Archives* 27, no. 2 (November 1975), 130–32.

"The kindness of our little friend": James Madison, quoted in J. H. Hollander's notes to Herbert Adams and Jared Sparks, "A Sketch of Haym Solomon," *Publications of the American Jewish Historical Society* (1894), 10.

"We have therefore to desire": *Letters of Delegates to Congress, 1774–1789: October 1, 1779–March 31 1780*, Volume 14, (Washington: Library of Congress, 1987), 264.

"as sudden as a clap of thunder"; "The riches of St. Eustachius"; "a vast magazine of military stores of all kinds": J. F. Jameson, "St Eustatius in the American Revolution", *The American Historical Review* 8 (1903): 683.

"You can have no idea, sir": John Adams to Robert Livingston, February 21, 1782, *The Diplomatic Correspondence of the American Revolution*, Volume 3 (Washington: John C. Rives, 1857).

"What blockheads"; "Upon every dispatch we receive": Godfrey Basil Mundy, *Life of Rodney* (London: James Carpenter & Son, 1836), 149.

"nest of villains"; "Commerce, commerce alone": Sir George Rodney to Philip Stephens, Barbados, June 29, 1781, *The Life and Correspondence of the Late Admiral Lord Rodney*, edited by Godfrey Basil Mundy (London: J. Murray, 1830), 117.

"one of the people called Jews of the City of Philadelphia": Jonas Phillips to President and Members of the Convention, available online at http://press-pubs.uchicago.edu/founders/documents/a6_3s11.html.

Notes to pages 205–226 [Chapter 10]

"he kept his troops impeccably in order": *Federal Republican*, August 30, 1814.

"tremendous and unusual": Description of the day's weather can be found in the *Boston Daily Advertiser*, September 1, 1814.

"magnificent black horse": Jon Latimer, *1812: War with America* (Cambridge, MA: Harvard University Press, 2009), 328.

"hogshead of rum": *Hallowell Gazette,* October 5, 1814.

"Such a war God considers as his own cause": John H. Stevens, "The duty of union in a just war," online at http://babel.hathitrust.org/cgi/pt?id=loc.ark %3A%2F13960%2Ft50g43w9r;page=root;view=image;size=100;seq=11; num=5.

"At this moment...your minds are harassed and your bosoms tortured": David Osgood, *A solemn protest against the late declaration of war, in a discourse, delivered on the next Lord's day after the tidings of it were received* (Cambridge, MA: Hilliard and Metcalf, 1812), 3.

"the law of nature and nations": Thomas Jefferson to Abraham Baldwin, quoted in William Dawson Johnston, *History of the Library of Congress: Volume I, 1800–1864* (Washington: U.S. Government Printing Office, 1904), 36.

"I learn from the newspapers that the Vandalism": Thomas Jefferson to Samuel H. Smith, September 21, 1814.

"something analytical, something chronological"; Thomas Jefferson to George Washington, quoted in Johnston, 148.

"From these three fountains...flow these three emanations": Lisa Jardine, *Francis Bacon: Discovery and the Art of Discourse* (New York: Cambridge University Press, 1974), 97.

"a blueprint of his own mind": Arthur Bestor, quoted in *Thomas Jefferson's Library: A Catalogue with the Entries in His Own Order,* edited by James Gilreath and Douglas L. Wilson (Washington, D.C.: Library of Congress, 1989), 3.

"because of the medley it presents to the mind": Johnston, 144.

For more information on the "copy of the Quran that he had purchased": See Kevin Hayes, "How Thomas Jefferson Read the Qur'an," *Early American Literature* 39, no. 2 (2004): 247–61.

"Providence has reserved": George Sale, *The Koran: Commonly Called the Alcoran of Mohammad* (London: L. Hawes, W. Clarke, R. Collins, 1764), viii.

"The idolatry of the Arabs": Ibid., 20.

"Mr. Jefferson's Library": *Federal Republican,* October 11, 1814.

"Congress are about purchasing": *Salem Gazette,* October 21, 1814.

"To be acquainted with the various laws and constitutions of civilized nations": George Sale's introduction to *The Koran: Commonly Called the Alcoran of Mohammed* (Philadelphia: J. W. Moore, 1856), iv.

"We understand that Mr. Jefferson's invaluable collection": "Jefferson's Library," *Portland Gazette* and *Maine Advertiser,* November 7, 1814.

"abounded with productions of atheistical, irreligious, and immoral character": *Federal Republican,* January 31, 1815.

"which bye the bye would be the largest": *Alexandria Gazette,* November 17, 1814.

"make the most of the bad bargain": *Alexandria Gazette Commercial and Political,* November 17, 1814.

"To Thomas Jefferson, esquire": *Georgetown Daily Federal Republican,* October 18, 1814, quoted in Johnston, 91–95.

"English works of progress and speculative freedom": Ibid., 74.

"a number of negroes, horses, and cattle"; "neither shows himself to be the heir": *American State Papers: Documents, Legislative and Executive, of the*

Congress of the United States, Issue 36 (Washington: Gales and Seaton, 1834), 448.

"many books of irreligious and immoral tendency" and subsequent quotations from the Congressional debate: "Mr. Jefferson's Library," *Virginia Patriot,* February 8, 1815.

"the friends of the bill replied with fact, wit, and argument": Annals of Congress, House of Representatives, 13th Congress, 3rd Session: 1105–6.

"The next generation will, we confidently predict, blush at the objections made in Congress to the purchase of Mr. Jefferson's library": *Washington City Weekly Gazette,* July 12, 1817, quoted in Johnston, 90.

"God and a religious president, or... Jefferson and no god": *The Gazette of the United States,* September 13, 1800.

"Murder, robbery, rape, adultery, and incest": *Jenks' Portland Gazette,* October 13, 1800.

"a sect by myself": Jefferson, letter to Ezra Stiles Ely, June 25, 1819, available online at http://founders.archives.gov/documents/Jefferson/98-01-02-0542.

"oracle"; "Divest yourself of all bias"; "Shake off all the fears": Jefferson, letter to Peter Carr, August 10, 1787, available online at http://founders.archives .gov/documents/Jefferson/01-12-02-0021

"the several sects"; "Let us reflect"; "It does me no injury": Thomas Jefferson, *Notes on the State of Virginia* (London: John Stockdale, 1787), 265–67.

Notes to pages 229–254 [Chapter 11]

"great houses": Omar ibn Said, quoted in Ala Alryyes, *A Muslim American Slave* (Madison: University of Wisconsin Press, 2011), 89.

"Then there came to our country"; "weak, small, evil man called Johnson": Ibid., 62–63.

"I have faith in Him who lights up the darkness": The earliest translation of Omar ibn Said's brief autobiography refers specifically to his recapture occurring on a new moon (Alryyes, 89), which calls for recitation of the text known as "His Supplication When He Looked at the New Crescent Moon," available online at www.al-islam.org/sahifa-al-kamilah-sajjadiyya -imam-zain-ul-abideen/43-his-supplication- when-he-looked-new-crescent.

"Run-Away": *Raleigh Star,* November 1, 1810.

"Passing himself as a free man": *The Star* (Raleigh, NC), October 18, 1810.

"negroes, moores, molatoes": Virginia law of 1682, quoted in John Brown Dillon and Benjamin Douglass, *Oddities of Colonial Legislation in America* (Indianapolis: Robert Douglass, 1879), 200–1.

"The introduction of Mohammedan slaves": Elizabeth Donnan, *Documents illustrative of the history of the slave trade to America* (Washington, D.C.: Carnegie Institution, Division of Historical Research, 1930), 358.

"The conferring of baptisme": James Kirke Paulding, *Slavery in the United States* (Harper & Brothers, 1836), 147.

"No other God but Money, nor Religion but Profit"; "Talk to a Planter of the Soul of a Negro": W. M. Jernegan, "Slavery and Conversion in the Colonies," *American Historical Review* 21 (1916): 516.

"greatly to be pitied": Peter Kalm, *Travels into North America,* Volume 1 (London: Printed for T. Lowndes, 1773), 311.

"the religious instruction of the negroes"; "I am perfectly satisfied, from long observation"; "plantations under religious instruction": *Proceedings of the meeting in Charleston, S. C., May 13–15, 1845, on the religious instruction of the Negroes: together with the report of the committee, and the address to the public* (Charleston: B. Jenkins, 1845), 19, 21–22, 26.

"The Negro, like other men, is innately religious": Haven Perkins, "Religion for Slaves: Difficulties and Methods," *Church History* 10, no. 3 (September 1941): 228–45.

"My long-crushed spirit rose": Frederick Douglass, *Narrative of the Life of Frederick Douglass* (London: H. G. Collins, 1851), 68.

"I saw white spirits and black spirits": *The Confessions of Nat Turner, the Leader of the Late Insurrection in Southampton, Va.* (Baltimore: Thomas R. Gray, 1831), 10–11.

"He told me, with great solemnity": Douglass, 65.

"Laboring in the field": *The Confessions of Nat Turner*, 10.

"Job would often leave the Cattle, and withdraw into the Woods to pray": Thomas Bluett, *Some Memoirs of the Life of Job, the Son of Solomon, the High Priest of Boonda in Africa; Who was a Slave About Two Years in Maryland; and Afterwards Being Brought to England, was Set Free, and Sent to His Native Land in the Year 1734* (London: Richard Ford, 1734), 19–20.

"could not speak one Word of English": Bluett, 21.

"As to his Religion": Ibid., 51.

"though sixty-five years of age"; "Prince was educated and perhaps is still nominally at least a Mahomedian": *Commercial Advertiser*, April 4, 1828.

"The Mohammedan Africans": Charles Colock Jones, *The Religious Instruction of the Negroes in the United States* (Savannah: Thomas Purse, 1842), 125.

"dreams, visions, trances, voices": Ibid., 125.

"In the name of God, the merciful, the compassionate": Alryyes, 51.

"perfect allusion to slavery": Ibid., 18.

"Blessed be He in whose hand is the *mulk*": Ibid., 51.

"To pray, I said: Praise be to Allah"; "And now I pray": Ibid., 75.

"earlier pages of the manuscript": John Franklin Jameson, quoted in Alryyes, 87.

"Among these are the Moors or Morescos, who were driven out of Spain about the end of the sixteenth century": *History of the captivity and sufferings of Mrs. Maria Martin: who was six years a slave in Algiers, two of which she was confined in a dark and dismal dungeon, loaded with irons for refusing to comply with the brutal request of a Turkish officer* (W. Crary, 1807), 9.

"Mohammedan Forbearance": *New-Hampshire Patriot*, October 30, 1810.

"Treatment of Negro slaves in Morocco"; "The Moors, or Moselmen, purchase their slaves from Tombuctoo"; "Being in the daily habit"; "While we contrast"; "Now that the abominable slave trade": *Connecticut Courant*, June 17, 1817.

"A Convert from Mohammedanism": *Boston Reporter*, September 1, 1837.

"venerable coloured man": *North Carolina University* 3 (1854): 307; this early magazine profile of Omar ibn Said is also included in Alryyes, 209–11.

"On the morning of the 25th of January": "Further Particulars from Bahia," *Gloucester Telegraph*, April 11, 1835.

"Being of feeble constitution": 1837 description of Omar ibn Said, found in Alryyes, 217.

"Mohammedanism has been supplanted in his heart": Ibid., 211.
"Since I cannot leave a guard to hold it," Sherman to Ulysses S Grant; "the nights were made hideous with smoke": Fayetteville resident Alice Campbell, quoted in Emily Farrington Smith, *Fayetteville, North Carolina: An All-American History* (Charleston: History Press, 2011), 85.
"*O people of America*": Ibid., 71.
"*Are you confident that He who is in heaven*": Ibid., 53.

Notes to pages 257–278 [Chapter 12]

"A modest building, somewhat gray": Thomas Buchanan Read, *The Poetical Works of Thomas Buchanan Read: Lyric poems. Sylvia; or, the last shepherd. Miscellaneous. Airs from Alpland* (1894), 44.
"never was solitude better personified": Mary Moody Emerson, *The Selected Letters of Mary Moody Emerson*, edited by Nancy Craig Simmons (Athens: University of Georgia Press, 1993), 149.
"never to put that ring on": Mary Moody Emerson, quoted in Ralph Waldo Emerson's remembrance of her, published in *The Complete Works* of 1904, Volume 10, Lectures and Biographical Sketches, online at http://www.bartleby.com/90/1015.html.
"Her blue eyes flashed like steel and stabbed like swords"; "She was thought to have the power of saying more disagreeable things": Quoted in the notes of F. B. Sanborn, *The Personality of Emerson* (Boston: The Merrymount Press, 1903), 29.
"Our Stranger": *The Selected Letters of Mary Moody Emerson*, 152.
"If you sail to India, you may see sixty millions of people bowing to thirty millions of gods": Elijah Parish, *Sermons, Practical and Doctrinal* (Boston: Crocker & Brewster, 1826), 61.
"Noah foretold": Elijah Parrish, *Sacred Geography: Or, A Gazetteer of the Bible* (Boston: Samuel T. Armstrong, 1813). Parrish borrowed liberally in his "gazetteer" and made no distinction between his words and those of others. Much of this description, for example, is originally from Robert Orme's *A History of the Military Transactions of the British Nation in Indostan* (1763).
"My Dear Waldo"; "I will send some of those he gave to me, if you have not met them": *The Selected Letters of Mary Moody Emerson*, 152.
"If Aunt Mary finds out": Ralph Waldo Emerson, *Journals of Ralph Waldo Emerson, 1849–1855* (Boston: Houghton Mifflin, 1912), 118.
"I am proud to belong to a religion which has taught the world both tolerance and universal acceptance": Vivekananda, Addresses at the Parliament of Religions, Chicago, 1893, online at http://www.ramakrishna.org/chcgfull.htm.
"The Hindus dwelt in the All": *Margaret and Her Friends: Or, Ten Conversations with Margaret Fuller Upon the Mythology of the Greeks and Its Expression in Art, Held at the House of the Rev. George Ripley* (Boston: Roberts Brothers, 1895), 25.
"Boston finds India a fascinating topic, and its swarthy representatives are always well received"; "physician, editor, traveler, lecturer, mother and housekeeper": "Causerie from Boston," *Worcester Sunday Spy*, March 18, 1894.

"women are the lords of creation"; "They are called the free women of India":
Alice Bunker Stockham, *Karezza: Ethics of Marriage* (Chicago: Alice B.
Stockham & Co., 1896), 68.

"In Sanskrit mythology, the feminine is represented" and other quotes from
Matilda Gage: *Woman, Church and State: A Historical Account of the Status
of Woman Through the Christian Ages: With Reminiscences of Matriarchate*
(Chicago: C. H. Kerr, 1893), 23–30.

"maxims from the sacred books": Gage, *Woman, Church and State*, 28.

"Man has ever manifested," Elizabeth Cady Stanton, address to the New
York State Legislature in 1860: *Elizabeth Cady Stanton, Feminist as
Thinker: A Reader in Documents and Essays*, edited by Ellen Carol DuBois
and Richard Cándida Smith (New York: New York University Press,
2007), 164.

"her native costume of soft white draperies": *Worcester Sunday Spy*, March 18,
1894.

"crowded with ladies": *Wheeling Sunday Register*, June 3, 1894.

"faddish"; "flighty": *The Duluth News Tribune*, July 28, 1902.

"Excellency George Washington": *The Independent Gazetteer* (Philadelphia),
May 23, 1787.

"Hymn to the Hindu God of Love": *Independent Gazeteer*, May 23, 1787.

Translation of the Letters of a Hindoo Rajah: Elizabeth Hamilton's book written
in the voice of a "Rajah" was first published in London in 1796.

"A spirit of sublime devotion": *New York Mercantile Advertiser*, June 12, 1800.

"Shah Coolen": *Commercial Advertiser*, October 5, 1801.

"note how Krishna wantoned in the wood": *The Indian Song of Songs* (London:
Trubner & Co., 1875), 16.

"We believe the profanity mentioned": "Article 7: Letters of Shahcoolen," *The
Boston Review*, February 1805.

"We also have reason to believe": "Self Immolation," *Otsego Herald*, October 2,
1817.

"the celebrated Hindoo reformer": "From England," *American Repertory*,
November 22, 1822.

"In the morning I bathe my intellect": Henry David Thoreau, *Walden* (New
York: Library of America, 1985), 559.

"A strain of music reminds me": Thoreau, *On the Concord and the Merrimack
Rivers* (New York: Library of America, 1985), 141.

"King Trishanku": Henry Wadsworth Longfellow, *Poems of Henry Wadsworth
Longfellow* (New York: Houghton Mifflin, 1880), 378.

"Passage to India": Walt Whitman, *Leaves of Grass* (New York: James Redfield,
1872).

"sage of Concord"; "I think Emerson is more than a brilliant fellow": Meade
Minnigerode and Herman Melville, *Some Personal Letters of Herman
Melville and a Bibliography* (New York: E. B. Hackett, 1922), 32–34.

"the Hindoo whale": Melville, *Moby-Dick* (New York: Harper & Brothers,
1851), chapter 55.

"unspeakable, wild, Hindoo odor about it": Ibid., chapter 96.

"Oh, thou dark Hindoo half of nature": Ibid., chapter 116.

"the dread Vishnoo"; "When Brahma, or the God of Gods": Ibid., chapter 82.

"to the average Western mind it is the nearest approach to a Torricellian vacuum of intelligibility": Oliver Wendell Holmes, *The Works of Oliver Wendell Holmes* (New York: Houghton Mifflin, 1892), 307.

"representative life"; "the arcana of the gods": Ralph Waldo Emerson, quoted in Phyllis Cole, *Mary Moody Emerson and the Origins of Transcendentalism: A Family History* (New York: Oxford University Press, 2002), 3–4.

Notes to pages 281–302 [Chapter 13]

"I appear before you to bear my testimony to the truth of 'Mormonism,'" Brigham Young, "Testimony to the Divinity of Joseph Smith's Mission…": A Discourse by President Brigham Young, Delivered in the Bowery, Great Salt Lake City, August 31, 1856, quoted in G. D. Watt, *Journal of Discourses By Brigham Young, President of the Church of Jesus Christ of Latter-day Saints, His Two Counsellors, the Twelve Apostles, and Others*, Volume 4 (London: Latter-day Saints Book Depot, 1857), 33.

"During our evening conversations, Joseph would occasionally give us some of the most amusing recitals that could be imagined": Lucy Mack Smith, *History of Joseph Smith* (Salt Lake City: Improvement Era, 1902), 82–83.

"And now, behold, I say unto you that you shall go unto the Lamanites": Doctrines and Covenants, 28:8.

"Was it by any act of ours that this people were driven into their midst?": Brigham Young quoted in *Journal of Discourses*, 41.

"a slum in the wilderness": Anthony Wallace, *Death and Rebirth of the Seneca* (New York: Random House, 1970), 184.

"not be merely overrun, but destroyed"; "Town Destroyer": Ibid., 143.

"yell and sing like demented people": Arthur C. Parker, "The Code of Handsome Lake, the Seneca Prophet," in New York State's *Education Department Bulletin* (Albany: University of the State of New York, 1912), 20.

Henry Simmons's sermon connecting Christian and Iroquois creation stories can be found in David Swatzler, *A Friend Among the Seneca: The Quaker Mission to Cornplanter's People* (Mechanicsburg: Stackpole Books, 2000), 27–30.

"letters, pen, and tilling the field": quoted in Jill Kinney, "Letters, Pen, and Tilling the Field: Quaker Schools Among the Seneca Indians on the Allegany River, 1798–1852" (PhD diss., University of Rochester, 2009).

"My son, do no ill": *The Ohio Primer, or An Introduction to Spelling & Reading* (Pittsburgh: H. Holdship, 1826), 10.

"immediate divine revelation": See *Letters of Elias Hicks: including also a few short essays written on several occasions, mostly illustrative of his doctrinal views* (New York: Isaac Hopper, 1834), 25.

"yellow skin and dried bones"; "some strong power"; "Niio!": Parker, 21–22.

"My, uncle"; "Never have I seen"; "clear swept space"; "clothed in fine clean raiment"; "Their cheeks were painted"; "He who created": Ibid., 24.

"Some speculated": For more on the possible Quaker influence on Handsome Lake's visions, and suspicions about his motives, see Kenney, 34–39.

"How the White Race came to America": Edward Cornplanter's addendum to the Code of Handsome Lake can be found in Parker, 16.

"I am happy to learn"; "Go on then, brother": Jefferson's Indian Addresses, "To Brother Handsome Lake," November 3, 1802.

"Burned-Over District": I use here the most commonly repeated form of Charles Finney's phrase. As he used it himself, upstate New York was "a burnt district," and it's worth noting his original usage had a bit more ambivalence than is usually remembered. He wrote not only of the "wild excitement" that passed through the region, but also of its often "spurious" nature. See *Charles G. Finney: An Autobiography* (Westwood: Fleming H. Revell Company, 1908), 78.

"combination of polygamy and polyandry": Charles Nordhoff, quoted in the introduction to *Free Love in Utopia: John Humphrey Noyes and the Origin of the Oneida Community*, George Wallingford Noyes and Lawrence Foster, eds. (Champaign: University of Illinois Press, 2001), ix.

"We were last week visited by the famous chief, Red Jacket": *Palmyra Gazette*, reprinted in the *New Bedford Mercury*, September 13, 1822. This news report is also partially quoted in Lori Taylor, "Telling Stories about Mormons and Indians," doctoral dissertation (Albany: State University of New York, 2000), 343.

"It is impossible to know": For further factors that make plausible this meeting of an Iroquois chief and the founder of Mormonism, see Taylor, 342–347.

"That inasmuch as any man drinketh wine or strong drink among you, behold it is not good": Doctrine and Covenants (The Church of Jesus Christ of Latter-day Saints), 89:1–21, online at https://www.lds.org/scriptures/dc-testament/dc/89.1-21.

"In localities of Utah, Idaho, and other states where the Mormon faith is prevalent": A. E. Fife, "The Legend of the Three Nephites Among the Mormons," *The Journal of American Folk-Lore* 53 (January–March 1940): 1–49.

"given power over death so as to remain on the earth until Jesus comes again": Book of Mormon, 3 Nephi 28:6.

Notes to pages 305–326 [Chapter 14]

"One morning in the early autumn of 1852": A description of the temple dedication ceremony, first printed just after the ceremony in the *San Francisco Whig*, was republished a few months later in the *Salem* (Massachusetts) *Register*, December 27, 1852.

"joss houses": For an early explanation of this derivation, see Eugene R. Smith, ed., *The Gospel in All Lands* (New York: Missionary Society of the Methodist Episcopal Church, 1886), 54: "In China these places are not often spoken of as temples. The word commonly used both by merchants and missionaries is Joss-house. Its derivation is from the Portuguese *Dios*, which again is from the Latin *Deus*, 'God.'"

"This splendid vessel": *Daily Alta California*, April 23, 1852.

"They were a novelty, a wonder": Otis Gibson, *The Chinese in America* (Cincinnati: Hitchcock & Walden, 1877), 224.

"our elder brethren": Henry Huntly Haight, quoted in Ira Condit, *The Chinaman as We See Him* (New York: Fleming H. Revell Company, 1900), 18.

"The Chinese have opened": Otis Gibson, *The Chinese in America* (Cincinnati: Hitchcock & Walden, 1877), 72.

"There is a strong feeling": Frank Soulé, John H. Gihon, James Nisbet, and Jim Nisbe, *The Annals of San Francisco* (New York: D. Appleton & Company, 1855), 378–379. Also quoted in Gibson, 226.

"A foreign miner's tax": Ibid., 228.

"Their display of numerous fanciful flags": Ibid., 225.

"The China Boys feel proud": Norman Assing, quoted in *The Annals of San Francisco*, 288

"the most gorgeous robes"; "a most horrible discord"; "an ear-splitting blast"; "These ceremonies": *San Francisco Whig*, republished in the *Salem Register* (Massachusetts), December 27, 1852.

"Immigrants separated from their native place": *Native Place, City, and Nation: Regional Networks and Identities in Shanghai, 1853–1937* (Berkeley: University of California Press, 1995), 8.

"The ancients who wished to illustrate illustrious virtue": "The Great Learning," James Legge, *The Life and Teachings of Confucious* (London: Trübner & Co., 1867), 266.

"China is made up of prefectures and counties": Quoted in Goodman, 13. "Such statements," Goodman continues, "resembled in structure the concentric logic of the Confucian text 'The Great Learning' [and] also served strategic purposes, defusing threats both from the state and hostile locals...."

"If we do not resist": Quoted in Goodman, 170.

Huiguan as religious organizations: "Huiguan were established to promote native-place sentiment for two very practical reasons: to provide a place where people from the same locale could pray to their common gods and where dead compatriots could be buried if the family could not afford to have the body shipped home." In Guanhua Wang, *In Search of Justice: The 1905–1906 Chinese Anti-American Boycott* (Cambridge, MA: Harvard University Press, 2002), 100. For more on the social and community organizing roles huiguans played, see Mark Lai, *Becoming Chinese American: A History of Communities and Institutions* (Lanham: Rowman Altamira, 2004), 46–54.

"Sir: — We wish to call your attention to the fact...": Six Companies letter to H. H. Ellis, Report of the Joint Special Commission on Chinese Immigration, 44th Congress, 2nd Session, Congressional edition, Volume 1734 (1877), 46.

"of every religious persuasion": "Additional Articles to the Treaty Between the United States of America and the Ta Tsing Empire," in William Frederick Mayers, ed., *Treaties Between the Empire of China and Foreign Powers* (Shanghai: North China Herald, 1897), 94.

"A-he, a Chinaman": *Daily Alta California* 2, no. 301 (October 9, 1851).

"China, as it is"; "Chinamen and a few Chinese women": Gibson, 64.

"It is not customary with the Chinese": Ibid., 66.

"The Creator has prepared": William Speer, *The Oldest and the Newest Empire: China and the United States* (Cincinnati: National Publishing Co., 1870), 488.

"gods many and lords many": "One of the principal Chinese 'joss-houses'": Gibson, 72–73.

"John Chinaman"; "some idea of what they might expect": *San Francisco Chronicle*, May 31, 1876: 5; also excerpted in Thomas Tweed and Stephen Prothero, eds., *Asian Religions in America* (New York: Oxford University Press, 1999) 70–73.

"For a long time our celestial residents"; "stirring up quite a revival": *San Francisco Chronicle*, May 30, 1876; also quoted in Gibson, 86–88.

"Nowhere in the civilized world": *Los Angeles Herald*, October 6, 1875.

"Plain Language from Truthful James": Bret Harte, *Overland Monthly*, September 1870.

"the worst poem I ever wrote": Harte, quoted in S. R. Elliott, "Glimpses of Bret Hart," *Reader* 10 (1907): 124.

"as historians including Ronald Takaki have noted": For Takaki's reading of Harte's work, see his *Iron Cages: Race and Culture in Nineteenth Century America* (New York: Knopf, 1979), 224.

"The *Secret Service* series of novels": This popular line of dime store detective stories was published in New York by Frank Tousey from 1899 to 1925.

"On a spring morning in the aftermath": "Chinese Worship Destroyed Joss," *Los Angeles Herald*, April 26, 1906.

"Across the street was the new Buddhist temple some young Chamber of Commerce Chinatown Chinese were trying to build, by themselves": Jack Kerouac, *The Dharma Bums* (New York: Penguin, 1976), 115.

Notes to pages 329–345 [Chapter 15]

"Five Ks": See Sikh Rehat Maryada, Section 6, Chapter 13, *Article XXIV*; available online at http://sgpc.net/rehat_maryada/section_six.html.

"I bow with heart and mind to the Holy Sword": Guru Gobind Singh, quoted in Rajinder Singh, "Glimpses of Guru Gobind Singh Ji," online at http://www.info-sikh.com/PageG92.html.

"We cannot get white men who will remain steadily at their work": *Bellingham Herald*, Sept. 5, 1907.

"Have We a Dusky Peril?"; "The land of the Hindus harbors 300,000,000 souls"; "Bellingham, Sept. 15, 1906": *Puget Sound American*, September 16, 1906.

"At the present rate at which they are coming": Rev. J. R. Macartney, *Bellingham Herald*, November 2, 1907.

"The long-expected cry": *New York Times*, September 6, 1907.

"two crumbling shacks"; "a great, calm, ungrammatical man of unbounded tact"; "What are you doing, boys?": *Collier's* writer Will Irwin, quoted in the *Bellingham Herald*, October 9, 1907.

"The Hindus have a love for jewelry": *Bellingham Herald*, September 5, 1907.

"in view of the Bellingham riots": Cornel Chang, *Pacific Connections: The Making of the U.S.-Canadian Borderlands*, 107.

"All that the State Department can do": *New York Times*, September 7, 1907.

Of the more than seven thousand Indians who emigrated to the Pacific coast: According to Bruce Labrack, the historian of Sikhism in America, counting Sikhs as 90 percent of early immigrants from India "is a conservative number. The actual number of Sikh immigrants is 95 percent." See Anju Kaur, "Smithsonian Distorts Sikh American History," *Sikh News Network*, April 8, 2014.

"The Hindu is the most undesirable immigrant in the state": Quoted in Karen Leonard, *Making Ethnic Choices: California's Punjabi Mexican Americans* (Philadelphia: Temple University Press, 2010), 24.

"brown": For the role of California's miscegenation laws in shaping Sikh-Mexican unions, see Leonard, 68–69.

"papers for a Sikh temple in Berkeley were granted in 1912": *San Francisco Call* 111, no. 176, May 24, 1912.

"initiated nearly twice as much litigation": See Leonard, 52.

"the burly Hindu": *San Francisco Call* 105, no. 135, April 14, 1909.

"My dear old and saintly father"; "Thank God, I am not a Christian; I can work on Sundays, too"; and other quotations from Bhagat Singh Thind are from *House of Happiness*, an autobiography compiled from lectures delivered in the 1920s and published by the author (Salt Lake City, 1931).

United States v. Bhagat Singh Thind: Documents relating to the U.S. Supreme Court case involving Thind can be found in *Asian Americans and the Supreme Court: A Documentary History*, edited by Hyung-chan Kim (New York: Greenwood Press, 1992), 204–15.

Notes to pages 347–367 [Chapter 16]

"pakkai": Bunyu Fujimura, *Though I Be Crushed* (Los Angeles: Nembutsu Press, 1985), 55.

"Never in military history": Douglas MacArthur, quoted in Geoffrey Miles White, *Remembering the War in the Pacific* (Manoa: University of Hawaii, 1991), 170.

"like rats in a wired cage": "That Damned Fence," anonymous poem from the Poston Relocation Center, online at http://parentseyes.arizona.edu/wracamps/thatdamnedfence.html.

"concentration camps": For a list of prominent figures at the time who referred to the internment camps by this term, see James Hirabayashi, " 'Concentration Camp' or 'Relocation Center': What's in a Name?," *Japanese American National Musuem Quarterly* 9, no. 3 (1994).

497 Germans, 83 Italians, 1,221 Japanese: Memo from W. F. Kelly, Chief Supervisor of Border Patrol, December 9, 1941.

"Buddhist and Shinto missions": Alan Hynd, *Betrayal from the East* (New York, McBride, 1943), 131. Hynd's lack of evidence supporting such claims is noted by Duncan Williams. For an example of the book sold as nonfiction see the advertisement for the Pelican Book Shop in the *St. Petersburg Times*, November 21, 1943. For an example of its portrayal as a novel, see "Slap the Jap," *New York Times*, April 25, 1945.

"Buddhaheads": Robert Asahina, *Just Americans* (New York, Penguin, 2007), 60. Asahina notes that when used as a phrase of derision by mainland Japanese Americans directed at those from Hawaii, the term had the double reference of "Buddha" and *buta*, Japanese for "pig." In this sense, it also may have concerned supposed stubbornness (pigheadedness) of immigrant families reluctant to assimilate through conversion.

"Buddhists were more likely than Christians to maintain their native language": As one account recalls this and related tendencies: "[Japanese Americans] who were Buddhist thought of themselves as the true Japanese because they retained their original religion. Those who became Protestant did so to seek better acceptance in mainstream society." Florence Hongo, quoted by Richard Watanabe, "So What Is a Buddhahead?," www-hsc.usc.edu/~rwatanab/buddha.htm.

"Subscription rolls of such publications": See Tetsuden Kashima, *Judgment Without Trial: Japanese American Imprisonment During World War II* (Seattle: University of Washington Press, 2011), 31.

"The cherry blossoms on Mount Yoshino": Fujimura, 98.

"That Privates Yamamoto and Shiomichi died for their country"; "But the above feeling is only the joy of reason": Ibid. As mentioned above, while I refer to the second soldier as "Shiomichi" here and throughout, Fujimura uses the name "Shiomitsu," it seems, in error.

"We are from the FBI"; "Wholesale Jap Raids": Ibid., 50–51. Subsequent dialogue from Fujimura's account of his interrogation appears on pages 54–55.

"like livestock": Ibid., 62.

"asphyxiation": Ibid., 92.

"This impermanent world": Ibid., 57.

"Though I know"; "For over twenty years": Ibid., 98.

"I guess I might as well tell you that we're in action now"; "was as good as any": Hisaye Yamamoto, "After Johnny Died," *Pacific Citizen*, December 1, 1945.

"that unlikely place of wind": Hisaye Yamamoto, *Seventeen Syllables and Other Stories* (New Brunswick: Rutgers University Press, 2001), 20.

"who had died soon after he learned to walk": Yamamoto, "After Johnny Died."

"What would I know about God?": Yamamoto, *Seventeen Syllables and Other Stories*, 69.

"All this is a temporary aberration": From the biographical information on Pfc. Joe Shiomichi provided by the 442nd Veterans Club of Honolulu.

"Okaa-san, mother, this will probably be the last letter I write to you in my poor Japanese": Fujimura, 99.

"his pregnant wife waved from the platform as his train left the station": Vanessa De La Torre, "'Relocated' idealist lived — and died — devoutly 'pro-American,'" *Imperial Valley Press*, July 5, 2004.

"A child's death" and subsequent citations from the memorial service sermon: Fujimura, 98–99.

"shortened the Pacific war by two years": Major General Charles Willoughby, quoted in *United States Commission on Wartime Relocation and Internment of Civilians, Personal Justice Denied: Report of the Commission on Wartime Relocation and Internment of Civilians* (Seattle: University of Washington Press, 1997), 256.

"only crosses and stars": Yamamoto, *Seventeen Syllables and Other Stories*, 169.

"Protestant-Catholic-Jew": Will Herberg's classic book on mid-twentieth-century religious diversity in America was first published in 1955.

"one of the great patriotic shrines in the nation"; "vacant lot"; and all other quoted remarks in the section on religious symbols on U.S. military graves comes from the hearings of the Subcommittee on Public Lands, Congressional meeting minutes, H. J. Res 338-342-342, 82nd Congress.

"We probably owe it to her and the grace of God": Joseph McCarthy, *Major Speeches and Debates of Senator Joe McCarthy* (Washington: U.S. Government Printing Office, 1953), 275.

"You seem to have altogether too many soldiers": Fujimura, 114.

Notes to pages 369–398 [Chapter 17]

"For ten years a new nation has grown": The Human Be-in organizers' press release is reproduced in Gene Anthony, *The Summer of Love: Haight-Ashbury at Its Highest* (San Francisco: Last Gasp, 1995), 147.

"Turn on, tune in, drop out": Timothy Leary's remarks at the Be-in can be seen online at https://www.youtube.com/watch?v=IPSzTBP5PAU.

"Mr. Haight-Ashbury": Michael McClure, appearing in a KPIX-TV documentary, which aired in San Francisco in 1967 and can be found online at https://diva.sfsu.edu/collections/sfbatv/bundles/189371.

"building an electric Tibet in California": Bowen, quoted in Kramer, 45.

"You mean to say you have a telephone in your meditation room?": "Electric Tibet, baby!": Ibid., 46.

"a serious religious occasion." Ibid., 52.

"Never before had America, or the world": Michael Bowen, *The Royal Maze*, Chapter 1, Part 1; online at http://www.royalmaze.com/my-odyssey-the-first-human-be-in/chapter-one-part-1/.

"I was on a mission from God [and] from John Cooke to do that Be-In," Michael Bowen, quoted in Robert Greenfield, *Timothy Leary: A Biography* (New York, Mariner Books, 2007), 300.

Amos Starr Cooke: Information on John Cooke's missionary forebear can be found in multiple sources, including Emily Carrie Hawley, *The Introduction of Christianity into the Hawaiian Islands* (Brattleboro: Press of E. L. Hildreth, 1922).

"While the natives stand confounded and amazed": Amos Starr Cooke, quoted in Edwin Grant Burrows, *Hawaiian Americans: An Account of the Mingling of Japanese, Chinese, Polynesian, and American Cultures* (New Haven: Yale University Press, 1947), 41.

"decided to take his youngest son on a 37,000-mile jaunt": *The Straits Times* (Singapore), March 25, 1935.

"Cole Porter was also on board": Details about Cole Porter's voyage on the *Franconia* can be found in Charles Schwartz, *Cole Porter: A Biography* (New York: Da Capo Press, 1979), 142–43, and Stephen Citron, *Noel & Cole: The Sophisticates* (New York: Oxford University Press, 1993), 136.

"a very popular means of entertainment in many intelligent families": *Columbus (GA) Enquirer-Sun*, July 31, 1892.

"a national industry which bids fair to rival that in chewing gum": "Ouija Prostration," *New York Times*, January 14, 1920.

"the performance is loose and flabby": *New York Times*, December 16, 1940.

"There's no hocus pocus mysticism": June Morrall, "1970s Interview with Alice Kent," online at http://www.halfmoonbaymemories.com/?p=11168.

"The root of all our difficulties, individual and social, is self-interest": Meher Baba, "Address to America," May 31, 1932. Quoted in C. B. Purdom, *The God-Man* (Myrtle Beach, SC: Meher Spiritual Center, 1971), 104–5.

"galactic telepathy": Millen Vermilyea's supposed ability to explore space psychically is mentioned in R. M. Decker's *35 Minutes to Mars* (Lakeville: Galde Books, 2004), 53–54. Decker refers to the first Mrs. Cooke by another of her many pseudonyms, Millen Belknap.

"a set of fantastic theories"; "dangerous"; "Suffering people": Rollo May, "Do You Remember When You Last Died?," *New York Times*, October 7, 1951.

"a milestone for Man comparable to his discovery of fire": L. Ron Hubbard, *Dianetics: The Modern Science of Mental Health* (New York: Hermitage House, 1950).

"money sickness"; "havingness": John Cooke's time in Tangier is discussed on *The Royal Maze*, a website maintained by several of his former students: "Black Magic in Tangier," online at http://www.royalmaze.com/black-magic -in-tangier/.

"I'd like to start a religion. That's where the money is": Quoted in Hugh B. Urban, *The Church of Scientology: A History of a New Religion* (Princeton: Princeton University Press), 58.

"The news was received with mixed emotions": *The Aberee*, "Scientology Acts to Legalize as Religion," April 1954.

"Nobody in Tangier is exactly what he seems to be": William Burroughs, "International Zone," in *Word Virus: The William S. Burroughs Reader* (New York: Grove, 2007), 128.

"one of the great hedonic mystic teachers": Timothy Leary, *Jail Notes* (New York: Grove, 1970), 133.

"certainly the greatest painter living": William Burroughs, letter to his parents, November 17, 1959, *Rub Out the Words: The Letters of William S. Burroughs, 1959–1974*, edited by Bill Morgan (New York: Ecco, 2012).

"euphoria and brilliant storms of laughter": Brion Gysin, quoted in *The Alice B. Toklas Cook Book* (New York: Harper & Brothers, 1954), 273.

"They were the first rich hippies I had ever seen": Brion Gysin, quoted in Terry Wilson, *Brion Gysin: Here to Go* (London: Creation Books, 2001), 81.

The Process: Brion Gysin's novel about the Cookes, first published in 1967, was reissued twenty years later by the Overlook Press.

"The method of directed recall is the method of Scientology": William Burroughs, letter to Allen Ginsberg, October 27, 1959, *The Letters of William S. Burroughs, 1945–1959*, edited by Oliver Harris (New York: Viking, 1993), 431.

"Somebody is reading a newspaper": William Burroughs, interview with the *Paris Review*, Fall 1965, online at http://www.theparisreview.org/interviews/ 4424/the-art-of-fiction-no-36-william-s-burroughs.

"about three feet off of a desk"; "Scientology has moved up into a bracket": L. Ron Hubbard, "Elementary Material: Know to Mystery Scale," lecture given January 7, 1955.

"We don't believe in sickness": L. Ron Hubbard, "Healing Promotion," September 1, 1962.

"had affected his mind": Meher Baba, quoted in Bhau Kalchuri, *Meher Prabhu: Lord Meher, The Biography of the Avatar of the Age, Meher Baba* (Asheville, NC: Manifestation, 1986), 5002.

"stepping right out of your pages": William Burroughs, letter to Brion Gysin, January 21, 1970, *Rub Out the Words: The Letters of William S. Burroughs, 1959–1974*, edited by Bill Morgan (New York: Ecco Press, 2012), 323.

"The Immortality Racket": Gysin's alternate titles are mentioned by John Geiger in *Nothing Is True—Everything Is Permitted: The Life of Brion Gysin* (New York: Disinformation Books, 2005), section 12.

"Like the Knights Templars of the 10th century": Isabella Paoli, "A synopsis of the true story of the transformation of American minds in the 1960s," wixarika.mediapark.net/en/assets/pdf/Roots_of_Awareness.pdf.

"a wizard that lives down the coast in Carmel Highlands": Bowen recalled the first words he heard about Cooke, and the tale of his "initiation," in unpublished chapters of his memoir, shared by one of Bowen's students, Mark Walker.

"as good a marker as any for the arrival of the counter culture as a mass movement": Hendrik Hertzberg, *Politics: Observations and Arguments: 1966–2004* (New York: Penguin, 2004), 555.

"It was the first time I did see a new society": Jerry Rubin, quoted in "OUT, DEMONS, OUT!" An oral history by Larry "Ratso" Sloman, Michael Simmons, and Jay Babcock, *Arthur* 13 (November 2004).

"We wanted to be a celebration of being alive": Jim Fouratt, quoted in "10,000 Chant 'L-O-V-E,'" *New York Times*, March 27, 1967.

"Acid actually played a very important role in the alteration of the American psyche": Allen Ginsberg, quoted in Sloman, Simmons, and Babcock, "OUT, DEMONS, OUT!"

"tune-in, turn-on, drop-out, jerk-off": William Hjortsberg, quoting Emmet Grogan, founder of the radical theater troupe the Diggers, in *Jubilee Hitchhiker: The Life and Times of Richard Brautigan* (New York: Counterpoint, 2013), 269.

Lewis Mumford's *The City in History*: I'm indebted to Joseph P. Laycock's article "Levitating the Pentagon: Exorcism as Politics, Politics as Exorcism," *Implicit Religion* 14, no. 3 (2011): 295–318, for making me aware of the connection between Lewis Mumford and Allen Cohen. See also Derek Taylor's *It Was Twenty Years Ago Today* (New York: Simon & Schuster, 1987) for other remembrances of the protest.

"One of the major works of scholarship of the twentieth century": This assessment of Mumford's book from the *Christian Science Monitor* appears in the backmatter of the 1968 Mariner Books edition.

"an effete and worthless baroque conceit": Lewis Mumford, *The City in History: Its Origins, Its Transformations, and Its Prospects* (New York: Harcourt, Brace & World, 1961), 432.

"turn orange and vibrate until all evil emissions had fled": *Time*, "Protest: The Banners of Dissent," October 27, 1967.

"now in the business of wholesale disruption and widespread resistance and dislocation of the American society": Jerry Rubin, quoted by Norman Mailer, "The Battle of the Pentagon," *Commentary*, April 1968.

"We're going to raise the Pentagon three hundred feet in the air": Abbie Hoffman, quoted in Mailer, "The Battle of the Pentagon."

"We didn't expect the building to actually leave terra firma": Keith Lampe, quoted in Sloman, Simmons, and Babcock, "OUT, DEMONS, OUT!"

"You think Abbie believed in a lot of that stuff?": Jim Fouratt, quoted in Sloman, Simmons, and Babcock, "OUT, DEMONS, OUT!"
"The smell of the drug, sweet as the sweetest leaves of burning tea": Mailer, "The Battle of the Pentagon."
"We Freemen, of all colors of the spectrum": Ibid.
"Ed Sanders and the Fugs are a bunch of crap": Kenneth Anger, quoted in Sloman, Simmons, and Babcock, "OUT, DEMONS, OUT!"
"the hippie element and weld it together with the hard line political reality": Jim Fouratt, quoted in Sloman, Simmons, and Babcock, "OUT, DEMONS, OUT!"
"Actually and expectedly, the hippies are wrong": "Protest: The Banners of Dissent," Time.
"The levitation of the Pentagon was a happening that demystified the authority of the military": Allen Ginsberg, quoted in Sloman, Simmons, and Babcock, "OUT, DEMONS, OUT!"
"M-14 rifles, bayonets, clubs, and stone faces": Mailer, "The Battle of the Pentagon."
"caught on like wildfire nationwide": Advertisement in The New Yorker, November 21, 1970.
"quintessential hippie tarot": online at http://www.tarotpassages.com/TNewT.htm.
"a gathering-together of younger people aware of the planetary fate that we are all sitting in the middle of": Allen Ginsberg, testimony before the Trial of the Chicago 7.
"the great crippled wizard": Timothy Leary, Jail Notes, 134.

Notes to pages 401–413 [Chapter 18]

"We are a nation of Christians and Muslims, Jews and Hindus, and non-believers": Barack Obama, January 20, 2009.
"I have been guided by the standard John Winthrop set": John F. Kennedy, January 9, 1961, online at http://en.wikisource.org/wiki/Address_of_President-Elect_John_F._Kennedy_Delivered_to_a_Joint_Convention_of_the_General_Court_of_the_Commonwealth_of_Massachusetts.
"Standing on the tiny deck of the Arabella in 1630 off the Massachusetts coast": Ronald Reagan, January 25, 1974, online at http://reagan2020.us/speeches/City_Upon_A_Hill.asp.
"The past few days when I've been at that window upstairs": Ronald Reagan, Farewell Address, January 12, 1989, online at http://www.nytimes.com/1989/01/12/news/transcript-of-reagan-s-farewell-address-to-american-people.html.
"It was right here, in the waters around us": Barack Obama, June 2, 2006, online at http://obamaspeeches.com/074-University-of-Massachusetts-at-Boston-Commencement-Address-Obama-Speech.htm.
"Be respectful": Dreams from My Father (New York: Random House, 2007), 154.
"I was not raised in a religious household": Barack Obama, The Audacity of Hope (New York: Random House, 2006), 202.
"Islam…is part of America": "President Obama makes remarks before hosting a dinner celebrating Ramadan," online at http://www.youtube.com/watch?v=uJ4rn5z0LNw.

"There need to be many more of us in here": Online at http://www.huffington post.com/2013/01/03/mazie-hirono-sworn-in_n_2404267.html.

Video of Cory Booker's Senate announcement: "Finishing the Work We Started," online at http://www.youtube.com/watch?v=NCm2meC1SS8.

Hate crimes since 9-11: Curt Anderson, "FBI: Hate Crimes vs. Muslims Rise," Associated Press, November 25, 2002.

2010 Gallup poll: Online at http://www.gallup.com/poll/125312/religious -prejudice-stronger-against-muslims.aspx.

"Regardless of what we look like": Michael Laris, Jerry Markon, and William Branigin, "Wade Michael Page, Sikh Temple Shooter, Identified as Skinhead Band Leader," Washington Post, August 6, 2012.

Hate crime rates: Online at http://www.aclu.org/maps/map-nationwide-anti -mosque-activity.

"on the spot where for long years wonderful cures had been performed"; "in carriages, in wagons, on horses": Le Baron Bradford Prince, Spanish Mission Churches of New Mexico (Cedar Rapids: Torch Press, 1915), 317.

"a small amount of sacred earth": Ibid., 321.

"How and when the healing virtues": Ibid., 317.

"Visitors to El Santuario come from all over the world": Online at http://www .elsantuariodechimayo.us/Santuario/Pocito.html.

Index

About the Author

Peter Manseau is the author of the memoir *Vows*, the novel *Songs for the Butcher's Daughter*, and the travelogue *Rag and Bone*. He has won the National Jewish Book Award, the American Library Association's Sophie Brody Medal for Outstanding Achievement in Jewish Literature, the Ribalow Prize for Fiction, and a 2012 National Endowment for the Arts Literature Fellowship. A founding editor of KillingTheBuddha.com and coauthor (with Jeff Sharlet) of *Killing the Buddha: A Heretic's Bible*, he received his doctorate in religion from Georgetown University and is currently a fellow in American religious history at the Smithsonian's National Museum of American History. He lives with his family in Annapolis, Maryland.